Melancthon Woolsey Stryker

Church Praise Book

A selection of hymns and tunes for Christian Worship

Melancthon Woolsey Stryker

Church Praise Book
A selection of hymns and tunes for Christian Worship

ISBN/EAN: 9783337038304

Printed in Europe, USA, Canada, Australia, Japan

Cover: Foto ©Lupo / pixelio.de

More available books at **www.hansebooks.com**

THE
CHURCH PRAISE BOOK:

A SELECTION OF HYMNS AND TUNES

FOR

CHRISTIAN WORSHIP.

"*Let the high praises of God be in their mouth, and a two-edged sword in their hand.*"

"*That at the name of Jesus every knee should bow; and every tongue should confess that Jesus Christ is Lord, to the glory of God the Father.*"

NEW YORK AND CHICAGO:
BIGLOW & MAIN, PUBLISHERS.

PREFACE.

THIS manual is offered to the Church as a compact hand-book for the united praise of the entire congregation—"young men and maidens, old men and children."

It is a critical selection from the ever enriching store of Christian song;—not a library. It is believed, however, that its seven hundred and twenty-eight hymns will abundantly meet all the requirements of public worship, and be found, in many themes, exceptionally rich.

The music, widely chosen, is neither frigid nor flippant, but lovable, and, because devout, *enduring*.

The book is an advance, but a conservative one; by no means presuming against the resonant memories of the American Church, nor, with a startling originality, disjoining the wedded hands of old and cherished adaptations. It, however, contains much more music than any similar collection, and, with what is familiar and precious, is blended the stately river-flow of the noblest German chorals, and the best of the modern, but already classic, English church-songs, whose purity and fervor are deep wells of worship, and whose clear melody and decisive movement will rapidly endear them to the very children.

We venture to say that an honest study will find none of the book impracticable or uninteresting.

Great labor has been given to secure the utmost accuracy in the authorial data. We believe that, in this regard, no similar American book can show such scrupulous editing.

Familiarity of use will find the indices sufficient for a book of these contents; the simple but careful classification, with the clear page-headings, rendering superfluous an array of stanza-lines, topics, scripture texts, etc.

The symmetrical page, with its type distinct even to aged eyes; the presence of its suitable tune with each hymn; the convenient size; the careful presswork; the durable binding and the moderate cost; are subordinate but cumulative pleas for favor.

Acknowledgment is hereby made to OLIVER DITSON & Co., A. S. BARNES & Co., and others, for authority to print a number of copyright tunes. Thanks are rendered to HOUGHTON, MIFFLIN & Co. for the use of two hymns by OLIVER WENDELL HOLMES, LL.D.; and to RAY PALMER, D.D., EDWIN F. HATFIELD, D.D., WM. H. WALTER, D.Mus., NATHAN B. WARREN, D.Mus., S. BURT SAXTON, and many other friends, for the free use of their hymns and tunes, and for many gracious suggestions.

We beg leave to suggest the desirability of having an active and well-trained chorus choir, and of holding stated meetings for the musical drill of the entire congregation; and we would urge a hearty interest in the book at all the firesides of the churches using it.

We submit our labor of love to all Christian people, as heartily Evangelical and Catholic; and pray Him "who inhabits the praises of Israel," that He will own and bless it to the fostering of His worship by "ALL THE PEOPLE."

M. WOOLSEY STRYKER,
HUBERT P. MAIN.

SEPT. 1881.

TABLE OF CONTENTS.

HYMNS.

Morning and Evening,	2– 20	Consecration,	440–464
The Lord's Day,	21– 54	Submission,	465–491
The House of God,	55– 72	The Ministry,	492–494
The Trinity,	73– 85	The House of God,	495–498
God the Father,	86–136	Baptism,	499–502
Jesus Christ,	137–152	The Lord's Supper,	503–549
The Advent,	153–157	Childhood,	550–561
The Nativity,	158–177	Wedlock,	562
His Ministry,	178–182	The Year,	563–568
The Cross,	183–191	Harvest,	569–577
His Resurrection,	192–208	National,	578–582
His Ascension,	209–212	Fasting Days,	583–585
The Ascended Lord,	213–219	The Church,	586–590
The Royal Priest,	220–228	All Saints,	591–603
The Holy Ghost,	229–246	Revival,	604–609
The Inspired Scriptures,	247–253	Missions,	610–636
Need of Christ,	254–261	Labor,	637–642
Salvation,	262–287	Aspiration,	643–645
Repentance,	288–305	Death,	646–664
Penitence,	306–327	Resurrection,	665–671
Faith,	328–369	The Second Advent,	672–692
Love,	370–402	The Last Judgment,	693–698
Hope,	403–425	Heaven,	699–726
Prayer,	426–439	Eternity,	727

Our Lord's Prayer.

OUR Father, which art in Heaven, Hallowed be thy name.
Thy Kingdom come. Thy will be done in Earth, as it is in Heaven.
Give us this day our daily bread.
And forgive us our debts, as we forgive our debtors.
And lead us not into temptation, but deliver us from Evil.
For Thine is the Kingdom, and the Power, and the Glory, forever.
Amen.

The Nicene Creed.

"I BELIEVE IN ONE GOD, THE FATHER ALMIGHTY, Maker of Heaven and earth, and of all things visible and invisible: and in ONE LORD JESUS CHRIST, the only begotten Son of God, Begotten of His Father before all worlds; God of God, Light of Light, Very God of Very God, Begotten, not made, being of one substance with the Father: By Whom all things were made; Who for us men and for our salvation, came down from Heaven, and was incarnate by the Holy Ghost of the Virgin Mary, and was made Man; And was crucified also for us under Pontius Pilate. He suffered and was buried; and the third day He rose again according to the Scriptures; and ascended into heaven, and sitteth on the right hand of the Father; And He shall come again with glory, to judge both the quick and the dead; Whose kingdom shall have no end.

And I believe in the HOLY GHOST, The Lord and Giver of Life, Who proceedeth from the Father and the Son, Who with the Father and the Son together is worshipped and glorified, Who spake by the Prophets. And I believe one Catholic and Apostolic Church. I acknowledge one Baptism for the remission of sins; And I look for the Resurrection of the dead, and the Life of the world to come. Amen."

THE CHURCH PRAISE BOOK.

1 Alleluia. 7s.   EDWARD J. HOPKINS, 1867.

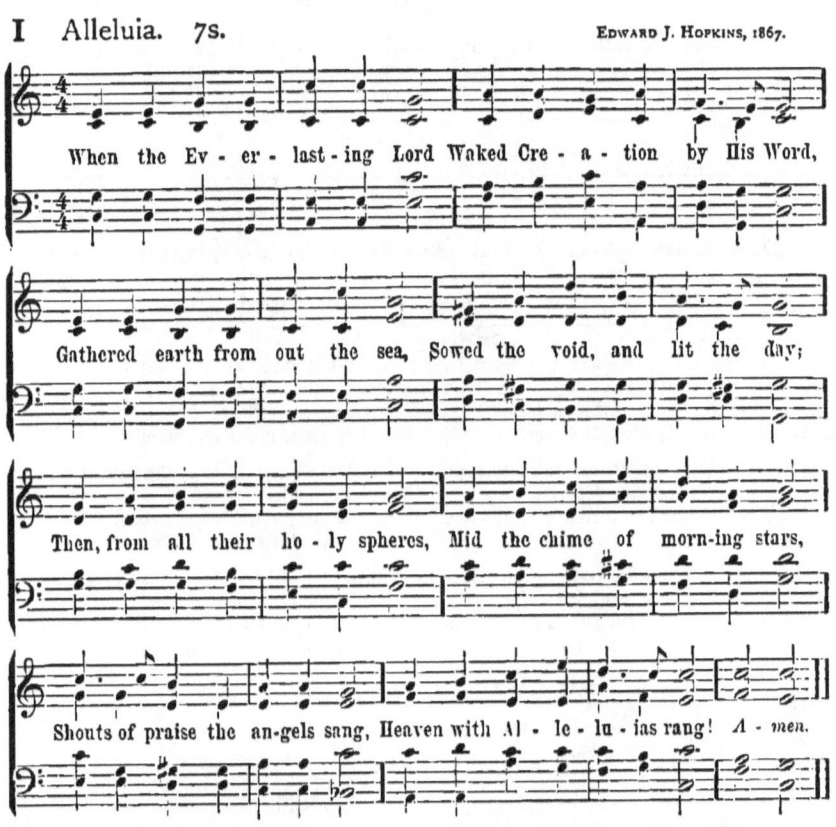

When the Ev-er-last-ing Lord Waked Cre-a-tion by His Word,
Gathered earth from out the sea, Sowed the void, and lit the day;
Then, from all their ho-ly spheres, Mid the chime of morn-ing stars,
Shouts of praise the an-gels sang, Heaven with Al-le-lu-ias rang! A-men.

2 When the Everlasting Word,
Cradled Babe,—"Arm of the Lord,"
Led a brighter, holier day,
By the Star of Bethlehem's ray;
Then again the heavenly throng,
Poured a flood of thrilling song,
"Praise the God of peace"—they sang,
Earth with Alleluias rang!

3 With a glad, harmonious voice,
All adoring hearts rejoice;
Heaven-taught, evermore, they raise
Hymns of faith, and love, and praise;
Till shall break that purest morn
When, the Earth and Heaven new-born,
Angel songs with saints' shall blend
Alleluias without end.   Amen.

Anon, 1880.

Morning.

2 Duke Street. L. M.   John Hatton, 1790.

A-wake, my soul! and, with the sun, Thy dai-ly stage of du-ty run;
Shake off dull sloth, and joy-ful rise, To pay thy morn-ing sac-ri-fice.

2 Wake, and lift up thyself, my heart!
And with the angels bear thy part,
Who, all night long, unwearied sing
High praise to the eternal King.

3 All praise to Thee, who safe hast kept,
And hast refreshed me, whilst I slept;
Grant, Lord! when I from death shall wake,
I may of endless light partake.

4 Lord! I my vows to Thee renew;
Disperse my sins as morning dew;
Guard my first springs of thought and will,
And with Thyself my spirit fill.

5 Direct, control, suggest, this day,
All I design, or do, or say;
That all my powers, with all their might,
In Thy sole glory may unite.
Thomas Ken, 1697. a.

3

New every morning is the love
Our waking and uprising prove;
Thro sleep and darkness safely brought,
Restored to life, and power, and thought.

2 New mercies each returning day,
Hover around us while we pray;
New perils past, new sins forgiven,
New thoughts of God, new hopes of heaven.

3 If, on our daily course, our mind
Be set to hallow all we find,
New treasures still, of countless price,
God will provide for sacrifice.

4 The trivial round, the common task,
Will furnish all we need to ask,
Room to deny ourselves, a road
To bring us daily nearer God.

5 Only, O Lord! in Thy dear love
Fit us for perfect rest above;
And help us, this and every day,
To live more nearly as we pray.
John Keble, 1827.

4

My God! how endless is Thy love!
  Thy gifts are every evening new;
And morning mercies from above
  Gently distill, like early dew.

2 Thou spread'st the curtains of the night,
  Great Guardian of my sleeping hours!
Thy sovereign word restores the light,
  And quickens all my drowsy powers.

3 I yield my powers to Thy command;
  To Thee I consecrate my days;
Perpetual blessings, from Thy hand,
  Demand perpetual songs of praise.
Isaac Watts, 1709.

Morning and Evening.

5 Nicæa. P. M.   John B. Dykes, 1861.

Holy, holy, holy, Lord God Almighty!
Early in the morning our song shall rise to Thee;
Holy, holy, holy! Merciful and Mighty!
God in Three Persons, blessed Trinity! A-men.

  2 Holy, holy, holy! all the saints adore Thee,
     Casting down their golden crowns around the glassy sea;
    Cherubim and Seraphim falling down before Thee,
     Which wert, and art, and evermore shalt be.

  3 Holy, holy, holy! though the darkness hide Thee,
     Though the eye of sinful man Thy glory may not see;
    Only Thou art holy: there is none beside Thee,
     Perfect in power, in love, and purity.

  4 Holy, holy, holy! Lord God Almighty!
     All Thy works shall praise Thy name, in earth, and sky, and sea:
    Holy, holy, holy! merciful and mighty;
     God in Three Persons, blessed Trinity! Amen.

Reginald Heber, 1819.

Morning and Evening.

6 Luton. L. M.
GEORGE BURDER, 1778.

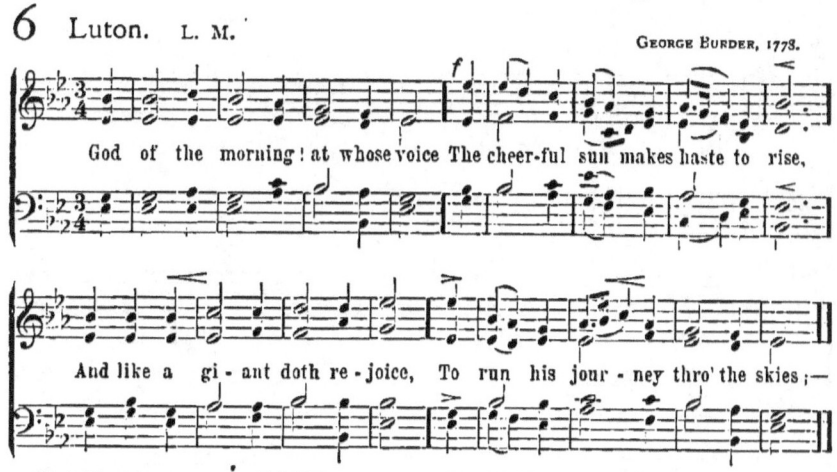

God of the morning! at whose voice The cheerful sun makes haste to rise, And like a giant doth rejoice, To run his journey thro' the skies;—

2 Oh! like the sun, may I fulfill
  Th' appointed duties of the day;
With ready mind, and active will,
  March on, and keep my heavenly way.

3 But I shall rove and lose the race,
  If God, my Sun, shall disappear,
And leave me in the world's wide maze
  To follow every wandering star.

4 Lord! Thy commands are clean and pure,
  Enlightening our beclouded eyes;
Thy threatenings just, Thy promise sure,
  Thy gospel makes the simple wise.

5 Give me Thy counsel for my guide,
  And then receive me to Thy bliss;
All my desires and hopes beside
  Are faint, and cold, compared with this.
              Isaac Watts, 1709.

7 Hebron. L. M.
LOWELL MASON, 1830.

Thus far the Lord has led me on, Thus far His power prolongs my days; And every evening shall make known Some fresh memorial of His grace.

Morning and Evening.

2 Much of my time has run to waste,
And I, perhaps, am near my home;
But He forgives my follies past,
He gives me strength for days to come.

3 I lay my body down to sleep,—
Peace is the pillow for my head;
While well-appointed angels keep
Their watchful stations round my bed.

4 Thus, when the night of death shall come,
My flesh shall rest beneath the ground,
And wait Thy voice to rouse my tomb,
With sweet salvation in the sound.
Isaac Watts, 1709.

8 Evening Hymn. L. M.   Thomas Tallis, 1565.

Glo-ry to Thee, my God! this night, For all the blessings of the light:
Keep me, oh! keep me, King of kings! Beneath Thine own al-might-y wings.

2 Forgive me, Lord! for Thy dear Son,
The ill that I this day have done;
That with the world, myself, and Thee,
I, ere I sleep, at peace may be.

3 Teach me to live, that I may dread
The grave as little as my bed:
Teach me to die, that so I may
Rise glorious at the awful day.

4 Oh! may my soul on Thee repose,
And may sweet sleep mine eyelids close;
Sleep, that shall me more vig'rous make,
To serve my God when I awake.

5 When in the night I sleepless lie,
My soul with heavenly thoughts supply:
Let no ill dreams disturb my rest,
No powers of darkness me molest.
Thomas Ken, 1697, a.

9

O Jesus, Lord of heavenly grace,
Thou Brightness of Thy Father's face,
Thou Fountain of eternal light,
Whose beams disperse the shades of night!

2 Come, holy Sun of heavenly love!
Send down Thy radiance from above,
And to our inmost hearts convey
The Holy Spirit's cloudless ray.

3 Oh! hallowed thus be every day!
Let meekness be our morning ray,
And faithful love our noon-day light,
And hope our sunset, calm and bright.

4 O Christ! with each returning morn,
Thine image to our hearts is borne;
Oh! may we ever clearly see
Our Saviour and our God in Thee!
Lat., *Ambrose*, 390.
Tr., *John Chandler*, 1837.

Morning and Evening.

10 Temple. 8s & 4s.   EDWARD J. HOPKINS. 1867.

2 And when morn again shall call us
    To run life's way,
May we still, whate'er befall us
    Thy will obey.
From the power of evil hide us,
In the narrow pathway guide us,
Nor Thy smile be e'er denied us
    The livelong day.

3 Guard us waking, guard us sleeping,
    And when we die,
May we in Thy mighty keeping
    All peaceful lie:
When the last dread call shall wake us,
Do not Thou our God forsake us,
But to reign in glory take us
    With Thee on high. Amen.

V. 1, *Reginald Heber*, 1827.
V. 2, *William Mercer*, 1864.
V. 3, *Richard Whately*, 1860.

Morning and Evening.

11 St. Vincent. L. M. J. UGLOW, arr., 1861.

Great God, to Thee my even-ing song, With humble grat-i-tude I raise:
O let Thy mer-cy tune my tongue, And fill my heart with lively praise. A-men.

2 Seal my forgiveness in the blood
  Of Jesus; His dear name alone
I plead for pardon, gracious God!
  And kind acceptance at Thy throne.

3 Let this bless'd hope mine eyelids close;
  With sleep refresh my feeble frame;
Safe in Thy care may I repose,
  And wake with praises to Thy name.
  Anne Steele, 1760.

12 Twilight. 6s & 5s. JOSEPH BARNBY, 1868.

Now the day is o-ver, Night is draw-ing nigh,
Shadows of the eve-ning Steal a-cross the sky. A-men.
  evening Steal a-cross the sky.

2 Jesus, give the weary
  Calm and sweet repose,
With Thy tend'rest blessing
  May our eyelids close.

3 When the morning wakens,
  Then may I arise
Pure, and fresh, and sinless,
  In Thy Holy Eyes. Amen.
  Sabine Baring-Gould, 1865, ab.

Evening.

13 Brown. C. M.   Wm. B. Bradbury, 1844.

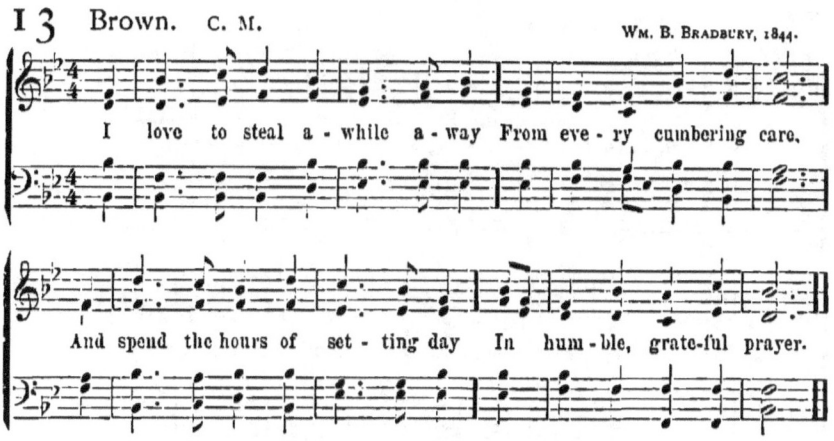

I love to steal a-while a-way From eve-ry cumbering care, And spend the hours of set-ting day In hum-ble, grate-ful prayer.

2 I love in solitude to shed
   The penitential tear,
And all His promises to plead,
   Where none but God can hear.

3 I love to think on mercies past,
   And future good implore,
And all my cares and sorrows cast
   On Him whom I adore.

4 I love by faith to take a view
   Of brighter scenes in heaven;
The prospect doth my strength renew,
   While here by tempests driven.

5 Thus, when life's toilsome day is o'er,
   May its departing ray
Be calm as this impressive hour,
   And lead to endless day!

Phœbe H. Brown, 1818.

14

The twilight falls, the night is near,
   I fold my work away,
And kneel to One who bends to hear
   The story of the day.

2 The old, old story; yet I kneel
   To tell it at Thy call,
And cares grow lighter as I feel.
   That Jesus knows them all.

3 Thou knowest all: I lean my head;
   My weary eyelids close;
Content and glad awhile to tread
   This path, since Jesus knows.

4 And He has loved me: all my heart
   With answering love is stirred,
And every anguished pain and smart
   Finds healing in the word.

5 So here I lay me down to rest,
   As nightly shadows fall,
And lean confiding on His breast
   Who knows and pities all.

Unknown.

15

How sweet, thro long-remembered years,
   His mercies to recall,   [fears,
And, pressed with wants, and griefs, and
   To trust His love for all.

2 How sweet to look in thoughtful hope,
   Beyond this fading sky,
And hear Him call His children up
   To His fair home on high.

3 Calmly the day forsakes our heaven,
   To dawn beyond the west;
So let my soul, in life's last even,
   Retire to glorious rest.

Leonard Bacon, 1845.

Evening.

16 St. Leonard. C. M.   Henry Hiles.

The shadows of the evening hours Fall from the dark'ning sky;
Upon the fragrance of the flowers The dews of evening lie;
Before Thy throne, O Lord of heav'n! We kneel at close of day;
Look on Thy children from on high, And hear us while we pray.

2 The sorrows of Thy servants, Lord!
  Oh, do not Thou despise:
But let the incense of our prayers
  Before Thy mercy rise.
The brightness of the coming night
  Upon the darkness rolls;
With hopes of future glory chase
  The shadows from our souls.

3 Slowly the rays of daylight fade;
  So fade within the heart
The hopes in earthly love and joy
  That, one by one, depart;
Slowly the bright stars, one by one,
  Within the heavens shine;
Give us, O Lord! fresh hopes in heaven,
  And trust in things divine.

Adelaide Anne Procter, 1858.

Evening.

17 Lux Benigna. P.
J. B. DYKES, 1868.

Lead, kindly Light, a-mid th'en-circling gloom, Lead Thou me on;
The night is dark, and I am far from home, Lead Thou me on.
Keep Thou my feet; I do not ask to see
The dis-tant scene; one step e-nough for me. A-men.

2 I was not ever thus, nor prayed that Thou
    Shouldst lead me on;
I loved to choose and see my path; but now
    Lead Thou me on.
I loved the garish day; and, spite of fears,
Pride ruled my will: remember not past
    years.

3 So long Thy power has blest me, sure it
    Will lead me on   [still
O'er moor and fen, o'er crag and torrent,
    The night is gone,   [till
And with the morn those angel faces smile,
Which I have loved long since, and lost
    awhile. Amen.

John H. Newman, 1833.

Evening.

18 Last Beam. P.
Portuguese.

Fading, still fading, the last beam is shining; Father in heaven, the day is declining;
Safety and innocence fly with the light, Temptation and danger walk forth with the night;
From the fall of the shade till the morning bells chime, Shield me from danger, save me from crime.
Father, have mercy, Father, have mercy, Father, have mercy thro Jesus Christ our Lord. *Amen.*

2 Father in heaven, oh, hear when we call!
Hear, for Christ's sake, who is Saviour of all;
Feeble and fainting, we trust in Thy might;
In doubting and darkness, Thy love be our light;
Let us sleep on Thy breast while the night taper burns,
Wake in Thine arms when morning returns.
    Father, have mercy, etc. Amen.

Unknown.

Evening.

19 Eventide. 10s. WILLIAM H. MONK 1860.

A - bide with me! fast falls the e - ven - tide; The dark-ness deep - ens; Lord, with me a - bide! When oth - er help - ers fail, and comforts flee, Help of the helpless, O a - bide with me! A - men.

2 Swift to its close ebbs out life's little day;
Earth's joys grow dim, its glories pass away
Change and decay in all around I see;
O Thou Who changest not, abide with me.

3 I need Thy presence every passing hour;
What but Thy grace can foil the tempter's power?
Who, like Thyself, my guide and stay can be?
Through cloud and sunshine, Lord, abide with me.

4 I fear no foe, with Thee at hand to bless:
Ills have no weight, and tears no bitterness.
Where is death's sting? where, grave, thy victory?
I triumph still, if Thou abide with me.

5 Hold Thou Thy Cross before my closing eyes;
Shine through the gloom, and point me to the skies;
Heaven's morning breaks, and earth's vain shadows flee;
In life, in death, O Lord, abide with me. Amen.

Henry F. Lyte, 1847.

Evening.

20 Emmaus. 10s.   John Goss, 1872.

The day is gent-ly sink-ing to a close, Faint-er and yet more faint the sunlight glows, O Brightness of Thy Fa-ther's glo-ry, Thou, E-ter-nal Light of Light, be with us now. A-men.

2 Our changeful lives are ebbing to an end,
Onward to darkness and to death we tend;
O Conqueror of the grave, be Thou our Guide,
Be Thou our Light in death's dark eventide.

3 Thou, who in darkness walking didst appear
Upon the waves, and Thy disciples cheer,
When all is dark, may we behold Thee nigh,
And hear Thy voice, "Fear not, for it is I."

4 Come, Lord, in lonely days, when storms assail,
And earthly hopes and human succors fail,
Where Thou art present, darkness cannot be:
Midnight is glorious noon, O Lord, with Thee.

5 In that last sunset, when the stars shall fall,
May we arise, awakened by Thy call,
With Thee, O Lord, for ever to abide
In that blest day which has no eventide. Amen.

Christopher Wordsworth, 1862.

The Lord's Day.

21 Communion. 10s.   MENDELSSOHN.

Still, still with Thee, when pur-ple morn-ing break-eth, When the bird wak-eth, and the shad-ows flee; Fair-er than morning, lov-li-er than day-light, Dawns the sweet con-cious-ness, I am with Thee. A-men.

  2 Alone with Thee, amid the mystic shadows,
    The solemn hush of nature newly born;
  Alone with Thee, in breathless adoration,
    In the calm dew and freshness of the morn.

  3 So shall it be at last, in that bright morning,
    When the soul waketh, and life's shadows flee;
  Oh, in that hour, fairer than daylight-dawning,
    Shall rise the glorious thought—I am with Thee. Amen.
                                          Harriet B. Stowe, 1854, ab.

22 Amantus. S. M.   C. BRYAN. 1862.

Hail to the Sab-bath day: The day di-vine-ly given;

The Lord's Day.

When men to God their ho-mage pay, And earth draws near to heaven.

2 Lord! in this sacred hour
　Within Thy courts we bend,
And bless Thy love, and own Thy power,
　Our Father and our Friend!

3 But Thou art not alone
　In courts by mortals trod;
Nor only is the day Thine own
　When man draws near to God:

4 Thy temple is the arch
　Of yon unmeasured sky;
Thy Sabbath, the stupendous march
　Of grand eternity.

5 Lord! may that holier day
　Dawn on Thy servant's sight;
And purer worship may we pay
　In heaven's unclouded light.
　　　　　Stephen G. Bulfinch, 1832.

23　Meinhold.　7s & 8s.　　　German.

{ Light of light! en-lighten me,　Now a-new the day is dawn-ing; }
{ Sun of grace! the shadows flee,　Brighten Thou my Sabbath morn-ing; }
With Thy joy-ous sunshine blest, Hap-py is my day of rest.

2 Let me with my heart to-day,
　Holy, holy, holy, singing,
Rapt a while from earth away,
　All my soul to Thee upspringing,
Have a foretaste only given
How they worship Thee in heaven.

3 Hence all care, all vanity,
　For the day to God is holy;
Come, Thou glorious Majesty!
　Deign to fill this temple lowly;
Naught to-day my soul shall move,
Simply resting in Thy love.
　　　　　Tr. Catherine Winkworth.

The Lord's Day.

24 Hodnet. 7s & 6s.   Sigismund Thalberg, 1850.

{ O day of rest and gladness! O day of joy and light! }
{ O balm of care and sadness, [omit] .... } Most beautiful, most bright!

{ On Thee, the high and lowly, Before th' eternal throne, }
{ Sing, "Holy! Ho-ly! Ho-ly!" [omit] .... } To the great God Triune.

2 On thee, at the creation,
   The light first had its birth:
On thee, for our salvation,
   Christ rose from depths of earth;
On thee, our Lord, victorious,
   The Spirit sent from heaven,
And thus on Thee, most glorious,
   A triple light was given.

3 To-day on weary nations
   The heavenly manna falls;
To holy convocations
   The silver trumpet calls,

Where gospel light is glowing
   With pure and radiant beams,
And living water flowing
   With soul-refreshing streams.

4 New graces ever gaining
   From this our day of rest,
We reach the rest remaining
   To spirits of the bless'd:
To Holy Ghost be praises,
   To Father and to Son;
The Church her voice upraises
   To Thee, bless'd Three in One!
       Christopher Wordsworth, 1862.

25 Lischer. H. M.   Fred. Schneider, 1840.

{ Welcome, delightful morn, Thou day of sa-cred rest! }   [toys,
{ I hail Thy kind return; Lord! make these moments bless'd: } From the low train of mortal

The Lord's Day.

I soar to reach im-mor-tal joys; I soar to reach im-mor-tal joys.

2 Now may the King descend,
  And fill His throne of grace!
Thy sceptre, Lord! extend,
  While saints address Thy face:
Let sinners feel Thy quickening word,
And learn to know and fear the Lord.

3 Descend, celestial Dove!
  With all Thy quickening powers;
Disclose a Saviour's love,
  And bless these sacred hours;
Then shall my soul new life obtain,
Nor Sabbath's e'er be spent in vain.
Hayward, 1806.

26 Silver Street. S. M. ISAAC SMITH, 1770.

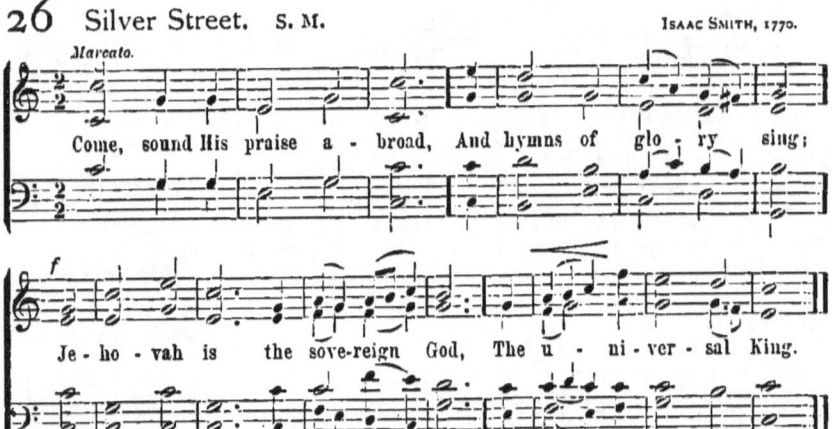

Come, sound His praise a-broad, And hymns of glo-ry sing;
Je-ho-vah is the sove-reign God, The u-ni-ver-sal King.

2 He formed the deeps unknown
  He gave the seas their bound;
The watery worlds are all His own,
  And all the solid ground.

3 Come, worship at His throne;
  Come, bow before the Lord:
We are His works, and not our own;
  He formed us by His word.

4 To-day attend His voice,
  Nor dare provoke His rod;
Come, like the people of His choice,
  And own your gracious God.
Isaac Watts, 1719.

27
STAND up, and bless the Lord,
  Ye people of His choice!
Stand up, and bless the Lord, your God,
  With heart, and soul, and voice.

2 God is our strength and song,
  And His salvation ours:
Then be His love in Christ proclaimed,
  With all our ransomed powers.

3 Stand up, and bless the Lord,—
  The Lord, your God, adore,
Stand up, and bless His glorious name,
  Henceforth, for evermore,
James Montgomery, 1825.

The Lord's Day.

28 Peterborough. C. M. Ralph Harrison, 1786.

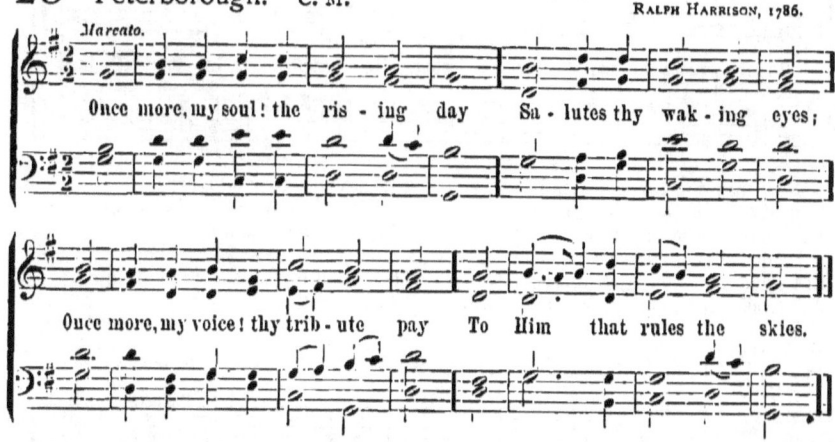

2 Night unto night His name repeats,
  The day renews the sound;
Wide as the heaven, on which He sits,
  To turn the seasons round.

3 'Tis He supports my mortal frame,—
  My tongue shall speak His praise;

My sins would rouse His wrath to flame,
  And yet His wrath delays.

4 Great God! let all my hours be Thine,
  Whilst I enjoy the light;
Then shall my sun in smiles decline,
  And bring a pleasing night.
Isaac Watts, 1707.

29 Halle. 7s. Peter Ritter, 1792.

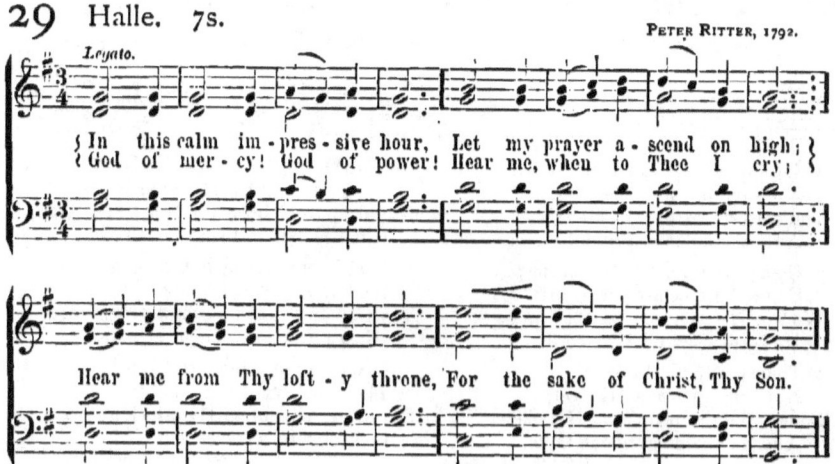

The Lord's Day.

2 With the morning's early ray,
　While the shades of night depart,
Let Thy beams of light convey
　Joy and gladness to my heart:
Now o'er all my steps preside,
And for all my wants provide.

3 Oh! what joy that word affords,—
　"Thou shalt reign o'er all the earth;"
King of kings, and Lord of lords!
　Send Thy gospel-heralds forth:
Now begin Thy boundless sway,
Usher in the glorious day.
Thomas Hastings, 1831.

30

Praise the name of God most high,
Praise Him, all below the sky,
Praise Him, all ye heavenly host,
Father, Son, and Holy Ghost;
As through countless ages past,
Evermore His praise shall last.
Anon, 1827.

31 Holley. 7s.
George Hews, 1835.

Soft-ly now the light of day Fades up-on my sight a-way;
Free from care, from la-bor free, Lord! I would commune with Thee.

2 Thou, whose all-pervading eye
　Naught escapes, without, within!
Pardon each infirmity,
　Open fault, and secret sin.

3 Soon, for me, the light of day
　Shall for ever pass away;
Then, from sin and sorrow free,
　Take me, Lord! to dwell with Thee.

4 Thou who, sinless, yet hast known
　All of man's infirmity!
Then, from Thine eternal throne,
　Jesus! look with pitying eye.
George W. Doane, 1824.

32

In the morning hear my voice,
Let me in Thy light rejoice;
God, my Sun! my strength renew,
Send Thy blessing down like dew.

2 When the evening skies display
Richer pomp than noon's array,
Be the shades of death to me
Bright with immortality.

3 When the round of care is run,
And the stars succeed the sun,
Songs of praise with prayer unite,
Crown the day, and hail the night
James Montgomery, 1825.

The Lord's Day.

33 Hursley. L. M.   Peter Ritter, 1792.

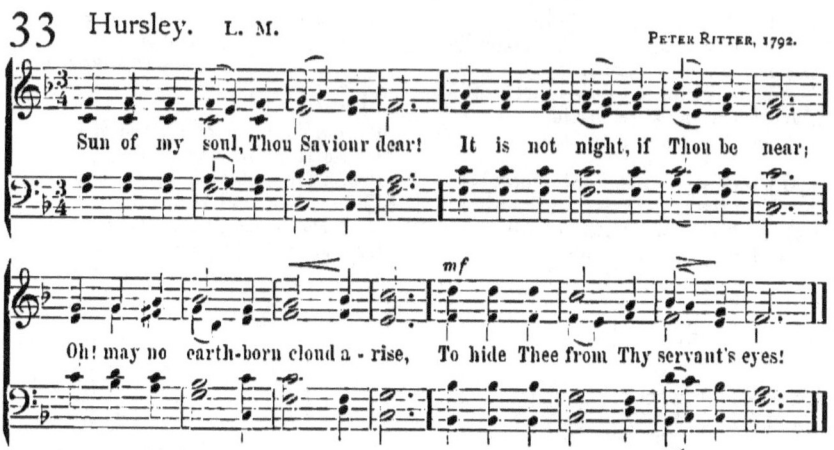

Sun of my soul, Thou Saviour dear! It is not night, if Thou be near;
Oh! may no earth-born cloud a-rise, To hide Thee from Thy servant's eyes!

2 When the soft dews of kindly sleep
My wearied eyelids gently steep,
Be my last thought, how sweet to rest
For ever on my Saviour's breast!

3 Abide with me from morn till eve,
For without Thee I cannot live;
Abide with me when night is nigh,
For without Thee I dare not die.

4 If some poor wandering child of Thine
Have spurned to-day the voice divine,
Now, Lord! the gracious work begin;
Let him no more lie down in sin.

5 Watch by the sick; enrich the poor,
With blessings from Thy boundless store;
Be every mourner's sleep to-night,
Like infant's slumbers, pure and light!

6 Come near and bless us when we wake,
Ere through the world our way we take;
Till, in the ocean of Thy love,
We lose ourselves in heaven above.
    John Keble, 1827.

34

Millions within Thy courts have met,
  Millions, this day, before Thee bowed;
Their faces Zion-ward were set,
  Vows with their lips to Thee they vowed.

2 Soon as the light of morning broke
  O'er island, continent, or deep,
Thy far-spread family awoke,
  The Lord's day round the world, to keep.

3 From east to west, the sun surveyed,
  From north to south, adoring throngs;
And still, when evening stretched her shade,
  The stars came out to hear their songs.

4 And not a prayer, a tear, a sigh,
  Hath failed this day some suit to gain;
To those in trouble Thou wert nigh;
  Not one hath sought Thy face in vain.

5 Yet one prayer more!—and be it one,
  In which both heaven and earth accord
Fulfill Thy promise to Thy Son;
  Let all that breathe call Jesus Lord!
    James Montgomery, 1853.

35

Away from every mortal care,
  Away from earth, our souls retreat;
We leave this worthless world afar,
  And wait and worship near Thy seat.

2 Father! my soul would still abide
  Within Thy temple, near Thy side;
But, if my feet must hence depart,
  Still keep Thy dwelling in my heart.
    Isaac Watts, 1709.

The Lord's Day.

36 Wavertree. L. M.   W. Shore.

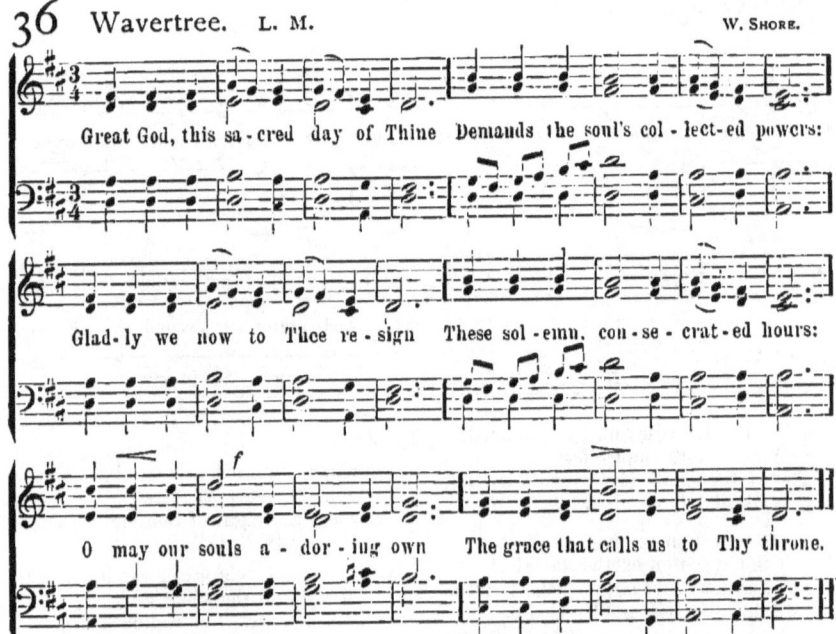

Great God, this sacred day of Thine Demands the soul's collected powers:
Gladly we now to Thee resign These solemn, consecrated hours:
O may our souls adoring own The grace that calls us to Thy throne.

2 All-seeing God! Thy piercing eye
   Can every secret thought explore;
May worldly cares our bosoms fly,
   And where Thou art intrude no more:
O may Thy grace our spirits move,
And fix our minds on things above.

3 Thy Spirit's powerful aid impart,
   And bid Thy word, with life divine,
Engage the ear and warm the heart:
   Then shall the day indeed be Thine;
Then shall our souls adoring own
The grace that calls us to Thy throne.
Anne Steele, 1760.

37

When, streaming from the eastern skies,
The morning light salutes mine eyes,
O Sun of righteousness divine!
On me with beams of mercy shine;
Chase the dark clouds of guilt away,
And turn my darkness into day.

2 And when, to heaven's all glorious King,
My morning sacrifice I bring,
And, mourning o'er my guilt and shame,
Ask mercy in my Saviour's name,
Then, Jesus! cleanse me with Thy blood,
And be my Advocate with God.

3 When each day's scenes and labors close,
And wearied nature seeks repose,
With pard'ning mercy richly blessed,
Guard me, my Saviour! while I rest;
And, as each morning sun shall rise,
Oh! lead me onward to the skies.

4 And, at my life's last setting sun,
My conflicts o'er, my labors done,
Jesus! Thy heavenly radiance shed,
To cheer and bless my dying bed;
And, from death's gloom, my spirit raise,
To see Thy face, and sing Thy praise.
William Shrubsole, Jr., 1813.

The Lord's Day.

38 Marlow. C. M.   John Chetham, 1740.

Marcato.

This is the day the Lord hath made; He calls the hours His own:
Let heaven re-joice, let earth be glad, And praise sur-round the throne.

2 To-day He rose and left the dead,
   And Satan's empire fell;
To-day the saints His triumph spread,
   And all His wonders tell.

3 Hosanna! in the highest strains,
   The church on earth can raise!
The highest heavens, in which He reigns,
   Shall give Him nobler praise.
         Isaac Watts, 1719.

39

With joy we hail the sacred day,
   Which God hath called His own;
With joy the summons we obey
   To worship at His throne.

2 Thy chosen temple, Lord! how fair!
   Where willing vot'ries throng,
To breathe the humble, fervent prayer,
   And pour the choral song.

3 Spirit of grace! Oh! deign to dwell
   Within Thy church below;
Make her in holiness excel,
   With pure devotion glow.

4 Let peace within her walls be found;
   Let all her sons unite,
To spread with grateful zeal around
   Her clear and shining light.
         Harriet Auber, 1829.

40

How sweetly breaks the Sabbath dawn
   Along the eastern skies!
So, when the night of time hath gone,
   Eternity shall rise.

2 What quiet reigns o'er earth and sea,
   Through all the silent air!
So calm may we, this Sabbath, be,
   And free from worldly care.

3 Thus let Thy peace, O Lord! pervade
   Our bosoms, all our days;
And let each passing hour be made
   A herald of Thy praise.
         Edwin F. Hatfield, 1840.

41

And now another week begins,
   This day we call the Lord's;
This day He rose, who bore our sins,—
   For so His word records.

2 Come, then, ye saints! and grateful sing
   Of Christ, our risen Lord,—
Of Christ, the everlasting King,—
   Of Christ, th' incarnate Word.

3 Hail! mighty Saviour! Thee we hail!
   Who fillest the throne above;
Till heart and flesh together fail,
   We'll sing Thy matchless love.
         Thomas Kelly, 1809, a.

The Lord's Day.

42

Again the Lord of life and light
  Awakes the kindling ray,
Unseals the eyelids of the morn,
  And pours increasing day.

2 Oh! what a night was that, which wrapt
  A guilty world in gloom!
Oh! what a sun which broke, this day,
  Triumphant from the tomb!

3 The powers of darkness leagued in vain
  To bind our Lord in death;
He shook their kingdom when He fell,
  With His expiring breath.

4 And now His conquering chariot wheels
  Ascend the lofty skies;
While, broke beneath His powerful cross,
  Death's iron sceptre lies.

5 This day be grateful homage paid,
  And loud hosannas sung;
Let gladness dwell in every heart,
  And praise on every tongue.

6 Ten thousand differing lips shall join
  To hail this welcome morn,
Which scatters blessings, from its wings,
  On nations yet unborn.
      Mrs. Anna Letitia Barbauld, 1772, a.

43 Spohr. L. M.   L. Spohr.

Thine earthly Sabbaths, Lord, we love,
But there's a nobler rest above;
To that our longing souls aspire,
With cheerful hope and strong desire.

2 No more fatigue, no more distress,
Nor sin nor death shall reach the place;
No groans shall mingle with the songs
Which warble from immortal tongues.

3 No rude alarms of raging foes;
No cares to break the long repose;
No midnight shade, no clouded sun,
But sacred, high, eternal noon.

4 O long-expected day begin!
Dawn on this world of woe and sin;
Fain would we leave this weary road,
To sleep in death, and rest in God.
      Philip Doddridge, 1737.

44

Sweet is the light of Sabbath-eve,
  And soft the sunbeams lingering there.
For these blest hours, the world I leave,
  Wafted on wings of faith and prayer.

2 The time—how lovely and how still;
  Peace shines and smiles on all below,—
The plain, the stream, the wood, the hill,—
  All fair with evening's setting glow.

3 Nor will our days of toil be long,
  Our pilgrimage will soon be trod;
And we shall join the ceaseless song,—
  The endless Sabbath of our God.
      James Edmeston, 1820.

The Lord's Day.

45 Vigils. C. M.   W. A. MOZART.

Blest day of God! most calm, most bright, The first, the best of days;
The laborer's rest, the saint's delight, The day of prayer and praise.

2 My Saviour's face made thee to shine;
   His rising thee did raise,
And made thee heavenly and divine
   Beyond all other days.

3 The first-fruits oft a blessing prove
   To all the sheaves behind;

And they the day of Christ who love,
   A happy week shall find.

4 This day I must with God appear;
   For, Lord, the day is Thine;
Help me to spend it in Thy fear,
   And thus to make it mine.

John Mason, 1683.

46 Sabbath. 7s.   LOWELL MASON, 1824.

Safely thro another week, God has brought us on our way;
Let us now a blessing seek, (Omit)............ Waiting in His courts to-day: Day of all the week the best, Emblem of eternal rest: Day of all the week the best, Emblem of eternal rest.

2 While we pray for pard'ning grace,
   Through the dear Redeemer's name,
Show Thy reconciléd face,
   Take away our sin and shame;
From our worldly cares set free,
May we rest, this day, in Thee.

3 May Thy gospel's joyful sound
   Conquer sinners, comfort saints;
Make the fruits of grace abound,
   Bring relief for all complaints:
Thus may all our Sabbaths prove,
Till we join the church above.

John Newton, 1779, a.

The Lord's Day.

47 Russia. 8s & 7s.   D. BORTNIANSKY, 1818.

Saviour! breathe an evening blessing, Ere repose our spirits seal;
Sin and want we come confessing; Thou canst save, and Thou canst heal.
Though the night be dark and dreary, Darkness cannot hide from Thee;
Thou art He who, never weary, Watchest where Thy people be.

2 Though destruction walk around us,
  Though the arrow past us fly,
Angel guards from Thee surround us,
  We are safe if Thou art nigh.
Should swift death this night o'ertake us,
  And our couch become our tomb,
May the morn in heaven awake us,
  Clad in light and deathless bloom.
James Edmeston, 1820.

48

SEE the clouds upon the mountains,
  Rolling, rising, melt away,
Light, forth flowing from its fountain,
  Pours an unobstructed ray.
So before Thy presence fading,
  Lord, may every shadow fly;
Chase the gloom my soul invading,
  With the sunbeam of Thine eye.

2 Lo! it dawns, the Sabbath morning
  Streams with radiance all divine;
Sanctity Thy courts adorning,
  Beautiful with grace they shine.
Holiness becomes Thy dwelling,
  Peerless sovereign of the sky
Princely palaces excelling,
  Pomp of earthly majesty.

3 Rise, my soul, the day is breaking,
  Gladdened nature drinks the light;
From the sleep of darkness waking,
  Put off all the clouds of night.
Take the rest this day is bringing,
  Best of all our earthly days,
Enter thou His gates with singing,
  Tread the hallowed floor with praise.
William B. Collyer, 1837.

The Lord's Day.

49 St. Ann's. C.M. Wm. Croft. 1708.

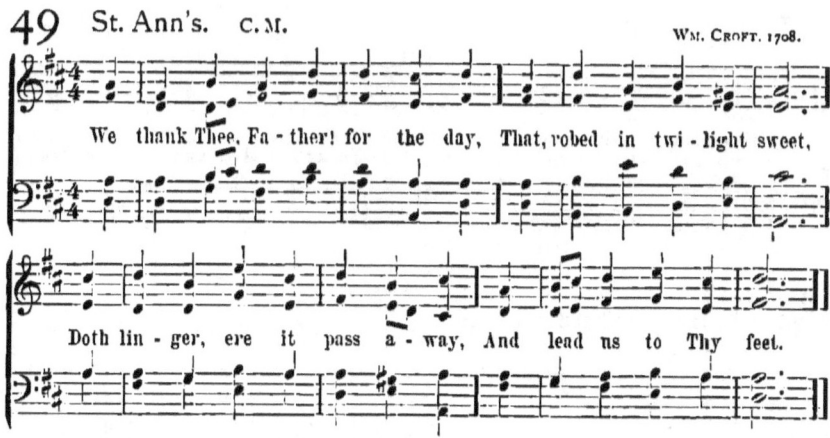

We thank Thee, Father! for the day, That, robed in twilight sweet, Doth linger, ere it pass away, And lead us to Thy feet.

2 We thank Thee for its healing rest
To weary toil and care;
Its praise, within Thy temple blessed—
Its holy balm of prayer.

3 We thank Thee for its living bread,
That did our hunger stay;
The manna, by Thine angels shed,
Around our desert way.

4 Oh! grant, that, when this span of life,
In evening shade, shall close,—
And all its vanity and strife
Tend to their long repose,—

5 We, for the sake of Him, who died,
Our Advocate and Friend,
May share that Sabbath, at Thy side,
Which never more shall end.
Lydia H. Sigourney, 1850.

50

When the worn spirit wants repose
And sighs her God to seek,
How sweet to hail the evening's close
That ends the weary week!

2 How welcome is the early dawn
That opens on the sight,
When first the soul-reviving morn
Sheds forth new rays of light!

3 Blest day! thine hours too soon will cease,
Yet, while they gently roll,
Breathe, heavenly Spirit, Source of peace,
A Sabbath o'er my soul.

4 Soon will my pilgrimage be done,
The world's long week be o'er,
That Sabbath dawn which needs no sun,
That day which fades no more.
James Edmeston, 1820.

51

God of the sunlight hours! how sad
Would evening shadows be,
Or night, in deeper sable clad,—
If aught were dark to Thee!

2 How mournfully that golden gleam
Would touch the thoughtful heart,
If, with its soft, retiring beam,
We saw Thy love depart!

3 But, though the gathering gloom may hide
Those gentle rays awhile,
Yet they, who in Thy house abide,
Shall ever share Thy smile.

4 Then let creation's volume close,
Though every page be bright;
On Thine, still open, we repose
With more intense delight.
Maria Grace Saffery, 1834, a

The Lord's Day.

52 Leighton. S.M. HENRY W. GREATOREX, 1849.

Still, still with Thee, my God! I would desire to be;
By day, by night, at home, abroad, I would be still with Thee:

2 With Thee, when dawn comes in,
  And calls me back to care;
Each day returning to begin
  With Thee, my God! in prayer:

3 With Thee, amid the crowd
  That throngs the busy mart,
To hear Thy voice, 'mid clamor loud,
  Speak softly to my heart:

4 With Thee, when day is done,
  And evening calms the mind;
The setting, as the rising, sun
  With Thee my heart would find.

5 With Thee, in Thee by faith
  Abiding I would be;
By day, by night, in life, in death,
  I would be still with Thee.
        James Drummond Burns, 1856.

53
Holy, delightful day,
  Day of divine delight!
We hailed thy gladsome morning ray;
  We bless thine evening bright.

2 Dear Lord! the day was bright,
  Because the day was Thine;
This full, this manifold delight,
  Was it not all divine?

3 Repeat the gladness here!
  Fulfill the bliss above!
Thy day, the everlasting year,
  Th' eternal joy, Thy love.
        Thomas H. Gill, 1860.

54
The day of praise is done;
  The evening shadows fall;
Yet pass not from us with the sun,
  True Light that lightenest all!

2 Around Thy throne on high,
  Where night can never be,
The white-robed harpers of the sky
  Bring ceaseless hymns to Thee.

3 Too faint our anthems here;
  Too soon of praise we tire;
But oh, the strains how full and clear
  Of that eternal choir!

4 Yet, Lord! to Thy dear will
  If Thou attune the heart,
We in Thine angels' music still
  May bear our lower part.

5 Shine Thou within us, then,
  A day that knows no end,
Till songs of angels and of men
  In perfect praise shall blend.
        John Ellerton, 1867.

The House of God.

55 Greenville. 8s 7s & 4. *J. J. Rousseau, 1751.*

In Thy name, O Lord! as-sem-bling, We, Thy peo-ple, now draw near;
D. C. Hear with meekness, Hear with meekness,—Hear Thy word with god-ly fear.

Teach us to re-joice with trembling; Speak, and let Thy ser-vants hear.—

2 While our days on earth are lengthened,
   May we give them, Lord, to Thee;
Cheered by hope, and daily strengthened,
   May we run, nor weary be,
      Till Thy glory
   Without clouds in heaven we see.

3 There, in worship purer, sweeter,
   Thee Thy people shall adore;
Tasting of enjoyment greater
   Far than thought conceived before;
      Full enjoyment,
   Full, unmixed, and evermore.
         Thomas Kelly, 1809.

56
Great Jehovah! we adore Thee,
   God, the Father, God, the Son,
God, the Spirit, joined in glory
   On the same eternal throne;
      Endless praises
   To Jehovah, Three in One.
         William Goode, 1811, a.

57
Lord! dismiss us with Thy blessing,
   Fill our hearts with joy and peace;
Let us each, Thy love possessing,
   Triumph in redeeming grace;
      Oh! refresh us,
   Traveling through this wilderness.

2 Thanks we give and adoration,
   For Thy gospel's joyful sound;
May the fruits of Thy salvation
   In our hearts and lives abound:
      May Thy presence
   With us, evermore, be found.

3 So, whene'er the signal's given,
   Us from earth to call away,
Borne on angels' wings to heaven,
   Glad the summons to obey,
      We shall surely
   Reign with Christ in endless day.
         John Fawcett, 1774.

58 Hendon. 7s.   *C. H. A. Malan, 1828.*

Lord! we come be-fore Thee now: At Thy feet we humbly bow; Oh! do not our

The House of God.

suit dis-dain;—Shall we seek Thee, Lord! in vain? Shall we seek Thee, Lord! in vain?

2 Lord! on Thee our souls depend,
In compassion, now descend;
Fill our hearts with Thy rich grace,
Tune our lips to sing Thy praise.

3 In Thine own appointed way,
Now we seek Thee, here we stay;
Lord! we know not how to go,
Till a blessing Thou bestow.

4 Send some message, from Thy word,
That may joy and peace afford;
Let Thy Spirit now impart
Full salvation to each heart.
William Hammond, 1745.

59
To Thy temple I repair,
Lord! I love to worship there,
When, within the veil, I meet
Christ before the mercy-seat.

2 While Thy glorious praise is sung,
Touch my lips, unloose my tongue,
That my joyful soul may bless
Thee, the Lord, my Righteousness.

3 From Thy house, when I return,
May my heart within me burn,
And at evening let me say,
"I have walked with God to-day."
James Montgomery, 1812.

60 Monkland. 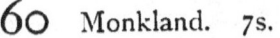 7s.

Arr. by JOHN P. WILKES, 1861.

Now may He, who, from the dead, Brought the Shepherd of the sheep,
Je-sus Christ, our King and Head, All our souls in safe-ty keep.

2 May He teach us to fulfill
   What is pleasing in His sight;
Perfect us in all His will,
   And preserve us day and night!

3 To that dear Redeemer's praise,
   Who the covenant sealed with blood,
Let our hearts and voices raise
   Loud thanksgivings to our God.
John Newton, 1779.

The House of God.

61 St. Godric. H. M.
JOHN B. DYKES, 1861.

Lord of the worlds above, How pleas-ant and how fair
The dwell-ings of Thy love, Thy earth-ly tem-ples are! To
Thine a-bode my heart aspires With warm de-sires to see my God.

2 Oh! happy souls who pray,
   Where God appoints to hear!
Oh! happy men who pay
   Their constant service there!
They praise Thee still; and happy they,
Who love the way to Zion's hill.

3 They go from strength to strength,
   Through this dark vale of tears,
Till each arrives at length,
   Till each in heaven appears;
Oh! glorious seat, when God, our King,
Shall thither bring our willing feet.
                              Isaac Watts, 1719.

62

O Zion! tune thy voice,
   And raise thy hands on high;
Tell all the earth thy joys,
   And boast salvation nigh;
Cheerful in God, arise and shine,
While rays divine stream all abroad.

2 He gilds thy morning face
   With beams that cannot fade;
His all-resplendent grace
   He pours around thy head;
The nations round thy form shall view,
With lustre new, divinely crowned.

3 In honor to His name,
   Reflect that sacred light;
And loud that grace proclaim,
   Which makes thy darkness bright;
Pursue His praise, till sovereign love,
In worlds above, the glory raise.

4 There, on His holy hill,
   A brighter sun shall rise,
And, with His radiance, fill
   Those fairer, purer skies;
While, round His throne, ten thousand stars,
In nobler spheres, His influence own.
                           Philip Doddridge, 1740.

The House of God.

63 Mear. C. M. *Unknown, 1740.*

A-rise, O King of grace! a-rise, And en-ter to Thy rest;
Lo! Thy church waits, with long-ing eyes, Thus to be owned and blest.

2 Here let the Son of David reign,
   Let God's Anointed shine;
   Justice and truth His court maintain,
   With love and power divine.

3 Here let Him hold a lasting throne;
   And, as His kingdom grows,
   Fresh honors shall adorn His crown,
   And shame confound His foes.
                            Isaac Watts, 1719.

64 Lanesboro'. C. M. *Wm. Dixon, 1790.*

Early, my God! without de-lay, I haste to seek Thy face; My thirsty spir-it
faints a-way, My thirsty spir-it faints a-way, Without Thy cheering grace.

2 I've seen Thy glory and Thy power
   Through all Thy temple shine;
   My God! repeat that heavenly hour,
   That vision so divine.

3 Not life itself, with all its joys,
   Can my best passions move;
   Or raise so high my cheerful voice,
   As Thy forgiving love.
                            Isaac Watts, 1719.

The House of God.

65 Dalston. S. P. M.   Aaron Williams, 1763.

How pleased and blessed was I, To hear the people cry,—
"Come, let us seek our God to-day!" Yes, with a cheerful zeal.
We haste to Zion's hill, And there our vows and honors pay.

2 Zion! thrice happy place,
  Adorned with wondrous grace,
And walls of strength embrace thee round;
  In thee our tribes appear
  To praise, and pray, and hear
The sacred gospel's joyful sound.

3 There David's greater Son
  Has fixed His royal throne;
He sits for grace and judgment there:
  He bids the saint be glad,
  He makes the sinner sad,
And humble souls rejoice with fear.

4 May peace attend thy gate,
  And joy within thee wait,
To bless the soul of every guest!
  The man who seeks thy peace,
  And wishes thine increase,—
A thousand blessings on him rest!

5 My tongue repeats her vows;
  "Peace to this sacred house!"
For there my friends and kindred dwell:
  And, since my glorious God
  Makes thee His blest abode,
My soul shall ever love thee well.
Isaac Watts 1719.

66

The Lord Jehovah reigns,
  His royal state maintains,
His head with awful glories crowned;
  Arrayed in robes of light,
  Begirt with sovereign might,
And rays of majesty around.

2 Upheld by Thy commands,
  The world securely stands,
And skies and stars obey Thy word;
  Thy throne was fixed on high
  Before the starry sky;
Eternal is Thy kingdom, Lord!

The House of God.

3 Let floods and nations rage,
And all their powers engage—
Let swelling tides assault the sky—
The terrors of Thy frown
Shall beat their madness down;
Thy throne forever stands on high.

4 Thy promises are true;
Thy grace is ever new;
There fixed, Thy church shall ne'er remove;
Thy saints, with holy fear,
Shall in Thy courts appear,
And sing Thine everlasting love.
Isaac Watts, 1719.

67

'Tis heaven begun below
To hear Christ's praises flow
In Zion, where His name is known:
What will it be above
To sing redeeming love,
And cast our crowns before His throne!

2 Oh, what sweet company
We then shall hear and see!
What harmony will there abound!
When souls unnumbered sing
The praise of Zion's King,
Nor one dissenting voice is found!

3 With everlasting joy,
Such as will never cloy,
We shall be filled, nor wish for more;
Bright as meridian day,
Calm as the evening ray,
Full as a sea without a shore.

4 Till that blest period come,
Zion shall be my home;
And may I never thence remove,
Till from the church below
To that on high I go,
And there commune in perfect love.
Joseph Swain, 1792.

68 Laban. S. M.
LOWELL MASON, 1830.

Come, we that love the Lord! And let our joys be known: Join in a song with sweet accord, And thus surround the throne.

2 Let those refuse to sing,
That never knew our God;
But children of the heavenly King
May speak their joys abroad.

3 The men of grace have found
Glory begun below;
Celestial fruits on earthly ground
From faith and hope may grow.

4 The hill of Zion yields
A thousand sacred sweets
Before we reach the heavenly fields,
Or walk the golden streets.

5 Then let our songs abound,
And every tear be dry;
We're marching thro Immanuel's ground,
To fairer worlds on high.
Isaac Watts, 1707.

The House of God.

69 Warwick. C. M. *Samuel Stanley, 1800.*

My soul! how lovely is the place, To which thy God resorts! 'Tis heaven to see His smiling face, Though in His earthly courts.

2 There the great Monarch of the skies
  His saving power displays,
And light breaks in upon our eyes,
  With kind and quickening rays.

3 There, mighty God! Thy words declare
  The secrets of Thy will;
And still we seek Thy mercy there,
  And sing Thy praises still.
            Isaac Watts, 1719.

70 Uxbridge. L. M. *Lowell Mason, 1824.*

How pleasant, how divinely fair, O Lord of hosts! Thy dwellings are With long desire my spirit faints, To meet th' assemblies of Thy saints.

2 Bless'd are the men, whose hearts are set
To find the way to Zion's gate;
God is their strength; and, through the road,
They lean upon their Helper, God.

3 Cheerful they walk with growing strength,
Till all shall meet in heaven at length;
Till all before Thy face appear,
And join in nobler worship there.
            Isaac Watts, 1719.

The House of God.

71 Mendon. L. M. — German, 1822.

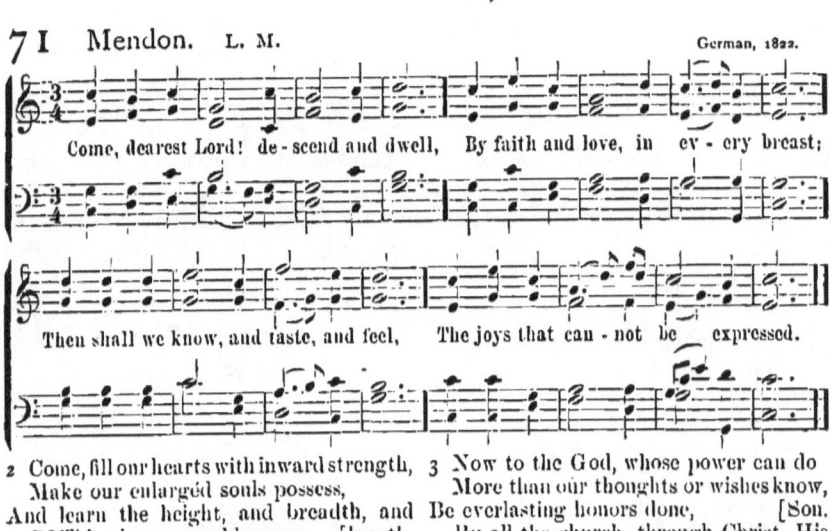

Come, dearest Lord! descend and dwell, By faith and love, in every breast;
Then shall we know, and taste, and feel, The joys that cannot be expressed.

2 Come, fill our hearts with inward strength,
  Make our enlarged souls possess,
And learn the height, and breadth, and
  Of Thine immeasurable grace. [length,

3 Now to the God, whose power can do
  More than our thoughts or wishes know,
Be everlasting honors done, [Son.
  By all the church, through Christ, His
Isaac Watts, 1709.

72 Truro. L. M. — Charles Burney, 1769.

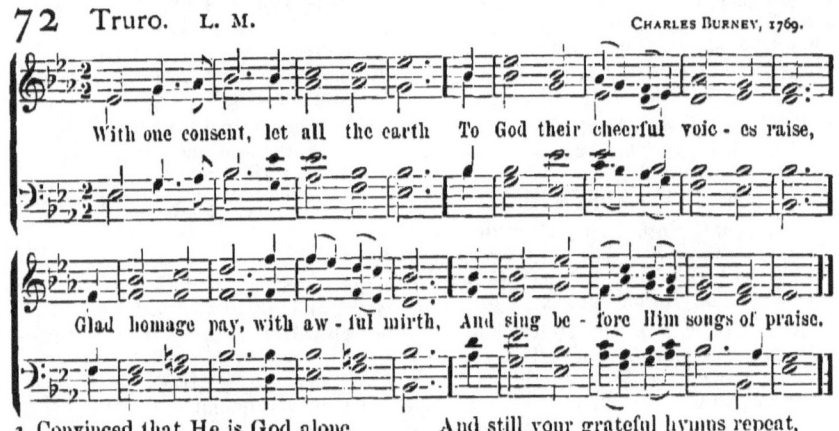

With one consent, let all the earth To God their cheerful voices raise,
Glad homage pay, with awful mirth, And sing before Him songs of praise.

2 Convinced that He is God alone,
    From whom both we and all proceed;
  We, whom He chooses for His own,
    The flock that He vouchsafes to feed.

3 Oh! enter, then, His temple gate,
    Thence to His courts devoutly press;

And still your grateful hymns repeat,
  And still His name with praises bless.

4 For He's the Lord, supremely good;
    His mercy is for ever sure;
  His truth, which always firmly stood,
    To endless ages shall endure.
Nahum Tate, 1696.

The Trinity.

73 Te Deum. L. M.   JOSEPH E. SWEETSER, 1849.

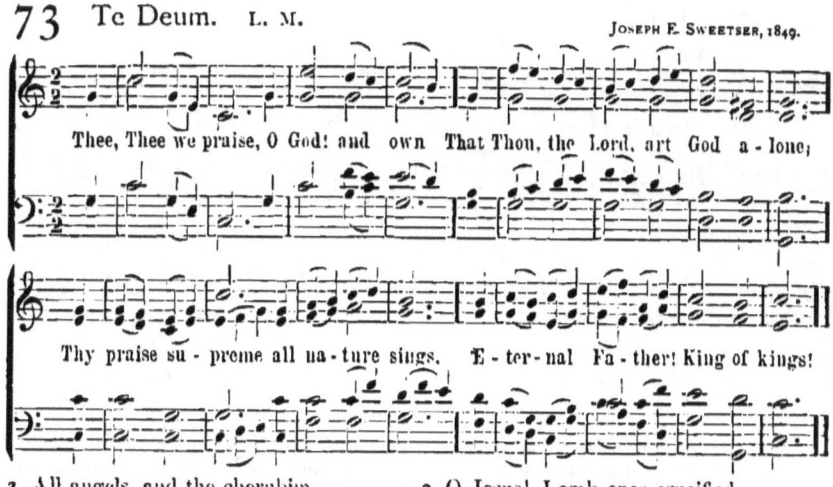

Thee, Thee we praise, O God! and own That Thou, the Lord, art God alone;
Thy praise supreme all nature sings. Eternal Father! King of kings!

2 All angels, and the cherubim,—
The heavenly host,—the seraphim,—
Cease not to cry,—"Be Thou adored,
O holy, holy, holy Lord!"

3 The heavens and earth are full of Thee,—
Thy glory, power, and majesty;
Th' apostles, prophets, martyrs, raise
To Thee their loudest songs of praise.

4 Thy holy church, o'er all the earth,
Exulting owns, with hallowed mirth,—
Infinite majesty is Thine,
Father eternal! Power divine!

5 Thee, too, O Christ! they all confess,—
Thee, King of glory! Thee they bless;
The Father's Son Thou art alone,—
Partaker of th' eternal throne.

6 Thee, Father, Son, and Holy Ghost!
Thy saints, with all the heavenly host,
Confess, proclaim, extol, adore,
From day to day, for evermore.
Latin, *Ambrose* (?), 390.
Tr. *Edwin F. Hatfield*, 1871.

74

O holy, holy, holy Lord!
Bright in Thy deeds and in Thy name,
Forever be Thy name adored,
Thy glories let the world proclaim!

2 O Jesus! Lamb once crucified
To take our load of sins away,—
Thine be the hymn, that rolls its tide
Along the realms of upper day!

3 O holy Spirit! from above,
In streams of light and glory given,
Thou source of ecstasy and love,
Thy praises ring through earth and [heaven!

4 O God Triune! to Thee we owe
Our every thought, our every song;
And ever may Thy praises flow
From saint and seraph's burning tongue!
James Wallis Eastburn, 1819.

75

The Lord is King; lift up thy voice,
O earth! and, all ye heavens! rejoice;
From world to world the joy shall ring,—
The Lord omnipotent is King.

2 Alike pervaded by His eye,
All parts of His dominion lie;
This world of ours and worlds unseen,
There is no boundary between.

3 Oh! when His wisdom can mistake,
His might decay, His love forsake,
Then may His children cease to sing,—
The Lord omnipotent is King.
Josiah Conder, 1824. a.

The Trinity.

76 Dix. 7s.
Conrad Kocher, 1838, arr.

Holy, holy, holy Lord God of hosts, e-ter-nal King!
By the heavens and earth a-dored! An-gels and arch-an-gels sing,
Chant-ing ev-er-last-ing-ly To the bless-ed Trin-i-ty.

2 Since by Thee were all things made,
   And in Thee do all things live,
Be to Thee all honor paid;
   Praise to Thee let all things give,
      Singing everlastingly
      To the blessèd Trinity.

3 Thousands, tens of thousands, stand
   Spirits bless'd, before the throne,
Speeding thence at Thy command;
   And, when Thy commands are done,
      Singing everlastingly
      To the blessèd Trinity.

4 Cherubim and seraphim
   Veil their faces with their wings;
Eyes of angels are too dim
   To behold the King of kings,
      While they sing eternally
      To the blessèd Trinity.

5 Thee, apostles, prophets, Thee,
   Thee, the noble martyr band,
Praise with solemn jubilee;
   Thee, the church in every land,
      Singing everlastingly
      To the blessèd Trinity.

6 Hallelujah! Lord! to Thee,
   Father, Son, and Holy Ghost,
Godhead One, and Persons three!
   Join with us the heavenly host,
      Singing everlastingly
      To the blessèd Trinity.
                          Christopher Wordsworth, 1862.

77

God of mercy, God of grace!
Show the brightness of Thy face;
Shine upon us, Saviour! shine;
Fill Thy church with light divine;
And Thy saving health extend
Unto earth's remotest end.

2 Let the people praise Thee, Lord!
Be by all that live adored:
Let the nations shout and sing,
Glory to their Saviour King;
At Thy feet their tributes pay,
And Thy holy will obey.

3 Let the people praise Thee, Lord!
Earth shall then her fruits afford;
God to man His blessing give;
Man to God devoted live;
All below, and all above,
One in joy, and light, and love.
                          Henry Francis Lyte, 1834.

The Trinity.

78 Italy. 6s & 4s. FELICE GIARDINI, 1769.

Come, Thou almighty King! Help us Thy name to sing, Help us to praise: Father! all glorious, O'er all victorious, Come, and reign o'er us, Ancient of days!

2 Come, Thou incarnate Word!
Gird on Thy mighty sword;
  Our prayer attend:
Come, and Thy people bless,
And give Thy word success;
Spirit of holiness!
  On us descend.

3 Come, holy Comforter!
Thy sacred witness bear,
  In this glad hour:
Thou, who almighty art,
Now rule in every heart,
And ne'er from us depart,
  Spirit of power!

4 To the great One in Three
The highest praises be,
  Hence, evermore!
His sovereign majesty
May we in glory see,
And to eternity
  Love and adore.
        Charles Wesley, 1757.

79
Thou, whose almighty word
Chaos and darkness heard,
  And took their flight,

Hear us, we humbly pray,
And, where the gospel's day
Sheds not its glorious ray,
  "Let there be light!"

2 Thou! who didst come to bring,
On Thy redeeming wing,
  Healing and sight,
Health to the sick in mind,
Sight to the inly blind,—
Oh! now to all mankind
  "Let there be light!"

3 Spirit of truth and love,
Life-giving holy Dove!
  Speed forth Thy flight:
Move o'er the waters' face,
Bearing the lamp of grace,
And, in earth's darkest place,
  "Let there be light!"

4 Blessed and holy Three,
All-glorious Trinity,—
  Wisdom, Love, Might!
Boundless as ocean's tide
Rolling in fullest pride,
Through the world, far and wide,—
  "Let there be light!"
        John Marriott, 1813.

The Trinity

80 Amsterdam. 7s & 6s. P.   JAMES NARES, 1750.

Meet and right it is to sing. In every time and place.
Glo-ry to our heav'nly King. The God of truth and grace: Join we, then, with sweet accord,
All in one thanksgiving join: Ho-ly, ho-ly, ho-ly Lord! E-ternal praise be Thine.

2 Thee the first born sons of light,
  In choral symphonies,
Praise by day, day without night,
  And never, never cease:
Angels, and archangels, all
  Praise the mystic Three in One,
Sing, and stop, and gaze, and fall,
  O'erwhelmed before Thy throne.

3 Vying with the heavenly choir
  Who chant Thy praise above,
We on eagle's wings aspire—
  The wings of faith and love:
Thee they sing with glory crowned;
  We extol the slaughtered Lamb:
Lower if our voices sound,
  Our theme is still the same.

4 Father, God! Thy love we praise,
  Which gave Thy Son to die:
Jesus, full of truth and grace,
  Alike we glorify:
Spirit, Comforter Divine!
  Praise by all to Thee be given,
Till we in full chorus join,
  And earth is turned to heaven.
Charles Wesley, 1749.

81

RISE, my soul! and stretch thy wings,
  Thy better portion trace;
Rise, from transitory things,
  Tow'rds heaven, thy native place
Sun, and moon, and stars decay,
  Time shall soon this earth remove;
Rise, my soul! and haste away,
  To seats prepared above.

2 Rivers to the ocean run,
  Nor stay in all their course;
Fire ascending seeks the sun;
  Both speed them to their source:
So a soul, that's born of God,
  Pants to view His glorious face;
Upward tends to His abode,
  To rest in His embrace.

3 Cease, ye pilgrims! cease to mourn,
  Press onward to the prize;
Soon our Saviour will return,
  Triumphant in the skies:
Yet a season,—and you know,
  Happy entrance will be given,
All our sorrows left below,
  And earth exchanged for heaven.
Robert Seagrave, 1742, a.

The Trinity.

82   Arthur's Seat.   H. M.   *John Goss.*

To Him that chose us first, Before the world began; To Him that bore the curse To save rebellious man; To Him that formed our hearts anew Is endless praise and glory due.

2 The Father's love shall run
　Through our immortal songs;
We bring to God, the Son,
　Hosannas on our tongues:
Our lips address the Spirit's name,
With equal praise, and zeal the same.

3 Let every saint above,
　And angel round the throne,
For ever bless and love
　The sacred Three in One:
Thus heaven shall raise His honors high,
When earth and time grow old and die.
　　　　　　　　　　Isaac Watts, 1709.

83
We give immortal praise
　To God the Father's love,
For all our comforts here,
　And better hopes above:
He sent His own eternal Son
To die for sins that man had done.

2 To God, the Son, belongs
　Immortal glory too,
Who bought us with His blood
　From everlasting woe:
And now He lives, and now He reigns,
And sees the fruit of all His pains.

3 To God the Spirit's name,
　Immortal worship give,
Whose new-creating power
　Makes the dead sinner live:
His work completes the great design,
And fills the soul with joy divine.

4 Almighty God! to Thee
　Be endless honors done,—
The undivided Three,
　The great, mysterious One!
Where reason fails with all her powers,
There faith prevails and love adores.
　　　　　　　　　　Isaac Watts, 1709.

84   Lyman.   H. M.   *L. van Beethoven.*

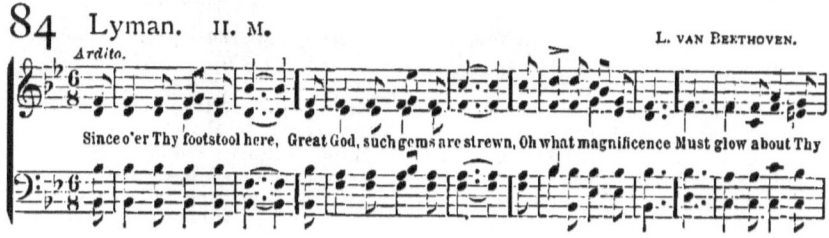

Since o'er Thy footstool here, Great God, such gems are strewn, Oh what magnificence Must glow about Thy

The Trinity.

throne! So brilliant these but drops of light— There o-cean tides roll deep and bright.

2 If night's blue-curtained sky,
　With constellations wrought,
Like royal canopy,
　With matchless diamonds fraught,
Be, Lord, Thy temples outer vail,
What splendor at the shrine must dwell!

3 Can our dim eyes endure
　That noon of living rays!
These spirits, so impure,
　Upon Thy glory gaze!
In mercy, Lord, anoint our sight,
And fit us for that world of light.
　　　　　　　W. A. Muhlenberg, 1823, a.

85　Integer.　11s & 5.　　F. F. FLEMMING, 1810.

Praise ye the Father! for His loving kindness, Tenderly cares He for His erring children; Praise Him, ye an-gels, praise Him in the heavens, Praise ye Je-ho-vah!

2 Praise ye the Saviour! great is His compassion,
Graciously cares He for His chosen people;
Young men and maidens, ye old men and children,
　　Praise ye the Saviour!

3 Praise ye the Spirit! Comforter of Israel,
Sent of the Father and the Son to bless us;
Praise ye the Father, Son and Holy Spirit,
　　Praise ye the Triune God.
　　　　　　Elizabeth Charles.

God the Father.

86 Grostete. L. M. — Henry W. Greatorex, 1849.

God of my life! through all my days, My grateful powers shall sound Thy praise; The song shall wake with opening light, And warble to the silent night.

2 When anxious cares would break my rest,
And griefs would tear my throbbing breast,
Thy tuneful praises, raised on high,
Shall check the murmur and the sigh.

3 When death o'er nature shall prevail,
And all its powers of language fail;
Joy through my swimming eyes shall break,
And mean the thanks I cannot speak.

4 But, oh! when that last conflict's o'er,
And I am chained to flesh no more,—
With what glad accents shall I rise
To join the music of the skies!
Philip Doddridge, 1740.

87

My God, my King, Thy various praise
Shall fill the remnant of my days;
Thy grace employ my humble tongue,
Till death and glory raise the song.

2 The wings of every hour shall bear
Some thankful tribute to Thine ear;
And every setting sun shall see
New works of duty done for Thee.

3 Let distant times and nations raise
The long succession of Thy praise;
And unborn ages make my song
The joy and triumph of their tongue.

4 But who can speak Thy wondrous deeds?
Thy greatness all our thoughts exceeds;
Vast and unsearchable Thy ways!
Vast and immortal be Thy praise!
Isaac Watts, 1719.

88

Sing to the Lord a joyful song;
  Lift up your hearts, your voices raise;
To us His gracious gifts belong,
  To Him our songs of love and praise.

2 For life and love, for rest and food,
  For daily help and nightly care,
Sing to the Lord, for He is good,
  And praise His name, for it is fair:

3 For strength to those who on Him wait,
  His truth to prove, His will to do,
Praise ye our God, for He is great,
  Trust in His name, for it is true:

4 For joys untold that daily move
  Round those who love His sweet employ,
Sing to our God, for He is love,
  Exalt His name, for it is joy:

5 For life below, with all its bliss,
  And for that life, more pure and high,
That inner life, which over this
  Shall ever shine, and never die.
John S. B. Monsell, 1852.

God the Father.

89 Huguenot. 10s. LOUIS BOURGEOIS, 1551.

In-fi-nite God! Thou great un-ri-valed One! Whose light e-clip-ses that of yon-der sun; Compared with Thee, how dim his beau-ty seems! How quenched the ra-diance of his gold-en beams!

2 O God! Thy creatures in one strain agree;—
All, in all times and places, speak of Thee;—
Even I, with trembling heart, and stammering tongue,
Attempt Thy praise, and join the general song.

3 All present through infinitude of space,
Thou art Thyself Thine own vast dwelling-place;
Soul of our soul! whom yet no sense of ours
Discerns, eluding our most active powers.

4 Light unapproachable surrounds Thy throne,
Darkness of glory veils Thee still unknown;
Unknown,—yet dwelling in our inmost part,
Teaching deep wisdom, Sovereign of the heart.

5 Oh then repeat the truth that never tires;
No God is like the God my soul desires;
He, at whose voice heaven trembles, even He,—
Great as He is,—knows how to stoop to me.

Fr. *Madame Guyon*. 1710.

God the Father.

90 Trust. 8s & 7s. F. Mendelssohn Bartholdy, 1840, alt.

God, my King, Thy might confessing, Ev-er will I bless Thy name;
Day by day Thy throne addressing, Still will I Thy praise proclaim.

2 Honor great our God befitteth;
  Who His majesty can reach?
Age to age His works transmitteth,
  Age to age His power shall teach.

3 They shall talk of all Thy glory,
  On Thy might and greatness dwell,
Speak of Thy dread acts the story,
  And Thy deeds of wonder tell.

4 Nor shall fail from memory's treasure,
  Works by love and mercy wrought—
Works of love surpassing measure,
  Works of mercy passing thought.

5 All Thy works, O Lord, shall bless Thee,
  Thee shall all Thy saints adore;
King supreme shall they confess Thee,
  And proclaim Thy sovereign power.
              Richard Mant, 1832.

91

God is love; His mercy brightens
  All the path in which we rove;
Bliss He wakes, and woe He lightens;
  God is wisdom, God is love.

2 Chance and change are busy ever;
  Man decays, and ages move;
But His mercy waneth never;
  God is wisdom, God is love.

3 Ev'n the hour, that darkest seemeth,
  Will His changeless goodness prove;
From the gloom His brightness streameth,
  God is wisdom, God is love.

4 He with earthly cares entwineth
  Hope and comfort from above;
Every where His glory shineth;
  God is wisdom, God is love.
              John Bowring, 1825.

92

Music! bring thy sweetest treasures,
  Dulcet melody and chord,
Link the notes with loveliest measures,
  To the glory of the Lord.

2 Wing the praise from every nation,
  Sweetest instruments employ,
Raise the chorus of creation,
  Swell the universal joy.

3 Far away be gloom and sadness;
  Spirits with seraphic fire!   [ness!
Tongues with hymns, and hearts with glad-
  Higher sound the chords, and higher.

4 To the Father, to the Saviour,
  To the Spirit, Source of light,
As it was, is now, and ever,
  Praise in heaven's supremest height.
              James Edmeston, 1837.

God the Father.

93 Devotion. 8s & 7s. Edmund S. Carter.

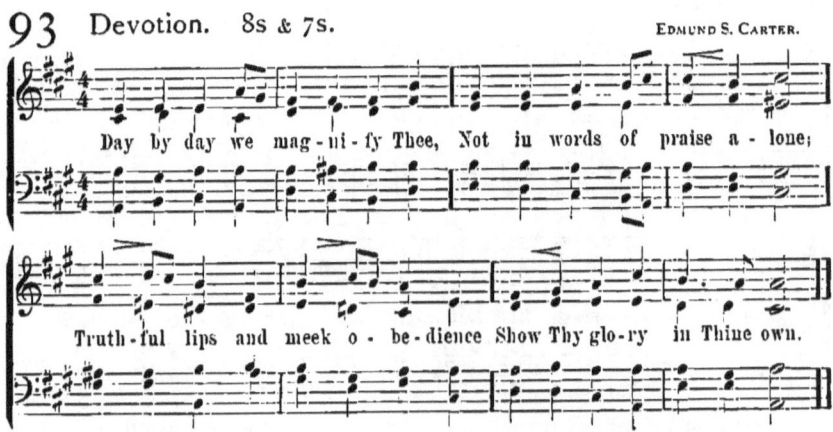

Day by day we mag-ni-fy Thee, Not in words of praise a-lone;
Truth-ful lips and meek o-be-dience Show Thy glo-ry in Thine own.

2 Day by day we magnify Thee,
  When, for Jesus' sake we try
Every wrong to bear with patience,
  Every sin to mortify.

3 Day by day we magnify Thee,
  Till our days on earth shall cease,
Till we rest from these our labors,
  Waiting for Thy day in peace.
                          Unknown.

94

Praise to Thee, Thou great Creator!
  Praise to Thee from every tongue;
Join, my soul, with every creature,
  Join the universal song.

2 Father! source of all compassion!
  Pure, unbounded grace is Thine:
Hail the God of our salvation,
  Praise Him for His love divine!

3 For ten thousand blessings given,
  For the hope of future joy,
Sound His praise thro' earth and heaven,
  Sound Jehovah's praise on high!

4 Praise to God, the great Creator,
  Father, Son, and Holy Ghost;
Praise Him, every living creature,
  Earth and heaven's united host.

5 Joyfully on earth adore Him,
  Till in heaven our song we raise;
Then enraptured fall before Him,
  Lost in wonder, love, and praise!
                        John Fawcett, 1782.

95

Take me, O my Father! take me,
  Take me, save me, through Thy Son;
That, which Thou wouldst have me, make me,
  Let Thy will in me be done.

2 Long from Thee my footsteps straying,
  Thorny proved the way I trod;
Weary come I now, and praying—
  Take me to Thy love, my God!

3 Fruitless years with grief recalling,
  Humbly I confess my sin;
At Thy feet, O Father! falling,
  To Thy household take me in.

4 Freely now to Thee I proffer
  This relenting heart of mine;
Freely, life and soul I offer—
  Gift unworthy love like Thine.

5 Father! take me; all forgiving,
  Fold me to Thy loving breast;
In Thy love for ever living,
  I must be for ever blessed!
                        Ray Palmer, 1864.

God the Father.

96 Henry. C. M. S. B. Pond, 1834.

The Lord de-scend-ed from a-bove, And bowed the heavens most high;
And un-der-neath His feet He cast The dark-ness of the sky.

2 On cherubim and seraphim,
　Full royally He rode,
And, on the wings of mighty winds,
　Came flying all abroad.

3 He sat serene upon the floods,
　Their fury to restrain;
And He, as sovereign Lord and King,
　For evermore shall reign.
　　　　　Thomas Sternhold, 1549, a.

97 Meditation. C. M. S. P. Tuckerman, 1843.

Grave.
Keep si-lence, all cre-a-ted things! And wait your Mak-er's nod;
My soul stands trembling, while she sings The hon-ors of her God.

2 Life, death, and hell, and worlds unknown,
　Hang on His firm decree;
He sits on no precarious throne,
　Nor borrows leave to be.

3 My God! I would not long to see
　My fate with curious eyes,—

What gloomy lines are writ for me,
　Or what bright scenes may rise:
4 In Thy fair book of life and grace,
　May I but find my name,
Recorded in some humble place,
　Beneath my Lord, the Lamb.
　　　　　Isaac Watts, 1706, a.

God the Father.

98 Old Hundredth. L. M.   Louis Bourgeois, 1552.

Be-fore Je-ho-vah's aw-ful throne, Ye na-tions! bow with sa-cred joy;

Know that the Lord is God a-lone; He can cre-ate, and He de-stroy.

2 His sovereign power, without our aid,
  Made us of clay, and formed us men;
And when, like wandering sheep we strayed,
  He brought us to His fold again.

3 We are His people, we His care,—
  Our souls, and all our mortal frame:
What lasting honors shall we rear,
  Almighty Maker! to Thy name?

4 We'll crowd Thy gates with thankful songs,
  High as the heavens our voices raise;
And earth, with her ten thousand tongues,
  Shall fill Thy courts with sounding praise.

5 Wide as the world is Thy command,
  Vast as eternity Thy love;
Firm as a rock Thy truth must stand,
  When rolling years shall cease to move.
        Isaac Watts, 1719, v. 1, a. by J. Wesley.

99

From all that dwell below the skies,
  Let the Creator's praise arise;
Let the Redeemer's name be sung,
  Through every land, by every tongue.

2 Eternal are Thy mercies, Lord!
  Eternal truth attends Thy word;
Thy praise shall sound from shore to shore,
  Till suns shall rise and set no more.
        Isaac Watts, 1719.

100

All people, that on earth do dwell!
  Sing to the Lord with cheerful voice;
Him serve with mirth, His praise forth tell,
  Come ye before Him and rejoice.

2 Know that the Lord is God indeed;
  Without our aid He did us make;
We are His flock, He doth us feed,
  And for His sheep, He doth us take.

3 Oh! enter, then, His gates with praise;
  Approach with joy His courts unto;
Praise, laud, and bless His name always,
  For it is seemly so to do.

4 For why? the Lord, our God, is good,
  His mercy is for ever sure;
His truth at all times firmly stood,
  And shall from age to age endure.
        William Kethe, 1561.

101

Praise God, from whom all blessings flow;
Praise Him, all creatures here below!
Praise Him above, ye heavenly host!
Praise Father, Son, and Holy Ghost.
        Thomas Ken, 1697, a.

God the Father.

102 Winchester. L. M.
German, 1690.

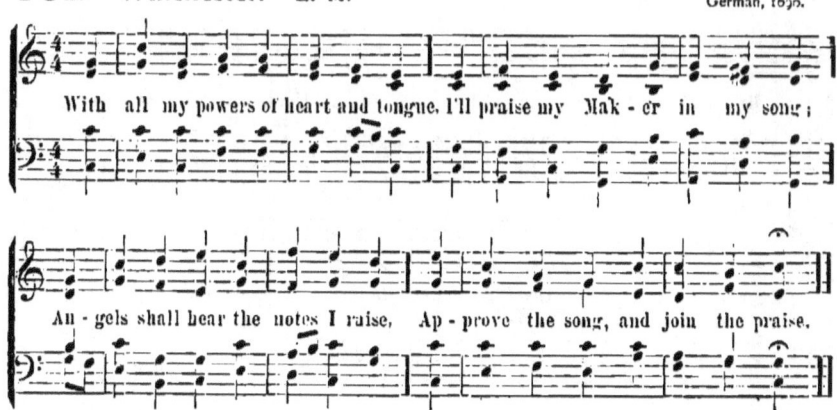

2 To God I cried, when troubles rose;
He heard me, and subdued my foes;—
He did my rising fears control,
And strength diffused through all my soul.

3 I'll sing Thy truth and mercy, Lord!
I'll sing the wonders of Thy word;
Not all Thy works and names below
So much Thy power and glory show.
Isaac Watts, 1719.

103 Bowen. L. M.
F. J. Haydn.

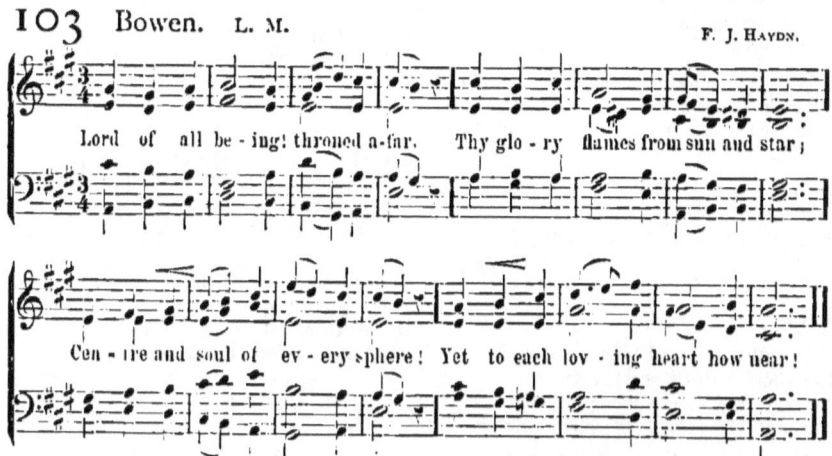

2 Sun of our life! Thy quickening ray
Sheds on our path the glow of day;
Star of our hope! Thy softened light
Cheers the long watches of the night.

3 Our midnight is Thy smile withdrawn;
Our noontide is Thy gracious dawn;
Our rainbow arch Thy mercy's sign;
All, save the clouds of sin, are Thine.

God the Father.

4 Lord of all life, below, above!
Whose light is truth, whose warmth is love,
Before Thine ever-blazing throne,
We ask no lustre of our own.

5 Grant us Thy truth to make us free,
And kindling hearts that burn for Thee,
Till all Thy living altars claim
One holy light, one heavenly flame.
Oliver Wendell Holmes, 1848.

104

High in the heavens, eternal God!
Thy goodness in full glory shines;
Thy truth shall break through every cloud,
That veils and darkens Thy designs.

2 For ever firm Thy justice stands,
As mountains their foundations keep;
Wise are the wonders of Thy hands;
Thy judgments are a mighty deep.

3 Life, like a fountain rich and free,
Springs from the presence of the Lord;
And, in Thy light, our souls shall see,
The glories promised in Thy word.
Isaac Watts, 1719.

105 Rapture. C. P. M.
EDWARD HARWOOD, 1760.

Begin, my soul! th' exalted lay, Let each enraptured thought obey, And praise th' Almighty name; Lo! heaven and earth, and seas, and skies, In one melodious concert rise, To swell th' inspiring theme.

2 Ye angels! catch the thrilling sound,
While all th' adoring thrones around,
  His boundless mercy sing:
Let every listening saint above
Wake all the tuneful soul of love,
  And touch the sweetest string.

3 Let man, by nobler passions swayed,
The feeling heart, the judging head,
  In heavenly praise employ;
Spread His tremendous name around
Till heaven's broad arch rings back the sound,
  The general burst of joy.
John Ogilvie, 1749.

God the Father.

106 Guyon. 10s 6s & 10s. W. H. WALTER, 1872.

I love my God, but with no love of mine, For I have none to give; I love Thee, Lord, but all the love is Thine,

For by Thy life I live; I am as nothing, and rejoice to be Emptied and lost, and swallow'd up in Thee.

2 Thou, Lord, alone art all Thy children need,
  And there is none beside;
From Thee the streams of blessedness proceed,
  In Thee the blest abide;
Fountain of life and all abounding grace,
Our source, our centre, and our dwelling-place.
      Madame Jeanne M. B. de la M. Guyon, 1710.

107 Sunlight. 6s & 5s. SAMUEL SMITH, 1871.

Summer suns are glowing Over land and sea, Happy light is flowing Bountiful and free;

Everything rejoices In the mellow rays, All earth's thousand voices Swell the psalm of praise.

God the Father.

2 God's free mercy streameth
   Over all the world,
And His banner gleameth
   Everywhere unfurled:
Broad and deep and glorious,
   As the heaven above,
Shines in might victorious
   His eternal Love.

3 We will never doubt Thee,
   Though Thou veil Thy light:
Life is dark without Thee;
   Death with Thee is bright:
Light of light! shine o'er us
   On our pilgrim way,
Go Thou still before us
   To the endless day.
            Wm. Walsham How, 1871.

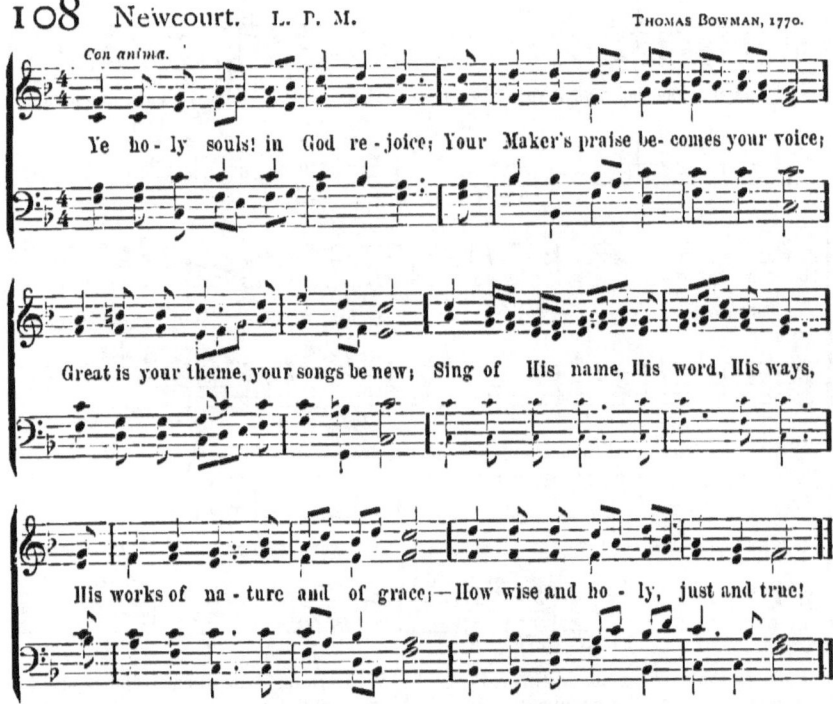

108 Newcourt. L. P. M.   Thomas Bowman, 1770.

Con anima.

Ye ho-ly souls! in God re-joice; Your Maker's praise be-comes your voice;

Great is your theme, your songs be new; Sing of His name, His word, His ways,

His works of na-ture and of grace;—How wise and ho-ly, just and true!

2 Justice and truth He ever loves;
And the whole earth His goodness proves;
  His word the heavenly arches spread;
How wide they shine from north to south!
And, by the spirit of His mouth,
  Were all the starry armies made.

3 I'll praise my Maker with my breath;
And, when my voice is lost in death,
  Praise shall employ my nobler powers:
My days of praise shall ne'er be past,
While life, and thought, and being last,
  Or immortality endures.
            Isaac Watts, 1719.

God the Father.

109 Creation. L. M. F. J. Haydn, 1795.

The spacious firmament on high, With all the blue ethereal sky,
And spangled heavens, a shining frame, Their great Original proclaim.
Th' unwearied sun, from day to day, Does his Creator's power display,
And publishes, to every land, The work of an Almighty hand.

2 Soon as the evening shades prevail,
The moon takes up the wondrous tale;
And nightly, to the listening earth,
Repeats the story of her birth:—
Whilst all the stars that round her burn,
And all the planets in their turn,
Confirm the tidings, as they roll,
And spread the truth from pole to pole.

3 What though, in solemn silence, all
Move round the dark terrestrial ball?
What though no real voice, nor sound,
Amidst their radiant orbs be found?—
In reason's ear they all rejoice,
And utter forth a glorious voice;
For ever singing as they shine,—
"The hand that made us is divine."

Joseph Addison, 1712.

God the Father.

110 Antiphon. 8s & 7s. FRANZ SCHUBERT, 1817.

Lord, Thy glory fills the heaven; Earth is with its fullness stor'd; Unto Thee be glory given, Ho-ly, ho-ly, ho-ly Lord! Heav'n is still with anthems ringing; Earth takes up the an-gels' cry, Ho-ly, ho-ly, ho-ly singing, Lord of hosts, Thou Lord most high, Lord of hosts, Thou Lord most high.

2 Ever thus in God's high praises,
   Brethren, let our tongues unite,
While our thoughts His greatness raises,
   And our love His gifts excite:
With His seraph train before Him,
   With His holy church below,
Thus unite we to adore Him,
   Bid we thus our anthem flow.

3 Lord, Thy glory fills the heaven;
   Earth is with its fullness stored;
Unto Thee be glory given,
   Holy, holy, holy Lord!
Thus Thy glorious name confessing,
   We adopt the angels' cry,
Holy, holy, holy, blessing
   Thee, the Lord our God most high!
            Richard Mant, 1837, alt.

God the Father.

111 Pleiades. 7s & 5s. JOHN H. HOPKINS, 1846.

God hath made the moon, whose beam Shimmers soft o'er hill and stream, Lighting with her silv'ry gleam All our lonely way. She with star-companions bright, Silvers all the hours of night; Then fades in o-ver-whelming light, Lost in per-fect day.

2 God hath made the glorious sun,
Through his daily course to run;
From the dawn till day is done
 Brightly shineth he.
When his circling round is o'er,
And we see him here no more,
He rises on a brighter shore,
 Far beyond the sea.

3 God hath sent me here below,
In my daily life to show,
Constant love to friend and foe,
 As He showed for me.
When we here have closed our eyes,
Sunk where death's dark ocean lies,
To worlds of glory may we rise,
 Lighted, Lord, by Thee!
   John H. Hopkins, 1846.

112 Dundee. C. M. Scotch Psalter, 1615.

Mak-er of earth, to Thee a-lone Per-pet-ual rest be-longs;

God the Father.

To Thee bright choirs a-round Thy throne Pour forth their end-less songs.

2 But we, as sinless now no more,
  Are doomed to toil and pain;
Yet exiles on a foreign shore
  May sing the heavenly strain.

3 Father, whose promise binds Thee still
  To make the captive free,
Grant us to mourn the deeds of ill
  That banish us from Thee.

4 And, mourning, grant us faith to rest
  Upon Thy love and care;
Till Thou restore us with the blest,
  The joys of heaven to share.
                    Tr. J. M. Neale, 1863.

113

My God, my everlasting hope,
  I live upon Thy truth;
Thy hands have held my childhood up,
  And strengthened all my youth.

2 Still has my life new wonders seen
  Repeated every year;
Behold, my days that yet remain,
  I trust them to Thy care.

3 Cast me not off when strength declines,
  When hoary hairs arise;
And round me let Thy glory shine,
  Whene'er Thy servant dies.
                    Isaac Watts, 1719.

114 St. Frances. C. M.   G. A. LÖHR, 1866.

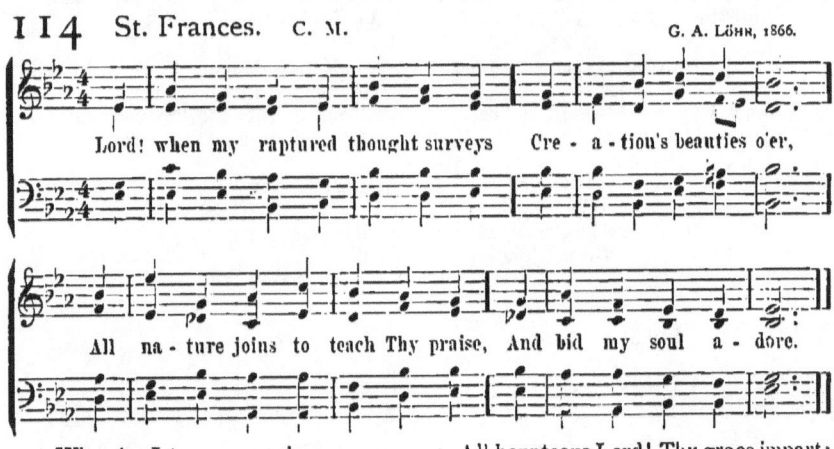

Lord! when my raptured thought surveys Cre-a-tion's beauties o'er,
All na-ture joins to teach Thy praise, And bid my soul a-dore.

2 Where'er I turn my gazing eyes,
  Thy radiant footsteps shine;
Ten thousand pleasing wonders rise,
  And speak their source divine.

3 All-bounteous Lord! Thy grace impart;
  Oh! teach me to improve
Thy gifts, with ever-grateful heart,
  And crown them with Thy love.
                    Anne Steele, 1760.

God the Father.

115 Bemerton. C. M.   H. W. Greatorex, 1849.

How are Thy servants bless'd, O Lord! How sure is their defence!
E - ter - nal Wis - dom is their guide, Their help, Om - ni - po - tence.

2 In foreign realms, and lands remote,
  Supported by Thy care,
Through burning climes they pass unhurt,
  And breathe in tainted air.

3 When by the dreadful tempest borne
  High on the broken wave,
They know Thou art not slow to hear,
  Nor impotent to save.

4 The storm is laid, the winds retire,
  Obedient to Thy will;
The sea, that roars at Thy command,
  At Thy command is still.

5 In midst of dangers, fears, and deaths,
  Thy goodness we'll adore;
We'll praise Thee for Thy mercies past,
  And humbly hope for more.

6 Our life, while Thou preserv'st that life,
  Thy sacrifice shall be;
And death, when death shall be our lot,
  Shall join our souls to Thee.

Joseph Addison, 1712, a.

116 St. Peter. C. M.   A. R. Reinagle, 1826.

Yes, I will bless Thee, O my God: Through all my mor - tal days,

God the Father.

And to e-ter-ni-ty pro-long Thy vast, Thy bound-less praise.

2 Nor shall my tongue alone proclaim
  The honors of my God:
My life, with all its active powers,
  Shall spread Thy praise abroad.

3 Not death itself shall stop my song,
  Though death will close my eyes:
My thoughts shall then to nobler heights
  And sweeter raptures rise.

4 There shall my lips, in endless praise,
  Their grateful tribute pay;
The theme demands an angel's tongue,
  And an eternal day.
    Ottiwell Heginbothom, 1768, a.

117

My Saviour! my almighty Friend!
  When I begin Thy praise,
Where will the growing numbers end,—
  The numbers of Thy grace?

2 Thou art my everlasting trust;
  Thy goodness I adore;
And, since I knew Thy graces first,
  I speak Thy glories more.

3 My feet shall travel all the length
  Of the celestial road;
And march, with courage, in Thy strength,
  To see my Father God.

4 When I am filled with sore distress
  For some surprising sin,
I'll plead Thy perfect righteousness,
  And mention none but Thine.

5 How will my lips rejoice to tell
  The vict'ries of my King!
My soul, redeemed from sin and hell,
  Shall Thy salvation sing.
    Isaac Watts, 1719.

118

Sing to the Lord Jehovah's name,
  And in His strength rejoice;
When His salvation is our theme,
  Exalted be our voice.

2 With thanks, approach His awful sight
  And psalms of honor sing;
The Lord's a God of boundless might,—
  The whole creation's King.

3 Come, and with humble souls adore;
  Come, kneel before His face:
Oh! may the creatures of His power
  Be children of His grace!

4 Now is the time;—He bends His ear,
  And waits for your request;
Come, lest He rouse His wrath, and swear,
  "Ye shall not see my rest."
    Isaac Watts, 1719.

119

Awake, my soul! to sound His praise,
  Awake, my harp! to sing;
Join, all my powers! the song to raise,
  And morning incense bring.

2 Among the people of His care,
  And through the nations round,
Glad songs of praise will I prepare,
  And there His name resound.

3 Be Thou exalted, O my God!
  Above the starry train;
Diffuse Thy heavenly grace abroad,
  And teach the world Thy reign.

4 So shall Thy chosen sons rejoice,
  And throng Thy courts above;
While sinners hear Thy pard'ning voice,
  And taste redeeming love.
    Joel Barlow, 1785.

God the Father.

120 Geneva. C. M.   John Cole, 1800.

When all Thy mer-cies, O my God! My ris-ing soul sur-veys,
Transport-ed with the view I'm lost, In won-der, love, and praise.

2 Unnumbered comforts, to my soul,
   Thy tender care bestowed,
Before my infant heart conceived
   From whom these comforts flowed.

3 Ten thousand thousand precious gifts
   My daily thanks employ;
Nor is the least a cheerful heart,
   That tastes those gifts with joy.

4 Through every period of my life,
   Thy goodness I'll pursue;
And after death, in distant worlds,
   The glorious theme renew.

5 Through all eternity, to Thee
   A joyful song I'll raise:
For, oh! eternity's too short
   To utter all Thy praise!
                    Joseph Addison, 1712.

121 Clarendon. C. M.   Isaac Tucker, 1800.

Sweet is the mem-'ry of Thy grace, My God, my heavenly King!
Let age to age Thy right-eous-ness, In sounds of glo-ry, sing.

God the Father.

2 God reigns on high,—but ne'er confines
    His goodness to the skies;
Through the whole earth His bounty shines,
    And every want supplies.

3 Creatures, with all their endless race,
    Thy power and praise proclaim;
But saints, who taste Thy richer grace,
    Delight to bless Thy name.
                    Isaac Watts, 1719.

122 Laus Deo. 8s & 7s.   JAMES A. JOHNSON, 1857.

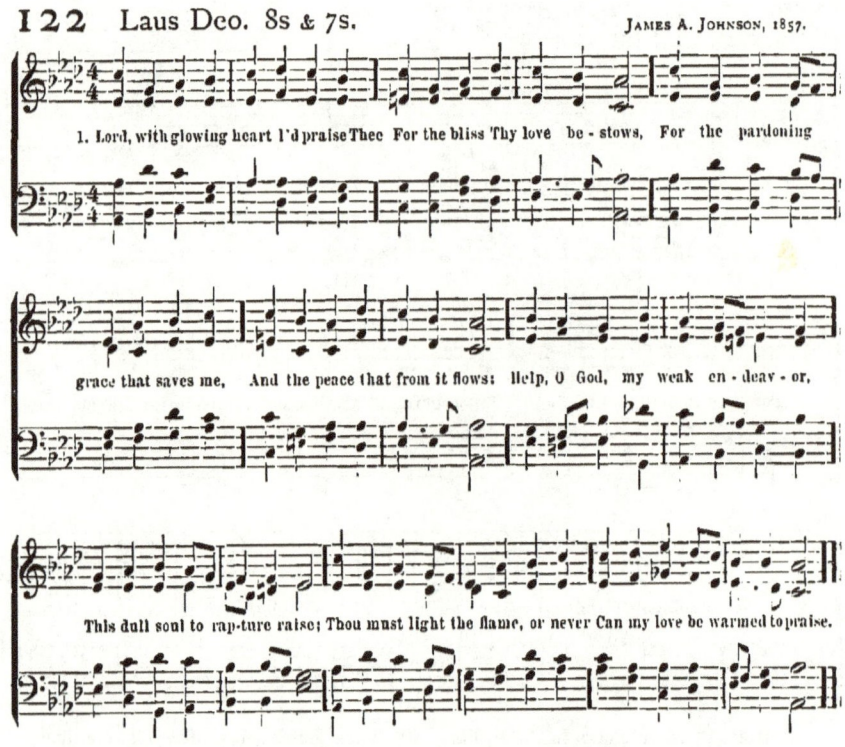

1. Lord, with glowing heart I'd praise Thee For the bliss Thy love bestows, For the pardoning grace that saves me, And the peace that from it flows: Help, O God, my weak endeavor, This dull soul to rapture raise; Thou must light the flame, or never Can my love be warmed to praise.

2 Praise, my soul, the God that sought thee,
    Wretched wanderer, far astray;
Found thee lost, and kindly brought thee
    From the paths of death away:
Praise, with love's devoutest feeling,
    Him who saw thy guilt-born fear,
And, the light of hope revealing,
    Bade the blood-stained cross appear.

3 Lord, this bosom's ardent feeling
    Vainly would my lips express;
Low before Thy footstool kneeling,
    Deign Thy suppliant's prayer to bless.
Let Thy grace, my soul's chief treasure,
    Love's pure flame within me raise;
And since words can never measure,
    Let my life show forth Thy praise.
                    Francis Scott Key, 1816.

God the Father.

123 "Ein Feste Burg." P. M.   Martin Luther, 1521.

Our God stands firm, a Rock and Tower, A Shield when dan-ger press-es;
A read-y help in ev-ery hour, When doubt or pain dis-tress-es!
For our ma-lignant foe Unswerving aims his blow; His fear-ful arms the while. Dark pow'r and dark-er guile; His hid-den craft is match-less.

2 Our strength is weakness in the fight;
  Our courage soon defection;
But comes a Warrior clad in might,
  A Prince of God's election!
    Who is this wondrous Chief,
    That brings this glad relief?
    The field of battle boasts
    Christ Jesus, Lord of hosts,
Still conq'ring and to conquer!

3 Then Lord, arise, lift up Thine arm!
  With mighty succor stay us!
Oh, turn aside the deadly harm,
  When Satan would betray us;
    That, rescued by Thy hand,
    In triumph we may stand,
    And round Thy foot-stool crowd,
    In joy to sing aloud
High praise to our Redeemer!

V. 1, 2. tr. fr. *Martin Luther*, 1529.
V. 3, *R. Corbet Singleton*, 1867.

God the Father.

124

To FATHER, Son and Holy Ghost,
  For ever be outpouring
All glory, from the heavenly host,
  And saints on earth adoring:
    Through time's remotest bound
    That chorus shall resound,
    And swell for evermore,
    Like stormy ocean's roar;
  Through endless ages rolling.
W. R. Whittingham.

125 God's Love. 7s & 6s. P.   W. F. SHERWIN, 1872.

Grander than ocean's sto-ry Or songs of forest trees— Pur-er than breath of morning Or evening's gentle breeze— Clearer than mountain ech-oes Ring out from peaks a-bove— Rolls on the glorious an-them Of God's e-ter-nal love!

2 Dearer than any lovings,
    The truest friends bestow;
  Stronger than all the yearnings,
    A mother's heart can know;
  Deeper than earth's foundations,
    And far above all thought;
  Broader than heaven's high arches—
    The love that Christ has brought.

3 Richer than all earth's treasure,
    The wealth my soul receives;
  Brighter than royal jewels,
    The crown that Jesus gives;
  Wondrous the condescension,
    And grace beyond degree!
  I would be ever singing
    The love of Christ to me.
W. F. Sherwin, 1871.

God the Father.

126 Teneriffe. C. M.   Geo. F. Root, 1860.

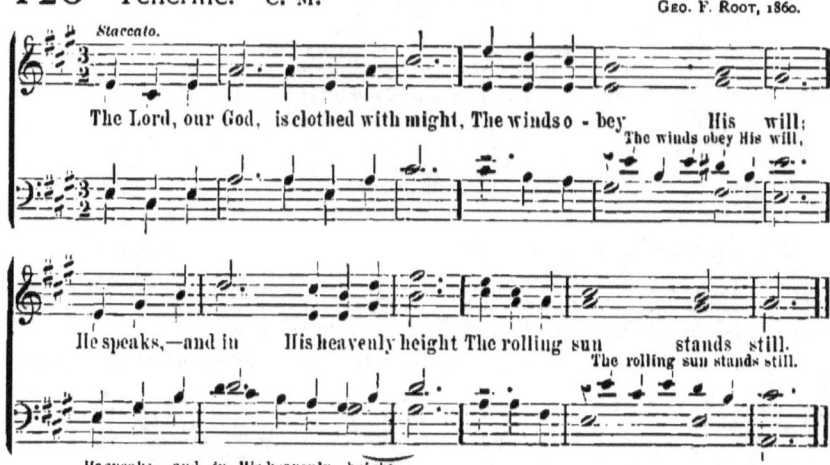

2 Howl winds of night! your force com-
  Without His high behest,   [bine;
Ye shall not, in the mountain pine,
  Disturb the sparrow's nest.

3 His voice sublime is heard afar,
  In distant peals it dies;
He yokes the whirlwind to His car,
  And sweeps the howling skies.

4 Ye nations! bend, in reverence bend;
  Ye monarchs! wait His nod,
And bid the choral song ascend
  To celebrate our God.
            H. K. White, 1806, alt.

127

Praise ye the Lord, ye' immortal choirs
  That fill the worlds above;
Praise Him who form'd you of His fires,
  And feeds you with His love.

2 Shine to His praise, ye crystal skies,
  The floor of His abode;
Or veil in shade your myriad eyes
  Before your brighter God.

3 Shout to the Lord, ye surging seas!
  In your eternal roar,
Let wave to wave resound His praise,
  And shore reply to shore.
            Isaac Watts, 1706.

128 Monsell. S. M.   Joseph Barnby, 1868.

God the Father

My soul, a-dor-ing, pleads Thy word, And owns Thy mer-cy sweet.

2 Where'er Thy name is blest,
Where'er Thy people meet,
There I delight in Thee to rest,
And find Thy mercy sweet.

3 Light Thou my weary way,
Lead Thou my wand'ring feet,
That while I stay on earth I may
Still find Thy mercy sweet.

4 Thus shall the heavenly host
Hear all my songs repeat,
To Father, Son, and Holy Ghost,
Thy joy, Thy mercy sweet.
John S. B. Monsell, 1862.

129 Wartburg. L. M. *J. H. Schein, 1628.*

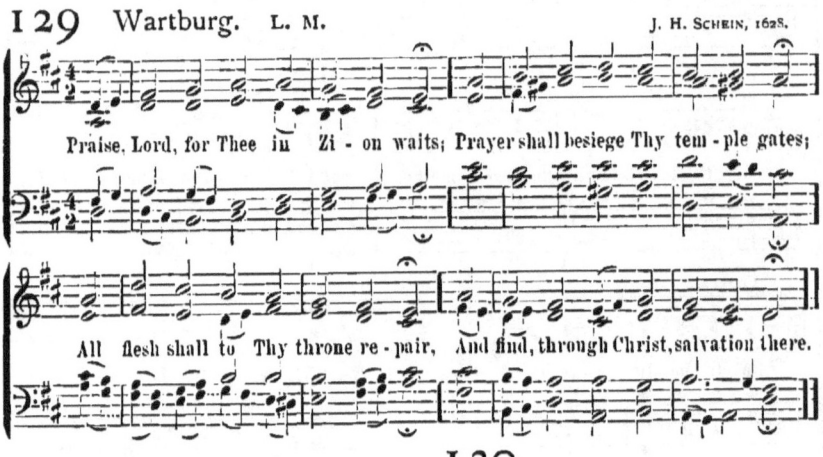

Praise, Lord, for Thee in Zi-on waits; Prayer shall besiege Thy tem-ple gates;
All flesh shall to Thy throne re-pair, And find, through Christ, salvation there.

2 Our spirits faint; our sins prevail;
Leave not our trembling hearts to fail;
O Thou that hearest prayer, descend,
And still be found the sinner's Friend.

3 How blest Thy saints, how safely led,
How surely kept, how richly fed:
Saviour of all in earth and sea,
How happy they who rest in Thee.

4 Lord, on our souls Thy spirit pour;
The moral waste within restore;
O let Thy love our spring-tide be,
And make us all bear fruit to Thee.
H. F. Lyte, 1834.

130

O Source divine, and Life of all,
The Fount of being's wondrous sea,
Thy depth would every heart appal,
That saw not Love supreme in Thee.

2 We shrink before Thy vast abyss,
Where worlds on worlds eternal brood;
We know Thee truly but in this,
That Thou bestowest all our good.

3 And so, 'mid boundless time and space,
O grant us still in Thee to dwell,
And through the ceaseless web to trace
Thy presence working all things well.
John Sterling, 1839.

God the Father.

131 Sabaoth. P. M.   Wm. B. Bradbury, 1867.

Ho-ly, ho-ly, ho-ly is the Lord! Sing, O ye peo-ple, glad-ly adore Him:
Let the mountains tremble at His word; Let the hills be joy-ful be-fore Him;
Mighty in wisdom, boundless in mercy, Great is Je-ho-vah, King o-ver all.

CHORUS.
Ho-ly, ho-ly, ho-ly is the Lord. Let the hills be joy-ful be-fore Him.

2 Praise Him, praise Him! shout aloud for joy,
  Watchman of Zion, herald the story;
Sin and death His kingdom shall destroy;
  All the earth shall sing of His glory;
Praise Him, ye angels, ye who behold Him
  Robed in His splendor, matchless, divine.—*Cho.*

3 King eternal, blessèd be His name!
  So may His children gladly adore Him,
When in heaven we join the happy strain,
  When we cast our bright crowns before Him;
There in His likeness joyful awaking,
  There we shall see Him, there we shall sing.—*Cho.*

Frances J. Van Alstyne, 1869.

God the Father.

132 Westminster. C. M.   JAMES TURLE, 1852.

My God, how wonder-ful Thou art! Thy ma-jes-ty how bright!
How beau-ti-ful Thy mer-cy-seat, In depths of burn-ing light!

2 How dread are Thine eternal years,
   O everlasting Lord!
By prostrate spirits, day and night,
   Incessantly adored.

3 How beautiful, how beautiful,
   The sight of Thee must be,
Thine endless wisdom, boundless power,
   And awful purity!

4 Oh! how I fear Thee, living God!
   With deepest, tenderest fears,
And worship Thee with trembling hope,
   And penitential tears.

5 Yet I may love Thee too, O Lord!
   Almighty as Thou art,
For Thou hast stooped to ask of me
   The love of this poor heart.

6 No earthly father loves like Thee,
   No mother, half so mild,
Bears and forbears as Thou hast done
   With me, Thy sinful child.
             Fred. W. Faber, 1849.

133
Holy and reverend is the name
   Of our eternal King:
"Thrice holy Lord!" the angels cry;
   "Thrice holy!" let us sing.

2 With sacred awe pronounce His name,
   Whom words nor thoughts can reach;
A broken heart shall please Him more
   Than the best forms of speech.

3 Thou holy God! preserve my soul
   From all pollution free:
The pure in heart are Thy delight,
   And they Thy face shall see.
             John Needham, 1768.

134
I sing th' almighty power of God,
   That made the mountains rise,
That spread the flowing seas abroad,
   And built the lofty skies.

2 I sing the wisdom, that ordained
   The sun to rule the day;
The moon shines full at His command,
   And all the stars obey.

3 Lord! how Thy wonders are displayed,
   Where'er I turn mine eye,
If I survey the ground I tread,
   Or gaze upon the sky!

4 There's not a plant or flower below,
   But makes Thy glories known;
And clouds arise, and tempests blow,
   By order from Thy throne.
             Isaac Watts, 1715.

God the Father.

135 Lyons. 10s & 11s. F. J. Haydn, 1770.

Oh! worship the King, all-glorious above, Oh! gratefully sing His pow-er and love,
Our Shield and Defender, the Ancient of days, Pavilioned in splendor, and girded with praise.

2 Oh! tell of His might, oh! sing of His grace,
Whose robe is the light, whose canopy space;
His chariots of wrath the deep thunder-clouds form,
And dark is His path on the wings of the storm.

3 Thy bountiful care what tongue can recite!
It breathes in the air, it shines in the light;
It streams from the hills, it descends to the plain,
And sweetly distills in the dew and the rain.

4 Frail children of dust, and feeble as frail,
In Thee do we trust, nor find Thee to fail;
Thy mercies how tender, how firm to the end,
Our Maker, Defender, Redeemer, and Friend!

Robert Grant, 1830, ab.

136

Ye servants of God! your Master proclaim,
And publish abroad His wonderful name;
The name, all-victorious, of Jesus extol;
His kingdom is glorious, and rules over all.

2 God ruleth on high, almighty to save;
And still He is nigh—His presence we have:
The great congregation His triumph shall sing,
Ascribing salvation to Jesus, our King.

3 Then let us adore, and give Him His right,
All glory and power, and wisdom and might,
All honor and blessing, with angels above,
And thanks never ceasing, and infinite love.

Charles Wesley, 1744, ab.

Jesus Christ.

137 Rothwell. L. M. — WILLIAM TANSUR, 1743.

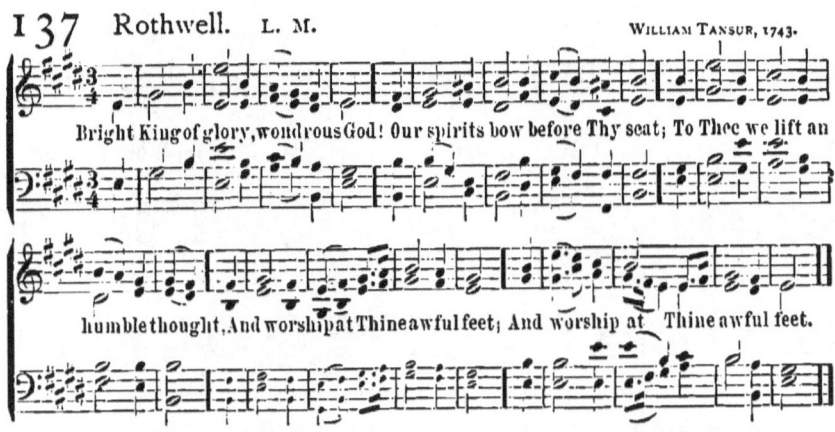

Bright King of glory, wondrous God! Our spirits bow before Thy seat; To Thee we lift an humble thought, And worship at Thine awful feet; And worship at Thine awful feet.

2 A thousand seraphs, strong and bright,
  Stand round the glorious Deity;
But who, amongst the sons of light,
  Pretends comparison with Thee?

3 Yet there is one, of human frame,—
  Jesus, arrayed in flesh and blood,—
Thinks it no robbery to claim
  A full equality with God.

4 Their glory shines with equal beams,
  Their essence is for ever one,
Though they are known by different names,
  The Father God, and God the Son.

5 Then let the name of Christ, our King,
  With equal honors be adored;
His praise let every angel sing,
  And all the nations own their Lord.
        Isaac Watts, 1707.

138

Ere the blue heavens were stretch'd abroad,
  From everlasting was the Word;
With God He was; the Word was God,
  And must divinely be adored.

2 Ere sin appeared, or Satan fell,
  He led the host of morning stars:
His generation who can tell?
  Or count the number of His years.

3 Mortals with joy behold His face,—
  Th' eternal Father's only Son;
How full of truth! how full of grace!
  When thro' His eyes the Godhead shone!

4 Archangels leave their high abode
  To learn new mysteries here, and tell
The love of our descending God,
  The glories of Immanuel.
        Isaac Watts, 1707.

139

What equal honors shall we bring,
  To Thee, O Lord, our God, the Lamb!
When all the notes, that angels sing,
  Are far inferior to Thy name?

2 Worthy is He that once was slain,—
  The Prince of peace, that groan'd and died,
Worthy to rise, and live, and reign,
  At His almighty Father's side.

3 Honor immortal must be paid,
  Instead of scandal and of scorn;
While glory shines around His head,
  And a bright crown without a thorn.

4 Blessings for ever on the Lamb,
  Who bore the curse for wretched men!
Let angels sound His sacred name,
  And every creature say,—Amen.
        Isaac Watts, 1707.

Jesus Christ.

140 Logos. 6s & 4s.   Hubert P. Main, 1881.

Jesus! Thy name I love, All other names above, Jesus, my Lord! Oh! Thou art all to me; Nothing to please I see, Nothing apart from Thee, Jesus, my Lord!

Copyright, 1881, by Biglow & Main.

2 Thou, blessèd Son of God!
Hast bought me with Thy blood,
  Jesus, my Lord!
Oh! how great is Thy love,
All other loves above,—
Love that I daily prove,
  Jesus, my Lord!

3 When unto Thee I flee,
Thou wilt my Refuge be,
  Jesus, my Lord!
What need I now to fear?
What earthly grief or care?
Since Thou art ever near,
  Jesus, my Lord!

4 Soon Thou wilt come again;
I shall be happy then,
  Jesus, my Lord!
Then Thine own face I'll see,
Then I shall like Thee be,
Then evermore with Thee,
  Jesus, my Lord!
       James George Deck (?), 1842.

141

Come, all ye saints of God!
Publish through earth abroad
  Christ Jesus' fame;
Tell what His love has done;
Trust in His name alone;
Shout to His lofty throne,—
  "Worthy the Lamb!"

2 Hence, gloomy doubts and fears!
Dry all your mournful tears!
  Join our glad theme;
Beauty for ashes bring,
Strike each melodious string,
Join heart and voice to sing,—
  "Worthy the Lamb!"

3 Hark! how the choirs above,
Filled with the Saviour's love,
  Dwell on His name!
There, too, may we be found,
With light and glory crowned,
While all the heavens resound,—
  "Worthy the Lamb!"
       James Boden, 1801.

Jesus Christ.

142 Angels. L. M.   Orlando Gibbons, 1623.

Now to the Lord a noble song! Awake, my soul! awake, my tongue! Hosanna to th' eternal name, And all His boundless love proclaim.

2 See where it shines in Jesus' face,—
The brightest image of His grace!
God, in the person of His Son,
Has all His mightiest works outdone.

3 The spacious earth and spreading flood
Proclaim the wise, the powerful God;
And Thy rich glories from afar
Sparkle in every rolling star.

4 But in His looks a glory stands,
The noblest labor of Thy hands;
The pleasing lustre of His eyes
Outshines the wonders of the skies.

5 Grace,—'tis a sweet, a charming theme;
My thoughts rejoice at Jesus' name:
Ye angels! dwell upon the sound;
Ye heavens! reflect it to the ground.

6 Oh! may I live to reach the place,
Where He unveils His lovely face,
Where all His beauties you behold,
And sing His name to harps of gold.
Isaac Watts, 1707.

143

O Christ! our King, Creator, Lord!
Saviour of all who trust Thy word!
To them who seek Thee ever near,
Now to our praises bend Thine ear.

2 In Thy dear cross a grace is found,—
It flows from every streaming wound,—
Whose power our inbred sin controls,
Breaks the firm bond, and frees our souls.

3 Thou didst create the stars of night;
Yet Thou hast veiled in flesh Thy light,
Hast deigned a mortal form to wear,
A mortal's painful lot to bear.

4 When Thou didst hang upon the tree;
The quaking earth acknowledged Thee;
When Thou didst there yield up Thy breath,
The world grew dark as shades of death.

5 Now in the Father's glory high,
Great Conqu'ror! never more to die,
Us by Thy mighty power defend,
And reign through ages without end.
Lat., Gregory I, 600.
Tr. Ray Palmer, 1858.

144

Let every heart exulting beat
  With joy, at Jesus' name of bliss:
With every pure delight replete,
  And passing sweet, its music is.

2 Oh! speak His glorious name abroad!
  Jesus let every tongue confess!
Let every heart and voice accord
  The Healer of our souls to bless.
Tr. John D. Chambers 1857.

Jesus Christ.

145 Covenant. L. M.   Joseph Barnby, 1872.

Je-sus, my Lord, my God, my All! Hear me, bless'd Saviour! when I call;
Hear me, and, from Thy dwelling-place, Pour down the rich-es of Thy grace:
Je-sus, my Lord! I Thee a-dore; Oh! make me love Thee more and more.

2 Jesus! too late I Thee have sought;
How can I love Thee as I ought?
And how extol Thy matchless fame,
The glorious beauty of Thy name?
Jesus, my Lord! I Thee adore;
Oh! make me love Thee more and more.

3 Jesus! what didst Thou find in me,
That Thou hast dealt so lovingly?
How great the joy that Thou hast brought,
So far exceeding hope or thought!
Jesus, my Lord! I Thee adore;
Oh! make me love Thee more and more.

4 Jesus! of Thee shall be my song;
To Thee my heart and soul belong;
All that I have or am is Thine,
And Thou, blest Saviour! Thou art mine:
Jesus, my Lord! I Thee adore;
Oh! make me love Thee more and more.
Henry Collins, 1852.

146

O Love, who ere life's earliest dawn
  On us Thy choice hast gently laid:
O Love, who here as Man wast born,
  And wholly like to us wast made:
O Love, we give ourselves to Thee,
Thine ever, only Thine to be.

2 O Love, who lovest us for aye,
  Who for our souls dost ever plead;
O Love, who didst our ransom pay,
  Whose power sufficeth in our stead:
O Love, we give ourselves to Thee,
Thine ever, only Thine to be.

3 O Love, who once shalt bid us rise
  From out this dying life of ours;
O Love, who once o'er yonder skies
  Shall set us in the fadeless bowers:
O Love, we give ourselves to Thee,
Thine ever, only Thine to be.
Tr. Cath. Winkworth, 1858.

Jesus Christ.

147 Burlington. C. M.   J. F. BURROWES, 1830.

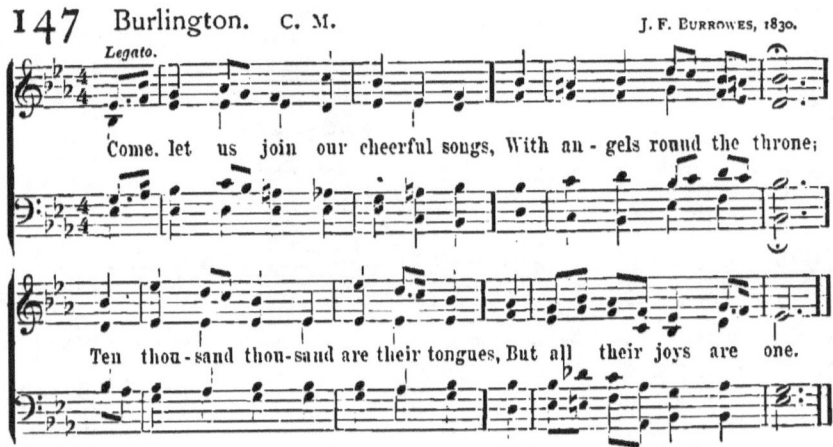

Come, let us join our cheerful songs, With an-gels round the throne; Ten thou-sand thou-sand are their tongues, But all their joys are one.

2 "Worthy the Lamb that died," they cry,
"To be exalted thus!"
"Worthy the Lamb," our lips reply,
"For He was slain for us!"

3 Jesus is worthy to receive
Honor and power divine;
And blessings, more than we can give,
Be, Lord! for ever Thine.

4 The whole creation join in one,
To bless the sacred name
Of Him, that sits upon the throne,
And to adore the Lamb.
Isaac Watts, 1707.

148

HOSANNA! raise the pealing hymn
To David's Son and Lord;
With cherubim and seraphim,
Exalt th' incarnate Word.

2 Hosanna! Sovereign, Prophet, Priest!
How vast Thy gifts, how free!
Thy blood, our life; Thy word, our feast;
Thy name, our only plea.

3 Hosanna! Master! lo! we bring
Our offerings to Thy throne;
Not gold, nor myrrh, nor mortal thing,
But hearts to be Thine own.

4 Hosanna! once Thy gracious ear
Approved a lisping throng;
Be gracious still, and deign to hear
Our poor but grateful song.

5 O Saviour! if redeemed by Thee,
Thy temple we behold,
Hosannas through eternity
We'll sing to harps of gold.
William H. Havergal, 1833.

149

JESUS is God! the glorious bands
Of holy angels sing
Songs of adoring praise to Him,
Their Maker and their King.

2 Backward our thoughts thro ages stretch,
Onward through endless bliss,—
For there are two eternities,
And both alike are His.

3 Jesus is God! Oh! could I now
But compass land and sea,
To teach and tell this single truth,
How happy should I be!

4 Oh! had I but an angel's voice,
I would proclaim so loud,
Jesus, the Good, the Beautiful,
Is everlasting God.
Frederic William Faber, 1862.

Jesus Christ.

150 Christus Rex. 7s & 6s.   German Choral.

Come, let us sing of Jesus, While hearts and accents blend;
Come, let us sing of Jesus, The sinner's only Friend.

2 We love to sing of Jesus,
  Who wept our path along;
We love to sing of Jesus,
  The tempted and the strong.

3 We love to sing of Jesus,
  Who died our souls to save;
We love to sing of Jesus,
  Triumphant o'er the grave.

4 Then let us sing of Jesus,
  While yet on earth we stay,
And hope to sing of Jesus
  Throughout eternal day.
        Geo. W. Bethune, 1850.

151 Benediction. 8s & 7s.   SAMUEL WEBBE, 1791.

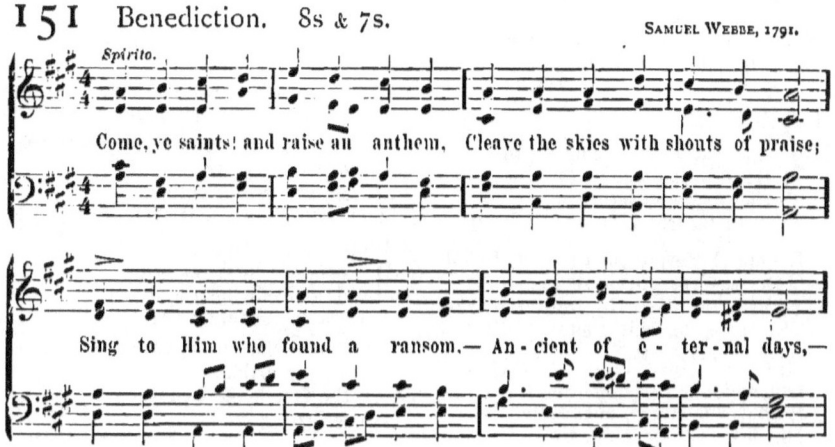

Come, ye saints! and raise an anthem, Cleave the skies with shouts of praise;
Sing to Him who found a ransom,— Ancient of eternal days,—

Jesus Christ.

2 High on yon celestial mountains,
  Stands His gem-built throne, all bright,
Midst incessant acclamations,
  Bursting from the sons of light:
    Zion's praises
  Are His chosen dwelling-place.

3 Bring your harps, and bring your odors,
  Sweep the string, and pour the lay,
View His works, behold His wonders,
  Let hosannas crown the day!
    He is worthy
  Of eternal, boundless praise.
            Job Hupton, 1806.

152 Horton. 7s.   XAVIER SCHNYDER, VON WARTENSEE, 1826.

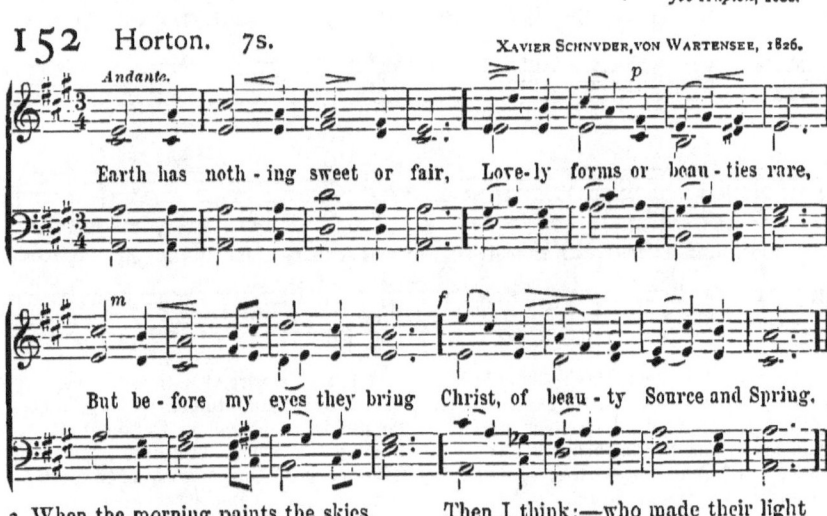

2 When the morning paints the skies,
When the golden sunbeams rise,
Then my Saviour's form I find
Brightly imaged on my mind.

3 When the day-beams pierce the night,
Oft I think on Jesus' light,—
Think,—how bright that light will be
Shining through eternity.

4 When, as moonlight softly steals,
Heaven its thousand eyes reveals,
Then I think;—who made their light
Is a thousand times more bright.

5 When I see, in spring-tide gay,
Fields their varied tints display,
Wakes the thrilling thought in me,—
What must their Creator be?

6 Lord of all that's fair to see!
Come, reveal Thyself to me;
Let me, 'mid Thy radiant light,
See Thine unveil'd glories bright.
          Ger., *Johann Scheffler*, 1657.
          Tr. *Frances Elizabeth Cox*, 1841.

The Advent.

153 Melita. L. M.   John B. Dykes, 1861.

O Wis-dom! spreading might-i-ly From out the mouth of God most high,

All na-ture sweetly or-der-ing, With-in Thy paths Thy children bring.

Draw near, O Christ, with us to dwell, In mer-cy save Thine Is-ra-el. A-men.

2 O Israel's Sceptre! David's Key!
Come Thou, and set death's captives free,
Unlock the gate that bars their road,
And lead them to the throne of God.
Draw near, O Christ, with us to dwell,
In mercy save Thine Israel.

3 O King! Desire of nations! come,
Lead sons of earth to heaven's high home,
Thou chief and precious Corner-stone,
Binding the severed into one.
Draw near, O Christ, with us to dwell,
In mercy save Thine Israel.
Fr. Horatio Nelson, 1857.

154 Antioch. C. M.   G. F. Handel, 1741.

Ardito.

Joy to the world, the Lord is come! Let earth re-ceive her King; Let

The Advent.

2 Joy to the earth,—the Saviour reigns;
　Let men their songs employ;
While fields and floods, rocks, hills, and plains
　Repeat the sounding joy.

3 No more let sins and sorrows grow,
　Nor thorns infest the ground;
He comes to make His blessings flow,
　Far as the curse is found.

4 He rules the world with truth and grace,
　And makes the nations prove
The glories of His righteousness,
　And wonders of His love.
　　　　　　　　Isaac Watts, 1709.

155

Hark the glad sound! the Saviour comes,—
　The Saviour promised long;
Let every heart prepare a throne,
　And every voice a song.

2 He comes, the pris'ners to release,
　In Satan's bondage held,
The gates of brass before Him burst,
　The iron fetters yield.

3 Our glad hosannas, Prince of peace!
　Thy welcome shall proclaim,
And heaven's eternal arches ring
　With Thy belovéd name.
　　　　　　Philip Doddridge, 1735.

156

Mortals! awake, with angels join,
　And chant the solemn lay;
Joy, love, and gratitude, combine
　To hail th' auspicious day.

2 In heaven the rapturous song began,
　And sweet seraphic fire
Through all the shining regions ran,
　And strung and tuned the lyre.

3 Swift, through the vast expanse, it flew,
　And loud the echo rolled;
The theme, the song, the joy was new,
　'T was more than heaven could hold.

4 Down to the portals of the sky
　Th' impetuous torrent ran;
And angels rushed, with eager joy,
　To bear the news to man.

5 Hark! the cherubic armies shout,
　And glory leads the song;
Good-will and peace are heard throughout
　Th' harmonious heavenly throng.

6 With joy the chorus we repeat—
　"Glory to God on high!"
Good-will and peace are now complete;
　Jesus was born to die.
　　　　　　　Samuel Medley, 1798.

The Advent.

157 Veni Immanuel. L. M.   Charles Gounod, 1872.

Draw nigh, draw nigh, Im-man-u-el, And ransom cap-tive Is-ra-el,

That mourns in lone-ly ex-ile here, Un-til the Son of God ap-pear.

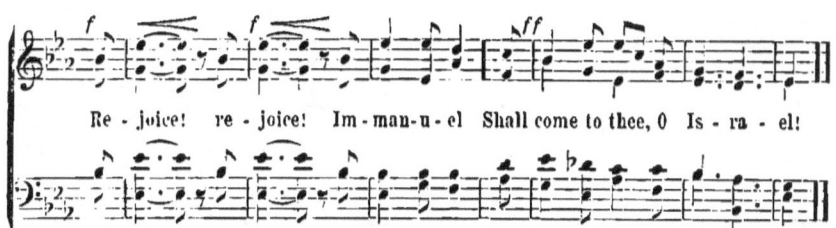

Re - joice! re - joice! Im-man-u-el Shall come to thee, O Is - ra - el!

2 Draw nigh, O Jesse's Rod, draw nigh,
To free us from the enemy;
From hell's abyss Thy people save,
And give us victory o'er the grave.
Rejoice! rejoice! Immanuel
Shall come to thee, O Israel!

3 Draw nigh, draw nigh, O Morning Star,
And bring us comfort from afar;
And banish far from us the gloom
Of sinful night and endless doom.
Rejoice! rejoice! Immanuel
Shall come to thee, O Israel!

4 Draw nigh, draw nigh, O David's Key,
The heavenly gate unfolds to Thee;
Make safe the way that leads on high,
And close the path to misery.
Rejoice! rejoice! Immanuel
Shall come to thee, O Israel!

5 Draw nigh, draw nigh, O Lord of Might,
Who once from Sinai's flaming height
Didst give the trembling tribes Thy Law,
In cloud, and majesty, and awe.
Rejoice! rejoice! Immanuel
Shall come to thee, O Israel!

Tr. *John M. Neale*, 1851.

The Nativity.

158 Carol. C. M. R. S. WILLIS, 1860.

It came upon the midnight clear, That glorious song of old, From angels bending near the earth, To touch their harps of gold: "Peace to the earth, good-will to men, From heaven's all-gracious King;" The world in solemn stillness lay, To hear the angels sing!

2 Still through the cloven skies they came
  With peaceful wings unfurled;
And still their heavenly music floats
  O'er all the weary world;
Above its sad and lowly plains
  They bend on hovering wing,
And ever o'er its Babel-sounds,
  The blessed angels sing.

3 Yet with the woes of sin and strife
  The world has suffered long;
Beneath the angel-strain have rolled
  Two thousand years of wrong;
And man, at war with man, hears not
  The love-song which they bring:
Oh! hush the noise, ye men of strife,
  And hear the angels sing!

4 And ye beneath life's crushing load
  Whose forms are bending low,
Who toil along the climbing way
  With painful steps and slow,
Look now! for glad and golden hours
  Come swiftly on the wing;
Oh! rest beside the weary road,
  And hear the angels sing!

5 For lo! the days are hast'ning on
  By prophet-bards foretold,
When with the ever-circling years
  Comes round the age of gold;
When peace shall over all the earth
  Its ancient splendors fling,
And all the world give back the song
  Which now the angels sing.

Edmund H. Sears. 1850.

The Nativity.

159 Zerah. C. M.   LOWELL MASON, 1837

To us a Child of hope is born, To us a Son is given;
Him shall the tribes of earth obey, Him all the hosts of heaven,
Him shall the tribes of earth obey, Him all the hosts of heaven.

2 His name shall be the Prince of Peace,
  For evermore adored;
The Wonderful, the Counselor,
  The great and mighty Lord.

3 His power, increasing, still shall spread;
  His reign no end shall know:
Justice shall guard His throne above,
  And peace abound below.
                  John Morrison, 1781, ab.

160

LET Israel, to the Prince of Peace,
  The loud hosanna sing;
With alleluias and with hymns,
  O Zion, hail thy King.

2 Renewed, the earth a robe of light,
  A robe of beauty, wears;
And, in new heavens, a brighter Sun
  Leads on the promised years.
                  Michael Bruce, 1781, ab.

161

FROM the faint day-spring's eastern goal,
  Far as the utmost west,
Come, sing we Christ, the Saviour, born
  Of virgin mother blest:

2 The Father of the age to come,
  In servant's form arrayed,
That, man, He might for man atone,
  And ransom whom He made.

3 A Shepherd, to the shepherd's fold
  The Lord of all is showed;
Celestial choristers rejoice,
  And angels sing to God.

4 Now glory, Jesus, be to Thee,
  Whom purest virgin bore,
With Father, and with Holy Ghost,
  Henceforth for evermore!
                  Richard Mant, 1837, ab.

The Nativity.

162 Yorkshire. 10s.   JOHN WAINWRIGHT, 1764.

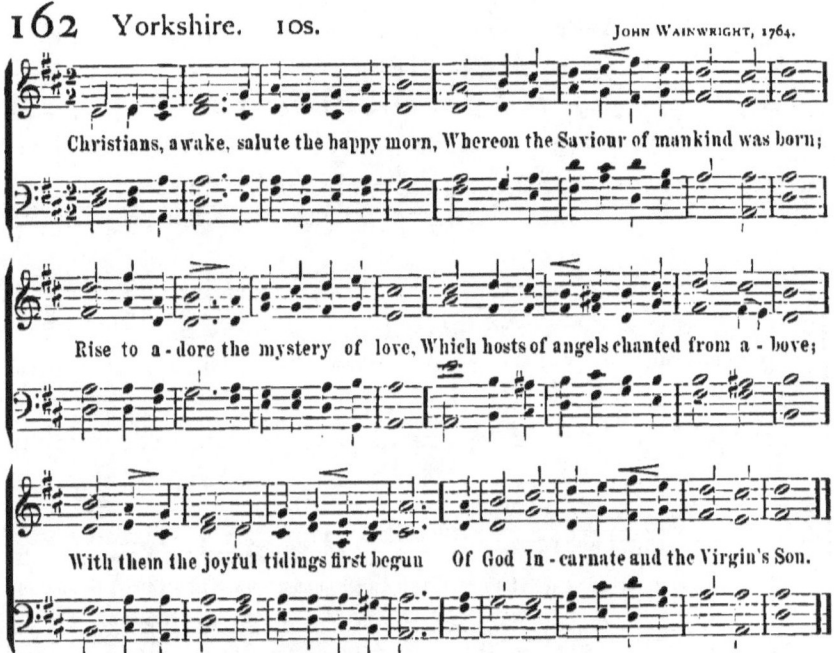

Christians, awake, salute the happy morn, Whereon the Saviour of mankind was born;
Rise to a-dore the mystery of love, Which hosts of angels chanted from a-bove;
With them the joyful tidings first begun Of God In-carnate and the Virgin's Son.

2 With burst of music the celestial choir
In hymns of joy, unknown before, conspire:
The praises of redeeming love they sang,
And heaven's whole arch with alleluias rang:
God's highest glory, was their anthem still,
Peace upon earth, and unto men good-will.

3 Oh may we keep and ponder in our mind,
God's wondrous love in saving lost mankind,
Trace we the Babe, who hath retrieved our loss,
From His poor manger to His bitter Cross;
Treading His steps, assisted by His grace,
Till man's first heavenly state again takes place.

4 Then may we hope, th' angelic thrones among,
To sing, redeem'd, a glad triumphal song;
He, that was born upon this joyful day,
Around us all His glory shall display;
Saved by His love, incessant we shall sing
Eternal praise to heaven's Almighty King.
                                  John Byrom, 1761.

The Nativity.

163 Herald Angels. 7s.   FELIX MENDELSSOHN, 1840.

2 Hail, the heaven-born Prince of Peace!
Hail, the Sun of Righteousness!
Light and life to all He brings,
Risen with healing in His wings.
Let us then with angels sing,
"Glory to the new-born King!
Peace on earth, and mercy mild;
God and sinners reconciled!"
    Hark! &c.

Charles Wesley, 1739.

The Nativity.

164 St. Laura.   11s & 10s.   W. A. Barrett.

Brightest and best of the sons of the morn-ing, Dawn on our dark-ness, and lend us Thine aid; Star of the East, the ho-ri-zon a-dorn-ing, Guide where our in-fant Re-deem-er is laid.

2 Cold on His cradle the dew-drops are shining
  Low lies His head with the beasts of the stall;
Angels adore Him, in slumber reclining,
  Maker, and Monarch, and Saviour of all.

3 Say, shall we yield Him, in costly devotion,
  Odors of Edom, and offerings divine?
Gems from the mountain, and pearls from the ocean,
  Myrrh from the forest, or gold from the mine?

4 Vainly we offer each ample oblation,
  Vainly with gold would His favor secure:
Richer, by far, is the heart's adoration;
  Dearer to God are the prayers of the poor.

5 Brightest and best of the sons of the morning,
  Dawn on our darkness, and lend us Thine aid!
Star of the East, the horizon adorning,
  Guide where our infant Redeemer is laid.

Reginald Heber, 1811.

The Nativity

165 Arthur's Seat. H. M. JOHN GOSS.

Hark! hark!—the notes of joy Roll o'er the heavenly plains, And seraphs find employ For their sublimest strains; Some new delight in heaven is known; Loud ring the harps around the [throne.

2 Hark! hark!—the sounds draw nigh,
   The joyful hosts descend;
Jesus forsakes the sky,
   To earth His footsteps bend;
He comes to bless our fallen race;
He comes with messages of grace.

3 Strike—strike the harps again,
   To great Immanuel's name;
Arise, ye sons of men!
   And all His grace proclaim;
Angels and men! wake every string,
'T is God the Saviour's praise we sing.
Andrew Reed, 1818.

166 Christmas. C. M. G. F. HANDEL, 1728.

Calm on the listening ear of night, Come heaven's me-lo-dious strains, Where wild Ju-de-a stretches far Her silver-mantled plains, Her silver-mantled plains.

The Nativity.

2 Celestial choirs, from courts above,
Shed sacred glories there,
And angels, with their sparkling lyres,
Make music on the air.

3 The answering hills of Palestine
Send back the glad reply;
And greet, from all their holy heights,
The day-spring from on high.

4 O'er the blue depths of Galilee
There comes a holier calm,
And Sharon waves, in solemn praise,
Her silent groves of palm.

5 "Glory to God!" the sounding skies
Loud with their anthems ring,—
"Peace to the earth, good-will to men,
From heaven's eternal King!"

Edmund H. Sears, 1851.

167 Bethlehem.   C. M.   I. B. Woodbury, 1855, arr.

While shepherds watched their flocks by night, All seated on the ground, The angel of the Lord came down And glory shone around. "Fear not," said he, for mighty dread Had seized their troubled mind; "Glad tidings of great joy I bring, To you and all man-kind."

2 "To you, in David's town, this day,
Is born of David's line,
The Saviour, who is Christ, the Lord;—
And this shall be the sign;
The heavenly Babe you there shall find,
To human view displayed,
All humbly wrapped in swaddling bands,
And in a manger laid.

3 Thus spake the seraph; and forthwith
Appeared a shining throng
Of angels, praising God, and thus
Addressed their joyful song:
"All glory be to God on high,
And to the earth be peace;
Good-will henceforth from heaven to men
Begin, and never cease!"

Nahum Tate, 1703.

The Nativity.

168 Adeste Fideles. P.   Marcos Portugal.

O come, all ye faithful, Joyfully triumphant, To Bethlehem hasten now with glad accord; Lo! in a manger Sits the King of angels; O come, let us adore Him, O come, let us adore Him. O come, let us adore Him, Christ the Lord.

2 Though true God of true God,
Light of Light eternal,
Our lowly nature He hath not abhorr'd:
Son of the Father,
Not made, but begotten:
O come, &c.

3 Raise, raise, choirs of angels!
Songs of loudest triumph,
Through heaven's high arches be your praises
Now to our God be [poured;
Glory in the highest;
O come, &c.
Tr. by W. Mercer.

169 Zephyr. L. M.   Wm. B. Bradbury, 1843.

When Jordan hushed his waters still, And silence slept on Zion's hill;

The Nativity.

When Bethlehem's shepherds through the night Watched o'er their flocks by starry light;

2 Hark! from the midnight hills around
A voice of more than mortal sound
In distant hallelujahs stole,
Wild murmuring o'er the raptured soul.

3 On wheels of light, on wings of flame,
The glorious hosts of Zion came;
High heaven with songs of triumph rung,
While thus they struck their harps, and sung:

4 "O Zion, lift thy raptured eye;
The long-expected hour is nigh;
Renewed, creation smiles again,
The Prince of Salem comes to reign.

5 "He comes to cheer the trembling heart,
Bid Satan and his host depart;
Again the Day-star gilds the gloom,
Again the bowers of Eden bloom."
Thomas Campbell, 1794.

170 Incarnation. L. M.   MARTIN LUTHER, 1523.

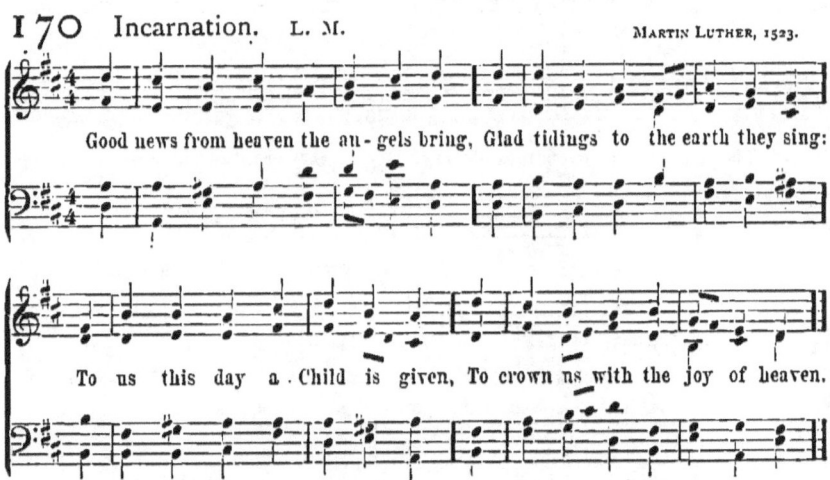

Good news from heaven the an-gels bring, Glad tidings to the earth they sing:
To us this day a Child is given, To crown us with the joy of heaven.

2 This is the Christ, our God and Lord,
Who in all need shall aid afford:
He will Himself our Saviour be,
From sin and sorrow set us free.

3 To us that blessedness He brings,
Which from the Father's bounty springs:
That in the heavenly realm we may
With Him enjoy eternal day.

4 Were earth a thousand times as fair,
Beset with gold and jewels rare,
She yet were far too poor to be
A narrow cradle, Lord, for Thee.

5 Ah, dearest Jesus, Holy child,
Make Thee a bed, soft, undefiled,
Within my heart, that it may be
A quiet chamber kept for Thee.
Martin Luther, 1535. Tr. Arthur T. Russell, 1848, ab.

The Nativity.

171 Hymn to Joy. 8s & 7s. L. VAN BEETHOVEN, 1824.

Hark! what mean those ho-ly voic-es, Sweetly warbling in the skies?
Sure, th' an-gel-ic host re-joic-es— Loud-est hal-le-lu-jahs rise.
Lis-ten to the wondrous sto-ry, Which they chant in hymns of joy;—
"Glo-ry in the high-est, glo-ry; Glo-ry be to God most high!"

2 "Peace on earth, good-will from heaven,
  Reaching far as man is found;
Souls redeemed, and sins forgiven;—
  Loud our golden harps shall sound.
Christ is born, the great Anointed;
  Heaven and earth His glory sing:
Glad, receive whom God appointed,
  For your Prophet, Priest, and King.

3 "Hasten, mortals! to adore Him;
  Learn His name, and taste His joy;
Till in heaven you sing before Him,—
  Glory be to God most high!"
Let us learn the wondrous story
  Of our great Redeemer's birth,
Spread the brightness of His glory,
  Till it cover all the earth.

John Cawood, 1819.

The Nativity.

172

COME, Thou long-expected Jesus!
  Born to set Thy people free;
From our fears and sins release us,
  Let us find our rest in Thee.
Israel's Strength and Consolation,
  Hope of all the earth Thou art;
Dear Desire of every nation,
  Joy of every longing heart.

2 Born, Thy people to deliver;
  Born a Child, and yet a King;
Born to reign in us for ever,
  Now Thy gracious kingdom bring.
By Thine own eternal Spirit,
  Rule in all our hearts alone;
By Thine all-sufficient merit,
  Raise us to Thy glorious throne.
  Charles Wesley, 1744.

173 Lux Mundi. 8s 7s & 4. ROBERT LOWRY, 1881.

An-gels, from the realms of glo-ry, Wing your flight o'er all the earth;
Ye who sang cre-a-tion's sto-ry, Now pro-claim Mes-si-ah's birth:
Come and worship, come and worship, Wor-ship Christ, the new-born King.

Copyright, 1881, by Big'ow & Ma'n.

2 Shepherds! in the fields abiding,
  Watching o'er your flocks by night,
God with man is now residing;
  Yonder shines the infant light;
    Come, and worship,—
  Worship Christ, the new-born King.

3 Sages! leave your contemplations;—
  Brighter visions beam afar;
Seek the great Desire of nations;

Ye have seen His natal star:
  Come, and worship—
Worship Christ, the new-born King.

4 Saints! before the altar bending,
  Watching long in hope and fear,—
Suddenly the Lord, descending,
  In His temple shall appear:
    Come, and worship—
  Worship Christ, the new-born King.
  James Montgomery, 1'19.

The Nativity.

174 St. Frances. C. M.   G. A. Löhr, 1866.

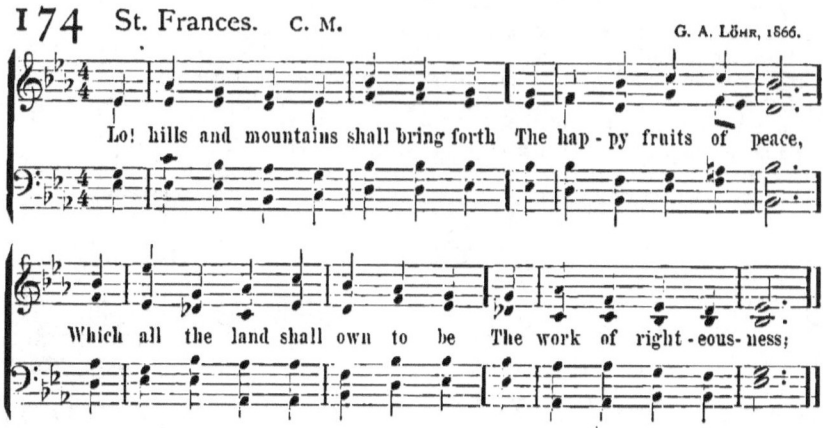

Lo! hills and mountains shall bring forth The hap-py fruits of peace,
Which all the land shall own to be The work of right-eous-ness;

2 While David's Son our needy race
Shall rule with gentle sway;
And from their humble neck shall take
Oppressive yokes away.

3 In every heart Thy awful fear
Shall then be rooted fast,
As long as sun and moon endure,
Or time itself shall last.

4 He shall descend like rain, that cheers
The meadow's second birth;
Or like warm showers, whose gentle drops
Refresh the thirsty earth.

5 In His blest days the just and good
Shall spring up all around:
The happy land shall everywhere
With endless peace abound.

6 To Him shall every king on earth
His humble homage pay;
And differing nations gladly join
To own His righteous sway.

7 For He shall set the needy free,
When they for succor cry;
Shall save the helpless and the poor
And all their wants supply.

8 For Him shall constant prayer be made,
Through all His prosperous days;
His just dominion shall afford
A lasting theme of praise.

9 Let earth be with His glory filled,
For ever bless His name;
Whilst to His praise the listening world
Their glad assent proclaim.
Metrical Psalm.

175

O Thou, who by a star didst guide
The wise men on their way,
Until it came and stood beside
The place where Jesus lay;

2 Although by stars Thou dost not lead
Thy servants now below,
Thy Holy Spirit, when they need,
Will show them how to go.

3 As yet we know Thee but in part:
But still we trust Thy word,
That blessed are the true in heart,
For they shall see the Lord.

4 O Saviour, give us then Thy grace,
To make us pure in heart,
That we may see Thee face to face
Hereafter, as Thou art.
John M. Neale, 1850.

The Nativity

176 Dix. 7s.   Conrad Kocher, 1838.

As with gladness men of old Did the guiding star behold;
As with joy they hailed its light, Leading onward, beaming bright;
So, most gracious Lord, may we Evermore be led to Thee.

2 As with joyful steps they sped
To that lowly manger-bed;
There to bend the knee before
Him whom heaven and earth adore;
So may we with willing feet
Ever seek the mercy-seat.

3 As they offered gifts most rare
At that manger rude and bare
So may we with holy joy,
Pure and free from sin's alloy,
All our costliest treasures bring,
Christ! to Thee, our heavenly King.

4 Holy Jesus! every day
Keep us in the narrow way:
And, when earthly things are past,
Bring our ransomed souls at last
Where they need no star to guide,
Where no clouds Thy glory hide.

5 In the heavenly country bright,
Need they no created light:
Thou its Light, its Joy, its Crown,
Thou its Sun which goes not down;
There for ever may we sing
Alleluias to our King.
William C. Dix, 1859.

177.

Ring again, ye starry chime!
'Tis the fullness of the time;
Shadows of the ages fly,
Love's bright banner fills the sky;
Earth's new birthday tell abroad,
Shout for joy, ye sons of God!

2 Let the Israel of faith
Gather now the spoils of death;—
Joy, as when the reapers come
Bearing high the harvest home.
Broken is th' oppressor's rod,
Burned the robes of war and blood.

3 Unto us the Child is born,
Unto us is given the Son;
His shall throne and kingdom be,
Heir of all Eternity.—
Let Thy government increase
Just and Wondrous Prince of Peace!

4 Counsel! Father! Mighty God!
Thou shalt ever be adored;
Thou didst lay Thy glory down,
Thou shalt wear the ages' crown!
Let us all that glory see,
Through Thy pure nativity.
M. Woolsey Stryker, 1881.

Christ's Ministry.

178 Horsley. C. M. — William Horsley, c. 1815.

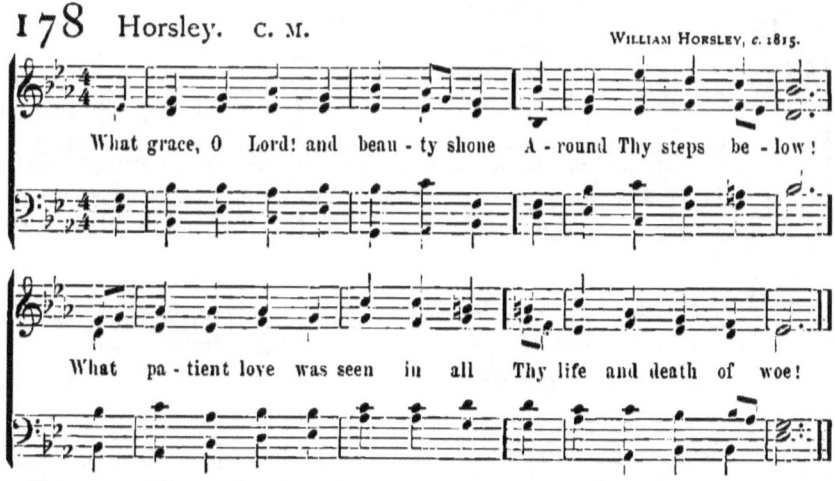

What grace, O Lord! and beau-ty shone A-round Thy steps be-low!
What pa-tient love was seen in all Thy life and death of woe!

2 For, ever on Thy burdened heart
   A weight of sorrow hung;
Yet no ungentle, murmuring word
   Escaped Thy silent tongue.

3 Thy foes might hate, despise, revile,
   Thy friends unfaithful prove;
Unwearied in forgiveness still,
   Thy heart could only love.

4 Oh! give us hearts to love like Thee;
   Like Thee, O Lord! to grieve
Far more for others' sins, than all
   The wrongs that we receive.
Edward Denny, 1839.

179

A PILGRIM through this lonely world,
   The blesséd Saviour passed;
A mourner all His life was He,
   A dying Lamb at last.

2 That tender heart that felt for all,
   For all its life-blood gave;
It found on earth no resting-place,
   Save only in the grave.

3 Such was our Lord; and shall we fear
   The cross with all its scorn?
Or love a faithless, evil world,
   That wreathed His brow with thorn?

4 No, facing all its frowns or smiles,
   Like Him, obedient still,
We homeward press, thro storm or calm,
   To Zion's blesséd hill.

5 In tents we dwell amid the waste,
   Nor turn aside to roam
In folly's paths; nor seek our rest,
   Where Jesus had no home.

6 Dead to the world, with Him who died
   To win our hearts, our love,
We, risen with our risen Head,
   In spirit dwell above.

7 By faith, His boundless glories there
   Our wondering eyes behold;
Those glories which eternal years
   Shall never all unfold.
Edward Denny, 1839.

180

THINE arm, O Lord, in days of old
   Was strong to heal and save:
It triumphed o'er disease and death,
   O'er darkness and the grave.

2 To Thee they went, the blind, the dumb,
   The palsied and the lame,
The leper with his tainted life,
   The sick with fevered frame.

Christ's Ministry.

181

3 And lo! Thy touch brought life and health,
Gave speech, and strength, and sight;
And youth renewed and frenzy calmed
Owned Thee, the Lord of Light:

4 And now, O Lord, be near to bless,
Almighty as of yore,
In crowded street, by restless couch,
As by Gennesareth's shore.

5 Be Thou our great Deliverer still,
Thou Lord of life and death;
Restore and quicken, soothe and bless
With Thine almighty breath.

6 To hands that work and eyes that see
Give wisdom's heavenly lore,
That whole and sick, and weak and strong
May praise Thee evermore.
                                Edward H. Plumptre, 1865.

Thou art the Way: to Thee alone
From sin and death we flee;
And he who would the Father seek,
Must seek Him, Lord, by Thee.

2 Thou art the Truth: Thy word alone
True wisdom can impart;
Thou only canst inform the mind,
And purify the heart.

3 Thou art the Life: the rending tomb
Proclaims Thy conquering arm;
And those who put their trust in Thee
Nor death nor hell shall harm.

4 Thou art the Way, the Truth, the Life;
Grant us that Way to know;
That Truth to keep, that Life to win,
Whose joys eternal flow.
                                George W. Doane, 1824.

182 Gratitude. L M.
Paul A. I. D. Bost, 1828.

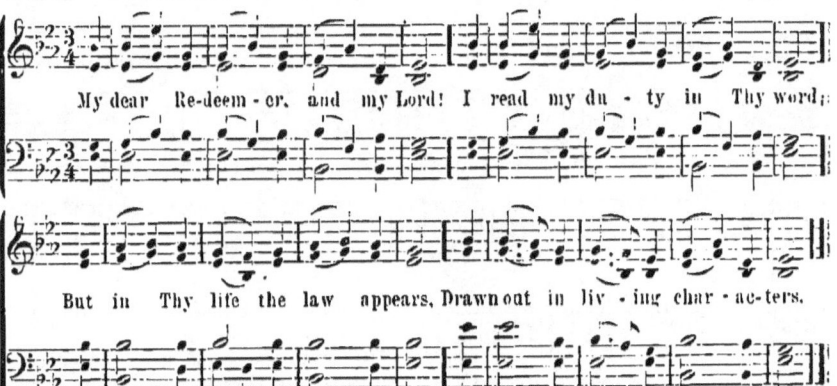

My dear Redeemer, and my Lord! I read my duty in Thy word;
But in Thy life the law appears, Drawn out in living characters.

2 Such was Thy truth, and such Thy zeal,
Such deference to Thy Father's will,
Such love and meekness, so divine,
I would transcribe, and make them mine.

3 Cold mountains and the midnight air
Witnessed the fervor of Thy prayer;
The desert Thy temptations knew,
Thy conflict and Thy vict'ry too.

4 Be Thou my pattern; make me bear
More of Thy gracious image here;
Then God, the Judge, shall own my name,
Among the foll'wers of the Lamb.
                                Isaac Watts, 1709.

The Cross.

183 Olive's Brow. L. M.
WM. B. BRADBURY, 1853.

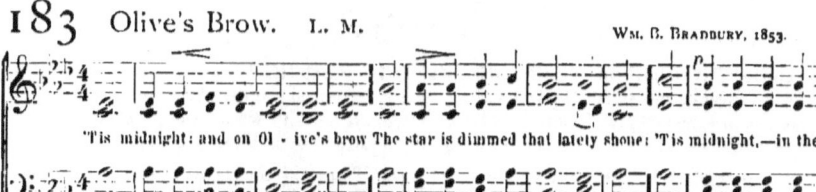

'Tis midnight; and on Olive's brow The star is dimmed that lately shone; 'Tis midnight,—in the

garden, now The suffering Saviour prays alone.

2 'Tis midnight,—and, from all removed,
Immanuel wrestles lone with fears;
E'en the disciple that He loved
Heeds not his Master's grief and tears.

3 'Tis midnight and for others' guilt
The Man of sorrows weeps in blood;
Yet He, who hath in anguish knelt,
Is not forsaken by His God.

4 'Tis midnight,—and, from ether-plains,
Is borne the song that angels know;
Unheard by mortals are the strains,
That sweetly soothe the Saviour's woe.
William B. Tappan, 1821.

184 Boston. C. M.
U. C. BURNAP, 1868.

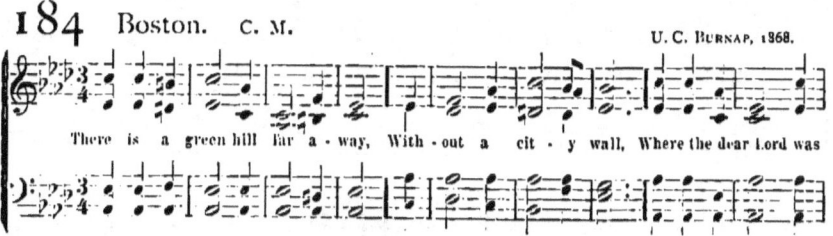

There is a green hill far away, Without a city wall, Where the dear Lord was

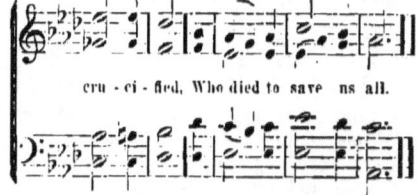

crucified, Who died to save us all.

2 We may not know, we cannot tell,
What pains He had to bear,
But we believe it was for us
He hung and suffered there.

3 He died that we might be forgiven,
He died to make us good,
That we might go at last to heaven,
Saved by His precious Blood.

4 There was no other good enough
To pay the price of sin;
He only, could unlock the gate
Of heaven, and let us in.

5 Oh, dearly, dearly, has He loved,
And we must love Him, too,
And trust in His redeeming Blood,
And try His works to do.
Cecil F. Alexander, 1848.

The Cross.

185 St. Drostane. L. M. J. B. DYKES, 1859.

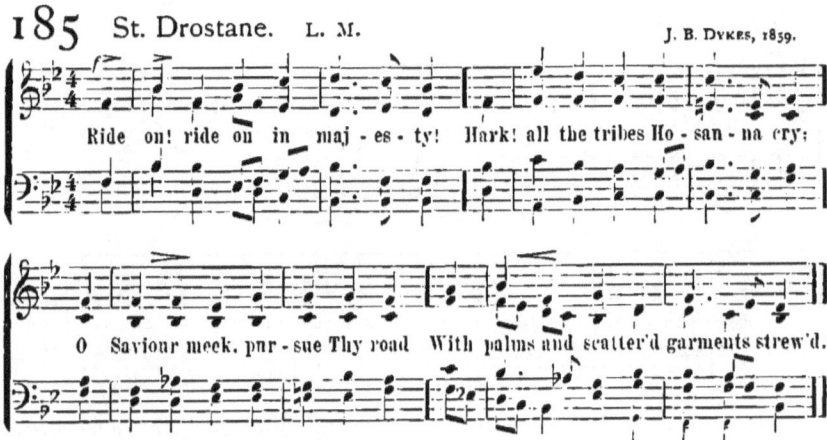

Ride on! ride on in majesty! Hark! all the tribes Hosanna cry;
O Saviour meek, pursue Thy road With palms and scatter'd garments strew'd.

2 Ride on! ride on in majesty!
In lowly pomp, ride on to die:
O Christ, Thy triumphs now begin
O'er captive death and conquer'd sin.

3 Ride on! ride on in majesty!
The angel armies of the sky
Look down with sad and wond'ring eyes
To see th' approaching Sacrifice.

4 Ride on! ride on in majesty!
The last and fiercest strife is nigh:
The Father on His sapphire throne
Awaits His own anointed Son.

5 Ride on! ride on in majesty!
In lowly pomp, ride on to die;
Bow Thy meek Head to mortal pain,
Then take, O God, Thy power, and reign.
Henry H. Milman, 1821.

186

CHRIST had His sorrows: when He shed
His tears, Jerusalem, for thee!
And when His trembling followers fled,
In His dark hour of agony.

2 Christ had His sorrows: so must thou
Who tread'st the path that Jesus trod;
Oh, then, like Him submissive bow,
Adore the sovereignty of God.

3 Christ had His joys: but they were not
The joys the son of pleasure boasts;
Ah no! 'twas when His spirit sought
Thy will, Thy glory, God of hosts!

4 Christ had His joys: and so hath he
Who feels the Spirit in his heart—
Who yields, O God, his all to Thee,
And loves Thy name for what Thou art.

5 Christ had His foes: the prince of hell
With all his legions sought His death!
See! human hearts with malice swell,
And murder feign affection's breath!

6 Christ had His foes: and so, if thou
Shalt with Him walk, and near Him live,
The cruel world will hate thee now,
And *thou* shalt suffer—and forgive!

7 Christ had His friends; His eye could trace,
Through the long train of coming years,
The chosen children of His grace,
The full reward of all His tears!

8 Christ had His friends: and *His are thine*,
If thou to Him hast bowed the knee:
And where those ransomed millions shine
Shall thy eternal mansion be.
N. E. Johnson, 1832.

The Cross.

187 Ashwell. L. M.
Lowell Mason, 1841.

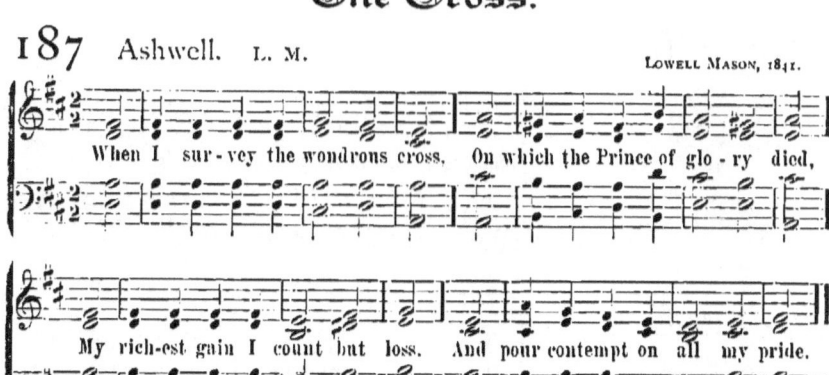

When I sur-vey the wondrous cross, On which the Prince of glo-ry died,
My rich-est gain I count but loss, And pour contempt on all my pride.

2 See from His head, His hands, His feet,
Sorrow and love flow mingled down;
Did e'er such love and sorrow meet,
Or thorns compose so rich a crown?

3 Forbid it, Lord, that I should boast,
Save in the death of Christ my God,

All the vain things that charm me most,
I sacrifice them to Thy blood.

4 Were the whole realm of nature mine,
That were a present far too small;
Love so amazing, so divine,
Demands my soul, my life, my all.
Isaac Watts, 1707.

188 Midnight. L. M.
Virgil C. Taylor, 1847.

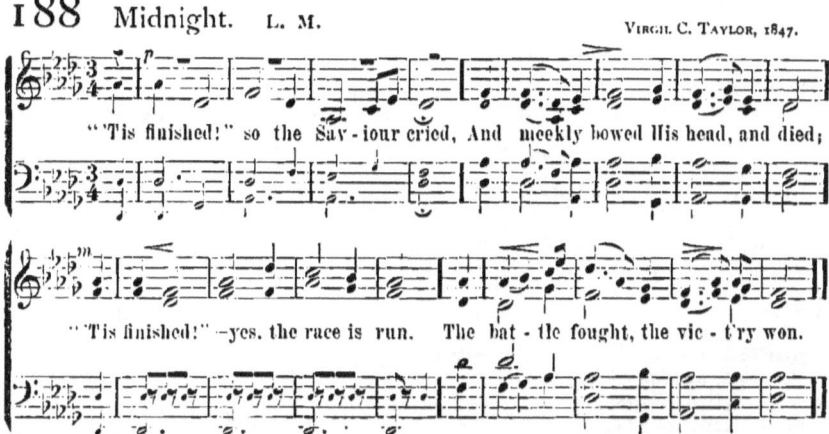

"'T is finished!" so the Sav-iour cried, And meekly bowed His head, and died;
"'T is finished!"—yes, the race is run. The bat-tle fought, the vic-t'ry won.

2 "'T is finished!"—Heaven is reconciled,
And all the powers of darkness spoiled;
Peace, love, and happiness, again
Return, and dwell with sinful men.

3 "'T is finished!"—let the joyful sound
Be heard through all the nations round;
"'T is finished!"—let the echo fly,
Thro heaven and hell, thro earth and sky.
Samuel Stennett, 1787.

The Cross.

189 Littledale. 7s & 6. ANON, 1874.

Jesus, in Thy dying woes,
Even while Thy life-blood flows,
Craving pardon for Thy foes: Hear us, Holy Jesus. Amen.

2 Saviour, for our pardon sue,
When our sins Thy pangs renew,
For we know not what we do;
   Hear us, Holy Jesus.

3 Oh, may we, who mercy need,
Be like Thee in heart and deed,
When with wrong our spirits bleed:
   Hear us, Holy Jesus.

4 Jesus, pitying the sighs
Of the thief, who near Thee dies,
Promising him Paradise:
   Hear us, Holy Jesus.

5 May we in our guilt and shame,
Still Thy love and mercy claim,
Calling humbly on Thy name:
   Hear us, Holy Jesus.

6 Jesus, loving to the end
Her whose heart Thy sorrows rend,
And Thy dearest human friend:
   Hear us, Holy Jesus.

7 May we all Thy loved ones be,
All one holy family,
Loving for the love of Thee:
   Hear us, Holy Jesus.

8 Jesus, whelmed in fears unknown,
With our evil left alone,
While no light from heaven is shown:
   Hear us, Holy Jesus.

9 When we vainly seem to pray,
And our hope seems far away,
In the darkness be our stay:
   Hear us, Holy Jesus.

10 Jesus, in Thy thirst and pain,
While Thy wounds Thy life-blood drain,
Thirsting more our love to gain:
   Hear us, Holy Jesus.

11 Jesus,—all our ransom paid,
All Thy Father's will obeyed,—
By Thy sufferings perfect made:
   Hear us, Holy Jesus.

12 Jesus,—all Thy labor vast,
All Thy woe and conflict past—
Yielding up Thy soul at last:
   Hear us, Holy Jesus.

13 May Thy life and death supply
Grace to live and grace to die,
Grace to reach the home on high:
   Hear us, Holy Jesus. Amen.

T. B. Pollock, 1871.

The Cross.

190 St. Anselm. 7s. J. H. HOPKINS, 1871.

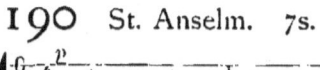

Bound up-on th' accursed tree, Faint and bleeding, who is He? By the eyes so pale and dim, Streaming blood, and writhing limb, By the flesh with scourges torn, By the crown of twisted thorn, By the side so deep-ly pierced, By the baffled, burning thirst, By the drooping, death-dew'd brow; Son of Man, 'tis Thou, 'tis Thou! A-men.

2 Bound upon th' accursèd tree,
Dread and awful, who is He?
By the sun at noonday pale,
Shivering rocks, and rending veil,
By the earth enwrapt in gloom,
By the saints who burst their tomb,
Eden promised ere He died
To the felon at His side;
Lord! our suppliant knees we bow!
Son of God! 'tis Thou! 'tis Thou!

3 Bound upon th' accursèd tree,
Dread and awful, who is He?
By the prayer for them that slew,
"Lord! they know not what they do!"
By the spoiled and empty grave,
By the souls He died to save,
By the conquest He hath won,
By the saints before His throne,
By the rainbow round His brow,
Son of God! 'tis Thou! 'tis Thou! Amen.
Henry Hart Milman, 1827.

The Cross.

191 Passion Choral. 7s & 6s. JOHANN LEONARD, (HASLER), 1601.

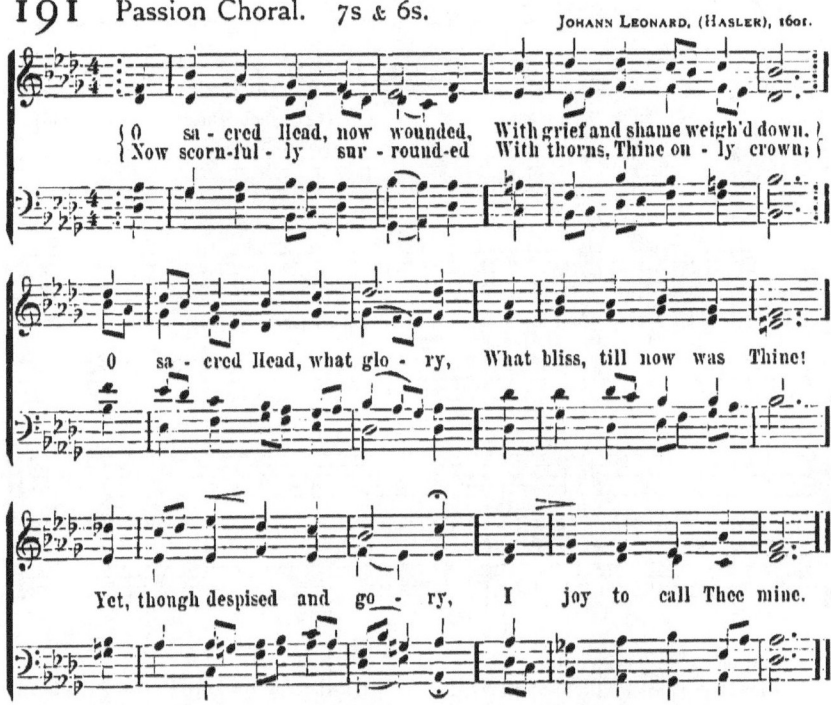

O sacred Head, now wounded, With grief and shame weigh'd down,
Now scornfully surrounded With thorns, Thine only crown;
O sacred Head, what glory, What bliss, till now was Thine!
Yet, though despised and gory, I joy to call Thee mine.

2 What Thou, my Lord! hast suffered
  Was all for sinners' gain;
Mine, mine was the transgression,
  But Thine the deadly pain:
Lo! here I fall, my Saviour!
  'Tis I deserve Thy place;
Look on me with Thy favor,
  Vouchsafe to me Thy grace.

3 What language shall I borrow
  To thank Thee, dearest Friend!
For this Thy dying sorrow,
  Thy pity without end?
Oh! make me Thine for ever;
  And should I fainting be,
Lord! let me never, never,
  Outlive my love to Thee!

4 And, when I am departing,
  Oh! part not Thou from me!
When mortal pangs are darting,
  Come, Lord! and set me free;
And, when my heart must languish
  Amidst the final throe,
Release me from mine anguish,
  By Thine own pain and woe.

5 Be near me when I'm dying,
  Oh! show Thy cross to me!
And, for my succor flying,
  Come, Lord! and set me free!
These eyes new faith receiving,
  From Jesus shall not move;
For He, who dies believing,
  Dies safely, through Thy love.

Ger., *Paul Gerhard*, 1656.
Tr. *James W. Alexander*, 1829.

The Resurrection.

192 Gethsemane. 7s.   RICHARD REDHEAD, 1853.

Go to dark Geth-sem-a-ne, Ye that feel the tempter's power.
Your Re-deem-er's con-flict see, Watch with Him one bit-ter hour;
Turn not from His griefs a-way; Learn of Je-sus Christ to pray.

2 Follow to the judgment-hall,
  View the Lord of life arraigned;
Oh! the wormwood and the gall!
  Oh! the pangs His soul sustained!
Shun not suffering, shame, or loss;
Learn of Him to bear the cross.

3 Calv'ry's mournful mountain climb;
  There, adoring at His feet,
Mark that miracle of time,
  God's own sacrifice complete:
"It is finished," hear Him cry;
Learn of Jesus Christ to die.

4 Early hasten to the tomb,
  Where they laid His breathless clay;
All is solitude and gloom;—
  Who hath taken Him away?
Christ is ris'n!—He meets our eyes;
Saviour! teach us so to rise.
          James Montgomery, 1820.

193

NEAR the tomb where Christ hath been
Weeping stands the Magdalene;
With the two disciples, she
Wonders where her Lord can be:
Looking in, they see the bed
Where the Lord hath laid His head.

2 Stooping down they see no more
Than the clothes which wrapp'd Him o'er;
Clothes which wound His feet, His brow,
Death's white vestments, useless now.
Two depart: but love and faith
Stronger are than sight, than death.

3 He was here: then she will wait
Watching early, watching late.
Where her Jesus last was seen,
There will wait the Magdalene.
Looking in with streaming eyes,
Angels twain she there espies.

The Resurrection.

194

4 Hark, with glad accord they cry,
Jesus lives, no more to die:
Thy dear Lord abides not here;
He is risen; do not fear;
Mary, wipe thy tears away,
See the place where Jesus lay,

5 Turning round she sees Him stand,
In the garden close at hand:
"Mary!" 'tis His accent now:
"Master; It is Thou, 'tis Thou!"—
We, with her, oh Christ adore,
Lord and Master, evermore!
Gerard Moultrie, 1867.

SURELY Christ thy griefs hath borne;
Weeping soul! no longer mourn;
View Him bleeding on the tree,
Pouring out His life for thee:
There thine every sin He bore;
Weeping soul! lament no more.

2 Cast thy guilty soul on Him,
Find Him mighty to redeem:
At His feet thy burden lay,
Look thy doubts and cares away:
Now, by faith, the Son embrace,
Plead His promise, trust His grace.
Augustus M. Toplady, 1759, ab.

195 Hastings. C. L. M.
THOMAS HASTINGS, 1832.

How calm and beau-ti-ful the morn, That gilds the sa-cred tomb,
Where Christ, the cru-ci-fied, was borne, And veiled in midnight gloom!
Oh! weep no more the Saviour slain! The Lord is risen—He lives a-gain.

2 Ye mourning saints! dry every tear
  For your departed Lord;
"Behold the place!—He is not here!"
  The tomb is all unbarred;
The gates of death were closed in vain;
The Lord is risen—He lives again.

3 How tranquil now the rising day!
  'Tis Jesus still appears,
A risen Lord, to chase away
  Your unbelieving fears:
Oh! weep no more your comforts slain;
The Lord is risen—He lives again.
Thomas Hastings, 1832.

The Resurrection.

196 Easter Hymn. 7s & 4s. P.   Lyra Davidica, 1709.

Christ the Lord is ris'n a-gain, Hal-le-lu-jah! Christ hath broken ev-ery chain; Hal-le-lu-jah! Hark, an-gel-ic voic-es cry, Hal-le-lu-jah! Singing evermore on high, Hal-le-lu-jah!

2 He who slumbered in the grave, Hallelujah!
Is exalted now to save; Hallelujah!
Now through Christendom it rings, Hallelujah!
That the Lamb is King of kings: Hallelujah!

3 Now He bids us tell abroad, Hallelujah!
How the lost may be restored, Hallelujah!
How the penitent forgiven, Hallelujah!
How we too may enter heaven: Hallelujah!

4 Thou, our Paschal Lamb indeed, Hallelujah!
Christ, Thy ransomed people feed! Hallelujah!
Take our sins and guilt away, Hallelujah!
That we all may sing for aye, Hallelujah!

M. Weiss, 1531.
Tr. Catherine Winkworth, 1858.

197

Holy Father! Holy Son! Hallelujah!
Holy Spirit! Three in One! Hallelujah!
Praise and glory be to Thee, Hallelujah!
Now, and through eternity. Hallelujah!

Anon, 1869.

The Resurrection.

198 Bremen. C. P. M.   Thomas Hastings, 1836.

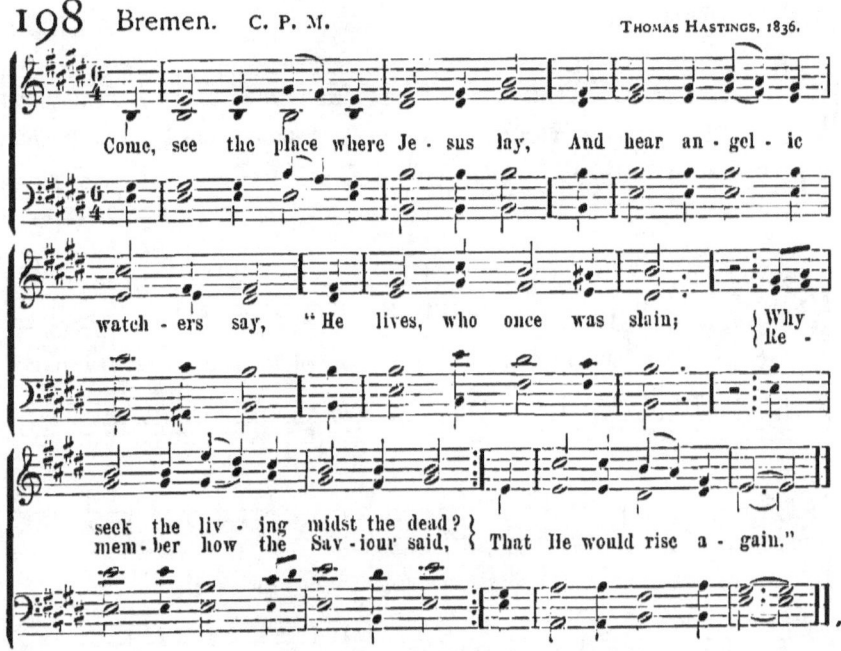

Come, see the place where Jesus lay,
And hear angelic watchers say,
"He lives, who once was slain;
Why seek the living midst the dead?
Remember how the Saviour said,
That He would rise again."

2 O joyful sound! O glorious hour,
When by His own almighty power
  He rose, and left the grave!
Now let our songs His triumph tell,
Who burst the bands of death and hell,
  And ever lives to save.

3 The First-Begotten of the dead,
For us He rose, our glorious Head,
  Immortal life to bring;
What, though the saints like Him shall die?
They share their Leader's victory,
  And triumph with their King.

4 No more they tremble at the grave
For Jesus will their spirits save,
  And raise their slumbering dust:
O risen Lord! in Thee we live,
To Thee our ransomed souls we give,
  To Thee our bodies trust.
Thomas Kelly, 1804.
Alt. Henry W. Baker, 1861.

199

Jesus, who died a world to save,
Revives and rises from the grave,
  By His almighty power:
From sin, and death, and hell, set free,
He captive leads captivity,
  And lives to die no more.

2 Children of God! look up and see
Your Saviour clothed in majesty,
  Triumphant o'er the tomb:
Give o'er your griefs, cast off your fears,
In heaven your mansions He prepares,
  And soon will take you home.

3 His church is still His joy and crown;
He looks with love and pity down
  On her He did redeem:
He tastes her joys, He feels her woes,
And prays that she may spoil her foes,
  And ever reign with Him.
William Hammond, 1745.

The Resurrection.

200 Resurrexit. P. M. A. S. Sullivan, 1873.

The Resurrection.

Christ is ris-en! Christ is ris-en! Earth and Heav'n pro-long the strain.

2 Lo, the chains of death are broken!
    Earth below, and Heaven above
Joy anew in every token
    Of Thy triumph, Lord of love!
He o'er earth and heaven shall reign
    At His Father's side,
Till He cometh once again,
    Bridegroom, to His Bride.
        Christ is risen! &c.

3 Angel legions, downward thronging,
    Hail the Lord of earth and skies!
Ye who watched with holy longing
    Till your Sun again should rise:—
He is risen! Earth, rejoice!
    Sing, ye starry train!
All things living, find a voice!
    Jesus lives again!
        Christ is risen! &c.
            Archer T. Gurney, 1862.

201 St. Albinus. 7s 8s & 4. H. J. GAUNTLETT, 1872.

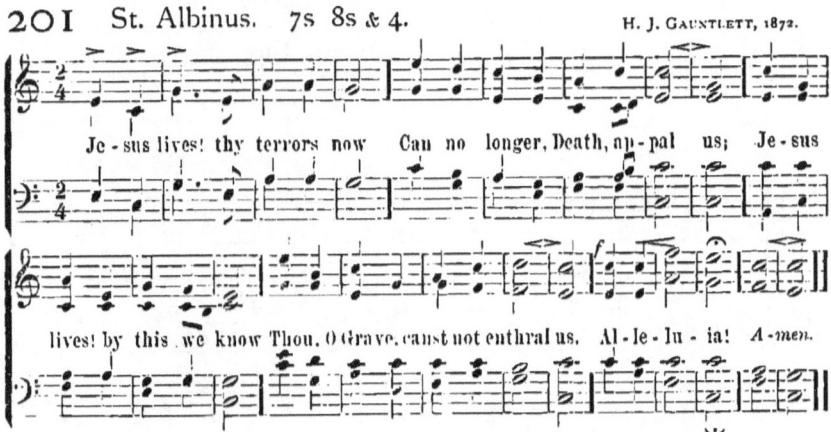

Je-sus lives! thy terrors now Can no longer, Death, ap-pal us; Je-sus lives! by this we know Thou, O Grave, canst not enthral us. Al-le-lu-ia! A-men.

2 Jesus lives! henceforth is death
    But the gate of life immortal;
This shall calm our trembling breath,
    When we pass its gloomy portal.
        Alleluia!

3 Jesus lives! for us He died;
    Then, alone to Jesus living,
Pure in heart may we abide,
    Glory to our Saviour giving.
        Alleluia!

4 Jesus lives! our hearts know well
    Naught from us His love shall sever;
Life, nor death, nor powers of hell
    Tear us from His keeping ever.
        Alleluia!

5 Jesus lives! to Him the throne
    Over all the world is given;
May we go where He is gone,
    Rest and reign with Him in heaven.
        Alleluia. Amen.
            C. F. Gellert, 1757. Tr. *F. E. Cox*, 1841.

The Resurrection

202 Mozart. 7s. W. A. Mozart, 1779.

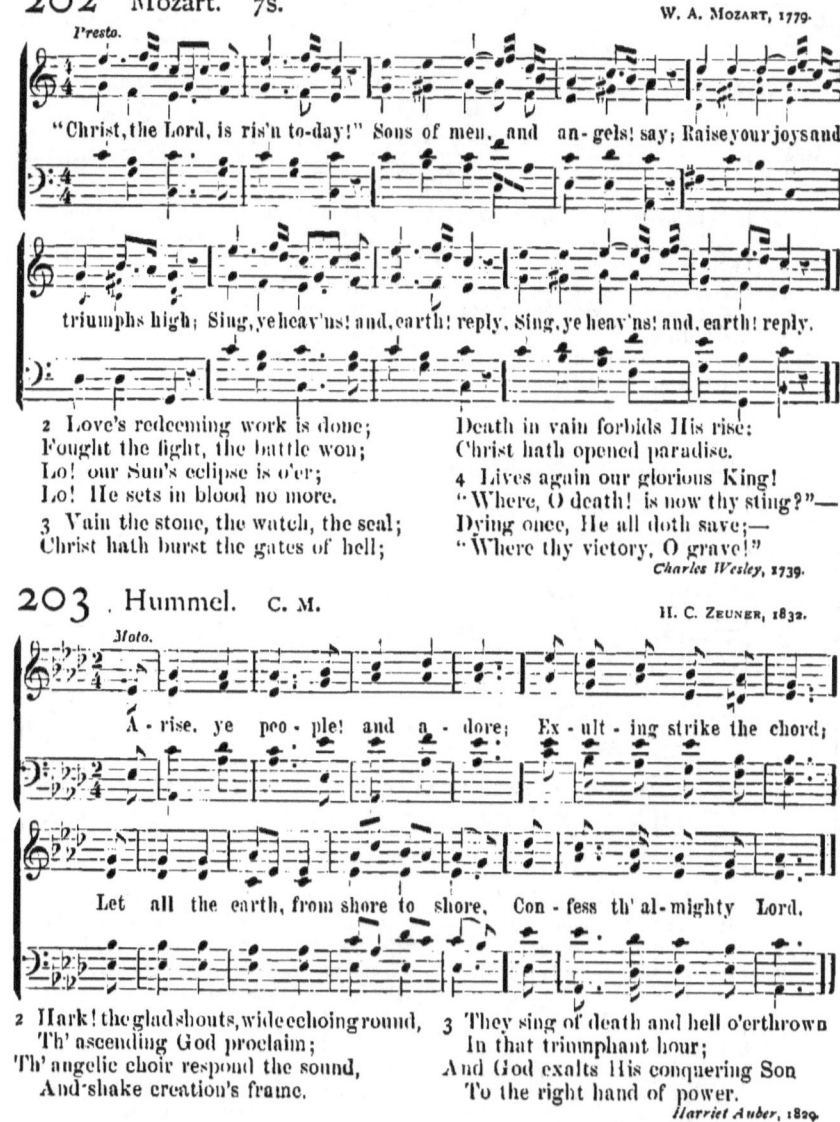

"Christ, the Lord, is ris'n to-day!" Sons of men, and angels! say; Raise your joys and triumphs high; Sing, ye heav'ns! and, earth! reply, Sing, ye heav'ns! and, earth! reply.

2 Love's redeeming work is done;
Fought the fight, the battle won;
Lo! our Sun's eclipse is o'er;
Lo! He sets in blood no more.

3 Vain the stone, the watch, the seal;
Christ hath burst the gates of hell;
Death in vain forbids His rise:
Christ hath opened paradise.

4 Lives again our glorious King!
"Where, O death! is now thy sting?"—
Dying once, He all doth save;—
"Where thy victory, O grave!"
Charles Wesley, 1739.

203 Hummel. C. M. H. C. Zeuner, 1832.

Moto.

A-rise, ye peo-ple! and a-dore; Ex-ult-ing strike the chord;
Let all the earth, from shore to shore, Con-fess th' al-mighty Lord.

2 Hark! the glad shouts, wide echoing round,
Th' ascending God proclaim;
Th' angelic choir respond the sound,
And shake creation's frame.

3 They sing of death and hell o'erthrown
In that triumphant hour;
And God exalts His conquering Son
To the right hand of power.
Harriet Auber, 1829.

The Resurrection.

204

1. Jesus, immortal King! arise;
   Assume, assert Thy sway;
   Till earth, subdued, its tribute bring,
   And distant lands obey.

2. Ride forth, victorious Conqueror, ride,
   Till all Thy foes submit;
   And all the powers of hell resign
   Their trophies at Thy feet.

3. Send forth Thy word, and let it fly,
   This spacious earth around;
   Till every soul, beneath the sun,
   Shall hear the joyful sound.

4. From sea to sea, from shore to shore,
   May Jesus be adored;
   And earth, with all her millions, shout
   Hosannas to the Lord.
   Aaron Crossley Hobart Seymour, 1810.

205

Ye choirs of new Jerusalem!
Your sweetest notes employ,
The paschal victory to hymn
In strains of holy joy.

2. For Judah's Lion bursts His chains,
   Crushing the serpent's head;
   And cries aloud, through death's domains,
   To wake th' imprisoned dead.

3. Devouring depths of hell their prey
   At His command restore;
   His ransomed hosts pursue their way
   Where Jesus goes before.

4. Triumphant in His glory now,
   To Him all power is given;
   To Him in one communion bow
   All saints in earth and heaven.

5. While we, His soldiers, praise our King,
   His mercy we implore,
   Within His palace bright to bring
   And keep us evermore.
   Lat. of Fulbert, 1020. Tr. Robert Campbell, 1850, a.

206 Messiah. 7s.
L. J. F. Herold, 1838.

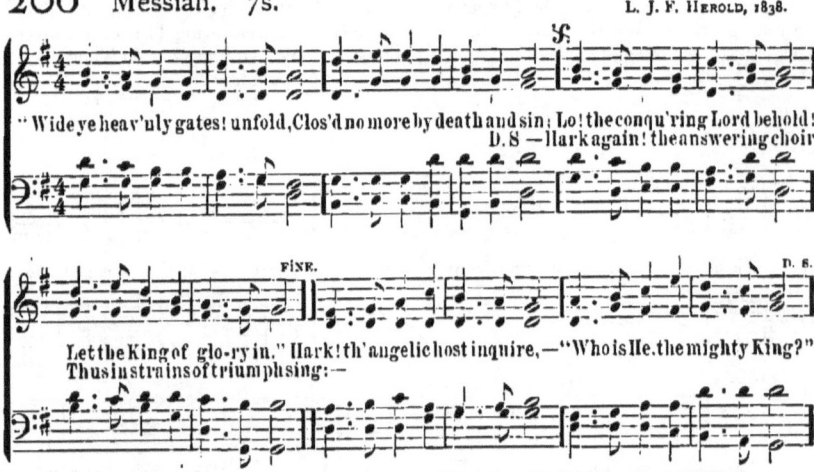

"Wide ye heav'nly gates! unfold, Clos'd no more by death and sin; Lo! the conqu'ring Lord behold! Let the King of glory in." Hark! th' angelic host inquire,—"Who is He, the mighty King?" Thus in strains of triumph sing:— D.S.—Hark again! the answering choir

2. "He, whose powerful arm alone
   On His foes destruction hurled;
   He, who hath the vict'ry won,
   He, who saved a ruined world:
   He, who God's pure law fulfilled,
   Jesus, the incarnate Word;
   He, whose truth with blood was sealed;
   He is heaven's all-glorious Lord."
   Harriet Auber, 1829.

The Resurrection.

207 Victory. 8s & 4.   G. P. A. PALESTRINA.

The strife is o'er, the bat-tle done; The vic-to-ry of life is won; The song of tri-umph has be-gun. Al-le-lu-ia!

2 The powers of death have done their worst,
But Christ their legions hath dispersed:
Let shouts of holy joy outburst,
    Alleluia!

3 The three sad days are quickly sped;
He rises glorious from the dead;
All glory to our risen Head!
    Alleluia!

4 He closed the yawning gates of hell,
The bars from heaven's high portals fell;
Let hymns of praise His triumphs tell!
    Alleluia!

5 Lord! by the stripes that wounded Thee,
From Death's dread sting Thy servants free,
That we may live and sing to Thee,
    Alleluia!
                Tr. *Francis Pott*, 1860.

208 St. Martin's.   C. M.   WM. TANSUR, 1735.

Th' e-ter-nal gates lift up their heads, The doors are o-pened wide; The King of glo-ry is gone up Un-to His Fa-ther's side.

The Ascension.

2 Thou art gone in before us, Lord,
  Thou hast prepared a place,
That we may be where now Thou art,
  And look upon Thy face.

3 And ever on Thine earthly path
  A gleam of glory lies;
A light still breaks behind the cloud
  That veils Thee from our eyes.

4 Lift up our thoughts, lift up our songs,
  And let Thy grace be given,
That while we linger yet below,
  Our hearts may be in heaven;

5 That where Thou art at God's right hand,
  Our hope, our love may be:
Dwell in us now, that we may dwell
  For evermore in Thee.

Cecil Frances Alexander, 1858.

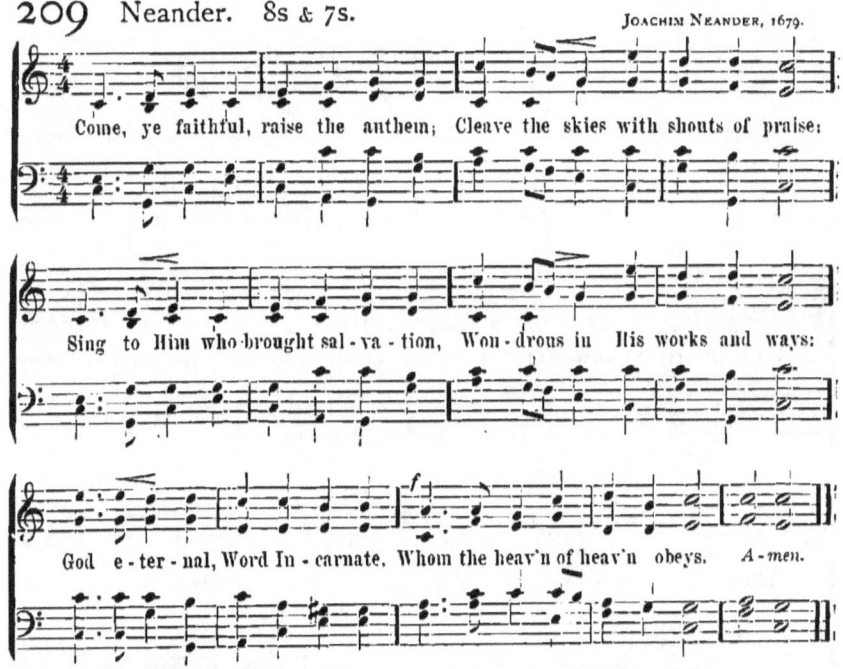

209 Neander. 8s & 7s. JOACHIM NEANDER, 1679.

Come, ye faithful, raise the anthem; Cleave the skies with shouts of praise;
Sing to Him who brought sal-va-tion, Won-drous in His works and ways:
God e-ter-nal, Word In-carnate, Whom the heav'n of heav'n obeys. A-men.

2 Ere He raised the lofty mountains,
  Formed the sea, or spread the sky,
Love eternal, free and boundless,
  Moved the Lord of life to die;
Fore-ordained the Prince of princes
  For the throne of Calvary.

3 Now above the sapphire pavement,
  High in unapproachéd light,
Lo! He lives and reigns for ever,
  Victor after hard-won fight,
Where the song of the redeeméd
  Rings unceasing day and night.

4 Trust Him then, ye fearful pilgrims;
  Who shall pluck you from His hand?
Pledged He stands for your salvation,—
  Pledged to give the promised land,—
Where, among the ransomed nations
  Ye, too, round His throne shall stand.

Job Hupton, 1806.

The Ascension.

210 Ascension. L. M.   Max Piutti, 1880.

Our Lord is ris-en from the dead; Our Jesus is gone up on high;
The powers of hell are captive led, Dragged to the por-tals of the sky;
There His tri-umphal char-iot waits, And an-gels chant the solemn lay:—
"Lift up your heads, ye heavenly gates! Ye ev-er-lasting doors! give way."

Copyright, 1880, by Biglow & Main.

2 "Loose all your bars of massy light,
   And wide unfold th' ethereal scene;
He claims these mansions as His right;
   Receive the King of glory in."
"Who is the King of glory?—who?"
   "The Lord, that all our foes o'ercame,
World, sin, and death, and hell o'erthrew;
   And Jesus is the Conqueror's name."

3 Lo! His triumphal chariot waits,
   And angels chant the solemn lay:—
"Lift up your heads, ye heavenly gates!
   Ye everlasting doors! give way."
"Who is the King of glory?—who?"—
   "The Lord, of glorious power possessed;
The King of saints and angels too;
   God over all, for ever blessed."
                          Charles Wesley, 1743.

The Ascension.

211 Nativity. C. M. *Henry Lahee.*

Lift up your heads, e-ter-nal gates, Un-fold, to en-ter-tain
The King of Glo-ry! see! He comes With His ce-les-tial train. A-men.

2 Who is the King of Glory, who?
  The Lord for strength renowned;
  In battle mighty; o'er His foes
    Eternal Victor crowned.
3 Lift up your heads, ye gates; unfold,
    In state to entertain

The King of Glory! see, He comes
  With all His shining train.
4 Who is the King of Glory, who?
  The Lord of hosts renowned;
  Of glory He alone is King,
    Who is with glory crowned. Amen.
  Tate & Brady, 1696.

212 Darwall. H. M. *John Darwall, 1770.*

Rejoice! the Lord is King!—Your God and King a-dore; Mortals! give thanks, and sing,
And triumph evermore: Lift up your hearts, lift up your voice, Rejoice! again, I say—rejoice!

2 His kingdom cannot fail;
    He rules o'er earth and heaven;
  The keys of death and hell
    Are to our Jesus given:
  Lift up your hearts,—lift up your voice,
  Rejoice! again, I say,—rejoice!

3 Rejoice in glorious hope;
    Jesus, the Judge, shall come,
  And take His servants up
    To their eternal home:
  We soon shall hear th' archangel's voice,
  The trump of God shall sound,—rejoice!
  Charles Wesley, 1746.

The Ascended Lord.

213 Frankfort. 8s & 7s.   J. C. BACH, 1680.

{ Jesus comes, His conflict over, Comes to claim His great reward; }
{ Angels round the Victor hover, Crowding to behold their Lord; } Haste, ye saints! your tribute bring, Crown Him, everlasting King.

2 Yonder throne, for Him erected,
Now becomes the Victor's seat;
Lo, the Man on earth rejected!
Angels worship at His feet:
Haste, ye saints! your tribute bring,
Crown Him, everlasting King.

3 Day and night they cry before Him,—
"Holy, holy, holy Lord!"
All the powers of heaven adore Him,
All obey His sovereign word:
Haste, ye saints! your tribute bring,
Crown Him, everlasting King.
Thomas Kelly, 1804.

214 Harwell. 8s & 7s.   LOWELL MASON, 1841.

{ Hark! ten thousand harps and voices Sound the note of praise above; }
{ Je-sus reigns, and heaven rejoices; Jesus reigns, the God of love: } See, He sits on yonder throne; Jesus rules the world alone. Halle-lujah, Halle-lujah, Halle-lujah! A-men.

2 King of glory! reign for ever—
Thine an everlasting crown;
Nothing, from Thy love, shall sever
Those whom Thou hast made Thine own;—
Happy objects of Thy grace,
Destined to behold Thy face.

3 Saviour! hasten Thine appearing;
Bring, oh, bring the glorious day,
When, the awful summons hearing,
Heaven and earth shall pass away;—
Then, with golden harps, we'll sing,—
"Glory, glory to our King!"
Thomas Kelly, 1804.

The Ascended Lord.

215 All Saints. 8s & 7s. *German Choral, 1698.*

"Who is this that comes from E-dom," All His rai-ment stained with blood,
To the slave pro-claiming freedom, Bring-ing and be-stow-ing good,
Glo-rious in the garb He wears, Glo-rious in the spoil He bears?

2 'Tis the Saviour, now victorious,
    Traveling onward in His might!
'Tis the Saviour! Oh! how glorious
    To His people is the sight!
Mighty to redeem the slave,
Jesus now is strong to save.

3 Mighty Victor! reign for ever;
    Wear the crown so dearly won;
Never shall Thy people, never,
    Cease to sing what Thou hast done;
Thou hast fought Thy people's foes;
Thou wilt heal Thy people's woes.
                    Thomas Kelly, 1839.

216

Look, ye saints!—the sight is glorious;
    See the "Man of sorrows" now!
From the fight returned victorious,
    Every knee to Him shall bow:
||: Crown Him! crown Him! :||
Crowns become the Victor's brow.

2 Crown the Saviour! angels! crown Him!
    Rich the trophies Jesus brings;
In the seat of power enthrone Him,
    While the heavenly concave rings:
||: Crown Him! crown Him! :||
Crown the Saviour, "King of kings!"

3 Sinners in derision crowned Him,
    Mocking thus the Saviour's claim;
Saints and angels! crowd around Him,
    Own His title, praise His name:
||: Crown Him! crown Him! :||
Spread abroad the Victor's fame.

4 Hark! those bursts of acclamation!
    Hark! those loud, triumphant chords!
Jesus takes the highest station;
    Oh! what joy the sight affords!
||: Crown Him! crown Him! :||
"King of kings, and Lord of lords."
                    Thomas Kelly, 1804.

The Ascended Lord.

217 Beecher. 8s & 7s. JOHN ZUNDEL, 1870.

Love di-vine, all love ex-cell-ing, Joy of heaven, to earth come down!
Fix in us Thy hum-ble dwelling, All Thy faith-ful mer-cies crown.
D.S. — Vis-it us with Thy sal-va-tion, En-ter ev-ery trem-bling heart.
Je-sus, Thou art all com-pas-sion, Pure, un-bound-ed love Thou art;

2 Breathe, oh, breathe Thy loving Spirit
  Into every troubled breast!
Let us all in Thee inherit,
  Let us find the promised rest:
Come, almighty to deliver,
  Let us all Thy life receive!
Speedily return, and never,
  Never more Thy temples leave!

3 Finish then Thy new creation,
  Pure, unspotted may we be;
Let us see our whole salvation
  Perfectly secured by Thee!
Changed from glory into glory,
  Till in heaven we take our place;
Till we cast our crowns before Thee,
  Lost in wonder, love, and praise.
          Charles Wesley, 1747.

218

SEE, the Conqueror mounts in triumph!
  See the King in royal state,
Riding on the clouds, His chariot,
  To His heavenly palace gate!
Hark! the choirs of angel voices
  Joyful alleluias sing,
And the portals high are lifted,
  To receive their heavenly King.

2 Who is this that comes in glory,
  With the trump of jubilee?
Lord of battles, God of armies,
  He has gained the victory;
He, who on the cross did suffer,
  He, who from the grave arose,
He has vanquished sin and Satan,
  He by death has spoiled His foes.

The Ascended Lord.

3 Thou hast raised our human nature,
   On the clouds to God's right hand;
There we sit in heavenly places,
   There with Thee in glory stand;
Jesus reigns, adored by angels;
   Man with God is on the throne;
Mighty Lord! in Thine ascension,
   We by faith behold our own.

4 Lift us up from earth to heaven,
   Give us wings of faith and love,
Gales of holy aspirations,
   Wafting us to realms above;
That, with hearts and minds uplifted,
   We with Christ our Lord may dwell,
Where He sits enthroned in glory,
   In the heavenly citadel.

5 So at last, when He appeareth,
   We from out our graves may spring,
With our youth renewed like eagles',
   Flocking round our heavenly King,
Caught up on the clouds of heaven,
   And may meet Him in the air,
Rise to realms where He is reigning,
   And may reign for ever there.
Christopher Wordsworth, 1863.

219   Conqueror.   6s & 4s.   JOHN ZUNDEL, 1854.

Rise, glorious Conqueror! rise, In-to Thy native skies; Assume Thy right: And where in / The clouds are many a fold, / backward roll'd, Pass thro those gates of gold, And reign in light! And reign in light!

2 Enter, incarnate God!
   No feet but Thine have trod
     The serpent down:
Blow the full trumpets, blow!
Wider yon portals throw!
Saviour! triumphant, go
   And take Thy crown!

3 Lion of Judah! hail!—
   And let Thy name prevail
     From age to age:
Lord of the rolling years!
Claim for Thine own the spheres;
For Thou hast bought with tears
   Thy heritage.
Matthew Bridges, 1848.

The Royal Priest.

220 Coronation.   C. M.   Oliver Holden, 1793.

All hail the power of Jesus' name! Let angels prostrate fall; Bring forth the royal diadem, And crown Him Lord of all; Bring forth the royal diadem, And crown Him Lord of all.

2 Let high-born seraphs tune the lyre,
  And, as they tune it, fall
Before His face who tunes their choir,
  And crown Him Lord of all.

3 Ye seed of Israel's chosen race,
  Ye ransomed of the fall,
Hail Him who saves you by His grace,
  And crown Him Lord of all.

4 Hail Him, ye heirs of David's line,
  Whom David Lord did call:

The God incarnate, Man Divine;
  And crown Him Lord of all.

5 Sinners! whose love can ne'er forget
  The wormwood and the gall,
Go, spread your trophies at His feet
  And crown Him Lord of all.

6 Let every tribe and every tongue,
  That bound creation's call,
Now shout in universal song
  The crownèd Lord of all.
                        Edward Perronet, 1779.

[SECOND TUNE.]

Miles Lane.   C. M.   William Shrubsole, 1779.

All hail the power of Je-sus' name! Let an-gels prostrate fall; Bring forth the royal di-a-dem, And crown Him, crown Him, crown Him, crown Him Lord of all.

The Royal Priest.

221 Ferguson. S. M.   Geo. Kingsley, 1843.

Crown Him with many crowns, The Lamb upon His throne; Hark! how the heavenly anthem drowns All music but its own!

2 Awake, my soul! and sing
  Of Him who died for Thee;
And hail Him as thy matchless King,
  Through all eternity.

3 Crown Him, the Lord of love!
  Behold His hands and side,—
Rich wounds, yet visible above
  In beauty glorified:

4 Crown Him, the Lord of peace!
  Whose power a sceptre sways,
From pole to pole, that wars may cease,
  Absorbed in prayer and praise:

5 Crown Him, the Lord of years!
  The Potentate of time,
Creator of the rolling spheres,
  Ineffably sublime!
        Matthew Bridges, 1847.

222

Awake, and sing the song
  Of Moses and the Lamb;
Wake, every heart, and every tongue!
  To praise the Saviour's name.

2 Sing of His dying love;
  Sing of His rising power;
Sing—how He intercedes above
  For those whose sins He bore.

3 Sing, till we feel our hearts
  Ascending with our tongues;
Sing, till the love of sin departs,
  And grace inspires our songs.

4 Sing on your heavenly way,
  Ye ransomed sinners! sing;
Sing on, rejoicing, every day,
  In Christ, th' eternal King.

5 Soon shall ye hear Him say,
  "Ye blessèd children! come;"
Soon will He call you hence away,
  And take His wanderers home.
        William Hammond, 1745.
        Alt. Martin Madan, 1760.

223

Enthroned is Jesus now
  Upon His heavenly seat;
The kingly crown is on His brow,
  The saints are at His feet.

2 They sing the Lamb of God,
  Once slain on earth for them;
The Lamb, thro' whose atoning blood
  Each wears his diadem.

3 Thy grace, O Holy Ghost!
  Thy blessed help supply,
That we may join that radiant host,
  Triumphant in the sky.
        Thomas James Judkin, 1837. a.

The Royal Priest.

224 Rathbun. 8s & 7s.   ITHAMAR CONKEY, 1847.

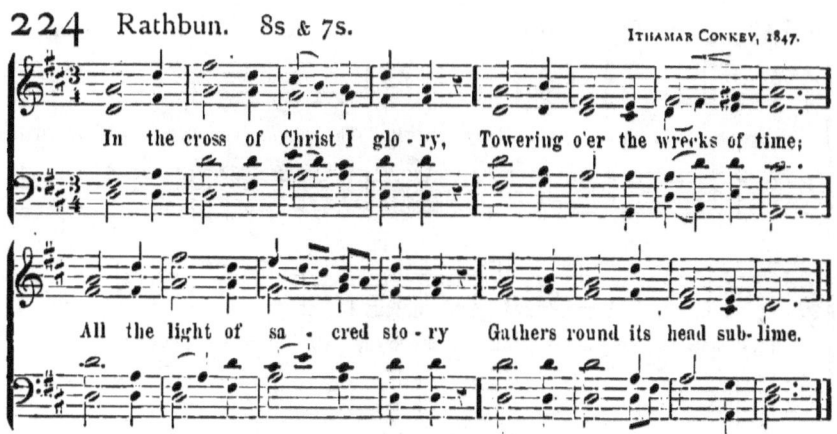

In the cross of Christ I glo-ry, Towering o'er the wrecks of time;
All the light of sa-cred sto-ry Gathers round its head sub-lime.

2 When the woes of life o'ertake me,
   Hopes deceive, and fears annoy,
Never shall the cross forsake me:
   Lo! it glows with peace and joy.

3 When the sun of bliss is beaming
   Light and love upon my way,
From the cross the radiance, streaming,
   Adds more lustre to the day.
               John Bowring, 1826.

225

HARK the notes of angels, singing,
   "Glory, glory to the Lamb!"
All in heaven their tribute bringing,
   Raising high the Saviour's name.

2 Ye, for whom His life was given!
   Sacred themes to you belong;
Come, assist the choir of heaven;
   Join the everlasting song.

3 See, th' angelic hosts have crowned Him,
   Jesus fills the throne on high;
Countless myriads, hovering round Him,
   With His praises rend the sky.

4 Filled with holy emulation,
   Let us vie with those above;
Sweet the theme—a free salvation!
   Fruit of everlasting love.

5 Endless life in Him possessing,
   Let us praise His precious name,
Glory, honor, power, and blessing,
   Be for ever to the Lamb!
               Thomas Kelly, 1804.

226

CHRIST, above all glory seated,
   King eternal, strong to save,
Dying, Thou hast death defeated;
   Buried, Thou hast spoiled the grave!

2 Thou art gone where now is given
   What no mortal might could gain,
On th' eternal throne of heaven,
   In Thy Father's power to reign.

3 There Thy kingdoms all adore Thee,
   Heaven above and earth below,
While the depths of hell before Thee
   Trembling and defeated bow.

4 We, O Lord, with hearts adoring,
   Follow Thee above the sky;
Hear our prayers Thy grace imploring,
   Lift our souls to Thee on high.

5 So when Thou again in glory
   On the clouds of heaven shalt shine,
We Thy flock may stand before Thee,
   Owned for evermore as Thine.
             James Russell Woodford, 1863. (?)

The Royal Priest.

227 Brooklyn. H. M.   John Zundel, 1852.

Fair shines the morning star, The silver trumpets sound, Their notes re-echoing far, While dawns the day a-round: Joy to the slave; the slave is free; It is the year of ju-bi-lee, It is the year of ju-bi-lee.

2 Blow ye the trumpet,—blow!—
   The gladly solemn sound;
Let all the nations know,
   To earth's remotest bound,—
The year of jubilee is come;
Return, ye ransomed sinners! home.

3 Extol the Lamb of God,—
   The all-atoning Lamb,
Redemption in His blood,
   Throughout the world proclaim;
The year of jubilee is come;
Return, ye ransomed sinners! home.

4 Ye, who have sold for naught
   Your heritage above!
Shall have it back unbought,
   The gift of Jesus' love;
The year of jubilee is come;
Return, ye ransomed sinners! home.
v. 1, James Montgomery, 1825.
v. 2, 3 & 4, Charles Wesley, 1750.

228

God is gone up on high,
   With a triumphant noise;
The clarions of the sky
   Proclaim th' angelic joys:
Join, all on earth! rejoice and sing,
Glory ascribe to glory's King.

2 All power to our great Lord
   Is by the Father given;
By angel hosts adored,
   He reigns supreme in heaven:
Join, all on earth! rejoice and sing,
Glory ascribe to glory's King.

3 Till all the earth, renewed
   In righteousness divine,
With all the hosts of God,
   In one great chorus join,
Join, all on earth! rejoice and sing,
Glory ascribe to glory's King.
Charles Wesley, 1746.

The Holy Ghost.

229 Bethune. L. M. U. C. Burnap, 1858.

Cre-a-tor Spir-it! by whose aid The world's foundations first were laid,
Come, vis-it ev-ery pi-ous mind, Come, pour Thy joys on human kind;
From sin and sor-row set us free, And make Thy temples worthy Thee.

2 O Source of uncreated light!
The Father's promised Paraclete!
Thrice holy Fount, thrice holy Fire!
Our hearts with heavenly love inspire;
Come, and Thy sacred unction bring,
To sanctify us while we sing.

3 Refine and purge our earthly parts;
But, Oh! inflame and fire our hearts;
Make us eternal truths receive,
And practice all that we believe;
Give us Thyself, that we may see
The Father and the Son, by Thee.

4 Immortal honors, endless fame,
Attend th' almighty Father's name!
The Saviour Son be glorified,
Who for lost man's redemption died!
And equal adoration be,
Eternal Paraclete! to Thee!

Lat., tr. John Dryden, 1690.

230 Federal Street. L. M. H. K. Oliver, 1832.

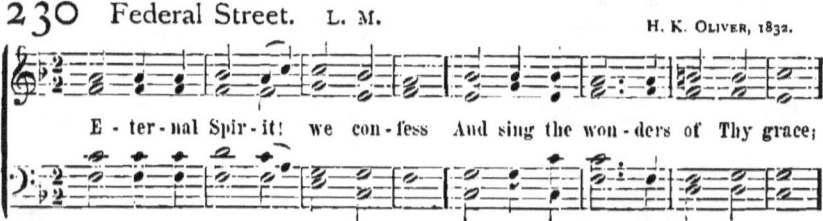

E-ter-nal Spir-it! we con-fess And sing the won-ders of Thy grace;

The Holy Ghost.

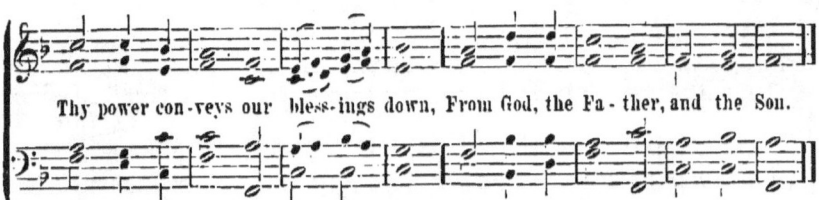

Thy power conveys our blessings down, From God, the Father, and the Son.

2 Enlightened by Thy heavenly ray,
Our shades and darkness turn to day;
Thine inward teachings make us know
Our danger, and our refuge too.

3 Thy power and glory work within,
And break the chains of reigning sin;
Do our imperious lusts subdue,
And form our wretched hearts anew.

4 The troubled conscience knows Thy voice,
Thy cheering words awake our joys;
Thy words allay the stormy wind,
And calm the surges of the mind.
Isaac Watts, 1709.

231

Spirit of power, and truth, and love,
Who sitt'st enthroned in light above!
Descend, and bear us on Thy wings,
Far from these low and fleeting things.

2 'Tis Thine the wounded soul to heal;
'Tis Thine to make the hardened feel;
Thine to give light to blinded eyes,
And bid the groveling spirit rise.

3 When faith is weak, and courage fails,
When grief or doubt our soul assails,
Who can, like Thee, our spirits cheer?
Great Comforter! be ever near.

4 Come Holy Spirit! like the fire;
With burning zeal our souls inspire;
Come, like the south wind, breathing balm,
Our joys refresh, our passions calm.

5 Come, like the sun's enlightening beam;
Come, like the cooling, cleansing stream;
With all Thy graces present be:—
Spirit of God! we wait for Thee.
Wm. Lindsay Alexander, 1849.

232

Come, blessèd Spirit, Source of light!
Whose power and grace are unconfined,
Dispel the gloomy shades of night,
The thicker darkness of the mind.

2 To mine illumined eyes, display
The glorious truths Thy word reveals,
Cause me to run the heavenly way,
Thy book unfold, and loose the seals.

3 Thine inward teachings make me know
The mysteries of redeeming love,
The emptiness of things below,
And excellence of things above.

4 While thro this dubious maze I stray,
Spread, like the sun, Thy beams abroad,
To show the dangers of the way,
And guide my feeble steps to God.
Benjamin Beddome, 1770.

233

Come, Holy Spirit, heavenly Dove!
My sinful maladies remove;
Be Thou my Light, be Thou my Guide,
O'er every thought and step preside.

2 The light of truth to me display,
That I may know and choose my way;
Plant holy fear within my heart,
That I from God may ne'er depart.

3 Conduct me safe, conduct me far,
From every sin and hurtful snare;
Lead me to God, my final rest,
In His enjoyment to be bless'd.

4 Lead me to holiness, the road
That I must take to dwell with God;
Lead to Thy word, that rules must give,
And sure directions how to live.
Simon Browne, 1720, a.

The Holy Ghost.

234 Bedford. C. M.   WILLIAM WHEALL, 1720.

My soul doth mag-ni-fy the Lord, My Spir-it doth re-joice
In God, my Saviour and my God; I hear His joy-ful voice.

2 I need not go abroad for joy,
  Who have a feast at home;
My sighs are turned into songs,
  The Comforter is come!

3 Down from above, the blessed Dove
  Is come into my breast,
To witness God's eternal love;
  This is my heavenly feast.
                    John Mason, 1683.

235

Our God, our God! Thou shinest here,
  Thine own this latter day:
To us Thy radiant steps appear;
  We watch Thy glorious way.

2 Not only olden ages felt
  The presence of the Lord;
Not only with the fathers dwelt
  Thy Spirit and Thy word.

3 Doth not the Spirit still descend,
  And bring the heavenly fire?
Doth not He still Thy church extend
  And waiting souls inspire?

4 Come, Holy Ghost, in us arise,
  Be this Thy mighty hour!
And make Thy willing people wise
  To know Thy day of power!
          Thomas Hornblower Gill, 1866, ab.

236

In Thy great name, O Lord! we come,
  To worship at Thy feet;
Oh! pour Thy Holy Spirit down
  On all that now shall meet.

2 Teach us to pray, and praise, and hear,
  And understand Thy word;
To feel Thy blissful presence near,
  And trust our living Lord.

3 Let sinners, Lord! Thy goodness prove,
  And saints rejoice in Thee;
Let rebels be subdued by love,
  And to the Saviour flee.
                 Joseph Hoskins, 1788.

237

Enthroned on high, almighty Lord!
  Thy Holy Ghost send down;
Fulfill in us Thy faithful word,
  And all Thy mercies crown.

2 Though, on our heads, no tongues of fire
  Their wondrous powers impart,
Grant, Saviour! what we more desire,
  Thy Spirit in our heart.

3 His love within us shed abroad,—
  Life's ever-springing well,
Till God in us, and we in God,
  In love eternal dwell.
                 Thomas Haweis, 1792.

The Holy Ghost.

238 St. Agnes. C. M.   J. B. Dykes, 1858.

Come, Holy Spirit, heavenly Dove, With all Thy quick'ning powers;
Kindle a flame of sacred love In these cold hearts of ours.

2 Look—how we grovel here below,
   Fond of these trifling toys!
Our souls can neither fly nor go,
   To reach eternal joys.

3 In vain we tune our formal songs,
   In vain we try to rise;
Hosannas languish on our tongues,
   And our devotion dies.

4 Dear Lord! and shall we ever live,
   At this poor dying rate?
Our love so faint, so cold to Thee,
   And Thine to us so great?

5 Come, Holy Spirit, heavenly Dove!
   With all Thy quickening powers;
Come, shed abroad a Saviour's love,
   And that shall kindle ours.
                Isaac Watts, 1707.

239

Eternal Spirit!—God of truth!
   Our contrite hearts inspire;
Kindle the flame of heavenly love,
   And feed the pure desire.

2 'Tis Thine to soothe the sorr'wing soul,
   With guilt and fears oppress'd;
'Tis Thine to bid the dying live,
   And give the weary rest.

3 Subdue the power of every sin,
   Whate'er that sin may be;
That we, in singleness of heart,
   May worship only Thee.

4 Then with our spirits witness bear,
   That we're the sons of God;
Redeemed from sin, and death, and hell,
   Through Christ's atoning blood.
                Thomas Cotterill, 1810.

240

Spirit Divine! attend our prayers,
   And make this house Thy home;
Descend with all Thy gracious powers,
   Oh! come, great Spirit! come.

2 Come as the light; to us reveal,
   Our emptiness and woe;
And lead us in those paths of life
   Where all the righteous go.

3 Come as the fire; and purge our hearts,
   Like sacrificial flame;
Let our whole soul an offering be
   To our Redeemer's name.

4 Come as the dove; and spread Thy wings,
   The wings of peaceful love;
And let Thy church on earth become
   Bless'd as the church above.
                Andrew Reed, 1829.

The Holy Ghost.

241 Olmutz. S. M. LOWELL MASON, 1824.

Come, Ho-ly Spir-it! come; Let Thy bright beams a-rise;
Dis-pel the dark-ness from our minds, And o-pen all our eyes.

2 Revive our drooping faith,
 Our doubts and fears remove,
And kindle in our breasts the flame
 Of never-dying love.

3 Convince us of our sin;
 Then lead to Jesus' blood,
And to our wondering view reveal
 The secret love of God.

4 Dwell ever in our hearts;
 Our minds from bondage free;
Then shall we know, and praise, and love,
 The Father, Son, and Thee.
Joseph Hart, 1759.

242

'Tis God the Spirit leads
 In paths before unknown;
The work to be performed is ours,
 The strength is all His own.

2 Supported by His grace,
 We still pursue our way;
And hope at last to reach the prize,
 Secure in endless day.

3 'Tis He that works to will,
 'Tis He that works to do;
His is the power by which we act,
 His be the glory too.
Benjamin Beddome, 1769.

243 Martyrdom. C. M. HUGH WILSON, 1768.

Spir-it of power and might! be-hold A world by sin destroyed;
Cre-a-tor Spir-it! as of old, Move on the form-less void.

The Holy Ghost.

244

Great Spirit! by whose mighty power
 All creatures live and move,
On us Thy benediction shower;
 Inspire our souls with love.

2 From death to life our spirits raise;
 Complete redemption bring;
New tongues impart, to speak the praise
 Of Christ, our God and King.

3 Thine inward witness bear, unknown
 To all the world beside;
Exulting, then, we feel and own
 Our Jesus glorified.
Thomas Haweis, 1792.

2 If sang the morning stars for joy,
 When nature rose to view,
What strains will angel-harps employ,
 When Thou shalt all renew?

3 And, if the sons of God rejoice
 To hear a Saviour's name,
How will the ransomed raise their voice,
 To whom the Saviour came!

4 So every kindred, tongue, and tribe,
 Assembling round the throne,
The new creation shall ascribe
 To sovereign love alone.
James Montgomery, 1825.

245 St. Cuthbert. 8 6 8 4. JOHN B. DYKES, 1860.

Our blest Re-deemer, ere He breathed His ten-der, last fare-well,

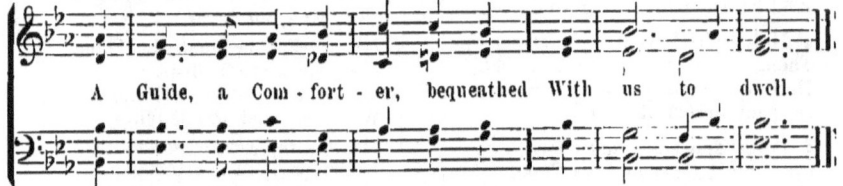

A Guide, a Com-fort-er, bequeathed With us to dwell.

2 He came sweet influence to impart,
 A gracious willing guest,
While He can find one troubled heart
 Wherein to rest.

3 And His that gentle voice we hear,
 Soft as the breath of even,
That checks each thought, that calms each
 And speaks of heaven. [fear,

4 And every virtue we possess,
 And every conquest won,
And every thought of holiness,—
 Are His alone.

5 Spirit of purity and grace,
 Our weakness, pitying, see;
O make our hearts Thy dwelling-place,
 And worthier Thee.

6 O praise the Father, praise the Son;
 Blest Spirit, praise to Thee;
All praise to God, the Three in One,
 The One in Three.
Harriet Auber, 1829, a.

The Holy Ghost.

246 Pleyel. 7s. IGNACE PLEYEL, 1790.

Holy Ghost! my soul inspire; Spirit of th' almighty Sire! Spirit of the Son divine! Comforter! Thy gifts be mine.

2 Holy Spirit! in my breast,
Grant that living faith may rest;
And subdue each rebel thought
To believe what Thou hast taught.

3 When around my sinking soul
Gathering waves of sorrow roll,
Spirit bless'd! the tempest still,
And with hope my bosom fill.

4 Holy Spirit! from my mind
Thought, and wish, and will unkind,
Deed and word unkind remove,
And my bosom fill with love.

5 Faith, and hope, and charity,
Comforter! descend from Thee:
Thou th' anointing Spirit art;
These Thy gifts to us impart!
Richard Mant, 1837.

247 C. M. Tune—CHERITH.

A GLORY gilds the sacred page,
Majestic, like the sun;
It gives a light to every age;—
It gives, but borrows none.

2 The hand, that gave it, still supplies
The gracious light and heat;
His truths upon the nations rise,—
They rise, but never set.

3 Let everlasting thanks be Thine,
For such a bright display,
As makes a world of darkness shine
With beams of heavenly day.

4 My soul rejoices to pursue
The steps of Him I love,
Till glory breaks upon my view,
In brighter worlds above.
William Cowper, 1772.

248 Cherith. C. M. L. SPOHR, 1840.

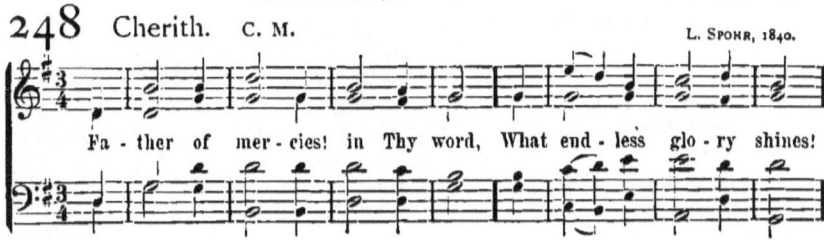

Father of mercies! in Thy word, What endless glory shines!

The Inspired Scriptures.

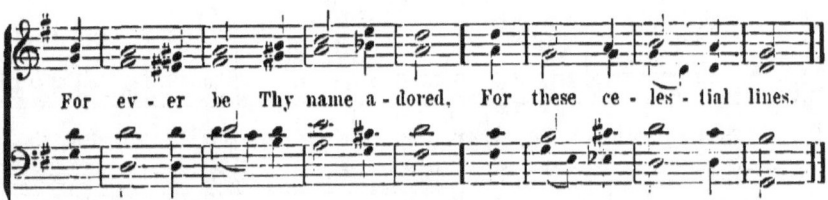

For ev-er be Thy name a-dored, For these ce-les-tial lines.

2 Oh! may these heavenly pages be
My ever dear delight;
And still new beauties may I see,
And still increasing light.

3 Divine Instructor, gracious Lord!
Be Thou for ever near;
Teach me to love Thy sacred word,
And view my Saviour there.
Anne Steele, 1760.

249
Laden with guilt, and full of fears,
I fly to Thee, my Lord!
And not a glimpse of hope appears,
But in Thy written word.

2 Oh! may Thy counsels, mighty God!
My roving feet command;
Nor I forsake the happy road,
That leads to Thy right hand.
Isaac Watts, 1709.

250 Burlington. C. M.   John F. Burrowes, 1830.

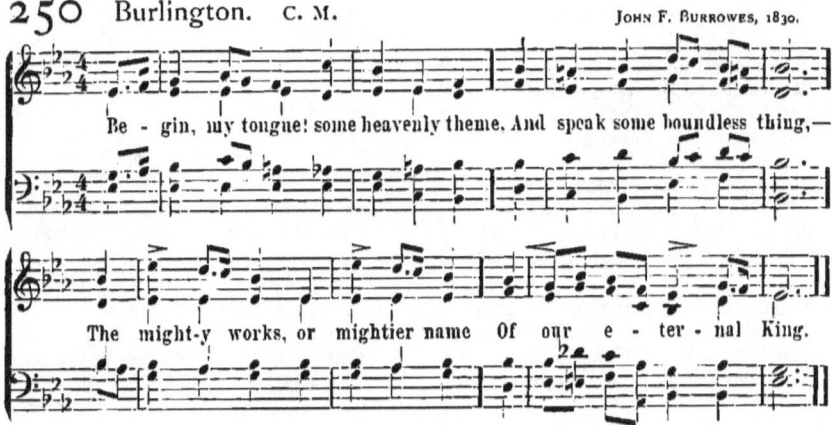

Be-gin, my tongue! some heavenly theme, And speak some boundless thing,—
The might-y works, or mightier name Of our e-ter-nal King.

2 Tell of His wondrous faithfulness,
And sound His power abroad;
Sing the sweet promise of His grace,
And the performing God.

3 Engraved as in eternal brass,
The mighty promise shines,
Nor can the powers of darkness raze
Those everlasting lines

4 His very word of grace is strong
As that which built the skies;
The voice that rolls the stars along
Speaks all the promises.
Isaac Watts, 1707.

The Inspired Scriptures.

251 Gilead. L. M.   E. H. Mehul, 1807.

The heavens declare Thy glo-ry, Lord! In ev-ery star Thy wis-dom shines;
But, when our eyes be-hold Thy word, We read Thy name in fair-er lines.

2 The rolling sun, the changing light,
  And nights and days Thy power confess;
But the bless'd volume Thou hast writ
  Reveals Thy justice and Thy grace.

3 Sun, moon, and stars convey Thy praise,
  Round the whole earth, and never stand;
So, when Thy truth began its race,
  It touched and glanced on every land.

4 Nor shall Thy spreading gospel rest,
  Till thro the world Thy truth has run;
Till Christ has all the nations bless'd,
  That see the light, or feel the sun.

5 Great Sun of Righteousness! arise;
  Bless the dark world with heavenly light;
Thy gospel makes the simple wise,
  Thy laws are pure, Thy judgments right.

6 Thy noblest wonders here we view,
  In souls renewed, and sins forgiven:
Lord! cleanse my sins, my soul renew,
  And make Thy word my guide to heaven.
                  Isaac Watts, 1719.

252

God, in the gospel of His Son,
Makes His eternal counsels known:
Where love in all its glory shines,
And truth is drawn in fairest lines.

2 Here sinners, of an humble frame,
May taste His grace, and learn His name;
May read, in characters of blood,
The wisdom, power, and grace of God.

3 Here faith reveals to mortal eyes
A brighter world beyond the skies;
Here shines the light which guides our way
From earth to realms of endless day.
                  Benjamin Beddome, 1787.

253 Canterbury. C. M.   Edward Blanck's, 1592.

How sad our state by na-ture is! Our sin—how deep it stains!

Need of Christ.

And Satan binds our captive minds, Fast in his slavish chains.

2 But there's a voice of sovereign grace,
Sounds from the sacred word;—
"Ho! ye despairing sinners! come,
And trust upon the Lord."

3 My soul obeys th' almighty call,
And runs to this relief;
I would believe Thy promise, Lord!
Oh! help my unbelief.
Isaac Watts, 1707.

254 Windham. L. M. Daniel Read, 1785.

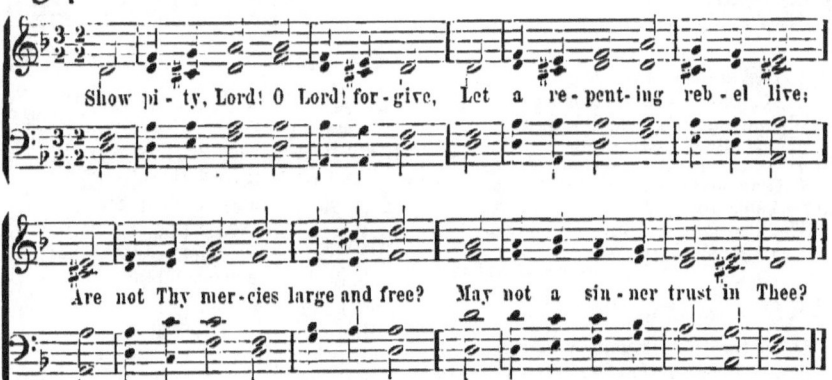

Show pity, Lord! O Lord! forgive, Let a repenting rebel live;
Are not Thy mercies large and free? May not a sinner trust in Thee?

2 My crimes though great, cannot surpass
The power and glory of Thy grace;
Great God! Thy nature hath no bound,
So let Thy pard'ning love be found.

3 Oh! wash my soul from every sin,
And make my guilty conscience clean;
Here on my heart the burden lies,
And past offences pain my eyes.

4 My lips with shame my sins confess,
Against Thy law, against Thy grace;
Lord! should Thy judgments be severe,
I am condemned but Thou art clear!
Isaac Watts, 1719.

255

From deep distress and troubled thoughts,
To Thee, my God! I raised my cries:
If Thou severely mark our faults,
No flesh can stand before Thine eyes.

2 But Thou hast built Thy throne of grace,
Free to dispense Thy pardons there;
That sinners may approach Thy face,
And hope and love, as well as fear.

3 Great is His love, and large His grace,
Through the redemption of His Son;
He turns our feet from sinful ways,
And pardons what our hands have done.
Isaac Watts, 1719.

Need of Christ.

256 Braden. S. M.   WM. B. BRADBURY, 1844

Oh! where shall rest be found.—Rest for the wea-ry soul?
'Twere vain the o-cean depths to sound, Or pierce to eith-er pole.

2 The world can never give
   The bliss for which we sigh;
'Tis not the whole of life to live,
   Nor all of death to die.

3 Here would we end our quest;
   Alone are found in Thee,
The life of perfect love,—the rest
   Of immortality.
               James Montgomery, 1819.

257

Dear Lord and Master mine!
   Thy happy servant see:
My Conqu'ror! with what joy divine
   Thy captive clings to Thee!

2 I love Thy yoke to wear,
   To feel Thy gracious bands,
Sweetly restrained by Thy care
   And happy in Thy hands.

3 No bar would I remove;
   No bond would I unbind;
Within the limits of Thy love
   Full liberty I find.

4 I would not walk alone,
   But still with Thee, my God,
At every step my blindness own,
   And ask of Thee the road.
               Thomas H. Gill, 1 67. (?)

258

Bless'd be Thy love, dear Lord!
   That taught us this sweet way,
Only to love Thee for Thyself,
   And for that love obey.

2 O Thou, our souls' chief Hope!
   We to Thy mercy fly;
Where'er we are, Thou canst protect,
   Whate'er we need, supply.

3 Whether we live or die,
   Both we submit to Thee;
In death we live, as well as life,
   If Thine in death we be.
               John Austin, 1668.

259

When shall Thy love constrain,
   And force me to Thy breast?
When shall my love return again
   To her eternal rest?

2 Ah! what avails my strife,
   My wandering to and fro?
Thou hast the words of endless life;
   Ah! whither shall I go?

3 Thy condescending grace
   To me did freely move;
It calls me still to seek Thy face,
   And stoops to ask my love.
               Charles Wesley, 1740.

Need of Christ.

260 Entreaty. 6s & 4s. P.   Thomas Hastings, 1832.

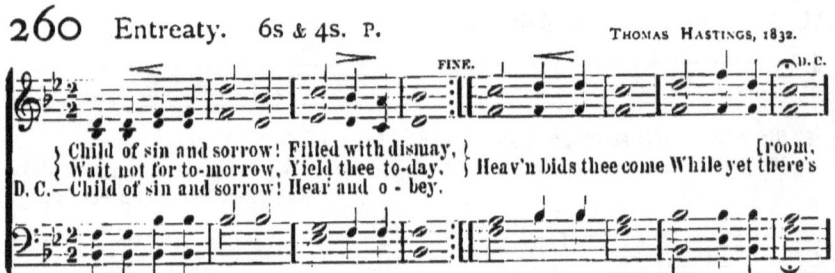

{ Child of sin and sorrow! Filled with dismay, }
{ Wait not for to-morrow, Yield thee to-day. } Heav'n bids thee come While yet there's [room.
D. C.—Child of sin and sorrow! Hear and o-bey.

2 Child of sin and sorrow,
　Why wilt thou die?
Come while thou canst borrow
　Help from on high:
Grieve not that love
Which from above,
Child of sin and sorrow,
　Would bring thee nigh.

3 Child of sin and sorrow,
　Thy moments glide,
Like the flitting arrow,
　Or the rushing tide;
Ere time is o'er,
Heaven's grace implore;
Child of sin and sorrow,
　In Christ confide.

4 Child of sin and sorrow!
　Where wilt thou be
Through that long to-morrow,
　Eternity?
Exiled from home,
Darkly to roam,
Child of sin and sorrow!
　Where wilt thou flee?
　　　　Thomas Hastings, 1832.

261 To-Day. 6s & 4s.   Lowell Mason, 1831.

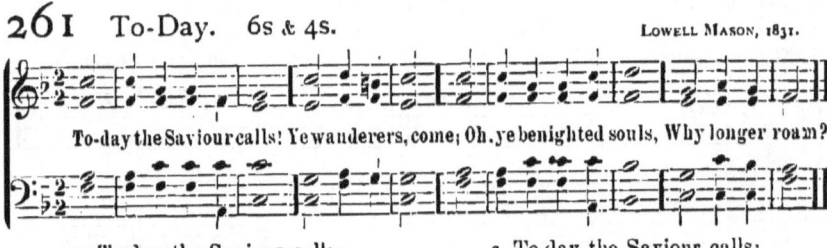

To-day the Saviour calls! Ye wanderers, come; Oh, ye benighted souls, Why longer roam?

2 To-day the Saviour calls;
　Oh, hear Him now;
Within these sacred walls
　To Jesus bow.

3 To-day the Saviour calls;
　For refuge fly;
The storm of justice falls,
　And death is nigh.

4 The Spirit calls to-day:
　Yield to His power;
Oh, grieve Him not away:
　'Tis mercy's hour.
　　　　Samuel F. Smith, 1831, alt.

Salvation.

262 Gloria in Excelsis. Unknown.

1. Glory be to | God on | high, || and on earth | peace, good- | will ˙ toward |ˈ men.
2. We praise Thee, we bless Thee, we | worship | Thee, || we glorify Thee, we give thanks
[to | Thee, for | Thy great | glory.

3. O Lord God, | heaven-ly | King, || God the | Father | Al- — | mighty!
4. O Lord, the only begotten Son, | Jesus | Christ! || O Lord God, Lamb of | God,
[Son] of the | Father!

5. That takest away the | sins ˙ of the | world˙ || have mercy | upon | us.
6. Thou that takest away the | sins ˙ of the | world! || re- | ceive our | prayer.
7. Thou that sittest at the right hand of | God the | Father! || have mercy | upon | us.

8. For Thou | only ˙ art | holy; || Thou | only | art the | Lord;
9. Thou only, O Christ! with the | Holy | Ghost, || art most high in the | glory ˙ of |
[God the | Father. || A- | men.

Salvation.

263 St. Barnabas. 8s 6s 8s & 7. W. H. MONK, 1872

Sal-va-tion! O the joy-ful sound, Glad ti-dings to our ears,
A sov'-reign balm for ev-'ry wound, A cor-dial for our fears.
Glo-ry, hon-or, praise and pow-er, Be un-to the Lamb for-ev-er!
Je-sus Christ is our Re-deemer; Al-le-lu-ia, praise the Lord! A-men.

2 Salvation! buried once in sin,
  At hell's dark door we lay;
But now we rise, by grace divine,
  And see a heavenly day.
     Glory, honor, &c.

3 Salvation! let the echo fly
  The spacious earth around,
While all the armies of the sky
  Conspire to raise the sound.
     Glory, honor, &c.

4 Salvation! O Thou bleeding Lamb,
  To Thee the praise belongs:
Our hearts shall kindle at Thy name,
  Thy name inspire our songs.
     Glory, honor, &c.   Amen.

Isaac Watts, 1709.

Salvation.

264 Cambridge. C. M.   John Randall, 1793.

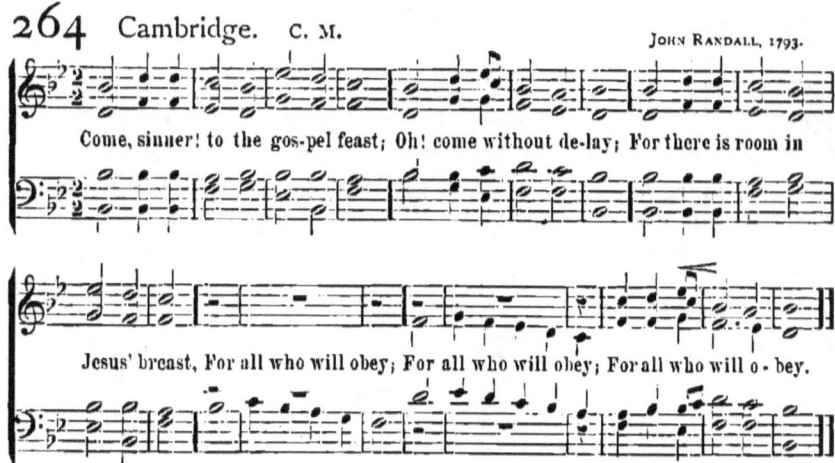

Come, sinner! to the gos-pel feast; Oh! come without de-lay; For there is room in Jesus' breast, For all who will obey; For all who will obey; For all who will o-bey.

2 There's room, in God's eternal love,
　To save Thy precious soul;
Room, in the Spirit's grace above,
　To heal and make thee whole.

3 There's room, within the church, redeem'd
　With blood of Christ divine;
Room, in the white-robed throng, conven'd,
　For that dear soul of thine.

4 There's room, in heaven among the choir,
　And harps and crowns of gold,
And glorious palms of vict'ry there,
　And joys that ne'er were told.

5 There's room, around thy Father's board,
　For thee and thousands more:
Oh! come and welcome to the Lord;
　Yea, come this very hour.
　　　　Frederic D. Huntington, 1843.

265

Let every mortal ear attend,
　And every heart rejoice;
The trumpet of the gospel sounds,
　With an inviting voice.

2 Rivers of love and mercy here
　In a rich ocean join;
Salvation in abundance flows,
　Like floods of milk and wine.

3 The happy gates of gospel grace
　Stand open night and day;
Lord! we are come to seek supplies,
　And drive our wants away.
　　　　Isaac Watts, 1707.

266

Sinner! the voice of God regard;
　'Tis Mercy speaks to-day;
He calls you by His sovereign word,
　From sin's destructive way.

2 Bow to the sceptre of His word,
　Renouncing every sin;
Submit to Him, your sovereign Lord,
　And learn His will divine.

3 His love exceeds your highest thoughts;
　He pardons like a God;
He will forgive your numerous faults,
　Through a Redeemer's blood.
　　　　John Fawcett, 1782.

267

The Head that once was crowned with
　Is crowned with glory now;　[thorns,
A royal diadem adorns
　The mighty Victor's brow.

Salvation.

2 The highest place that heaven affords
  Is His,—is His by right;
  "The King of kings, and Lord of lords,"
    And heaven's eternal Light:

3 The joy of all who dwell above,
    The joy of all below,
  To whom He manifests His love,
    And grants His name to know.

4 To them the cross, with all its shame,
    With all its grace, is given;
  Their name,—an everlasting name;
    Their joy,—the joy of heaven.

5 The cross He bore is life and health,—
    Though shame and death to Him;
  His people's hope, His people's wealth,
    Their everlasting theme.

Thomas Kelly, 1820.

268 Trisagion.   N. B. WARREN, 1857.

Therefore with angels and archangels, and with all the com-pa-ny of heav'n, we laud and mag-ni-fy Thy glo-ri-ous name, ev-ermore praising Thee, and saying, Ho-ly, ho-ly, ho-ly Lord God of Hosts; Heav'n and earth are full of Thy glo-ry: Glo-ry be to Thee, O Lord most high. A-men.

Salvation.

269 Woodland. C. M.
N. D. Gould, 1832.

Wouldst thou eternal life obtain? Now to the cross repair; There stand, and gaze, and weep, and pray, Where Jesus breathes His life away; Eternal life is there.

2 Go;—there, from every streaming wound,
Flows rich atoning blood;
That blood can cleanse the deepest stain,
Bid frowning justice smile again,
And seal thy peace with God.

3 Go;—at that cross thy heart, subdued,
With thankful love shall glow;
By wondrous grace thy soul set free,
Eternal life, from Christ, to thee,
A vital stream shall flow.
Ray Palmer, 1864.

270
The proudest heart that ever beat
Hath been subdued in me;
The wildest will that ever rose
To scorn Thy Word, or aid Thy foes,
Is quelled, my God, by Thee.

2 Thy will, and not my will be done;
My heart be ever Thine!
Confessing Thee, the mighty 'Word,'
I hail Thee, Christ, my God, my Lord,
And make Thy name my sign.
William Hone.

271 Calvary. 7s.
Johann Rosenmuller, 1655.

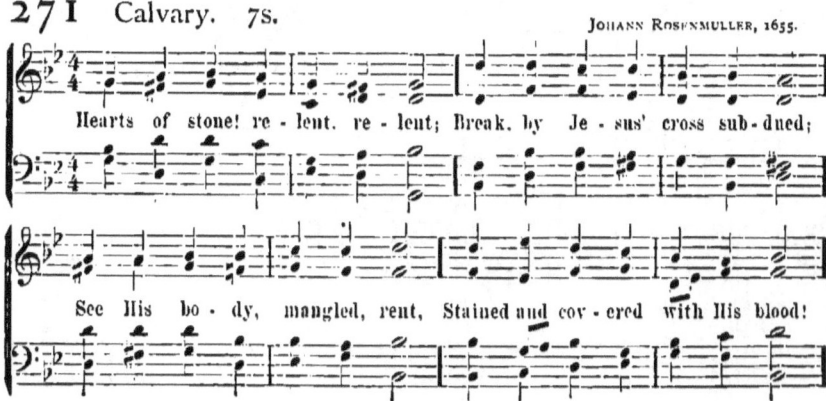

Hearts of stone! relent, relent; Break, by Jesus' cross subdued; See His body, mangled, rent, Stained and covered with His blood!

Salvation.

Sin-ful soul! what hast thou done? Cru-ci-fied th' e-ter-nal Son!

2 Yes, thy sins have done the deed;
Driven the nails that fixed Him there;
Crowned with thorns His sacred head;
Plunged into His side the spear;
Made His soul a sacrifice,—
While for sinful man He dies.

3 Wilt thou let Him bleed in vain,—
Still to death thy Lord pursue?
Open all His wounds again,
And the shameful cross renew?
No;—with all my sins I'll part,
Saviour! take my broken heart!
Ger., *Johann Cruger*, 1640.
Tr. *Charles Wesley*, 1745.

272 Bera. L. M.   J. E. GOULD, 1849.

Legato.

Come, let our voi-ces join to raise A sacred song of sol-emn praise;

God is a sov-ereign King; re-hearse His honors in ex-alt-ed verse.

2 Come, let our souls address the Lord,
Who framed our natures with His word;
He is our Shepherd;—we the sheep,
His mercy chose, His pastures keep.

3 Come, let us hear His voice to-day,
The counsels of His love obey;
Nor let our hardened hearts renew
The sins and plagues that Israel knew.

4 Seize the kind promise, while it waits,
And march to Zion's heavenly gates;
Believe,—and take the promised rest;
Obey,—and be for ever bless'd.
Isaac Watts, 1719.

273

Say, sinner! hath a voice within
Oft whispered to thy secret soul,
Urged thee to leave the ways of sin,
And yield thy heart to God's control?

2 Sinner! it was a heavenly voice,—
It was the Spirit's gracious call;
It bade thee make the better choice,
And haste to seek in Christ thine all.

3 Spurn not the call to life and light;
Regard, in time, the warning kind;
That call thou may'st not always slight,
And yet the gate of mercy find.
Abby Bradley Hyde, 1824.

Salvation.

274 Segur. 8s 7s & 4.   Joseph P. Holbrook, 1862.

Come, ye souls, by sin af-flict-ed! Bow'd with fruit-less sor-row down, By the per-fect law con-vict-ed, Through the cross, behold the crown; Look to Je-sus; Look to Je-sus; Mer-cy flows thro Him a-lone.

2 Take His easy yoke, and wear it;
  Love will make obedience sweet;
Christ will give you strength to bear it,
  While His wisdom guides your feet
    Safe to glory,
Where His ransomed captives meet.

3 Sweet, as home to pilgrims weary,
  Light to newly-opened eyes,
Or full springs in deserts dreary,
  Is the rest the cross supplies;
    All, who taste it,
Shall to rest immortal rise.
Joseph Swain, 1792.

275

Come, ye sinners! poor and wretched,
  Weak and wounded, sick and sore;
Jesus ready stands to save you,
  Full of pity, joined with power;
    He is able,
He is willing; doubt no more.

2 Ho! ye needy! come and welcome,
  God's free bounty glorify;
True belief, and true repentance,
  Every grace that brings us nigh,
    Without money,
Come to Jesus Christ and buy.

3 Let not conscience make you linger,
  Nor of fitness fondly dream;
All the fitness He requireth,
  Is to feel your need of Him;
    This He gives you;
'Tis the Spirit's rising beam.
Joseph Hart, 1753.

Salvation.

276 Blumenthal. 7s.   JACQUES BLUMENTHAL, 1849.

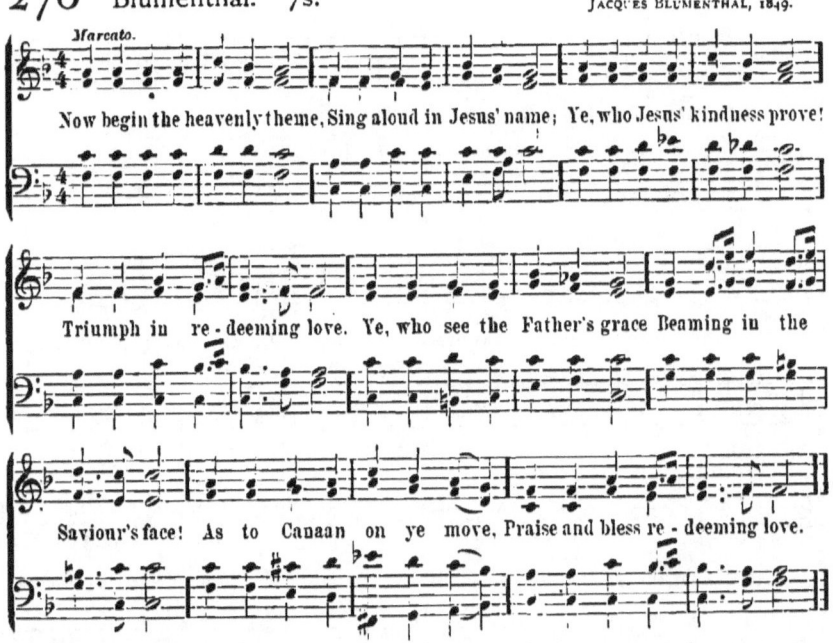

Now begin the heavenly theme, Sing aloud in Jesus' name; Ye, who Jesus' kindness prove! Triumph in re-deeming love. Ye, who see the Father's grace Beaming in the Saviour's face! As to Canaan on ye move, Praise and bless re-deeming love.

2 Mourning souls! dry up your tears;
Banish all your guilty fears;
See your guilt and curse remove,—
Cancelled by redeeming love.
Hither, then, your music bring;
Strike aloud each joyful string;
Mortals! join the hosts above,—
Join to praise redeeming love.
John Langford, 1763.

277

DEPTH of mercy, can there be
Mercy still reserved for me?
Can my God His wrath forbear?
Me, the chief of sinners, spare?
I have long withstood His grace,
Long provoked Him to His face;
Would not hearken to His calls;
Grieved Him by a thousand falls.

2 There for me the Saviour stands;
Shows His wounds, and spreads His hands;
God is love; I know, I feel;
Jesus weeps, and loves me still.
Now incline me to repent;
Let me now my fall lament;
Now my foul revolt deplore;
Weep, believe, and sin no more.
Charles Wesley, 1740.

278

Now, with angels round the throne,
  Cherubim and seraphim,
And the church for ever one,
  Let us swell the solemn hymn,—
To the Father of our Lord,
To the Spirit and the Word;
As it was all worlds before,
Is, and shall be evermore.
Josiah Conder, 1836.

Salvation.

279 Palestrina. L. M.   J. Mazzinghi, 1805.

Peace, troubled soul, whose plaintive moan Hath taught each scene the notes of woe;
Cease thy complaint, suppress thy groan, And let thy tears forget to flow;
Behold, the precious balm is found, To lull thy pain, to heal thy wound.

2 Come, freely come, by sin oppressed,
   Unburden here the weighty load;
Here find thy refuge, and thy rest,
   Safe on the bosom of thy God:
Thy God's thy Saviour,—glorious word!
That sheaths th' avenger's glittering sword.

3 As spring, the winter,—day, the night,—
   Peace, sorrow's gloom shall chase away;
And smiling joy, a seraph bright,
   Shall tend thy steps and near thee stay;
Whilst glory weaves th' immortal crown,
And waits to claim thee for her own.
          Walter Shirley, 1774.

280 Mishael. 7s & 6s. P.   L. van Beethoven, 1824.

Drooping souls, no longer mourn, Jesus still is precious, If to Him you

Salvation.

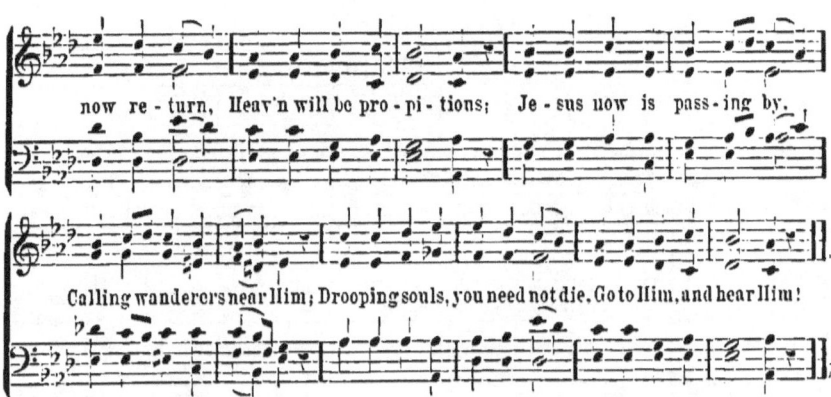

now re-turn, Heav'n will be pro-pi-tions; Je-sus now is pass-ing by.

Calling wanderers near Him; Drooping souls, you need not die, Go to Him, and hear Him!

2 He has pardon, full and free,
　Sorrowing souls to gladden;
Still He cries—"Come unto Me,
　Weary, heavy-laden!"
Though your sins, like mountains high,
　Rise, and reach to heaven,
Soon as you on Him rely,
　All shall be forgiven.

3 Precious is the Saviour's name,
　All His saints adore Him;
He to save the dying came;—
　Prostrate, bow before Him!
Wandering sinners! now return;
　Contrite souls! believe Him!
Jesus calls you; cease to mourn;
　Worship Him; receive Him.
　　　　　　　Thomas Hastings, 1831.

281　Harmony Grove.　L. M.　　　H. K. OLIVER, 1839.

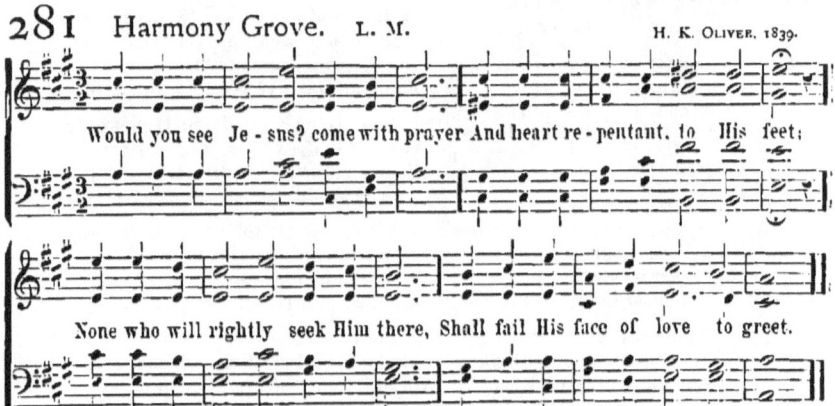

Would you see Je-sus? come with prayer And heart re-pentant, to His feet;

None who will rightly seek Him there, Shall fail His face of love to greet.

2 Would you see Jesus? come with faith,
And search the word His grace hath giv'n,
For help and guidance in the path
That leads to His abode in heaven.

3 Would you see Jesus? day by day
Let thought and converse be on high,
And hastening on the heavenward way,
With Jesus live with Jesus die.
　　　　　　　Unknown.

10

Salvation.

282 Sessions. L. M.   L. O. Emerson, 1847.

Deep in our hearts, let us record
The deeper sorrows of our Lord;
Behold the rising billows roll,
To overwhelm His holy soul!

2 Yet, gracious God! Thy power and love
Have made the curse a blessing prove;
Those dreadful sufferings of Thy Son
Atoned for sins which we had done.

3 The pangs of our expiring Lord
The honors of Thy law restored;
His sorrows made Thy justice known,
And paid for follies not His own.

4 Oh! for His sake, our guilt forgive,
And let the mourning sinner live:
The Lord will hear us in His name,
Nor shall our hope be turned to shame.
Isaac Watts, 1719.

283

Haste, traveler, haste! the night comes on,
And many a shining hour is gone;
The storm is gathering in the west,
And thou far off from home and rest.

2 The rising tempest sweeps the sky;
The rains descend, the winds are high;
The waters swell, and death and fear
Beset thy path, nor refuge near.

3 Oh, yet a shelter you may gain,
A covert from the wind and rain;
A hiding-place, a rest, a home,
A refuge from the wrath to come!

4 Then linger not in all the plain;
Flee for thy life; the mountain gain;
Look not behind; make no delay;
Oh, speed thee, speed thee on thy way!
Wm. Bengo Collyer, 1829.

284

When God's right arm is bared for war,
And thunders clothe His cloudy car,
We sing the Saviour of our race,
The Lamb our shield and hiding-place.

2 'Tis He, the Lamb, to Him we fly,
While the dread tempest passes by,
To Him, though guilty still we run,
And God still spares us for His Son.

3 While yet we sojourn here below,
Pollutions still our hearts o'erflow;
Fall'n, abject, mean, a sentenced race,
We deeply need a hiding-place.

4 Yet courage—days and years will glide,
And we shall lay these clods aside;
Shall be baptized in Jordan's flood,
And washed in Jesus' cleansing blood.

5 Then pure, immortal, sinless, freed,
We, through the Lamb, shall be decreed,—
Shall meet the Father face to face,
And need no more a hiding-place.
H. Kirke White, 1804. a.

Salvation

285 Rose Hill. L. M.   J. E. Sweetser, 1849.

"Come hith-er, all ye wea-ry souls! Ye heavy-lad-en sinners! come; I'll give you rest from all your toils. And raise you to My heavenly home."

2 "They shall find rest, that learn of Me;
   I'm of a meek and lowly mind;
But passion rages like the sea,
   And pride is restless as the wind.

3 "Bless'd is the man, whose shoulders take
   My yoke, and bear it with delight;
My yoke is easy to his neck,
   My grace shall make the burden light."

4 Jesus! we come at Thy command;
   With faith, and hope, and humble zeal;
Resign our spirits, to Thy hand,
   To mould and guide us at Thy will.
                     Isaac Watts, 1709.

286

BEHOLD! a Stranger's at the door!
He gently knocks,—has knocked before;
Has waited long—is waiting still;
You treat no other friend so ill.

2 But will He prove a friend indeed?
He will—the very friend you need;
The Man of Nazareth,—'tis He,
With garments dyed at Calvary.

3 Oh! lovely attitude!—He stands
With melting heart, and laden hands:
Oh! matchless kindness!—and He shows
This matchless kindness to His foes.

4 Admit Him, ere His anger burn;
His feet departed ne'er return;
Admit Him,—or the hour's at hand,
When, at His door, denied you'll stand.
                     Joseph Grigg, 1765.

287

JESUS, engrave it on my heart
That Thou the one thing needful art;
I could from all things parted be,
But never, never, Lord, from Thee.

2 Needful is Thy most precious blood
To reconcile my soul to God,
Needful is Thy indulgent care,
Needful Thy all-prevailing prayer.

3 Needful Thy presence, dearest Lord,
True peace and comfort to afford,
Needful Thy promise, to impart
Fresh life and vigor to my heart.

4 Needful art Thou, my Guide, my Stay,
Through all life's dark and weary way;
Nor less in death Thou'lt needful be
To bring my spirit home to Thee.

5 Then needful still, my God, my King,
Thy name eternally I'll sing!
Glory and praise be ever His—
The one thing needful Jesus is!
                     Samuel Medley, 1789.

Repentance.

288 Meditation. C. M.   S. P. Tuckerman, 1843.

There is a time we know not when, A place we know not where,
That marks the des-ti-ny of men, To glo-ry or de-spair.

2 There is a line by us unseen,
  That crosses every path,
The hidden boundary between
  God's patience and His wrath.

3 To pass that limit is to die,
  To die as if by stealth;
It does not quench the beaming eye,
  Or pale the glow of health.

4 The conscience may be still at ease,
  The spirits light and gay;
That which is pleasing still may please,
  And care be thrust away.

5 But on that forehead God has set
  Indelibly a mark—
Unseen by man, for man as yet
  Is blind and in the dark.

6 And still the doom'd man's path below
  May bloom as Eden bloomed—
He did not, does not, will not know,
  Or feel, that he is doomed.

7 Oh! where is this mysterious bourne
  By which our path is crossed;
Beyond which God Himself hath sworn
  That He who goes, is lost?

8 How far may we go on to sin?
  How long will God forbear?
Where does hope end, and where begin
  The confines of despair?

9 An answer from the skies is sent,—
  "Ye that from God depart,
While it is called to-day, repent,
  And harden not your heart."
        J. Addison Alexander. 1847.

289

O sinner, bring not tears alone,
  Or outward form of prayer,
But let it in thy heart be known
  That penitence is there

2 To smite the breast, the clothes to rend,
  God asketh not of thee;
Thy secret soul He bids thee bend
  In true humility.

3 O, let us, then, with heartfelt grief,
  Draw near unto our God,
And pray to Him to grant relief,
  And stay the lifted rod.

4 O righteous Judge, if Thou wilt deign
  To grant us what we need,
We pray for time to turn again,
  And grace to turn indeed.
        Tr. *John Chandler*, 1837, alt.

Repentance.

290 Meribah. C. P. M.   Lowell Mason, 1839.

Lo! on a narrow neck of land, 'Twixt two unbounded seas, I stand, Secure, insen-si-ble! A point of time, a moment's space, Removes me to yon heavenly place, Or shuts me up in hell.

2 O God! mine inmost soul convert,
And deeply, on my thoughtful heart,
  Eternal things impress:
Give me to feel their solemn weight,
And tremble on the brink of fate,
  And wake to righteousness.

3 Before me place, in dread array,
The pomp of that tremendous day,
  When Thou, with clouds, shalt come
To judge the nations at Thy bar;
And tell me, Lord! shall I be there
  To meet a joyful doom!
Charles Wesley, 1749.

3 Prevent, prevent it by Thy grace;
Be Thou, dear Lord! my hiding-place,
  In this th' accepted day;
Thy pard'ning voice, Oh! let me hear,
To still my unbelieving fear,
  Nor let me fall, I pray.

4 Among Thy saints let me be found,
Whene'er th' archangel's trump shall sound,
  To see Thy smiling face;
Then loudest of the throng I'll sing,
While heaven's resounding mansions ring
  With shouts of sovereign grace.
Selina Shirley, 1772, a.

291

When Thou, my righteous Judge! shalt come
To take Thy ransomed people home,
  Shall I among them stand?
Shall such a worthless one as I,
Who sometimes am afraid to die,
  Be found at Thy right hand?

2 I love to meet among them now,
Before Thy gracious feet to bow,
  Though humblest of them all;
How can I bear the piercing thought,
What, if my name should be left out,
  When Thou for them shalt call?

292

O Thou, that hear'st the prayer of faith!
Wilt Thou not save a soul from death,
  That casts itself on Thee?
I have no refuge of my own,
But fly to what my Lord hath done,
  And suffered once for me.

2 Slain in the guilty sinner's stead,
His spotless righteousness I plead,
  And His availing blood;
Thy merit, Lord! my robe shall be;
Thy merit shall atone for me,
  And bring me near to God.
Augustus M. Toplady, 1776.

Repentance.

293 Hamburg. L. M.   Arr. Lowell Mason, 1824.

A broken heart, my God, my King! Is all the sacrifice I bring; The God of grace will ne'er despise A broken heart for sacrifice.

2 My soul lies humbled in the dust,
And owns Thy dreadful sentence just;
Look down, O Lord! with pitying eye,
And save the soul condemned to die.

3 Create my nature pure within,
And form my soul averse to sin;
Let Thy good Spirit ne'er depart,
Nor hide Thy presence from my heart.

4 I cannot live without Thy light,
Cast out and banished from Thy sight:
Thy holy joys, my God! restore,
And guard me, that I fall no more.

5 Then will I teach the world Thy ways;
Sinners shall learn Thy sovereign grace;
I'll lead them to my Saviour's blood,
And they shall praise a pard'ning God.
Isaac Watts, 1719.

294

Buried in shadows of the night,
We lie, till Christ restores the light;
Wisdom descends to heal the blind,
And chase the darkness of the mind.

2 Our guilty souls are drowned in tears,
Till His atoning blood appears;
Then we awake from deep distress,
And sing the Lord, our Righteousness.
Isaac Watts, 1709.

295

When at Thy footstool, Lord! I bend,
And plead with Thee for mercy there,
Oh! think Thou of the sinner's Friend,
And for His sake receive my prayer.

2 Oh! think not of my shame and guilt,
My thousand stains of deepest dye;
Think of the blood which Jesus spilt,
And let that blood my pardon buy.

3 Think, Lord! how I am still Thine own,
The trembling creature of Thy hand!
Think how my heart to sin is prone,
And what temptations round me stand.

4 Oh! think upon Thy holy word,
And every plighted promise there;
How prayer should evermore be heard,
And how Thy glory is—to spare.

5 Oh! think not of my doubts and fears,
My strivings with Thy grace divine:
But think on Jesus' woes and tears,
And let His merits stand for mine.

6 Thine eye, Thine ear, they are not dull;
Thine arm can never shortened be;
Behold me here! my heart is full;
Behold, and spare, and succor me!
Henry Francis Lyte, 1833.

Repentance.

296 Tyndal. C. M.   Anon.

Jesus, Thou art the sinner's friend; As such I look to Thee; Now, in the fullness of Thy love, Now, in the fullness of Thy love, O Lord, remember me.

2 Remember Thy pure word of grace,
Remember Calvary,
Remember all Thy dying groans,
And then remember me.

3 Lord! I am guilty—I am vile,
But Thy salvation's free;
Then, in Thine all-abounding grace,
Dear Lord, remember me.

4 And when I close mine eyes in death,
When creature helps all flee;
Then, O my dear Redeemer God,
I pray, remember me.
    Richard Burnham, 1783, a.

297

O Jesus, Saviour of the lost,
My Rock and Hiding-place,
By storms of sin and sorrow tossed,
I seek Thy sheltering grace.

2 Guilty, forgive me Lord! I cry;
Pursued by foes, I come;
A sinner, save me, or I die—
An outcast, take me home.

3 And when I stand before Thy throne,
And all Thy glories see,
Still be my righteousness alone
To hide myself in Thee.
    Edward H. Bickersteth, 1849.

298

How oft, alas! this wretched heart
Has wandered from the Lord!
How oft my roving thoughts depart,
Forgetful of His word!

2 Yet sovereign mercy calls—"Return!"
Dear Lord! and may I come?
My vile ingratitude I mourn;
Oh! take the wanderer home.

3 Thy pard'ning love, so free, so sweet,
Dear Saviour! I adore;
Oh! keep me at Thy sacred feet,
And let me rove no more.
    Anne Steele, 1760.

299

O God of mercy! hear my call,
My loads of guilt remove;
Break down this separating wall,
That bars me from Thy love.

2 Give me the presence of Thy grace;
Then my rejoicing tongue
Shall speak aloud Thy righteousness,
And make Thy praise my song.

3 No blood of goats, nor heifer slain,
For sin could e'er atone:
The death of Christ shall still remain
Sufficient and alone.
    Isaac Watts, 1719.

Repentance.

300 Redemption. L. M. — M. CHERUBINI.

Jesus, the sinner's friend, to Thee, Lost and un-done for aid I flee;
Wea-ry of earth, my-self, and sin: O-pen Thine arms, and take me in.

2 Pity and heal my sin-sick soul;
'Tis Thou alone canst make me whole;
Dark, till in me Thine image shine,
And lost I am, till Thou art mine.

3 At last I own it cannot be
That I should fit myself for Thee:
Here, then, to Thee I all resign;
Thine is the work, and only Thine.

4 What shall I say Thy grace to move?
Lord, I am sin,—but Thou art love:
I give up every plea beside,—
Lord, I am lost—but Thou hast died.
Charles Wesley, 1739, a.

301

With broken heart and contrite sigh,
A trembling sinner, Lord! I cry;
Thy pard'ning grace is rich and free;
O God! be merciful to me!

2 I smite upon my troubled breast,
With deep and conscious guilt oppressed
Christ and His cross, my only plea;
O God! be merciful to me!

3 Far off I stand with tearful eyes,
Nor dare uplift them to the skies;
But Thou dost all my anguish see;
O God! be merciful to me!

4 Nor alms, nor deeds, that I have done,
Can for a single sin atone;
To Calvary alone I flee;
O God! be merciful to me!

5 And when, redeemed from sin and hell,
With all the ransomed throng I dwell,
My raptured song shall ever be,
God has been merciful to me!
Cornelius Elven, 1852.

302

Nature with open volume stands
  To spread her Maker's praise abroad;
And every labor of His hands
  Shows something worthy of a God:—

2 But in the grace that rescued man,
  His brightest form of glory shines;
Here, on the cross, 'tis fairest drawn,
  In precious blood and crimson lines.

3 Oh! the sweet wonders of that cross,
  Where God, the Saviour, loved and died!
Her noblest life my spirit draws
  From His dear wounds and bleeding side.

4 I would forever speak His name,
  In sounds to mortal ears unknown;
With angels join to praise the Lamb,
  And worship at His Father's throne.
Isaac Watts, 1707.

Repentance.

303 Anastasius. L. M.   Johann A. Freylinghausen, 1704.

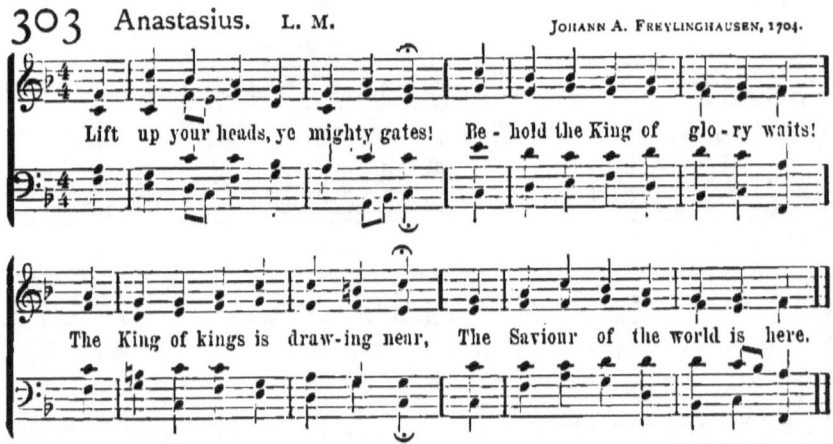

Lift up your heads, ye mighty gates! Behold the King of glory waits! The King of kings is drawing near, The Saviour of the world is here.

2 Life and salvation doth He bring,
Wherefore rejoice, and gladly sing:
Eternal praise, my God! to Thee!
Creator! wise is Thy decree.

3 Fling wide the portals of your heart,
Make it a temple, set apart
From earthly use for heaven's employ,
Adorned with prayer, and love, and joy.

4 Redeemer! come; I open wide
My heart to Thee; here, Lord! abide;
Let me Thine inner presence feel,
Thy grace and love in me reveal.

5 Thy Holy Spirit guide us on
Until our glorious goal be won!
Eternal praise, eternal fame,
Be offered, Saviour! to Thy name!
Ger., George Weissel, 1635.
Tr. Catherine Winkworth, 1855.

304

God calling yet!—shall I not hear?
Earth's pleasures shall I still hold dear?
Shall life's swift passing years all fly,
And still my soul in slumbers lie?

2 God calling yet!—shall I not rise?
Can I His loving voice despise,
And basely His kind care repay?
He calls me still; can I delay?

3 God calling yet!—and shall He knock,
And I my heart the closer lock?
He still is waiting to receive,
And shall I dare His Spirit grieve?

4 God calling yet!—I cannot stay;
My heart I yield without delay;
Vain world! farewell; from thee I part;
The voice of God hath reached my heart.
Ger., Gerhard Tersteegen, 1730.
Tr. Jane Borthwick, 1853, a.

305

Jesus, my All, to heaven is gone,
He whom I fix my hopes upon;
His track I see, and I'll pursue
The narrow way, till Him I view.

2 The way the holy prophets went,
The road that leads from banishment,
The King's highway of holiness,
I'll go; for all His paths are peace.

3 Lo! glad I come! and Thou, blest Lamb!
Shalt take me to Thee as I am;
Nothing but sin I Thee can give;
Nothing but love shall I receive.

4 Then will I tell, to sinners round,
What a dear Saviour I have found;
I'll point to Thy redeeming blood,
And say—Behold the way to God!
John Cennick, 1743, a.

Penitence.

306 Langran. 10s.   JAMES LANGRAN, 1863.

Weary of earth and laden with my sin, I look at heaven and long to enter in, But there no evil thing may find a home: And yet I hear a Voice that bids me "Come."

2 So vile I am, how dare I hope to stand
In the pure glory of that holy land?
Before the whiteness of that throne appear?
Yet there are hands stretch'd out to draw me near.

3 It is the voice of Jesus that I hear,
His are the hands stretch'd out to draw me near,
And His the blood that can for all atone,
And set me faultless there before the throne.

4 Yea, Thou wilt answer for me, righteous Lord:
Thine all the merits, mine the great reward;
Thine the sharp thorns, and mine the golden crown,
Mine the life won, and Thine the life laid down.

5 Naught can I bring, dear Lord, for all I owe,
Yet let my full heart what it can bestow;
Like Mary's gift let my devotion prove,
Forgiven greatly, how I greatly love.
Samuel J. Stone, 1865.

Penitence.

307 Remember Me. 10s.   T. Hewlett, 1872.

Slain for my soul, for all my sins de-famed, King, crown'd with thorns, with blas-phe-mies proclaimed, High o'er the clouds Thy roy-al Sign I see: Throned on Thy glo-ry, Lord, re-mem-ber me. A-men.

2 For Thy tormentors, for my pardon sue;
"Father, forgive, they know not what they do."
When they that pierc'd, when every eye, shall see
Thee in Thy kingdom, Lord, remember me.

3 Think of me now with all Thy sorrows press'd;
Think of me in Thy crowning of the blest;
Confess'd, besought, and worshipped on the Tree,
Lord, in Thy kingdom, still remember me.

4 'Mid all the thronging of Thy ransomed dead;
With all the Book of Life before Thee spread;
Toss'd, like a waif, upon the living sea
By angels parted, Lord, remember me.

5 Lord, ere I see Thy kingdom, let me see
Thy Paradise, and Paradise with Thee;
There while I rest, from death, from sorrow free,
Lord, in my resting still remember me. Amen.

Herbert Knyaston, 1862.

Penitence.

308 Litany. 7s.   John L. Hatton.

Saviour, when in dust to Thee, Low we bow th' adoring knee; When, repentant, to the skies Scarce we lift our streaming eyes; Oh! by all Thy pains and woe, Suffer'd once for man below, Bending from Thy throne on high, Hear our solemn lit-a-ny. A-men.

2 By Thy birth and early years,
By Thy human griefs and fears,
By Thy fasting and distress
In the lonely wilderness,
By Thy vict'ry in the hour
Of the subtle tempter's power;
Jesus, look with pitying eye;
Hear our solemn litany.

3 By Thy conflict with despair
By Thine agony of prayer,
By the purple robe of scorn,
By Thy wounds, Thy crown of thorn,
By Thy cross, Thy pangs, and cries,
By Thy perfect sacrifice;
Jesus, look with pitying eye;
Hear our solemn litany.

Penitence.

4 By Thy deep expiring groan
By the sealed sepulchral stone,
By Thy triumph o'er the grave,
By Thy power from death to save;
Mighty God, ascended Lord,
To Thy throne in heaven restored,
Prince and Saviour, hear our cry,
Hear our solemn litany. Amen.
Robert Grant, 1815.

309 Gloria Paschali. 8s & 7s. N. Decius, 1529, arr.

To God on high be thanks and praise For mercy ceasing never, Whereby no foe a hand can raise, Nor harm can reach us ever! With joy to Him our hearts ascend, The Source of peace, that knows no end. A peace that none can sever!

2 The honors paid Thy holy name,
To hear Thou ever deignest!
Then, God the Father, still the same,
Unshaken ever reignest!
Unmeasured stands Thy glorious might!
Thy thoughts, Thy deeds out-strip the light!
Our heaven Thou, Lord, remainest!

3 O Jesus Christ, our God and Lord,
Son of Thy heavenly Father,
O Thou who hast our peace restored,
And the lost sheep doth gather,
Thou Lamb of God, to Thee on high
From out our depths we sinners cry,
Have mercy on us, Jesus!
Nicholas Decius, 1529.

Penitence.

310 Dewitt. C. M.   U. C. Burnap, 1868.

I see the crowd in Pilate's hall, I mark their wrathful mien; Their shouts of "crucify" appall, With blasphemy between.

2 And of that shouting multitude
  I feel that I am one;
And in that din of voices rude,
  I recognize my own.

3 I see the scourges tear His back,
  I see the piercing crown,
And of that crowd who smite and mock
  I feel that I am one.

4 Around yon cross the throng I see,
  Mocking the Sufferer's groan;
Yet still my voice it seems to be,
  As if I mocked alone.

5 'Twas I that shed the sacred blood,
  I nailed Him to the tree,
I crucified the Christ of God,
  I joined the mockery.

6 Yet not the less that blood avails
  To cleanse away my sin;
And not the less that cross prevails
  To give me peace within.
          Horatius Bonar, 1857.

311

Oh! injured Majesty of heaven!
  Look from Thy holy throne:
A prostrate rebel owns, with grief,
  The treasons he hath done.

2 While love its grateful anthem swells,
  Tears mingle with the song:
My heart with tender anguish bleeds,
  That I such grace should wrong.

3 Remorse and shame my lips have sealed,
  But, O my Father! speak;
And all the harmony of heaven,
  Shall through the silence break.
          Philip Doddridge, 1749.

312

Dear Saviour! when my thoughts recall
  The wonders of Thy grace,
Low at Thy feet, ashamed, I fall,
  And hide this wretched face.

2 Shall love like Thine be thus repaid?
  Ah! vile, ungrateful heart!
By earth's low cares detained, betrayed,
  From Jesus to depart.

3 But He, for His own mercy's sake,
  My wandering soul restores;
He bids the mourning heart partake
  The pardon it implores.

4 Confirm the kind forgiving word,
  With pity in Thy face,
And I will own for ever, Lord!
  Thy condescending grace!
          Anne Steele, 1760, a.

Penitence.

313 Amsterdam. 7s & 6s. P.   JAMES NARES, 1750.

Lord, and is Thine anger gone,—And art Thou pacified!
After all that I have done, Dost Thou no longer chide!
Let Thy love my heart constrain,
All my restless passions sway: Keep me, lest I turn again
Out of the narrow way.

2 To the cross, Thine altar, bind
  Me with the cords of love;
Never let me freedom find
  From Thee, my Lord, to move:
That I never, never more
From my much-loved Master part,
To the posts of mercy's door,
  Oh nail my willing heart!

3 As the apple of Thine eye,
  Thy weakest servant keep;
Help me at Thy feet to lie,
  And there forever weep:
Tears of joy mine eyes o'erflow,
That I've any hope of heaven;
Much of love I ought to know,
  For I am much forgiven!
Charles Wesley, 1745, a.

314

Lord, I feel a carnal mind
  That hangs about me still,
Vainly though I strive to bind
  My own rebellious will;
Is not haughtiness of heart
  Gulf between my Lord and me?
Meek Redeemer! now impart
  Thine own humility!

2 Fain would I my Lord pursue,
  Be all my Saviour taught,
Do as Jesus bade me do,
  And think as Jesus thought:
But 'tis Thou must change my heart;
The good gift must come from Thee;
Meek Redeemer! now impart
  Thine own humility!

3 Let Thy cross my will control;
  Conform me to my Guide!
In the manger lay my soul,
  And crucify my pride!
Give me, Lord, Thy gentle heart;
Lowly Mind! my portion be!
Meek Redeemer! now impart
  Thine own humility!

4 Tear away my every boast;
  My stubborn mind abase;
Saviour, fix my only trust
  In Thy redeeming grace!
Give me a submissive heart,
From all self-dependence free;
Meek Redeemer! now impart
  Thine own humility!
Augustus M. Toplady, 1759, a.

Penitence.

315 Even Me. 8s 7s 6 7.
Wm. B. Bradbury, 1862.

{ Lord! I hear of showers of blessing, Thou art scattering full and free; }
{ Showers, the thirsty land re-freshing;—Let their bless-ing fall on me,— }
E-ven me,— e-ven me! Let their bless-ing fall on me.

2 Pass me not, O tender Saviour!
  Let me love and cling to Thee;
  I am longing for Thy favor;
    When Thou comest, call for me,—
      Even me.

3 Pass me not, O mighty Spirit!
  Thou canst make the blind to see;
  Witnesser of Jesus' merit,
    Speak the word of power to me,—
      Even me.

4 Have I long in sin been sleeping,
  Long been slighting, grieving Thee?
  Has the world my heart been keeping?
    Oh! forgive and rescue me,—
      Even me.

5 Love of God, so pure and changeless,—
  Blood of God, so rich and free,—
  Grace of God, so strong and boundless,—
    Magnify them all in me,—
      Even me.
Elizabeth Codner, 1860.

316 Webb. 7s & 6s.
G. J. Webb, 1830.

To-day Thy mercy calls me, To wash away my sin: How-ev-er great my trespass,
D. S.—Thy blood, O Christ! can cleanse me,
Whate'er I may have been, How-ev-er long from mercy I may have turned a-way,
And make me white to-day.

Penitence.

2 To-day Thy gate is open,
  And all who enter in
Shall find a Father's welcome,
  And pardon for their sin;
The past shall be forgotten,
  A present joy be given,
A further grace be promised—
  A glorious crown in heaven.

3 To-day the Father calls me;
  The Holy Spirit waits;
The blessed angels gather
  Around the heavenly gates;
No question will be asked me,
  How often I have come;
Although I oft have wandered,
  It is my Father's home.
                    Oswald Allen, 1862.

317 St. Hilda. 7s & 6s. E. HUSBAND.

O Jesus, Thou art standing Outside the fast-closed door, In lowly patience waiting To pass the threshold o'er: We bear the name of Christians. His name and sign we bear: Oh, shame, thrice shame upon us! To keep Him standing there.

2 O Jesus, Thou art knocking:
  And lo! that hand is scarred,
And thorns Thy brow encircle,
  And tears Thy face have marred:
Oh, love that passeth knowledge,
  So patiently to wait!
Oh, sin that hath no equal,
  So fast to bar the gate!

3 O Jesus, Thou art pleading
  In accents meek and low,—
"I died for you, my children,
  And will ye treat me so?"
O Lord, with shame and sorrow
  We open now the door:
Dear Saviour, enter, enter,
  And leave us nevermore!
                    W. W. How, 1854.

Penitence.

318 Walsal. C. M.
HENRY PURCELL, 1695.

Why should the chil-dren of a King, Go mourning all their days?
Great Com-fort-er! de-scend, and bring Some to-kens of Thy grace.

2 Dost Thou not dwell in all the saints,
And seal the heirs of heaven?
When wilt Thou banish my complaints,
And show my sins forgiven?

3 Assure my conscience of her part
In the Redeemer's blood;
And bear Thy witness with my heart,
That I am born of God.
Isaac Watts, 1709.

319 Pentecost. L. M.
WILLIAM BOYD, 1874.

Wea-ry of wand'ring from my God, And now made will-ing to re-turn,
I hear and bow me to the rod, For Thee, not with-out hope, I mourn.

2 O Jesus, full of pardoning grace,
More full of grace than I of sin;
Yet once again I seek Thy face:
Open Thine arms and take me in.

3 Thou know'st the way to bring me back,
My fallen spirit to restore:
O for Thy truth and mercy's sake,
Forgive, and bid me sin no more.
Charles Wesley, 1749, ab.

Penitence.

320 Manoah. C. M.   F. J. HAYDN, 1801.

Ap-proach, my soul! the mer-cy-seat, Where Jesus answers prayer;
There humbly fall before His feet, For none can perish there.

2 Thy promise is my only plea,
   With this I venture nigh:
Thou callest burdened souls to Thee,
   And such, O Lord! am I.

3 Bowed down beneath a load of sin,
   By Satan sorely pressed,
By war without and fears within,
   I come to Thee for rest.

4 Be Thou my shield and hiding-place
   That, sheltered near Thy side,
I may my fierce Accuser face,
   And tell him "Thou hast died."

5 Oh, wondrous love,—to bleed and die,
   To bear the cross and shame,
That guilty sinners, such as I,
   Might plead Thy gracious name!
                John Newton, 1779.

321

When, wounded sore, the stricken soul
   Lies bleeding and unbound,
One only hand, a piercéd hand,
   Can salve the sinner's wound.

2 When sorrow swells the laden breast,
   And tears of anguish flow,
One only heart, a broken heart,
   Can feel the sinner's woe.

3 When penitence has wept in vain
   Over some foul, dark spot,
One only stream, a stream of blood,
   Can wash away the blot.

4 'Tis Jesus' blood, that washes white,
   His hand, that brings relief;
His heart, that's touched with all our joys,
   And feeleth for our grief.

5 Lift up Thy bleeding hand, O Lord!
   Unseal that cleansing tide;
We have no shelter from our sin,
   But in Thy wounded side.
                Cecil F. Alexander, 1858.

322

With tears of anguish I lament,
   Here at Thy feet, my God!
My passion, pride, and discontent,
   And vile ingratitude.

2 Sure there was ne'er a heart so base,
   So false, as mine has been,—
So faithless to its promises,
   So prone to every sin?

3 How long, dear Saviour! shall I feel
   These struggles in my breast?
When wilt Thou bow my stubborn will,
   And give my conscience rest?

4 Break, sovereign grace! Oh! break the charm,
   And set the captive free;
Reveal, almighty God! Thine arm,
   And haste to rescue me.
                Samuel Stennett, 1787.

Penitence.

323. Come to Me.
Wm. B. Bradbury, 1853.

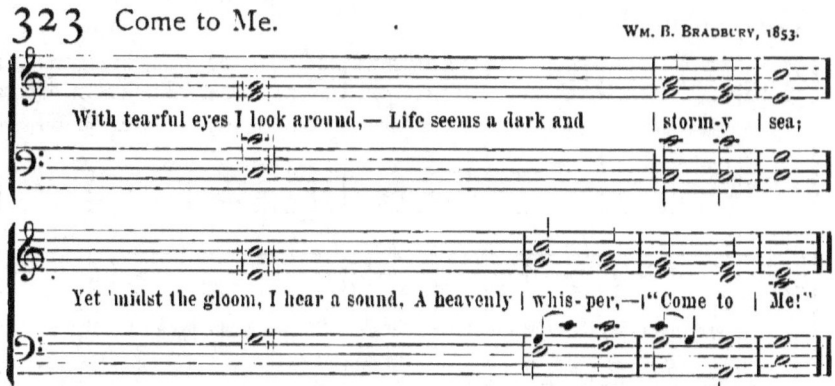

With tearful eyes I look around,— Life seems a dark and | storm-y | sea;
Yet 'midst the gloom, I hear a sound, A heavenly | whis-per,—|"Come to | Me!"

2 It tells me of a place of rest;
  It tells me where my | soul may | flee: ||
Oh! to the weary, faint, oppressed,
  How sweet the | bidding,— |
    "Come to | Me!"

3 When nature shudders, loth to part
  From all I love, en- | joy, and | see, ||
When a faint chill steals o'er my heart,
  A sweet voice | utters,— | "Come to | Me!"

4 "Come, for all else must fail and die;
  Earth is no resting- | place for | thee; ||
Heav'nward direct thy weeping eye,
  I am thy | portion;—| Come to | Me!"

5 O voice of mercy! voice of love!
  In conflict, grief, and | ag-o- | ny, ||
Support me, cheer me from above!
  And gently | whisper,— | "Come to | Me!"
Charlotte Elliott, 1841.

324. De Profundis.
Anon.

1 Out of the depths have I cried unto Thee, | O Lord! |
  Lord, hear my | voice: || Let Thine ears be at- | tentive to the | voice · of my sup- | pli | cations. ||

2 If Thou, Lord, shouldst mark iniquities, | O Lord! | who shall | stand? ||
  But there is forgiveness with | Thee, || That Thou mayest be | feared. ||

3 I wait for the Lord, | my soul doth wait, | And in His word do I | hope. ||
  My soul waiteth for the Lord more than they that watch for the | morning: || I say, more than they that watch for the | morning. ||

4 Let Israel hope in the Lord; | For with the Lord there is mercy, | and with Him is plenteous re- | demption. ||
  And He shall redeem | Israel || From all His in- | iquities. ||

Psalm cxxx.

Penitence.

325 Achor. 7s & 6s. JOHN H. CORNELL, 1865.

Lord God of my sal-va-tion, To Thee, to Thee I cry;
O let my sup-pli-ca-tion Ar-rest Thine ear on high.
Dis-tress-es round me thick-en, My life draws near the grave;
De-scend, O Lord, to quick-en, De-scend my soul to save.

2 Thy wrath lies hard upon me,
  Thy billows o'er me roll;
My friends all seem to shun me,
  And foes beset my soul.
Where'er on earth I turn me,
  No comforter is near;
Wilt Thou too, Father, spurn me?
  Wilt Thou refuse to hear?

3 No! banished and heart-broken
  My soul still clings to Thee;
The promise Thou hast spoken
  Shall still my refuge be.
So present ills and terrors
  May future joy increase;
And scourge me from my errors
  To duty, hope, and peace.
           H. F. Lyte, 1834.

Penitence.

326 Pelton. S. M.
J. M. Pelton, 1859.

Out of the depths of woe, To Thee, O Lord! I cry; Darkness surrounds me, but I know That Thou art ev-er nigh, That Thou art ev-er nigh.

2 I cast my hope on Thee;
　Thou canst, Thou wilt forgive;
　Wert Thou to mark iniquity,
　Who in Thy sight could live?

3 Humbly on Thee I wait,
　Confessing all my sin:
　Lord! I am knocking at Thy gate;
　Open, and take me in.

4 Glory to God above!
　The waters soon will cease;
　For, lo! the swift-returning dove
　Brings home the sign of peace.

5 Though storms His face obscure,
　And dangers threaten loud,
　Jehovah's covenant is sure,
　His bow is in the cloud.
　　　　　James Montgomery, 1822.

327 Gould's Chant.
John Edgar Gould, 1845.

From the recesses of a lowly spirit Our humble prayer ascends. O | Fa · ther! | hear it; ||
Borne on the trembling wings of | fear · and | meekness. || For- | give · its | weakness.

Penitence—Faith.

2 We know, we feel, how mean and how unworthy
The lowly sacrifice we | pour · be- | fore Thee;— ||
What can we offer Thee,—O | Thou · most | holy!— ||
But | sin · and | folly?

3 Lord! in Thy sight, who every bosom viewest,
Cold are our warmest vows, and | vain our | truest; ||
Thoughts of a hurrying hour—our | lips re- | peat them— ||
Our | hearts · for- | get them.

4 We see Thy hand—it leads us, it supports us;—
We hear Thy voice—it | counsels · and it | courts us:— ||
And then we turn away!—and | still · Thy | kindness ||
For- | gives · our | blindness.

John Bowring, 1823.

328 Faith. 10s.   JAMES FLINT, 1873.

Fierce was the billow wild, dark was the night, Oars labored heav-i-ly, foam glimmered white; Trembled the mar-i-ners, per-il was high; Then said the God of God, "Peace! it is I!"

2 Ridge of the mountain wave lower thy crest!
Wail of Euroclydon be thou at rest!
Sorrow can never be, darkness must fly,
Where saith the Light of light, "Peace! it is I."

3 Jesus, Deliverer, come Thou to me;
Soothe Thou my voyaging over life's sea;
Thou, when the storm of death roars, sweeping by,
Whisper, O Truth of truth,—"Peace! it is I!"

Anatolius, 458. Tr. John M. Neale, 1862.

Faith.

329 Vox Dilecti. C. M.   J. B. Dykes, 1868.

I heard the voice of Jesus say, "Come unto Me and rest;
lay down, thou weary one, lay down Thy head upon My breast;"
I came to Jesus as I was, Weary, and worn, and sad:
I found in Him a resting-place, And He has made me glad. A-men.

2 I heard the voice of Jesus say,
  "Behold! I freely give
The living-water; thirsty one!
  Stoop down, and drink and live:"
I came to Jesus, and I drank
  Of that life-giving stream;
My thirst was quenched, my soul revived,
  And now I live in Him.

3 I heard the voice of Jesus say,
  "I am this dark world's Light;
Look unto Me; thy morn shall rise,
  And all thy day be bright:"
I looked to Jesus, and I found,
  In Him, my Star, my Sun;
And, in that light of life, I'll walk
  Till traveling days are done.

Horatius Bonar, 1850.

Faith.

330
Oh! gift of gifts! Oh! grace of faith!
  My God! how can it be
That Thou who hast discerning love,
  Shouldst give that gift to me?
How many hearts Thou mightst have had
  More innocent than mine!
How many souls more worthy far
  Of that sweet touch of Thine!

2 Ah! Grace! into unlikeliest hearts
  It is Thy boast to come,
The glory of Thy light to find
  In darkest spots a home.
Thy choice, O God of goodness! then
  I lovingly adore;
Oh! give me grace to keep Thy grace,
  And grace t' inherit more.
Frederick Wm. Faber, 1848, ab.

331 Woodworth. L. M.   Wm. B. Bradbury, 1849.

Just as I am, without one plea, But that Thy blood was shed for me,
And that Thou bidd'st me come to Thee. O Lamb of God! I come—I come!

2 Just as I am, and waiting not
To rid my soul of one dark blot,
To Thee, whose blood can cleanse each spot,
  O Lamb of God! I come—I come!

3 Just as I am, though tossed about
With many a conflict, many a doubt,
Fightings and fears within, without,
  O Lamb of God! I come—I come!

4 Just as I am, poor, wretched, blind;
Sight, riches, healing of the mind,
Yea, all I need, in Thee to find,
  O Lamb of God! I come—I come!

5 Just as I am; Thou wilt receive,
Wilt welcome, pardon, cleanse, relieve;
Because Thy promise I believe,
  O Lamb of God! I come—I come!

6 Just as I am; Thy love unknown
Has broken every barrier down;
Now, to be Thine, yea, Thine alone,
  O Lamb of God! I come—I come!
Charlotte Elliott, 1836.

332
Complete in Thee! no work of mine
May take, dear Lord, the place of Thine;
Thy blood has pardon bought for me,
And I am now complete in Thee.

2 Complete in Thee—no more shall sin,
Thy grace has conquered, reign within;
Thy voice will bid the tempter flee,
And I shall stand complete in Thee.

3 Complete in Thee—each want supplied,
And no good thing to me denied,
Since Thou my portion, Lord, wilt be,
I ask no more—complete in Thee.

4 Dear Saviour! when, before Thy bar
All tribes and tongues assembled are,
Among Thy chosen may I be
At Thy right hand—complete in Thee.
Aaron Robarts Wolfe, 1852, 1857.

Faith.

333 Refuge. 7s.
JOSEPH P. HOLBROOK, 1862.

Jesus, lover of my soul, Let me to Thy bosom fly, While the billows near me roll, While the tempest still is high; Hide me, O my Saviour, hide, Till the storm of life is past; Safe into the haven guide, Oh, receive my soul at last.

2 Other refuge have I none,
  Hangs my helpless soul on Thee:
Leave, ah! leave me not alone,
  Still support and comfort me:
All my trust on Thee is stayed,
  All my help from Thee I bring;
Cover my defenceless head,
  With the shadow of Thy wing.

3 Plenteous grace with Thee is found,
  Grace to cover all my sin;
Let the healing streams abound,
  Make and keep me pure within.
Thou of life the Fountain art,
  Freely let me take of Thee:
Spring Thou up within my heart,
  Rise to all eternity.
Charles Wesley, 1743.

334 Martyn. 7s.
S. B. MARSH, 1834.

{ Mary to the Saviour's tomb Hasted at the early dawn, }
{ Spice she brought, and sweet perfume, But the Lord she loved was gone. }
D. C.—Trembling, while a crystal flood Issued from her weeping eyes.

Faith.

2 Jesus, who is always near,
   Though too often unperceived,
Came, His drooping child to cheer,
   Kindly asking why she grieved.
Though at first she knew Him not,
   When He called her by her name,
Then her griefs were all forgot,
   For she found He was the same.

3 Grief and sighing quickly fled
   When she heard His welcome voice;
Just before, she thought Him dead,
   Now, He bids her heart rejoice.

What a change His word can make,
   Turning darkness into day?
You who weep for Jesus' sake,
   He will wipe your tears away.

4 He who came to comfort her,
   When she thought her all was lost,
Will for your relief appear,
   Though you now are tempest-tost.
On His word your burden cast,
   On His love your thoughts employ;
Weeping for a while may last,
   But the morning brings the joy.
                        John Newton, 1779.

335 Sutherland.   H. M.   WM. B. BRADBURY, 1844.

2 I love my Shepherd's voice;
   His watchful eyes will keep
My wandering soul among
   The thousands of His sheep;
He feeds His flock, He calls their names,
His bosom bears The tender lambs.

3 My dear Almighty Lord,
   My Conqueror and my King,
Thy love, and power, and truth,
   Thy reigning grace I sing:
Subdued and clad, Behold I sit,
With willing heart, Before Thy feet.
                Isaac Watts, 1709, a.

Faith.

336 Portuguese Hymn. 11s.   MARCOS PORTUGAL.

How firm a foun-da-tion, ye saints of the Lord! Is laid for your faith, in His excellent word! What more can He say, than to you He hath said, You, who un-to Je-sus for refuge have fled? You, who un-to Je-sus for refuge have fled?

2 "Fear not, I am with thee, O be not dismayed,
For I am thy God, I will still give thee aid:
I'll strengthen thee, help thee, and cause thee to stand,
Upheld by My righteous, omnipotent hand.

3 "When through the deep waters I call thee to go,
The rivers of sorrow shall not overflow;
When through fiery trials thy pathway shall lie,
My grace, all-sufficient, shall be thy supply.

4 "E'en down to old age all My people shall prove
My sovereign, eternal, unchangeable love;
And then, when gray hairs shall their temples adorn,
Like lambs they shall still in My bosom be borne.

5 "The soul that on Jesus hath leaned for repose,
I will not, I will not desert to His foes;
That soul, though all hell should endeavor to shake,
I'll never, no never, no never forsake!"

George Keith (?) 1787.

Faith.

337 Clare. 7s & 6s. HUBERT P. MAIN, 1877.

In heaven-ly love a-bid-ing, No change my heart shall fear,
And safe is such con-fid-ing, For noth-ing changes here:
The storm may roar with-out me, My heart may low be laid,
But God is round a-bout me, And can I be dismayed?

Copyright, 1878, by Hubert P. Main.

2 Wherever He may guide me,
  No want shall turn me back;
My Shepherd is beside me,
  And nothing can I lack;
His wisdom ever waketh,
  His sight is never dim;
He knows the way He taketh,
  And I will walk with Him.

3 Green pastures are before me,
  Which yet I have not seen;
Bright skies will soon be o'er me,
  Where darkest clouds have been;
My hope I cannot measure,
  My path to life is free;
My Saviour has my treasure,
  And He will walk with me.
       Anna Latitia. Waring, 1850.

Faith.

338 Regent Square. 8s & 7s.   Henry Smart, 1867.

Now, my soul! thy voice up-raising, Tell, in sweet and mournful strain, How the Cru-ci-fied, en-dur-ing Grief, and wounds, and dy-ing pain, Free-ly of His love was of-fered, Sin-less was for sin-ners slain.

2 Through His heart the spear is piercing,
   Though His foes have seen Him die;
Blood and water thence are streaming
   In a tide of mystery,
Water from our guilt to cleanse us,
   Blood to win us crowns on high.

3 Jesus! may those precious fountains
   Drink to thirsty souls afford;
Let them be our cup and healing,
   And at length our full reward;
So a ransomed world shall ever
   Praise Thee, its redeeming Lord.
      Lat., *Maglorianus Santolius*, 1650.
      Tr. Henry Williams Baker, 1861.

339 Boylston. S. M.   Lowell Mason, 1832.

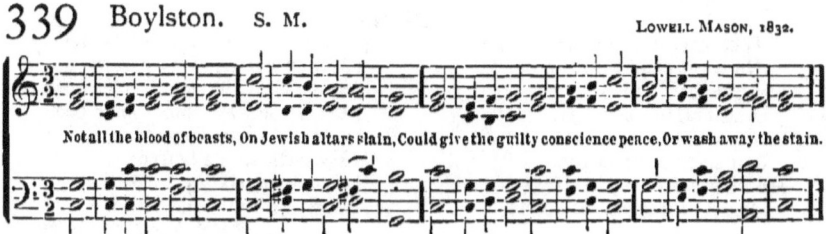

Not all the blood of beasts, On Jewish altars slain, Could give the guilty conscience peace, Or wash away the stain.

Faith.

2 But Christ, the heavenly Lamb,
  Takes all our sins away;—
A sacrifice of nobler name,
  And richer blood than they.

3 My faith would lay her hand
  On that dear head of Thine,
While, like a penitent I stand,
  And there confess my sin.
  Isaac Watts, 1709.

340

Like sheep we went astray,
  And broke the fold of God,—
Each wandering in a different way,
  But all the downward road.

2 How dreadful was the hour,
  When God our wanderings laid,
And did at once His vengeance pour,
  Upon the Shepherd's head!

3 How glorious was the grace,
  When Christ sustained the stroke!
His life and blood the Shepherd pays,
  A ransom for the flock.

4 But God shall raise His head,
  O'er all the sons of men,
And make Him see a numerous seed,
  To recompense His pain.
  Isaac Watts, 1709.

341 Coventry. C. M.

BENJAMIN CUZENS.

O Jesus! sweet the tears I shed, While at the cross I kneel,
Gaze at Thy wounded, faint-ing head, And all Thy sorrows feel.

2 'Twas for the sinful Thou didst die,
  And I a sinner stand:
What love speaks from Thy dying eye,
  And from each piercéd hand!

3 I know this cleansing blood of Thine
  Was shed, dear Lord! for me,—
For me, for all,—Oh! grace divine!—
  Who look by faith on Thee.

4 O Christ of God! O spotless Lamb!
  By love my soul is drawn;
Henceforth, for ever, Thine I am;
  Here life and peace are born.

5 In patient hope, the cross I'll bear,
  Thine arm shall be my stay;
And Thou, enthroned, my soul shalt spare
  On Thy great judgment-day.
  Ray Palmer, 1867.

Faith.

342 Miriam. 7s & 6s.
JOSEPH P. HOLBROOK, 1865.

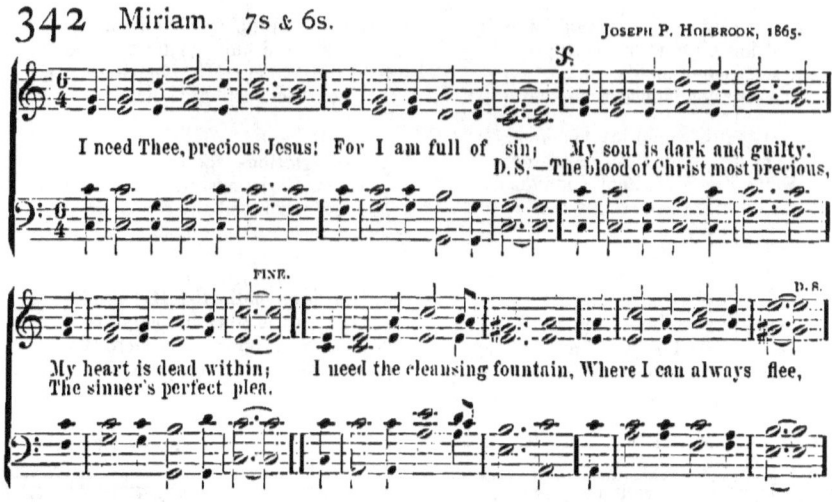

I need Thee, precious Jesus! For I am full of sin; My soul is dark and guilty.
D. S.—The blood of Christ most precious,
My heart is dead within; I need the cleansing fountain, Where I can always flee,
The sinner's perfect plea.

2 I need Thee blessèd Jesus!
  For I am very poor;
A stranger and a pilgrim,
  I have no earthly store;
I need the love of Jesus,
  To cheer me on my way,
To guide my doubting footsteps,
  To be my strength and stay.

3 I know no life divided,
  O Lord of life! from Thee;
In Thee is life provided
  For all mankind and me;
I know no death, O Jesus!
  Because I live in Thee;
Thy death it is which frees us
  From death eternally.

4 I need Thee blessèd Jesus,
  And hope to see Thee soon,
Encircled with the rainbow,
  And seated on Thy throne;
There, with Thy blood-bought children
  My joy shall ever be,
To sing Thy praise, Lord Jesus!
  To gaze, my Lord! on Thee!
Frederick Whitfield, 1859.
v. 3. fr. C. J. P. Spitta, 1833.

343

I've found a joy in sorrow,
  A secret balm for pain,
A beautiful to-morrow
  Of sunshine after rain;
I've found a branch of healing,
  Near every bitter spring;
A whispered promise stealing
  O'er every broken string.

2 I've found a glad hosanna
  For every woe and wail,
A handful of sweet manna,
  When grapes from Eshcol fail;
I've found a Rock of Ages,
  When desert wells were dry;
And, after weary stages,
  I've found an Elim nigh;—

3 My Saviour! Thee possessing,
  We have the joy, the balm,
The healing and the blessing,
  The sunshine and the psalm,
The promise for the fearful,
  The Elim for the faint,
The rainbow for the tearful,
  The glory for the saint.
Jane Fox Crewdson, 1860.

Faith.

344

My sins, my sins, my Saviour!
  They take such hold on me,
I am not able to look up,
  Save only, Christ, to Thee;
In Thee is all forgiveness,
  In Thee abundant grace,
My shadow and my sunshine
  The brightness of Thy face.

2 My sins, my sins, my Saviour!
  How sad on Thee they fall!
Seen through Thy gentle patience,
  I tenfold feel them all;
I know they are forgiven,
  But still, their pain to me
Is all the grief and anguish
  They laid, my Lord, on Thee.
  J. S. B. Monsell, 1863.

345

O WORD of God incarnate,
  O Wisdom from on high,
O Truth unchanged, unchanging,
  O Light of our dark sky!
We praise Thee for the radiance
  That from the hallowed page,
A lantern to our footsteps,
  Shines on from age to age.

2 The Church from her dear Master
  Received the gift divine,
And still that light she lifteth
  O'er all the earth to shine.
It is the golden casket
  Where gems of truth are stored,
It is the heaven-drawn picture
  Of Christ the living Word.

3 Oh, make Thy Church, dear Saviour,
  A lamp of burnished gold,
To bear before the nations
  Thy true light as of old;
Oh, teach Thy wandering pilgrims
  By this their path to trace,
Till, clouds and darkness ended,
  They see Thee face to face.
  W. W. How, 1867.

346 Melcombe. L. M.   SAMUEL WEBBE, 1790.

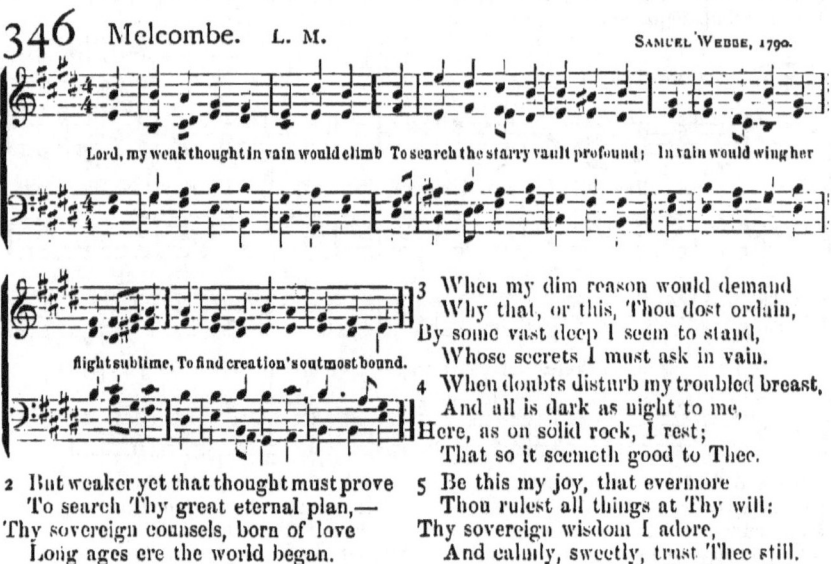

Lord, my weak thought in vain would climb To search the starry vault profound; In vain would wing her flight sublime, To find creation's outmost bound.

2 But weaker yet that thought must prove
To search Thy great eternal plan,—
Thy sovereign counsels, born of love
Long ages ere the world began.

3 When my dim reason would demand
Why that, or this, Thou dost ordain,
By some vast deep I seem to stand,
Whose secrets I must ask in vain.

4 When doubts disturb my troubled breast,
And all is dark as night to me,
Here, as on solid rock, I rest;
That so it seemeth good to Thee.

5 Be this my joy, that evermore
Thou rulest all things at Thy will;
Thy sovereign wisdom I adore,
And calmly, sweetly, trust Thee still.
  Ray Palmer, 1858.

Faith.

351 Kirke. L. M. — D. BORTNIANSKI, 1783.

My Lord! how full of sweet content, I pass my years of ban-ish-ment!
Where'er I dwell, I dwell with Thee, In heaven, in earth, or on the sea.

2 To me remains nor place, nor time;
My country is in every clime:
I can be calm and free from care
On any shore, since God is there.

3 While place we seek, or place we shun,
The soul finds happiness in none;
But with a God to guide our way,
'Tis equal joy, to go or stay.

4 Could I be cast where Thou art not,
That were indeed a dreadful lot;
But regions none remote I call,
Secure of finding God in all.

Fr. Madame de la Motte Guyon, 1722.
Tr. William Cowper, 1783, a.

352 Seasons. L. M. — IGNACE PLEYEL.

A poor blind child I wan-der here, If hap-ly I may feel Thee near:
I grope in darkness on my way, A-midst the blaze of gos-pel day.

2 Thee, only Thee, I fain would find,
And cast the world and flesh behind;
Thou, only Thou, to me be given,
Of all Thou hast in earth and heaven.

3 Lord! I am blind—be Thou my sight;
Lord! I am weak—be Thou my might;
A helper of the helpless be;
And let me find my all in Thee.

John Wesley, 1742, a.

Faith.

353 Lintz. H. M.   WM. B. BRADBURY, 1857.

Upward I lift mine eyes, From God is all my aid;
The God that built the skies, And earth and nature made:
God is the tower to which I fly; His grace is nigh in ev-ery hour.

2 My feet shall never slide,
   And fall in fatal snares,
Since God, my Guard and Guide,
   Defends me from my fears.
Those wakeful eyes, which never sleep,
Shall Israel keep when dangers rise.

3 Since Thou hast pledged Thy word
   To save my soul from death,
Shall I not trust my Lord
   To keep my mortal breath!
I'll go and come, nor fear to die,
Till, from on high, Thou call me home.
Isaac Watts, 1719.

354 Serenity. C. M.   WM. V. WALLACE, 1856.

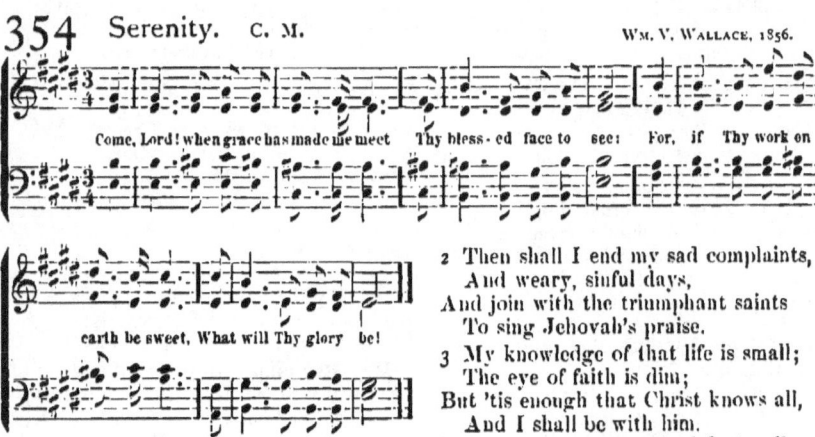

Come, Lord! when grace has made me meet Thy bless-ed face to see: For, if Thy work on earth be sweet, What will Thy glory be!

2 Then shall I end my sad complaints,
   And weary, sinful days,
And join with the triumphant saints
   To sing Jehovah's praise.

3 My knowledge of that life is small;
   The eye of faith is dim;
But 'tis enough that Christ knows all,
   And I shall be with him.
Richard Baxter, 1681.

Faith.

355 Ward. L. M.
Arr. Lowell Mason, 1830.

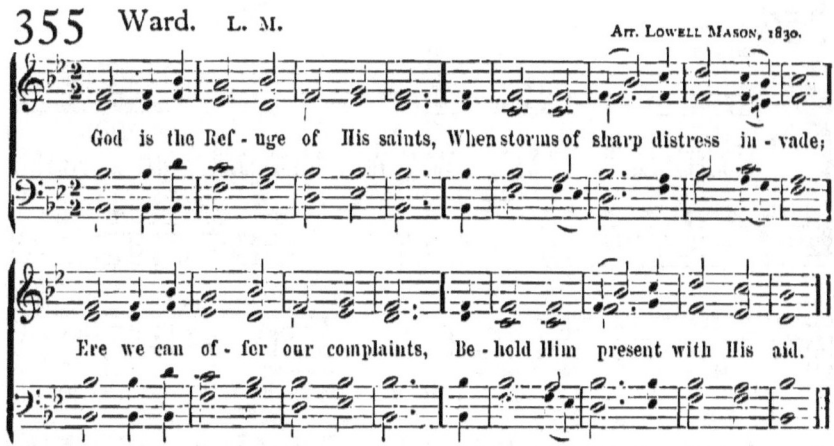

God is the Ref-uge of His saints, When storms of sharp distress in-vade;
Ere we can of-fer our complaints, Be-hold Him present with His aid.

2 Let mountains from their seats be hurled,
  Down to the deep, and buried there;
Convulsions shake the solid world;—
  Our faith shall never yield to fear.

3 Loud may the troubled ocean roar,—
  In sacred peace our souls abide,
While every nation, every shore,
  Trembles, and dreads the swelling tide.

4 There is a stream, whose gentle flow
  Supplies the city of our God;
Life, love, and joy still gliding through,
  And watering our divine abode:—

5 That sacred stream,—Thy holy word,—
  That all our raging fear controls:
Sweet peace Thy promises afford,
  And give new strength to fainting souls.

6 Zion enjoys her monarch's love,
  Secure against a threatening hour;
Nor can her firm foundations move,
  Built on His truth, and armed with power.
  Isaac Watts, 1719.

356
Lord! Thou hast searched and seen me through;
Thine eye commands, with piercing view,
My rising and my resting hours,
My heart and flesh, with all their powers.

2 My thoughts, before they are my own,
Are to my God distinctly known;
He knows the words I mean to speak,
Ere from my opening lips they break.

3 Within Thy circling power I stand;
On every side I find Thy hand;
Awake, asleep, at home, abroad,
I am surrounded still with God.

4 Amazing knowledge, vast and great!
What large extent! what lofty height!
My soul, with all the powers I boast,
Is in the boundless prospect lost.

5 Oh! may these thoughts possess my breast,
Where'er I rove, where'er I rest;
Nor let my weaker passions dare
Consent to sin, for God is there.
Isaac Watts, 1719.

357
He lives, the great Redeemer lives;
(What joy the blest assurance gives!)
And now, before His Father, God,
Pleads the full merits of His blood.

2 Repeated crimes awake our fears,
And justice armed with frowns, appears;
But in the Saviour's lovely face,
Sweet mercy smiles, and all is peace.

Faith.

3 Hence then, ye black, despairing thoughts!
Above our fears. above our faults,
His powerful intercessions rise,
And guilt recedes, and terror dies.

4 In every dark distressful hour,
When sin and Satan join their power,
Let this dear hope repel the dart,
That Jesus bears us on His heart.

5 Great Advocate, almighty Friend!—
On Him our humble hopes depend:
Our cause can never, never fail,
For Jesus pleads, and must prevail.

Anne Steele, 1760.

358 York. C. M.

Scotch Psalter, 1615.

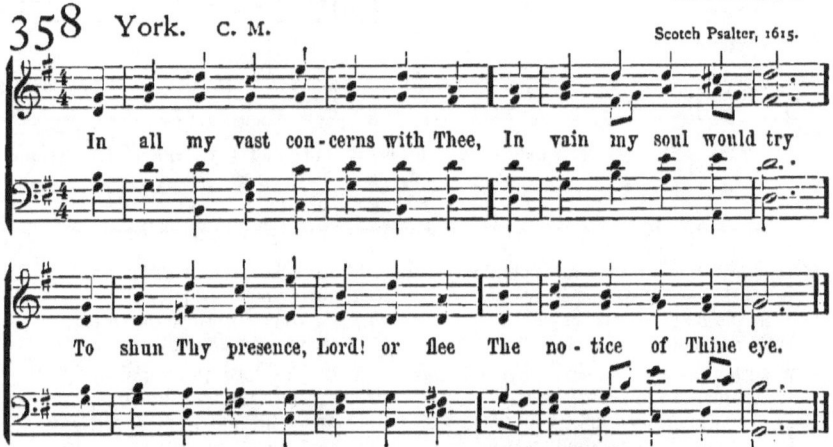

In all my vast concerns with Thee, In vain my soul would try
To shun Thy presence, Lord! or flee The notice of Thine eye.

2 Thine all-surrounding sight surveys
  My rising and my rest,
My public walks, my private ways,
  And secrets of my breast.

3 My thoughts lie open to the Lord,
  Before they're formed within;
And ere my lips pronounce the word,
  He knows the sense I mean.

4 Oh! wondrous knowledge, deep and high!
  Where can a creature hide?
Within Thy circling arms I lie,
  Beset on every side.

5 So let Thy grace surround me still,
  And like a bulwark prove,
To guard my soul from every ill,
  Secured by sovereign love.

Isaac Watts, 1719.

359

Thy way, O God! is in the sea,
  Thy path I cannot trace;
Nor comprehend the mystery
  Of Thine unbounded grace.

2 As in a glass, I dimly see
  The wonders of Thy love;
How little do I know of Thee,
  Or of the joys above!

3 'Tis but in part I know Thy will;—
  I bless Thee for the sight:
But soon Thy love will all reveal,
  In glory's clearer light!

4 With rapture I shall then survey
  Thy providence and grace;
And spend an everlasting day
  In wonder, love, and praise.

John Fawcett, 1782, a.

Faith.

360 St. Stephens. C. M.
William Jones, 1789.

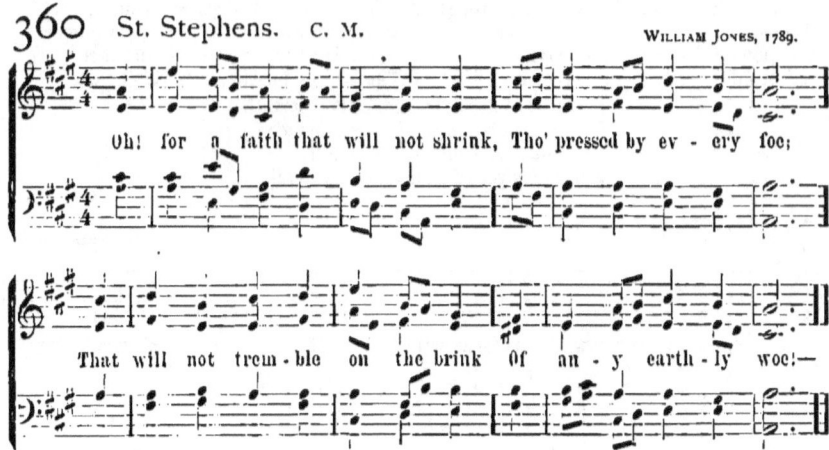

Oh! for a faith that will not shrink, Tho' pressed by ev-ery foe;
That will not trem-ble on the brink Of an-y earth-ly woe!—

2 That will not murmur nor complain,
　Beneath the chastening rod,
But, in the hour of grief or pain,
　Will lean upon its God;—

3 A faith, that shines more bright and clear
　When tempests rage without;
That, when in danger, knows no fear,
　In darkness, feels no doubt;—

4 A faith, that keeps the narrow way
　Till life's last hour is fled,
And, with a pure and heavenly ray,
　Lights up a dying bed!

5 Lord! give us such a faith as this;
　And then, whate'er may come,
We'll taste, ev'n here, the hallowed bliss
　Of an eternal home.
　　　　　　William H. Bathurst, 1830.

361
The roseate hues of early dawn,
　The brightness of the day,
The crimson of the sunset sky,
　How fast they fade away!

2 Oh! for the pearly gates of heaven!
　Oh! for the golden floor!
Oh! for the Sun of righteousness,
　That setteth never more!

3 Oh! for a heart that never sins!
　Oh! for a soul washed white!
Oh! for a voice to praise our King,
　Nor weary day or night!

4 Oh! by Thy love and anguish, Lord!
　Oh! by Thy life laid down,
Oh! that we fall not from Thy grace,
　Nor cast away our crown.
　　　　　　Cecil Frances Alexander, 1853.

362
Give me the wings of faith, to rise
　Within the veil, and see
The saints above,—how great their joys,
　How bright their glories be.

2 I ask them,—whence their victory came?
　They, with united breath,
Ascribe their conquest to the Lamb,—
　Their triumph to His death.

3 They marked the footsteps that He trod;
　His zeal inspired their breast;
And, foll'wing their incarnate God,
　Possess the promised rest.

4 Our glorious Leader claims our praise,
　For His own pattern given,
While the long cloud of witnesses
　Show the same path to heaven.
　　　　　　Isaac Watts, 1709.

Faith.

363 Migdol. L. M.   Lowell Mason, 1839.

'Tis by the faith of joys to come, We walk thro deserts dark as night;
Till we arrive at heaven, our home, Faith is our guide, and faith our light.

2 The want of sight she well supplies;
She makes the pearly gates appear;
Far into distant worlds she pries,
And brings eternal glories near.

3 Cheerful we tread the desert through,
While faith inspires a heavenly ray;
Though lions roar and tempests blow,
And rocks and dangers fill the way.

4 So Abr'am, by divine command,
Left his own house to walk with God;
His faith beheld the promised land,
And fired his zeal along the road.
    Isaac Watts, 1709.

4 Often I feel my sinful heart
Prone from my Jesus to depart;
And, though I oft have Him forgot,
His loving-kindness changes not.

5 So, when I pass death's gloomy vale;
And life, and mortal powers shall fail;
Oh! may my last expiring breath
His loving-kindness sing in death!

6 Then shall I mount and soar away
To the bright world of endless day;
Then shall I sing, with sweet surprise,
His loving-kindness in the skies!
    Samuel Medley, 1787.

364

Awake, my soul! in joyful lays,
And sing Thy great Redeemer's praise;
He justly claims a song from me,
His loving kindness is so free.

2 He saw me ruined in the fall,
Yet loved me, notwithstanding all,
And saved me from my lost estate;
His loving-kindness is so great.

3 Through mighty hosts of cruel foes,
Where earth and hell my way oppose,
He safely leads my soul along,
His loving-kindness is so strong.

365

Let me but hear my Saviour say,
"Strength shall be equal to thy day;"
Then I rejoice in deep distress,
Leaning on all sufficient grace.

2 I glory in infirmity,
That Christ's own power may rest on me;
When I am weak, then am I strong,
Grace is my shield, and Christ my song.

3 I can do all things, or can bear
All sufferings, if my Lord be there;
Sweet pleasures mingle with the pains,
While His kind hand my soul sustains.
    Isaac Watts, 1707.

Faith.

366 St. Ælred. 8s & 3.
John B. Dykes, 1862.

Fierce raged the tempest o'er the deep, Watch did Thine anxious servants keep,
But Thou wast wrapped in guileless sleep, Calm and still. A-men.

2 "Save, Lord, we perish," was their cry,
"O save us in our agony!"
Thy word above the storm rose high,
  "Peace, be still."

3 The wild winds hushed; the angry deep
Sank, like a little child, to sleep;
The sullen billows cease to leap,
  At Thy will.

4 So, when our life is clouded o'er,
And storm-winds drift us from the shore,
Say, lest we sink to rise no more,
  "Peace, be still." Amen.
  Godfrey Thring, 1858.

367 Sicily. 8s 7s & 4.
Sicilian Melody.

O my soul! what means this sad-ness? Wherefore art thou thus cast down?
{ Let thy griefs be turned to gladness, Bid thy rest-less fears be-gone;
{ Look to Je-sus, Look to Je-sus, And re-joice in His dear name. }

2 Though ten thousand ills beset thee,
  From without and from within,
Jesus saith, He'll ne'er forget thee,
  But will save from hell and sin:
    He is faithful
  To perform His gracious word.

3 Though distresses now attend thee,
  And thou tread'st the thorny road;
His right hand shall still defend thee;
  Soon He'll bring thee home to God;
    Therefore praise Him,—
  Praise the great Redeemer's name.
  John Fawcett, 1782.

Faith.

368 Tenderness. S. M.   EDWARD HAMILTON, 1857.

If, thro unruffled seas, Toward heav'n we calmly sail, With grateful hearts, O God, to Thee, We'll own the fav'ring gale.

2 But should the surges rise,
   And rest delay to come,
Blest be the sorrow—kind the storm,
   Which drives us nearer home.

3 Teach us, in every state,
   To make Thy will our own;
And when the joys of sense depart,
   To live by faith alone.
Augustus M. Toplady, 1776.

369 St. Olave. C. M.   JOSEPH BARNBY, 1861.

Lord Jesus! are we one with Thee? Oh! height, Oh! depth of love!
With Thee we died upon the tree, In Thee we live above.

2 Such was Thy grace, that, for our sake,
   Thou didst from heaven come down,
Thou didst of flesh and blood partake,
   In all our sorrows one.

3 Ascended now in glory bright,
   Still one with us Thou art;
Nor life, nor death, nor depth, nor height,
   Thy saints and Thee can part.

4 Soon, soon shall come that glorious day
   When, seated on Thy throne,
Thou shalt to wondering worlds display
   That Thou with us art one.
James George Deck, 1837.

Love.

370 Mornington. S. M. G. C. W. MORNINGTON, 1760.

My God, my Life, my Love! To Thee, to Thee I call;

I can-not live, if Thou re-move, For Thou art All in all.

2 Thy shining grace can cheer,
This dungeon where I dwell;
'Tis Paradise when Thou art here;
If Thou depart, 'tis hell.

3 Not all the harps above
Can make a heavenly place,
If God his residence remove,
Or but conceal His face.

4 Nor earth, nor all the sky,
Can one delight afford;
No, not a drop of real joy,
Without Thy presence, Lord!
Isaac Watts, 1707.

371 Love Divine. L. M. I. B. WOODBURY, 1848.

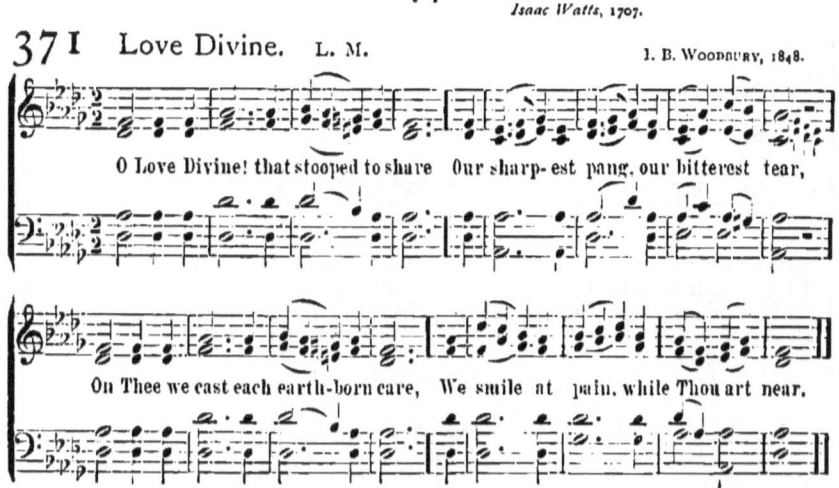

O Love Divine! that stooped to share Our sharp-est pang, our bitterest tear,

On Thee we cast each earth-born care, We smile at pain, while Thou art near.

Love.

2 Though long the weary way we tread,
 And sorrow crown each lingering year,
No path we shun, no darkness dread,
 Our hearts still whispering, Thou art near.

3 On Thee we fling our burdening woe,
 O Love Divine, for ever dear;
Content to suffer while we know,
 Living or dying, Thou art near.
Oliver W. Holmes, 1859.

372 Horbury. 6s & 4s.   John B. Dykes, 1860.

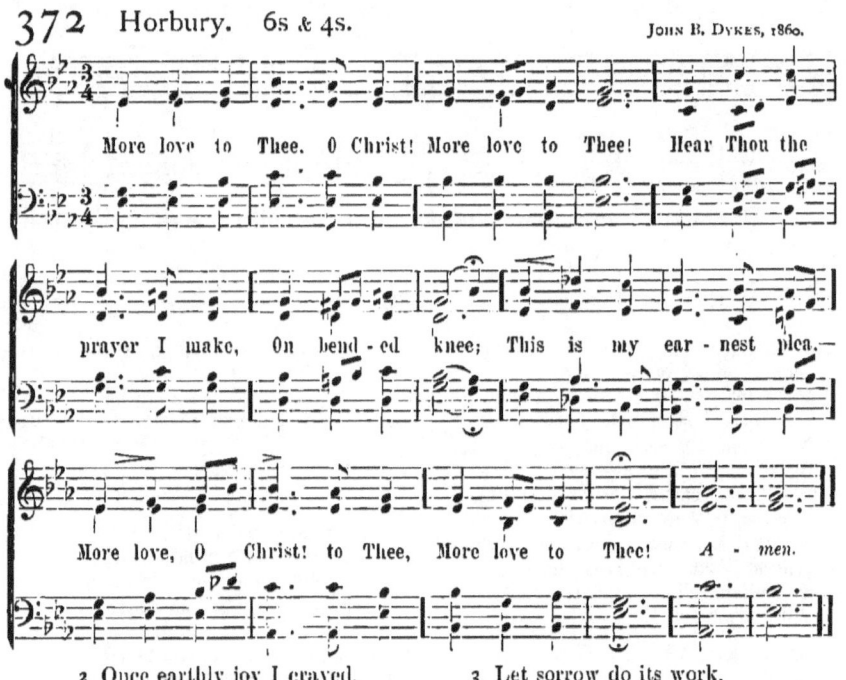

More love to Thee, O Christ! More love to Thee! Hear Thou the prayer I make, On bend-ed knee; This is my ear-nest plea,— More love, O Christ! to Thee, More love to Thee! A-men.

2 Once earthly joy I craved,
 Sought peace and rest;
Now Thee alone I seek,
 Give what is best:
This all my prayer shall be,—
More love, O Christ! to Thee,
 More love to Thee!

3 Let sorrow do its work,
 Send grief and pain;
Sweet are Thy messengers,
 Sweet their refrain,
When they can sing with me,—
More love, O Christ, to Thee,
 More love to Thee.

4 Then shall my latest breath
 Whisper Thy praise;
This be the parting cry
 My heart shall raise,—
This still its prayer shall be,—
More love, O Christ! to Thee,
 More love to Thee!
Elizabeth Prentiss, 1869.

Love.

373 Geer. C. M.
H. W. Greatorex, 1849.

*Jesus! these eyes have never seen That radiant form of Thine;
The veil of sense hangs dark between Thy blessed face and mine.*

2 I see Thee not, I hear Thee not,
  Yet Thou art oft with me;
And earth hath ne'er so dear a spot,
  As where I meet with Thee.

3 Yet, though I have not seen, and still
  Must rest in faith alone,
I love Thee, dearest Lord!—and will,
  Unseen, but not unknown.

4 When death these mortal eyes shall seal,
  And still this throbbing heart,
The rending veil shall Thee reveal,
  All glorious as Thou art!
  Ray Palmer, 1858.

374
I've found the Pearl of greatest price!
  My heart doth sing for joy;
And sing I must, for Christ is mine!
  Christ shall my praise employ.

2 Christ is my Prophet, Priest and King;
  My Prophet full of light,
My great High-Priest before the throne,
  My King of heavenly might.

3 Christ is my Peace; He died for me,
  For me He gave His blood;
And, as my wondrous Sacrifice,
  Offered Himself to God.

4 Christ Jesus is my All in All,—
  My Comfort, and my Love;
My Life below, and He shall be
  My Joy and Crown above.
  John Mason, 1683.

375
There is a name I love to hear,
  I love to sing its worth;
It sounds like music in mine ear,
  The sweetest name on earth.

2 It tells me of a Saviour's love,
  Who died to set me free;
It tells me of His precious blood,
  The sinner's perfect plea.

3 It tells me what my Father hath
  In store for every day,
And, though I tread a darksome path,
  Yields sunshine all the way.

4 It tells of One, whose loving heart
  Can feel my deepest woe,
Who in each sorrow bears a part,
  That none can bear below.

5 Then let me praise that charming name,
  'Tis music to mine ear;
Fain would I sound it out so loud,
  That earth and heaven should hear.
  Frederick Whitfield, 1859.
  v. 5. *Philip Doddridge*, 1740, a.

Love.

376 Ortonville. C. M. THOMAS HASTINGS, 1837.

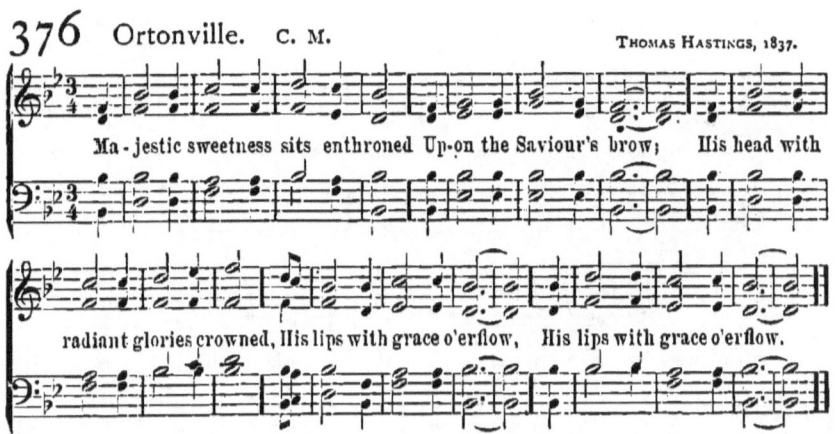

Ma-jestic sweetness sits enthroned Up-on the Saviour's brow; His head with radiant glories crowned, His lips with grace o'erflow, His lips with grace o'erflow.

2 No mortal can with Him compare
  Among the sons of men;
Fairer is He, than all the fair
  That fill the heavenly train.

3 He saw me plunged in deep distress;
  He flew to my relief;
For me He bore the shameful cross;
  And carried all my grief.

4 To Him I owe my life and breath,
  And all the joys I have;
He makes me triumph over death,
  And saves me from the grave.
          Samuel Stennett, 1787.

377

AMAZING grace!—how sweet the sound!
  That saved a wretch like me;
I once was lost, but now am found,
  Was blind, but now I see.

2 'Twas grace that taught my heart to fear,
  And grace my fears relieved;
How precious did that grace appear,
  The hour I first believed!

3 Through many dangers, toils and snares,
  I have already come;
'Tis grace has brought me safe thus far,
  And grace will lead me home.
          John Newton, 1779.

378

OH! for a thousand tongues to sing
  My dear Redeemer's praise!
The glories of my God and King,
  The triumphs of His grace.

2 My gracious Master and my God!
  Assist me to proclaim,
To spread, through all the earth abroad,
  The honors of Thy name.

3 Jesus—the name that charms our fears,
  That bid our sorrows cease;
'Tis music in the sinner's ears;
  'Tis life, and health, and peace.
          Charles Wesley, 1739.

379

OH! what amazing words of grace
  Are in the gospel found,
Suited to every sinner's case
  Who knows the joyful sound!

2 Come, then, with all your wants and
  Your every burden bring;   [wounds,
Here love, eternal love, abounds,—
  A deep, celestial spring.

3 This spring with living water flows,
  And living joy imparts;
Come, thirsty souls! your wants disclose,
  And drink with thankful hearts.
          Samuel Medley, 1789.

Love

380 Chesterfield. C. M.
Thomas Haweis, 1792.

O Jesus! King most wonderful, Thou Conqueror renowned;
Thou sweetness most ineffable, In whom all joys are found!

2 When once Thou visitest the heart,
  Then truth begins to shine;
Then earthly vanities depart;
  Then kindles love divine.

3 O Jesus, Light of all below!
  Thou Fount of life and fire!
Surpassing all the joys we know,
  All that we can desire,—

4 May every heart confess Thy name,
  And ever Thee adore;
And, seeking Thee, itself inflame
  To seek Thee more and more.

5 Thee may our tongues for ever bless,
  Thee may we love alone;
And ever in our lives express
  The image of Thine own.

Lat., *Bernard, of Clairvaux*, 1140.
Tr. *Edward Caswall*, 1849.

381 Heber. C. M.
Geo. Kingsley, 1833.

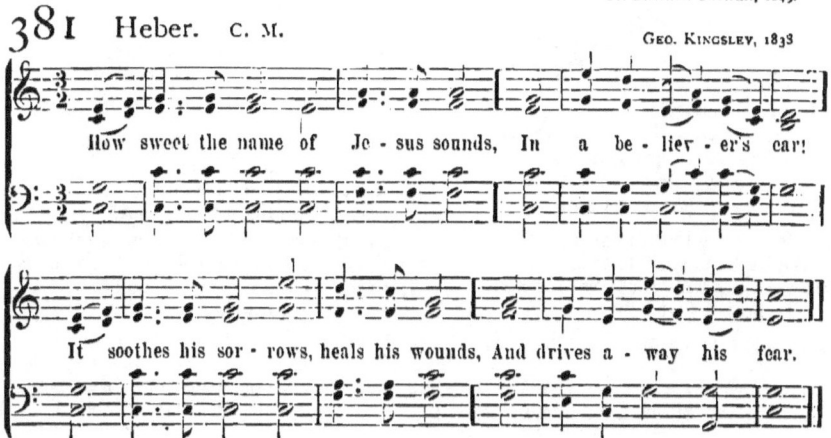

How sweet the name of Jesus sounds, In a believer's ear!
It soothes his sorrows, heals his wounds, And drives away his fear.

Love.

2 It makes the wounded spirit whole,
  And calms the troubled breast;
'Tis manna to the hungry soul,
  And, to the weary, rest.

3 Jesus!—my Shepherd, Husband, Friend!
  My Prophet, Priest, and King!
My Lord, my Life, my Way, my End!
  Accept the praise I bring.

4 Weak is the effort of my heart,
  And cold my warmest thought;
But, when I see Thee as Thou art,
  I'll praise Thee as I ought.

5 Till then, I would Thy love proclaim,
  With every fleeting breath;
And may the music of Thy name
  Refresh my soul in death.
            John Newton, 1779.

382 Federal Street. L. M. HENRY K. OLIVER, 1832.

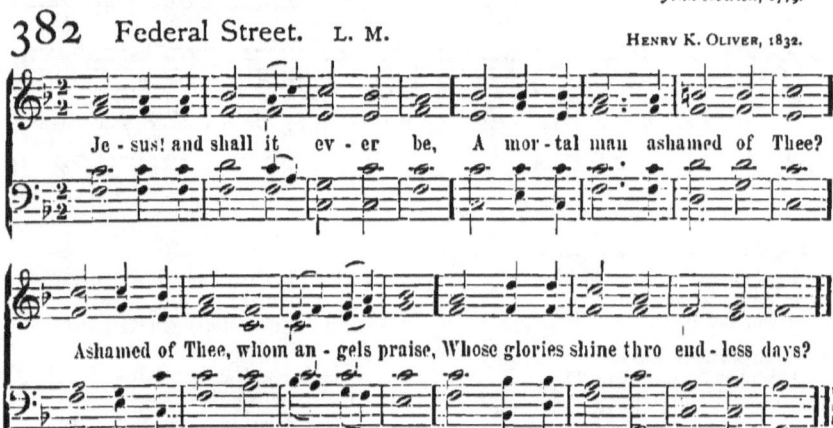

Jesus! and shall it ever be, A mortal man ashamed of Thee?
Ashamed of Thee, whom angels praise, Whose glories shine thro endless days?

2 Ashamed of Jesus! sooner far
Let evening blush to own a star;
He sheds the beams of light divine,
O'er this benighted soul of mine.

3 Ashamed of Jesus! oh, as soon
Let morning blush to own the sun;
He sheds the beams of light divine
O'er this benighted soul of mine.

4 Ashamed of Jesus! that dear Friend,
On whom my hopes of heaven depend!
No; when I blush, be this my shame,
That I no more revere His name.

5 Ashamed of Jesus! yes, I may,
When I've no guilt to wash away,
No tear to wipe, no good to crave,
No fears to quell, no soul to save.

6 Till then,—nor is my boasting vain,—
Till then, I boast a Saviour slain;

And, Oh! may this my glory be,
That Christ is not ashamed of me.
            Joseph Grigg, 1723.
        Alt. *Benjamin Francis, 1787.*

383

JESUS! Thy blood and righteousness
My beauty are,—my glorious dress;
Midst flaming worlds, in these arrayed,
With joy shall I lift up my head.

2 When, from the dust of death, I rise
To claim my mansion in the skies,
E'en then this shall be all my plea,—
"Jesus hath lived,—hath died for me."

3 Oh, let the dead now hear Thy voice;
Now bid Thy banished ones rejoice;
Their beauty this—their glorious dress,
Jesus! Thy blood and righteousness.
        Ger., *Nicholas Louis Zinzendorf, 1730.*
            Tr. *John Wesley, 1740.*

Love.

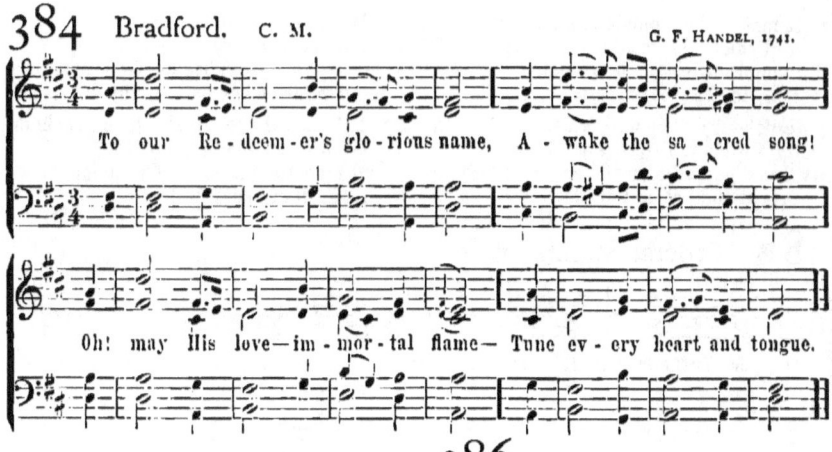

384 Bradford. C. M.   G. F. Handel, 1741.

To our Redeemer's glorious name, Awake the sacred song! Oh! may His love—immortal flame—Tune every heart and tongue.

2 His love what mortal thought can reach?
  What mortal tongue display?
Imagination's utmost stretch,
  In wonder, dies away.

3 Dear Lord! while we adoring pay
  Our humble thanks to Thee,
May every heart with rapture say,—
  "The Saviour died for me!"

4 Oh! may the sweet, the blissful theme,
  Fill every heart and tongue,
Till strangers love Thy charming name,
  And join the sacred song.
                    Anne Steele, 1760.

385

Eternal Sun of Righteousness!
  Display Thy beams divine,
And cause the glory of Thy face
  Upon my heart to shine.

2 Light, in Thy light! Oh! may I see,
  Thy grace and mercy prove,
Revived, and cheered, and blessed by Thee,
  The God of pard'ning love.

3 Lift up Thy countenance serene,
  And let Thy happy child
Behold, without a cloud between,
  The Godhead reconciled.
                    Charles Wesley, 1762.

386

My God! the covenant of Thy love,
  Abides for ever sure;
And, in its matchless grace, I feel
  My happiness secure.

2 Since Thou, the everlasting God,
  My Father art become;
Jesus, my Guardian, and my Friend,
  And heaven my final home;—

3 I welcome all Thy sovereign will,
  For all that will is love;
And, when I know not what thou dost,
  I wait the light above.
                    Philip Doddridge, 1740.

387

My God! the Spring of all my joys,
  The Life of my delights,
The glory of my brightest days,
  And Comfort of my nights!

2 In darkest shades, if He appear,
  My dawning is begun;
He is my soul's sweet Morning Star,
  And He my rising Sun.

3 The op'ning heavens around me shine,
  With beams of sacred bliss,
While Jesus shows His heart is mine,
  And whispers—I am His.
                    Isaac Watts, 1707.

Love.

388 Merton. C. M. — H. K. Oliver, 1842.

My God, I love Thee, not be-cause I hope for heaven thereby;
Nor yet be-cause, if I love not, I must for-ev-er die.

2 Thou, O my Jesus, Thou didst me
  Upon the cross embrace;
For me didst bear the nails and spear,
  And manifold disgrace;—

3 And griefs and torments numberless,
  And sweat of agony,
Yea, death itself; and all for one
  That was Thine enemy!

4 Then why O blessèd Jesus Christ,
  Should I not love Thee well?
Not for the hope of winning heaven,
  Nor of escaping hell;—

5 Not with the hope of gaining ought,
  Not seeking a reward;
But as Thyself has lovèd me,
  O ever-loving Lord!

6 Ev'n so I love Thee, and will love,
  And in Thy praise will sing;
Soley because Thou art my God,
  And my eternal King.

  Francis Xavier, ab. 1542.
  Tr. *Edward Caswall, 1849.*

389

The royal banner is unfurled,
  The cross is reared on high,
On which the Saviour of the world
  Is stretched in agony.

2 And, see! the spear hath pierced His side,
  And shed that sacred flood,
That holy reconciling tide,
  The water and the blood.

3 Hail, holy cross! from thee we learn
  The only way to heaven:
And, Oh! to Thee may sinners turn,
  And look, and be forgiven!

4 So let us praise the Saviour's name,
  And with exulting cry,
The triumph of the cross proclaim
  To all eternity.

  Lat. *Venantius Fortunatus, 580.*
  Tr. *John Chandler, 1837.*

390

O Jesus Christ! if aught there be
  That more than all beside,
In ever painful memory
  Must in my heart abide.

2 It is that deep ingratitude
  Which I to Thee have shown,
Who didst for me in tears and blood
  Upon the cross atone.

  Edward Caswall, 1849.

Love.

391 Carey. 8s & 5s. HUBERT P. MAIN, 1877.

Lord! 'tis not that I did choose Thee, That could never be; For this heart would still re-fuse Thee, Thou hast chosen me: Hast from all the sin that stained me, Washed and set me free; And un-to this end ordained me,—That I live to Thee.

Copyright, 1877, by Biglow & Main.

2 'Twas Thy sovereign mercy called me,
  Taught my opening mind;
Else the world had yet enthralled me,
  To Thy glories blind.
Now my heart owns none above Thee;
  For Thy grace I thirst;
Knowing well that, if I love Thee,—
  Thou didst love me first.
                Josiah Conder, 1837, alt.

392 Tune—ARIEL.

To Father, Son, and Holy Ghost,
The God, whom heaven's triumphant host
  And saints on earth adore;
Be glory as in ages past,
Is now, and shall for ever last,
  When time shall be no more.
                Tate & Brady, 1696, a.

393 Ariel. C. P. M. LOWELL MASON, 1836.

Oh! could I speak the matchless worth, Oh! could I sound the glo-ries forth,

Love.

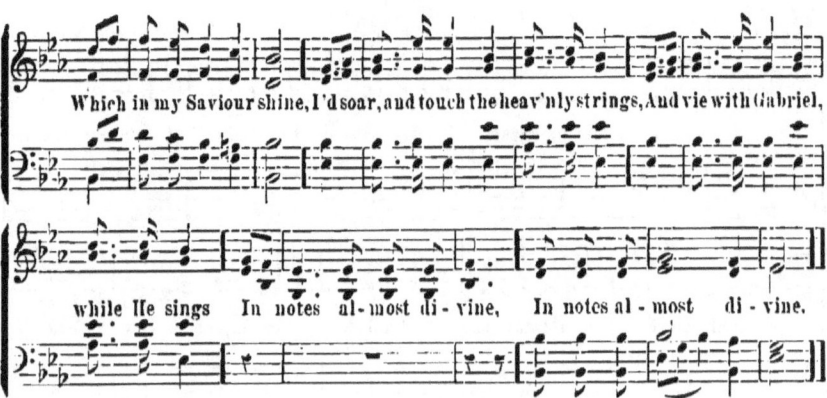

Which in my Saviour shine, I'd soar, and touch the heav'nly strings, And vie with Gabriel, while He sings In notes al-most di-vine, In notes al-most di-vine.

2 I'd sing the precious blood He spilt,
My ransom from the dreadful guilt
Of sin and wrath divine:
I'd sing His glorious righteousness,
In which all-perfect, heavenly dress
My soul shall ever shine.

3 I'd sing the characters He bears,
And all the forms of love He wears,
Exalted on His throne:
In loftiest songs of sweetest praise,
I would, to everlasting days,
Make all His glories known.
Samuel Medley, 1789.

394 Crusader's Hymn. P. M.
Ad. by R. S. Willis, 1850.

Fairest Lord Je-sus, Ru-ler of all nature, O Thou of God and man the Son; Thee will I cher-ish, Thee will I hon-or, Thou my soul's glo-ry, joy and crown.

2 Fair are the meadows,
Fairer still the woodlands,
Robed in the blooming garb of spring;
　Jesus is fairer,
　Jesus is purer,
Who makes the woeful heart to sing.

3 Fair is the sunshine,
Fairer still the moonlight,
And all the twinkling, starry host.
　Jesus shines brighter,
　Jesus shines purer,
Than all the angels heaven can boast.
Anon, 12th Century.

Love.

395 Nebo. S. M.
Thomas Hastings, 1843.

I was a wandering sheep, I did not love the fold; I did not love my Saviour's voice, I would not be con-trolled, I would not be con-trolled.

2 I was a wayward child,
   I did not love my home;
I did not love my Father's voice,
   I loved afar to roam.

3 Jesus my Shepherd is,—
   'Twas He that loved my soul;
'Twas He that washed me in His blood,
   'Twas He that made me whole;

4 'Twas He that sought the lost,
   That found the wandering sheep;
'Twas He that brought me to the fold,
   'Tis He that still doth keep.

5 I was a wandering sheep,
   I would not be controlled;
But now I love my Shepherd's voice,
   I love, I love the fold:
Horatius Bonar, 1843, ab.

396 Miller. L. M.
Hubert P. Main, 1870.

Earth has a joy unknown to heaven, The new-born peace of sins forgiven; Tears of such pure and deep delight, Ye an-gels, nev-er dimmed your sight.

2 Loud is the song, the heavenly plain
Is shaken with the choral strain;
And dying echoes, floating far,
Draw music from each chiming star.

3 But I amid your choirs shall shine,
And all your knowledge shall be mine;
Ye on your harps must lean to hear
A secret chord that mine will bear.
Augustus Lucas Hillhouse, 1822.

Love.

397 The Old Story. 7s & 6s. W. G. Fischer, 1869.

I love to tell the sto-ry Of unseen things above, Of Je-sus and His glory, Of Je-sus and His love. I love to tell the story, Because I know 'tis true; It sat-is-fies my longings As nothing else can do.

CHORUS.

I love to tell the story, 'Twill be my theme in glory, To tell the old, old story Of Jesus and His love.

2 I love to tell the story:
  'Tis pleasant to repeat
What seems each time I tell it,
  More wonderfully sweet.
I love to tell the story:
  For some have never heard
The message of salvation,
  From God's own holy Word.—Cho.

3 I love to tell the story;
  For those who know it best
Seem hungering and thirsting
  To hear it like the rest.
And when, in scenes of glory,
  I sing the NEW, NEW SONG,
'Twill be the OLD, OLD STORY
  That I have loved so long.—Cho.

Kate Hankey, 1867.

Love.

398. König der Ehren. P. M.
Würtemberg Gesangbuch.

Prais-es we're bringing to Je-sus, Al-mighty and Roy-al!
O my soul, ren-der thy voice to the heav-en-ly cho-ral!
Throng-ing a-bout; Psalt-'ry and harp a-wake out;
Let this praise song be heard o'er all. A-men.

2 Praises to Jesus, my soul! for thy wonderful saving;
His be the glory from Abraham's seed and all living!
He is thy light! Think thou, my soul, of His right;
Close with Amen the thanksgiving.

3 Angels and archangels, with your high music we're blending
Shouts of Redemption, as up to your ranks we're ascending:
Onward we go; Conquerors o'er the last foe;
Swelling the chorus unending! Amen.

Joachim Neander, 1679.
Tr. & 3 stanza added, M. W. Stryker, 1880.

399. Southminster. 7s.
ORLANDO GIBBONS, 1623.

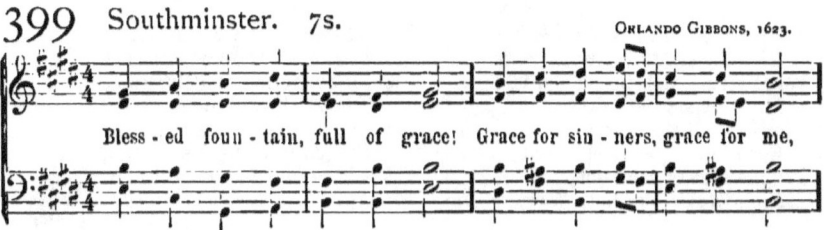

Bless-ed foun-tain, full of grace! Grace for sin-ners, grace for me,

Love.

To this source a-lone I trace What I am, and hope to be.

2 What I am, as one redeemed,
　Saved and rescued by the Lord;
Hating what I once esteemed,
　Loving what I once abhorred.

3 What I hope to be ere long,
　When I take my place above;
When I join the heavenly throng;
　When I see the God of love.

4 Then I hope like Him to be,
　Who redeemed His saints from sin,
Who I now obscurely see,
　Through a vail that stands between.

5 Blessèd fountain, full of grace!
　Grace for sinners, grace for me;
To this source alone I trace
　What I am, and hope to be.
　　　　　　　Thomas Kelly, 1839.

400

Saviour! teach me, day by day,
　Love's sweet lesson to obey;
Sweeter lesson cannot be,
　Loving Him who first loved me.

2 With a childlike heart of love,
　At Thy bidding may I move;
Prompt to serve and follow Thee,
　Loving Him who first loved me.

3 Teach me all Thy steps to trace,
　Strong to follow in Thy grace;
Learning how to love from Thee,
　Loving Him who first loved me.

4 Thus may I rejoice to show
　That I feel the love I owe;
Singing, till Thy face I see,
　Of His love who first loved me.
　　　　　　　Anon, 1854.

401　Stephanos.　8 5 8 3.　　Henry W. Baker, 1861, arr. 1871.

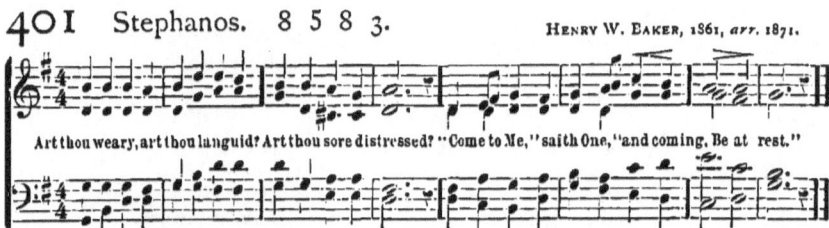

Art thou weary, art thou languid? Art thou sore distressed? "Come to Me," saith One, "and coming, Be at rest."

2 Hath He marks to lead me to Him,
　If He be my Guide?—
"In His feet and hands are wound-prints,
　And His side."

3 If I find Him, if I follow,
　What his guerdon here?—
"Many a sorrow, many a labor,
　Many a tear."

4 If I still hold closely to Him,
　What hath He at last?—
"Sorrow vanquished, labor ended,
　Jordan passed."

5 If I ask Him to receive me,
　Will He say me nay?
"Not till earth, and not till heaven
　Pass away."
　　　　　　Tr. *John M. Neale*, 1851.

Love.

402 Affiance. 10s.
JOSEPH BARNBY, 1872.

A-bide in me, O Lord, and I in Thee, From this good hour, O leave me nev-er-more; Then shall the dis-cord cease, the wound be healed, The life-long bleed-ing of the soul be o'er. A-men.

2 Abide in me; o'ershadow by Thy love
   Each half-formed purpose and dark thought of sin;
Quench ere it rise, each selfish, low desire,
   And keep my soul as Thine,—calm and divine.

3 As some rare perfume in a vase of clay,
   Pervades it with a fragrance not its own,
So, when Thou dwellest in a mortal soul,
   All heaven's own sweetness seems around it thrown.

4 Abide in me: there have been moments blest,
   When I have heard Thy voice and felt Thy power;
Then evil lost its grasp; and passion hushed,
   Owned the divine enchantment of the hour.

5 These were but seasons beautiful and rare;
   Abide in me, and they shall ever be;
Fulfil at once Thy precept and my prayer,
   Come, and abide in me, and I in Thee.

Harriet Beecher Stowe, 1855. (I)

Hope.

403 Wellerd. L. M.   Hubert P. Main, 1869.

Stand up, my soul! shake off thy fears, And gird the gos-pel ar-mor on,
March to the gates of end-less joy, Where Je-sus, Thy great Captain's gone.

2 Hell and thy sins resist thy course,
But hell and sin are vanquished foes,
Thy Jesus nailed them to the cross,
And sung the triumph when He rose.

3 Then let my soul march boldly on,
Press forward to the heavenly gate,
There peace and joy eternal reign,
And glittering robes for conquerors wait.

4 There shall I wear a starry crown,
And triumph in almighty grace,
While all the armies of the skies,
Join in my glorious Leader's praise.
    Isaac Watts, 1707.

404

The oath and promise of the Lord
Join to confirm His wondrous grace;
Eternal power performs the word,
And fills all heaven with endless praise.

2 Amid temptations, sharp and long,
My soul to this dear refuge flies;
Hope is my anchor, firm and strong,
While tempests blow, and billows rise.

3 The gospel bears my spirit up;
A faithful and unchanging God
Lays the foundation for my hope,
In oaths, and promises, and blood.
    Isaac Watts, 1709.

405

Thou, Saviour! art the living bread;
Thou wilt my every want supply;
Be Thee sustained, and cheered, and led,
I'll press through dangers to the sky.

2 What, though temptations oft distress,
And sin assails and breaks my peace?
Thou wilt uphold, and save, and bless,
And bid the storms of passion cease.

3 Then let me take Thy gracious hand,
And walk beside Thee onward still;
Till my glad feet shall safely stand,
For ever firm, on Zion's hill.
    Ray Palmer, 1833, ab.

406

O God! thou art my God alone;
Early to thee my soul shall cry;
A pilgrim in a land unknown,
A thirsty land, whose springs are dry,

2 Yet, through this rough and thorny maze,
I follow hard on Thee, my God!
Thy hand unseen upholds my ways,
I safely tread where Thou hast trod.

3 Better than life itself Thy love,
Dearer than all beside to me;
For whom have I in heaven above,
Or what on earth, compared with Thee?
    James Montgomery, 1822.

Hope.

407 Eloise. C. M. *Hubert P. Main, 1874.*

As pants the hart for cool-ing streams, When heat-ed in the chase,
So longs my soul, O God, for Thee, And Thy re-fresh-ing grace.

2 For Thee, my God, the living God,
My thirsty soul doth pine;
Oh, when shall I behold Thy face,
Thou Majesty divine!

3 Why restless, why cast down, my soul?
Trust God; who will employ
His aid for thee, and change these sighs
To thankful hymns of joy.
Nahum Tate, 1696.
Alt. H. F. Lyte, 1834.

408 Adrian. S. M. *J. E. Gould, 1846.*

Oh, cease, my wand'ring soul, On rest-less wing to roam;
All this wide world, to ei-ther pole, Hath not for thee a home.

2 Behold the ark of God!
Behold the open door!
Oh, haste to gain that dear abode,
And rove, my soul, no more.

3 There safe thou shalt abide,
There sweet shall be thy rest;
And every longing satisfied,
With full salvation blest.
W. A. Muhlenberg, 1826.

Hope.

409 Forelight. 10s. E. H. Thorne, 1872.

Joy-ful-ly, joy-ful-ly on-ward I move, Bound to the land of bright spir-its a-bove; An-gel-ic chor-is-ters sing as I come, Joy-ful-ly, joy-ful-ly, haste to thy home; A-men.

2 Soon will my pilgrimage end here below,
Home to that land of delight will I go;
Pilgrim and stranger no more shall I roam,
Joyfully, joyfully, resting at home,

3 Sounds of sweet melody fall on my ear;
Harps of the blessed, your voices I hear;
Rings with the harmony heaven's high dome,—
Joyfully, joyfully, haste to thy home.

4 Death, with thy weapons of war lay me low,
Strike, king of terrors, I fear not the blow;
Jesus hath broken the bars of the tomb!
Joyfully, joyfully, will I go home.

5 Bright will the morn of eternity dawn,
Death shall be banished, his scepter be gone;
Joyfully, then, shall I witness his doom,
Joyfully, joyfully, safely at home.

William Hunter, 1843.

Hope.

410 Olmutz. S. M.
Lowell Mason, 1824

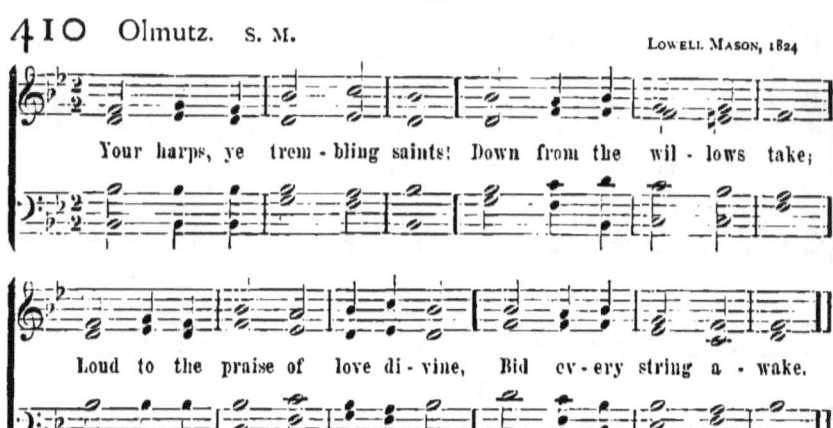

Your harps, ye trem-bling saints! Down from the wil-lows take;
Loud to the praise of love di-vine, Bid ev-ery string a-wake.

2 Though in a foreign land,
　We are not far from home;
And, nearer to our house above,
　We every moment come.

3 His grace will, to the end,
　Stronger and brighter shine;
Nor present things, nor things to come,
　Shall quench the spark divine.

4 The people of His choice
　He will not cast away;
Yet do not always here expect
　On Tabor's mount to stay.

5 When we in darkness walk,
　Nor feel the heavenly flame;
Then is the time to trust our God,
　And rest upon His name.

6 Soon shall our doubts and fears
　Subside at His control;
His loving kindness shall break through
　The midnight of the soul.

7 Still on His plighted love
　At all events rely;
The very hidings of His face
　Shall train thee up to joy.

8 Blest is the man, O God!
　That stays himself on Thee:—
Who waits for Thy salvation, Lord!
　Shall Thy salvation see
Augustus M. Toplady, 1772, ab.

411

Oh! what, if we are Christ's,
　Is earthly shame or loss?
Bright shall the crown of glory be,
　When we have borne the cross.

2 Keen was the trial once,
　Bitter the cup of woe,
When martyred saints, baptized in blood,
　Christ's sufferings shared below.

3 Bright is their glory now,
　Boundless their joy above,
Where on the bosom of their God,
　They rest in perfect love,

4 Lord! may that grace be ours,
　Like them, in faith, to bear
All that of sorrow, grief, or pain
　May be our portion here.

5 Enough, if Thou at last
　The word of blessing give,
And let us rest beneath Thy feet,
　Where saints and angels live.
Henry W. Baker, 1852.

Hope.

412 Liverpool. C. M.   Robert Wainwright, 1774. (1.

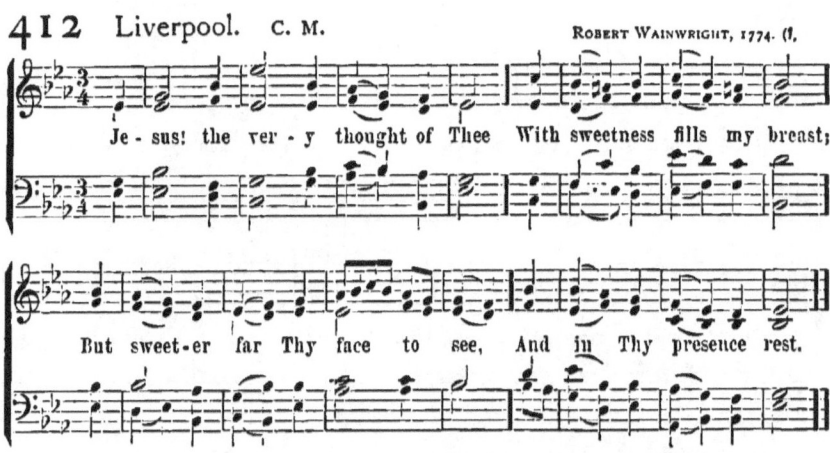

Je-sus! the ver-y thought of Thee With sweetness fills my breast;
But sweet-er far Thy face to see, And in Thy presence rest.

2 Nor voice can sing, nor heart can frame,
  Nor can the mem'ry find,
A sweeter sound than Thy blest name,
  O Saviour of mankind!

3 O Hope of every contrite heart!
  O Joy of all the meek!
To those who fall, how kind Thou art!
  How good to those who seek!

4 But what to those who find? Ah! this
  Nor tongue nor pen can show:
The love of Jesus,—what it is,
  None but His loved ones know.

5 Jesus! our only joy be Thou,
  As Thou our prize wilt be;
Jesus! be Thou our glory now,
  And through eternity!
        Lat., Bernard, of Clairvaux, 1140.
              Tr. Edward Caswall, 1849.

413

Thou lovely Source of true delight,
  Whom I unseen adore!
Unveil Thy beauties to my sight,
  That I may love Thee more.

2 Thy glory o'er creation shines;
  But, in Thy sacred word,
I read, in fairer, brighter lines,
  My bleeding, dying Lord.

3 'Tis here, whene'er my comforts droop,
  And sins and sorrows rise,
Thy love, with cheerful beams of hope,
  My fainting heart supplies.

4 But, ah! too soon the pleasing scene
  Is clouded o'er with pain;
My gloomy fears rise dark between,
  And I again complain.

5 Jesus, my Lord, my life, my light!
  Oh! come with blissful ray;
Break radiant through the shades of night,
  And chase my fears away.
              Anne Steele, 1760.

414

When I can read my title clear,
  To mansions in the skies,
I bid farewell to every fear,
  And wipe my weeping eyes.

2 Should earth against my soul engage,
  And hellish darts be hurled,
Then I can smile at Satan's rage,
  And face a frowning world.

3 Let cares like a wild deluge come,
  And storms of sorrow fall;
May I but safely reach my home,
  My God, my heaven, my all!
              Isaac Watts, 1707.

Hope.

415 Magdalene College. C. P. M.
William Hayes, 1749. (?)

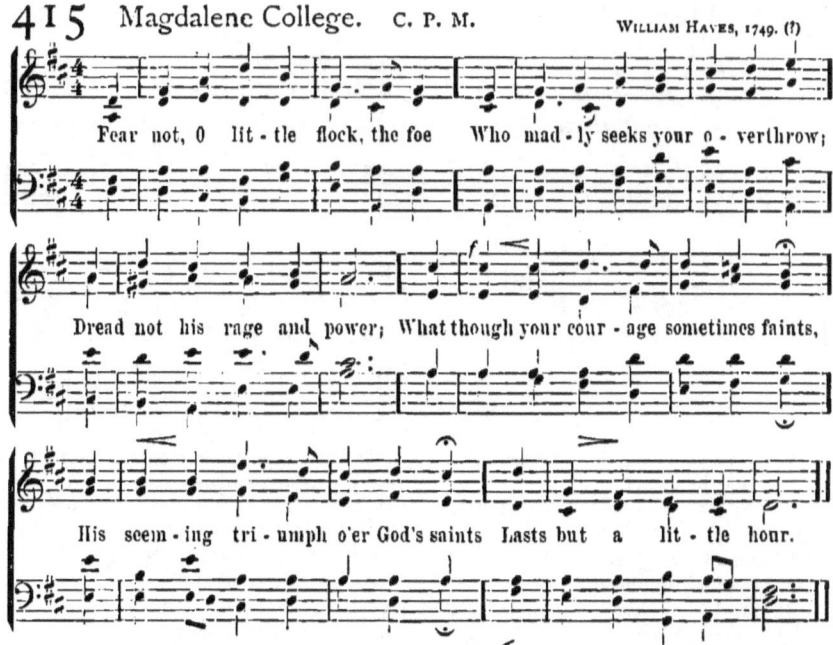

Fear not, O little flock, the foe Who madly seeks your overthrow;
Dread not his rage and power; What though your courage sometimes faints,
His seeming triumph o'er God's saints Lasts but a little hour.

2 Be of good cheer; your cause belongs
To Him who can avenge your wrongs;
   Leave all to Him, your Lord!
Though hidden yet from mortal eyes,
Salvation shall for you arise:
   He girdeth on His sword!

3 As true as God's own word is true,
Not earth nor hell with all their crew
   Against us shall prevail;
A jest and by-word are they grown;
God is with us, we are His own,
   Our victory cannot fail!

4 Amen, Lord Jesus, grant our prayer!
Great Captain, now Thine arm make bare,
   Fight for us once again!
So shall Thy saints and martyrs raise
A mighty chorus to Thy praise,
   World without end: Amen!

Gustavus Adolphus, 1631.
Tr. Catherine Winkworth, 1855, a.

416

O Lord! how happy should we be,
If we could cast our care on Thee,
   If we from self could rest;
And feel, at heart, that One above,
In perfect wisdom, perfect love,
   Is working for the best!

2 How far from this our daily life,
Ever disturbed by anxious strife,
   By sudden, wild alarms!
Oh! could we but relinquish all
Our earthly props, and simply fall
   On Thine almighty arms!—

3 Could we but kneel, and cast our load,
E'en while we pray, upon our God,
   From self entirely cease,
Leave all things to a Father's will,
And taste, before Him lying still,
   E'en in affliction, peace.

Joseph Anstice, 1836.

Hope.

417

Children of light! arise and shine;
Your birth, your hopes, are all divine,
　Your home is in the skies;
Oh! then, for heavenly glory born,
Look down on all, with holy scorn,
　That earthly spirits prize.

2 O blessèd Lord! we yet shall reign,
Redeemed from sorrow, sin, and pain,
　And walk with Thee in white:
We suffer now; but, Oh! at last
We'll bless Thee, Lord! for all the past,
　And own our cross was light.
　　　　　　　　Edward Denny, 1839.

418

O Lord! in sorrow I resign
My soul to that dear hand of Thine,
　Without reserve or fear;
That hand shall wipe my streaming eyes,
Or, into smiles of glad surprise,
　Transform the falling tear.

2 My sole possession is Thy love;
On earth beneath, in heaven above,
　I have no other store:
And though, with fervent suit I pray
And importune Thee, night and day,
　I ask Thee nothing more.
　　　　Fr. Madame de la Motte Guyon, 1710.
　　　　Tr. William Cowper, 1783, a

419 Monkland. 7s.　　　　Arr. John P. Wilkes, 1861.

Faint not, Christian! though the road, Leading to thy blest abode, Darksome be, and dangerous too, Christ, thy Guide, will bring thee through.

2 Faint not, Christian! though in rage
Satan would thy soul engage;
Gird on faith's anointed shield,
Bear it to the battle-field.

3 Faint not, Christian! though the world
Has its hostile flag unfurled;
Hold the cross of Jesus fast,
Thou shalt overcome at last.

4 Faint not, Christian! though within
There's a heart so prone to sin;
Christ, the Lord, is over all;
He'll not suffer thee to fall.
　　　　　　　　James H. Evans, 1833.

420

Joyful be the hours to-day;
　Joyful let the season be;
Let us sing, for well we may;
　Jesus! we shall sing of Thee.

2 Joyful are we now to own—,
　Rapture thrills us, as we trace
All the deeds Thy love hath done,
　All the riches of Thy grace.

3 'Tis Thy grace alone can save;
　Every blessing comes from Thee,—
All we have and hope to have,
　All we are and hope to be.
　　　　　　　　Thomas Kelly, 1853.

Hope.

421 Septuor. P. M.   Ad. fr. L. van Beethoven, 1799.
Con moto.

Head of the Church tri-umphant, We joy-ful-ly a-dore Thee;
Till Thou appear, Thy members here Shall sing like those in glo-ry;
We lift our hearts and voi-ces With blest an-tic-i-pa-tion,
And cry a-loud, And give to God The praise of our sal-va-tion!

2 Thou dost conduct Thy people
Through torrents of temptation;
   Nor will we fear
   While Thou art near,
The fire of tribulation;
We clap our hands exulting
In Thine almighty favor;
   Thy love divine
   That makes us Thine,
Shall keep us Thine forever!

3 By faith we see the glory
To which Thou shalt restore us;
   The world despise
   For that high prize
Which Thou hast set before us;
And if Thou count us worthy,
We each, as dying Stephen,
   Shall see Thee stand
   At God's right hand,
To take us up to heaven!
                 Charles Wesley, 1745.

Hope.

422   St. Hilda.   7s & 6s.   E. Husband.

A pilgrim and a stranger, I journey here below; Far distant is my country, The home to which I go: Here I must toil and travail, Oft weary and oppressed, But there my God shall lead me To everlasting rest.

2 It is a well-worn pathway;
  Many have gone before,—
The holy saints and prophets,
  The patriarchs of yore;
They trod the toilsome journey,
  In patience and in faith,
And them I fain would follow,
  Like them in life and death.

3 With them my thoughts are dwelling,
  'Tis there I long to be;
Come, Lord! and call Thy servant
  To blessedness with Thee!
Come, bid my toils be ended,
  Let all my wanderings cease;
Call from the wayside lodging,
  To the sweet home of peace!

4 There I shall dwell for ever,
  No more a stranger guest,
With all Thy blood-bought children,
  In everlasting rest:
The pilgrim toils forgotten,
  The pilgrim conflicts o'er,
All earthly griefs behind us,
  Eternal joys before!

Ger., *Paul Gerhardt*, 1667.
Tr. *Jane Borthwick* 1862.

Hope.

423 Clark. C. M.   HUBERT P. MAIN, 1869.

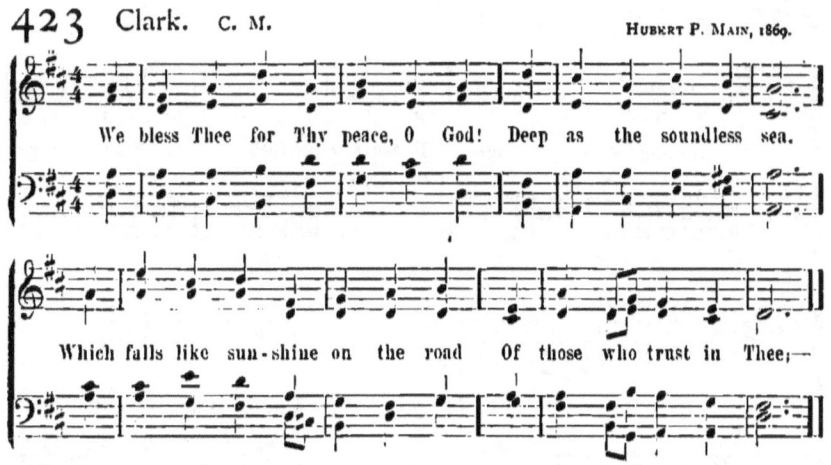

We bless Thee for Thy peace, O God! Deep as the soundless sea.
Which falls like sun-shine on the road Of those who trust in Thee;—

2 That peace which suffers and is strong,
   Trusts where it cannot see,
Deems not the trial way too long,
   But leaves the end with Thee;

3 That peace which flows serene and deep,
   A river in the soul,
Whose banks a living verdure keep;
   God's sunshine o'er the whole.

4 Such, Father! give our hearts such peace,
   Whate'er the outward be,
Till all life's discipline shall cease,
   And we go home to Thee.
                Anon, 1862.

424

God moves in a mysterious way
   His wonders to perform;
He plants His footsteps in the sea,
   And rides upon the storm.

2 Deep in unfathomable mines
   Of never-failing skill,
He treasures up His bright designs,
   And works His sovereign will.

3 Ye fearful saints! fresh courage take;
   The clouds, ye so much dread,
Are big with mercy, and shall break
   In blessings on your head.

4 Judge not the Lord by feeble sense,
   But trust Him for His grace;
Behind a frowning providence,
   He hides a smiling face.

5 His purposes will ripen fast,
   Unfolding every hour;
The bud may have a bitter taste,
   But sweet will be the flower.

6 Blind unbelief is sure to err,
   And scan his work in vain;
God is his own interpreter,
   And He will make it plain.
              William Cowper, 1772.

425

Our God, our help in ages past,
   Our Help for years to come,
Our Shelter from the stormy blast,
   And our eternal Home!—

2 Before the hills in order stood,
   Or earth received her frame,
From everlasting Thou art God,
   To endless years the same.

3 A thousand ages in Thy sight
   Are like an evening gone;
Short as the watch that ends the night,
   Before the rising sun.

Prayer.

4 Time, like an ever-rolling stream,
Bears all its sons away;
They fly forgotten, as a dream
Dies at the opening day.

5 Our God, our Help in ages past,
Our Hope for years to come!
Be Thou our Guard, while troubles last,
And our eternal Home.

Isaac Watts, 1719.

426 Brattle Street. C. M.   IGNACE PLEYEL, 1791.

{ While Thee I seek, protecting Power! Be my vain wishes stilled; }
{ And may this consecrated hour (Omit.) . . . . . } With better hopes be fill'd. Thy love the power of tho't bestow'd; To Thee my tho'ts would soar: Thy mercy o'er my life has flowed; That mercy I adore.

2 In each event of life, how clear,
Thy ruling hand I see!
Each blessing to my soul more dear,
Because conferred by Thee:
In every joy that crowns my days,
In every pain I bear,
My heart shall find delight in praise,
Or seek relief in prayer.

3 When gladness wings the favored hour,
Thy love my thoughts shall fill;
Resigned, when storms of sorrow lower,
My soul shall meet Thy will:
My lifted eye, without a tear,
The gathering storm shall see;
My steadfast heart shall know no fear;
That heart will rest on Thee.

Helen Maria Williams, 1786.

Prayer.

427 Prayer. 8s & 4.   John B. Dykes, 1868.

My God! is any hour so sweet, From blush of morn to evening star, As that which calls me to Thy feet— The hour of prayer?

2 Blest is the tranquil hour of morn,
   And blest that solemn hour of eve
When, on the wings of prayer upborne,
   The world I leave.

3 Then is my strength by Thee renewed;
   Then are my sins by Thee forgiven;
Then dost Thou cheer my solitude
   With hopes of heaven.

4 Lord! till I reach that blissful shore,
   No privilege so dear shall be,
As thus my inmost soul to pour
   In prayer to thee.
            Charlotte Elliott, 1834.

428

Jesus, my Saviour, look on me,
For I am weary and oppressed;
I come to cast myself on Thee;
   Thou art my Rest!

2 I am bewildered on my way;
Dark and tempestuous is the night;
Oh, shed Thou forth some cheering ray;
   Thou art my Light!

3 Thou wilt my every want supply
E'en to the end, whate'er befall;
Through life—in death—eternally,
   Thou art my All!
            Charlotte Elliott, 1863.

429 Byefield. C. M.   Thomas Hastings, 1843, arr.

Prayer is the soul's sincere desire, Unuttered or expressed; The motion of a hidden fire, That trembles in the breast.

Prayer.

2 Prayer is the burden of a sigh,
  The falling of a tear,
The upward glancing of an eye,
  When none but God is near.

3 Prayer is the simplest form of speech,
  That infant lips can try;
Prayer, the sublimest strains that reach
  The Majesty on high.

4 Prayer is the Christian's vital breath,
  The Christian's native air:
His watchword at the gates of death;
  He enters heaven with prayer.

5 Prayer is the contrite sinner's voice,
  Returning from his ways;
While angels in their songs rejoice,
  And cry—" Behold he prays!"

6 O Thou, by whom we come to God,—
  The Life, the Truth, the Way!
The path of prayer Thyself hast trod;
  Lord! teach us how to pray.
James Montgomery, 1819.

430

O Thou, who hast Thy servants taught
  That not by words alone,
But by the fruits of holiness,
  The life of God is shown!

2 While in Thy house of prayer we meet,
  And call Thee God and Lord,
Give us a heart to follow Thee,
  Obedient to Thy word.

3 Through all the dangerous paths of life,
  Uphold us as we go,
That with our lips, and in our lives,
  Thy glory we may show.
Henry Alford, 1844.

431 Seymour. 7s.
CARL MARIA VON WEBER, 1826.

Come, my soul! thy suit prepare; Jesus loves to answer prayer:
He Himself has bid thee pray, Therefore will not say thee nay.

2 Thou art coming to a King,
  Large petitions with thee bring;
For His grace and power are such,
  None can ever ask too much.

3 With my burden I begin,
  Lord! remove this load of sin;
Let Thy blood, for sinners spilt,
  Set my conscience free from guilt.

4 Lord! I come to Thee for rest,
  Take possession of my breast;
There Thy blood-bought right maintain,
  And without a rival reign.

5 While I am a pilgrim here,
  Let Thy love my spirit cheer;
As my Guide, my Guard, my Friend,
  Lead me to my journey's end.
John Newton, 1778.

Prayer.

432 Mercy-Seat. 11s & 10s.   Joseph Barnby, 1872.

Thou knowest, Lord, the wea-ri-ness and sor-row Of the sad heart that comes to Thee for rest; Cares of to-day, and burdens for to-mor-row, Blessings im-plored, and sins to be con-fessed; We come be-fore Thee at Thy gracious word, And lay them at Thy feet; Thou knowest, Lord. A-men.

2 Thou knowest all the past; how long and blindly
  On the dark mountains the lost wanderer strayed;
How the good Shepherd followed, and how kindly
  He bore it home, upon His Shoulders laid;
And healed the bleeding wounds, and soothed the pain,
And brought back life, and hope, and strength again

3 Thou knowest all the present; each temptation,
  Each toilsome duty, each foreboding fear;
All to each one assigned of tribulation,
  Or to belovéd ones, than self more dear;

Prayer.

All pensive memories, as we journey on,
  Longings for vanished smiles and voices gone.

4 Thou knowest all the future; gleams of gladness
  By stormy clouds too quickly overcast;
Hours of sweet fellowship and parting sadness,
  And the dark river to be crossed at last.
Oh! what could hope and confidence afford
  To tread that path; but this, Thou knowest Lord!

5 Thou knowest, not alone as God, all-knowing;
  As Man, our mortal weakness Thou hast proved:
On earth, with purest sympathies o'erflowing,
  O Saviour, Thou hast wept, and Thou hast loved;
And love and sorrow still to Thee may come,
And find a hiding-place, a rest, a home.

6 Therefore we come, Thy gentle call obeying,
  And lay our sins and sorrows at Thy feet;
On everlasting strength our weakness staying,
  Clothed in Thy robe of righteousness complete:
Then rising and refreshed, we leave Thy throne,
And follow on to know as we are known. Amen.
Jane Borthwick, 1854.

433   Naomi.   C. M.   Lowell Mason, 1836.

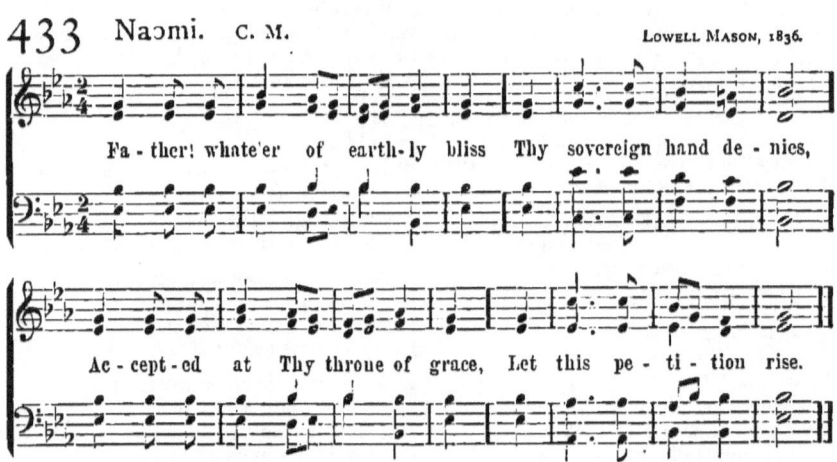

Father! whate'er of earth-ly bliss Thy sovereign hand de-nies,
Ac-cept-ed at Thy throne of grace, Let this pe-ti-tion rise.

2 "Give me a calm, a thankful heart,
  From every murmur free;
The blessings of Thy grace impart,
  And let me live to Thee.!

3 Let the sweet hope, that Thou art mine,
  My path of life attend;
Thy presence through my journey shine,
  And bless its happy end.
Anne Steele, 1760.

Prayer.

434 Retreat. L. M.
Thomas Hastings, 1840.

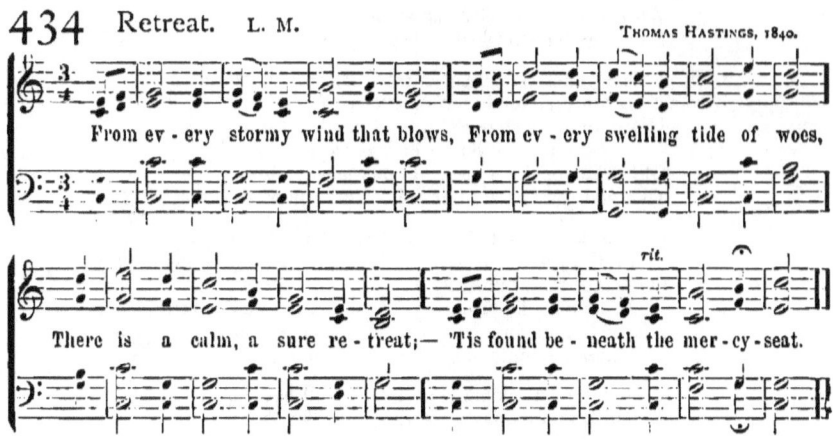

From ev-ery stormy wind that blows, From ev-ery swelling tide of woes,
There is a calm, a sure re-treat;— 'Tis found be-neath the mer-cy-seat.

2 There is a place where Jesus sheds
The oil of gladness on our heads,
A place, than all besides, more sweet;
It is the blood-bought mercy-seat.

3 There is a spot where spirits blend,
Where friend holds fellowship with friend;
Though sundered far, by faith they meet
Around one common mercy-seat.

4 There, there, on eagle wings we soar,
And time, and sense seem all no more;
And heaven comes down our souls to greet,
And glory crowns the mercy-seat.

5 Oh! may my hand forget her skill,
My tongue be silent, cold, and still,
This bounding heart forget to beat,
If I forget the mercy-seat!
Hugh Stowell, 1827.

435

Hast thou within a care so deep,
It chases from thine eyelids sleep?
To thy Redeemer take that care,
And change anxiety to prayer.

2 Hast thou a hope, from which thy heart
Would almost feel it death to part?
Entreat thy God that hope to crown,
Or give thee strength to lay it down.

3 Hast thou a friend, whose image dear
May prove an idol worshiped here?
Implore the Lord, that naught may be
A shade between Himself and thee.

4 Whate'er the care that breaks thy rest,
Whate'er the wish that swells thy breast,
Present to God that wish, that care,
And change anxiety to prayer.
Mrs. A. Julius.

436

Where high the heavenly temple stands,
The house of God not made with hands,
A great High Priest our nature wears,—
The Guardian of mankind appears.

2 Though now ascended up on high,
He bends on earth a brother's eye;
Partaker of the human name,
He knows the frailty of our frame.

3 Our Fellow-Sufferer yet retains
A fellow-feeling of our pains;
And still remembers, in the skies,
His tears, His agonies, and cries.

4 In every pang that rends the heart,
The Man of sorrows had a part;
He sympathizes with our grief,
And to the sufferer sends relief.
Michael Bruce, 1766.

Prayer.

437 Packer. C. M.   Hubert P. Main, 1869.

Oh! could I find from day to day, A nearness to my God;
Then should my hours glide sweet a-way, And live up-on Thy word.

2 Lord! I desire with Thee to live,
  A new from day to day,
In joys the world can never give,
  Nor ever take away.

3 O Jesus! come and rule my heart,
  And I'll be wholly thine;
And never, never more depart;
  For Thou art wholly mine.

4 Thus, till my last expiring breath,
  Thy goodness I'll adore;
And, when my flesh dissolves in death,
  My soul shall love Thee more.
         Benjamin Cleveland, 1790, a.

438
How can I, Lord, abide with Thee,
  Unless with Thee I speak?
How can I love Thee verily,
  And not Thy converse seek?

2 Doth not my soul, dear Lord, decline,
  Whene'er I faintly pray?—
When on that outstretched hand of Thine
  My doubting hand I lay?

3 My life were stopped, if prayer should fail,
  O soul of mine pray on!
Pray, weakling, till thou dost prevail,
  Pray till thy tears are gone!

4 Pray till thy Lord's own strength is thine!
  Still sweetly, strongly pray!
For ever breathe the air divine!
  Clasp thy dear Lord alway!
         Thomas H. Gill, 1856.

439
Alone with Thee, with Thee alone,
  I breathe the heavenly air;
Lord, what sweet wonders Thou hast shown
  Thy lonely worshipper!

2 Thou takest this rapt soul apart
  Into Thy secret place;
Thou keepest for this yearning heart
  The fullness of Thy grace.

3 For these blest eyes thou openest
  Full many a deep divine:
In these glad ears thou whisperest
  Some secret sweet of Thine.

4 The solitude, how populous!
  My Lord doth full appear;
The silence, how melodious!
  My Lord alone I hear.

5 O Lord, my God, mine all, mine own,
  Still grant these visits sweet;
Still meet Thy lover all alone!
  These blessed hours repeat.
         Thomas H. Gill, 1856.

Consecration.

440 Festival. 7s & 6s. P. — JOHN HEYWOOD.

Forth to the fight, ye ran-som'd, Might-y in God's own might,
Stem-ming the tide of bat-tle, Rout-ing the hosts of night.

CHORUS.
Lift ye the Blood-red Ban-ner, Wield ye the Spir-it's sword,
Raise ye the Christian's war cry— "The Cross of Christ the Lord!" A-men.

2 Fight, for the Lord is o'er you,
Fight, for He bids you fight;
There where the fray is thickest
Close with the hosts of night,
    Lift ye, &c.

3 Fear not the din of battle,
Follow where He has trod
Perfecting strength in weakness—
Jesus, Incarnate God!
    Lift ye, etc.

W. H. Kirby.

Consecration.

441 Disciple. 8s & 7s.   W. A. Mozart, ad. 1873.

Jesus, I my cross have taken, All to leave, and follow Thee;
Naked, poor, despised, forsaken, Thou, from hence, my all shalt be!
Perish every fond ambition, All I've sought, or hoped, or known;
Yet how rich is my condition, God and heaven are still my own!

2 Let the world despise and leave me;
  They have left my Saviour, too;
Human hearts and looks deceive me;
  Thou art not, like man, untrue;
And, while Thou shalt smile upon me,
  God of wisdom, love, and might!
Foes may hate, and friends may shun me;
  Show Thy face, and all is bright.

3 Man may trouble and distress me;
  'T will but drive me to Thy breast;
Life with trials hard may press me,
  Heaven will bring me sweeter rest:
Oh! 'tis not in grief to harm me;
  While Thy love is left to me;
Oh! 'twere not in joy to charm me,
  Were that joy unmixed with Thee.
              Henry Francis Lyte, 1825.

442

Sweet the moments, rich in blessing,
  Which before the cross I spend,
Life, and health, and peace possessing,
  From the sinner's dying Friend!
Here I'll sit, for ever viewing
  Mercy's streams in streams of blood:
Precious drops! my soul bedewing,
  Plead, and claim my peace, with God.

2 Here it is I find my heaven,
  While upon the Lamb I gaze;
Love I much?—I've much forgiven,—
  I'm a miracle of grace.
Love and grief my heart dividing,
  With my tears His feet I'll bathe;
Constant still in faith abiding,—
  Life deriving from His death.
              James Allen, 1757.
            Alt. *Walter Shirley, 1776.*

Consecration.

443 Roseville. 8s & 7s.
Hubert P. Main, 1875.

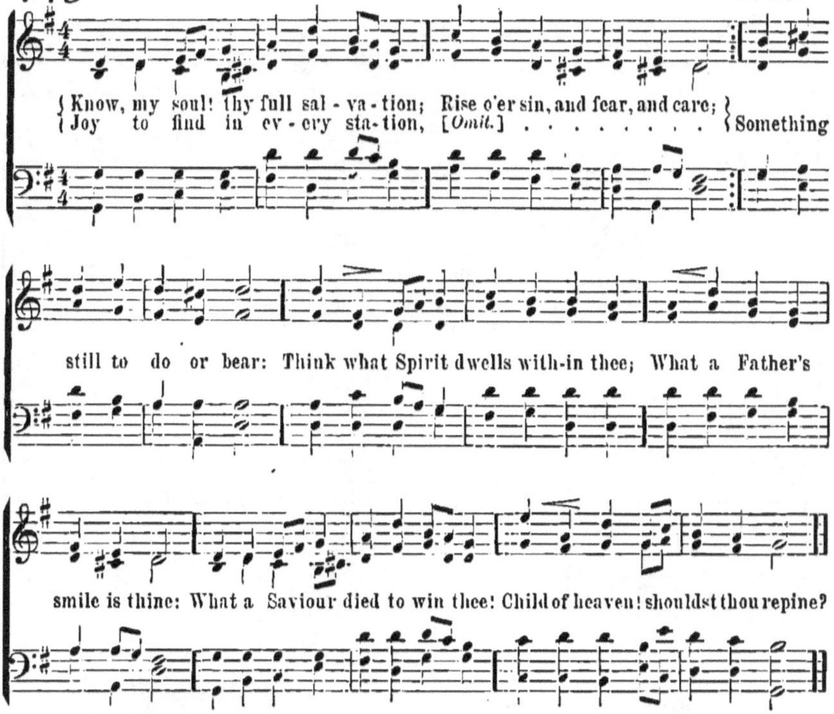

{ Know, my soul! thy full sal-va-tion; Rise o'er sin, and fear, and care; }
{ Joy to find in ev-ery sta-tion, [*Omit.*] . . . . } Something still to do or bear: Think what Spirit dwells with-in thee; What a Father's smile is thine: What a Saviour died to win thee! Child of heaven! shouldst thou repine?

2 Haste thee on from grace to glory,
   Armed by faith, and winged by prayer,
Heaven's eternal day's before thee,
   God's own hand shall guide thee there.
Soon shall close thy earthly mission,
   Swift shall pass thy pilgrim days,
Hope soon change to glad fruition,
   Faith to sight, and prayer to praise.
Henry Francis Lyte, 1825.

444 Pleyel. 7s.
Ignace Pleyel, 1790.

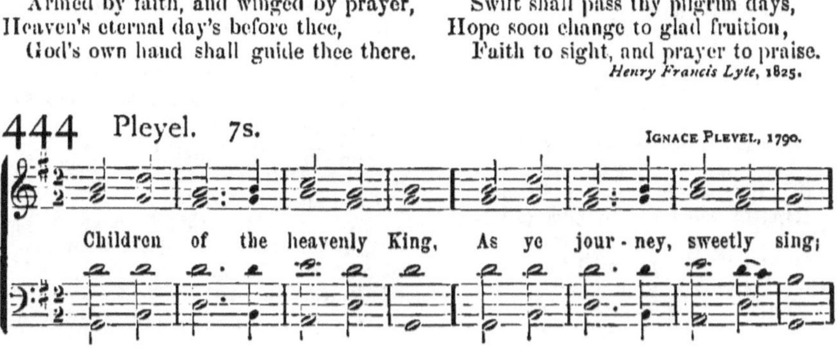

Children of the heavenly King, As ye jour-ney, sweetly sing;

Consecration.

Sing your Saviour's worthy praise, Glorious in His works and ways.

2 Ye are traveling home to God
In the way the fathers trod;
They are happy now, and ye
Soon their happiness shall see.

3 Shout, ye little flock, and blest!
You on Jesus' throne shall rest;
There your seat is now prepared;
There your kingdom and reward.

4 Fear not, brethren; joyful stand
On the borders of your land;
Jesus Christ, your Father's Son,
Bids you undismayed go on.

5 Lord, submissive make us go,
Gladly leaving all below;
Only Thou our Leader be,
And we still will follow Thee.
John Cennick, 1742.

445 Sentinel. 7s & 3. PHILIP ARMES, 1872.

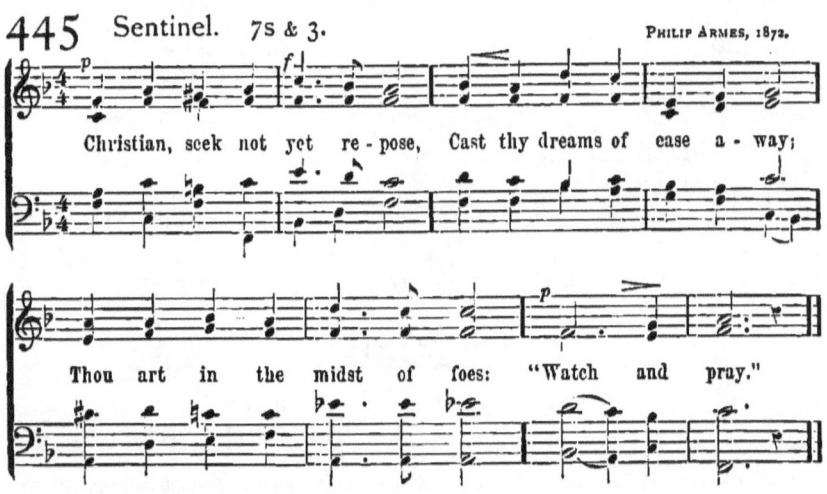

Christian, seek not yet repose, Cast thy dreams of ease away; Thou art in the midst of foes: "Watch and pray."

2 Principalities and powers,
  Must'ring their unseen array,
Wait for thy unguarded hours;
  "Watch and pray."

3 Gird thy heavenly armor on,
  Wear it ever night and day;
Near thee lurks the Evil One;
  "Watch and pray."

4 Hear the victors who o'ercame;
  Still they watch each warrior's way;
All with one deep voice exclaim
  "Watch and pray."

5 Hear, above all these, thy Lord,
  Him thou lovest to obey;
Hide within thy heart His word,
  "Watch and pray."
Charlotte Elliott, 1839, ab.

Consecration.

446 Maitland. C. M. GEORGE N. ALLEN, 1849.

I'm not ashamed to own my Lord, Or to defend His cause.
Maintain the honor of His word, The glory of His cross.

2 Jesus, my God!—I know His name,
His name is all my trust;
Nor will He put my soul to shame,
Nor let my hope be lost.

3 Firm as His throne His promise stands,
And He can well secure
What I've committed to His hands,
Till the decisive hour.
Isaac Watts, 1709.

447 Christmas. C. M. G. F. HANDEL, 1728.

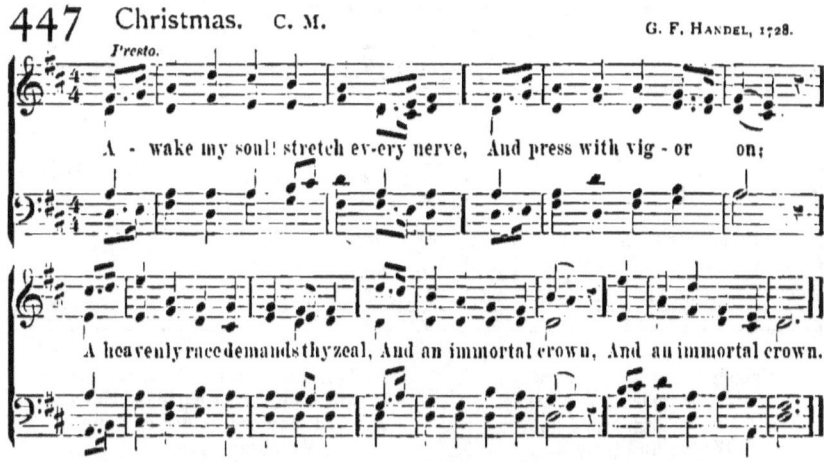

Presto.

Awake my soul! stretch ev-ery nerve, And press with vig-or on;
A heavenly race demands thy zeal, And an immortal crown, And an immortal crown.

2 A cloud of witnesses around
Hold thee in full survey;
Forget the steps already trod,
And onward urge thy way.

3 Blest Saviour! introduced by Thee,
Have I my race begun;
And, crowned with vict'ry, at Thy feet,
I'll lay my honors down.
Philip Doddridge, 1740.

Consecration.

448 St. Bartholomew. C. M.   A. MACDONALD.

The Son of God goes forth to war, A kingly crown to gain: His blood-red banner streams afar! Who follows in His train? Who best can drink His cup of woe, Triumphant over pain, Who patient bears His cross below, He follows in His train. A-men.

2 A glorious band, the chosen few,
  On whom the Spirit came:
Twelve radiant saints, their hope they knew,
  And mock'd the cross and flame:
They met the tyrant's brandish'd steel,
  The lion's gory mane;
They bow'd their necks the death to feel:
  Who follows in their train?

3 A noble army, men and boys,
  The matron and the maid,
Around the Saviour's throne rejoice,
  In robes of light arrayed:
They climb'd the steep ascent of heaven
  Through peril, toil, and pain:
O God! to us may grace be given
  To follow in their train.   Amen.
                            Reginald Heber, 1827.

Consecration.

449 Eisenach. P. M.   J. H. Schein, 1628.

Says Christ, our Champion,—follow Me; For-sake the world,—de-ny-ing
Your life its lust, and lib-er-ty, While liv-ing and when dy-ing;
Walk in My way, ye Christians all; Take up My cross and heed My call.

2 I am the light, I shine for you,
   With holiness o'erflowing;
I show the gleam of beacon true,
   And life with glory glowing;
Not one shall walk in gloom of night,
Who takes for guide My love, and light!

3 Then let us follow, confident,
   Our Master's love and leading,
And trust with faith and sure content,
   The Lord whose wounds are bleeding;
For he who flies the earthly strife,
Shall win no crown of heavenly life.
       Tr. *F. M. Finch*, 1880, ab.

450 Jerusalem. C. M.   L. Spohr, 1835.

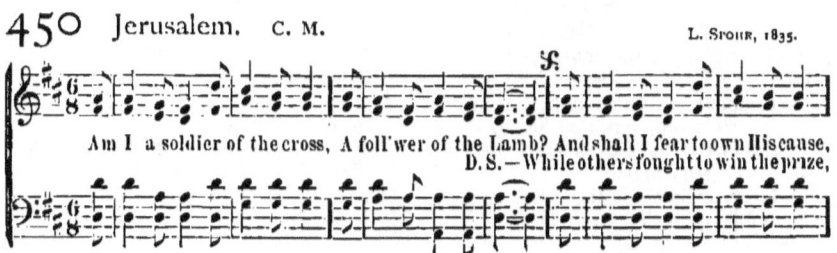

Am I a soldier of the cross, A foll'wer of the Lamb? And shall I fear to own His cause,
D. S.—While others fought to win the prize,

Consecration.

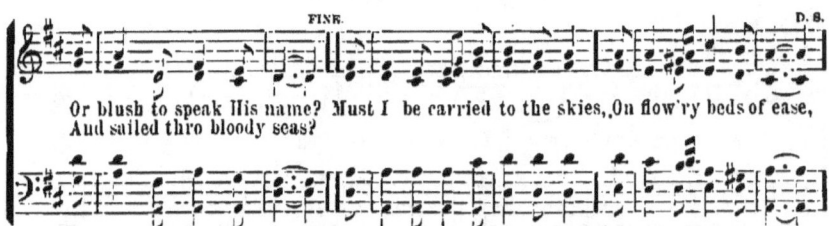

Or blush to speak His name? Must I be carried to the skies,
And sailed thro bloody seas? On flow'ry beds of ease,

2 Are there no foes for me to face?
 Must I not stem the flood?
Is this vile world a friend to grace,
 To help me on to God?
Sure, I must fight, if I would reign;
 Increase my courage, Lord!
I'll bear the toil, endure the pain,
 Supported by Thy word.
Isaac Watts, 1723.

That leads me to the Lamb!
Where is the blessedness I knew
 When first I saw the Lord?
Where is the soul-refreshing view
 Of Jesus and His word?

2 Return, O holy Dove! return,
 Sweet Messenger of rest!
I hate the sins that made Thee mourn,
 And drove Thee from my breast.
So shall my walk be close with God,
 Calm and serene my frame;
So purer light shall mark the road
 That leads me to the Lamb.
William Cowper, 1779.

451

Oh, for a closer walk with God,
 A calm and heavenly frame,
A light to shine upon the road,

452 Laban. S. M. *Lowell Mason, 1830.*

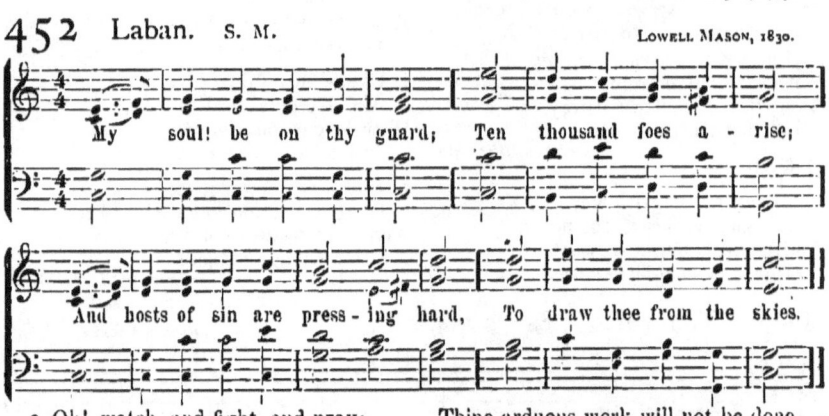

My soul! be on thy guard; Ten thousand foes arise;
And hosts of sin are pressing hard, To draw thee from the skies.

2 Oh! watch, and fight, and pray;
 The battle ne'er give o'er;
Renew it boldly every day,
 And help divine implore.
3 Ne'er think the vict'ry won,
 Nor once at ease sit down;

Thine arduous work will not be done,
 Till thou obtain the crown.
4 Fight on, my soul! till death
 Shall bring thee to thy God;
He'll take thee, at thy parting breath,
 Up to His bless'd abode.
George Heath, 1784.

Consecration.

453 Dennis. S. M.   Johann Georg Nägeli, 1792.

Andante.

A charge to keep I have, A God to glo-ri-fy;
A nev-er-dy-ing soul to save, And fit it for the sky:—

2 To serve the present age,
  My calling to fulfill,—
Oh! may it all my powers engage,—
  To do my Master's will.

3 Arm me with jealous care,
  As in Thy sight to live;
And, Oh! Thy servant, Lord! prepare
  A strict account to give.

4 Help me to watch and pray,
  And on Thyself rely;
Assured, if I my trust betray,
  I shall for ever die.
              Charles Wesley, 1762.

454

Come and rejoice with me;
  For once my heart was poor,
And I have found a treasury
  Of love, a boundless store.

2 Come and rejoice with me:
  I, who was sick at heart,
Have met with One who knows my case,
  And knows the healing art.

3 Come and rejoice with me;
  For I have found a Friend
Who knows my heart's most secret depths,
  Yet loves me without end.

4 I knew not of His love,
  And He had loved so long,
With love so faithful and so deep,
  So tender and so strong!

5 And now I know it all,
  Have heard and know His voice,
And hear it still from day to day:
  Can I enough rejoice?
              Elizabeth Charles, 1867.

455 Tamworth. 8s 7s & 4.   Charles Lockhart, 1769.

Marcato.

{ Guide me, O Thou great Je-ho-vah! Pilgrim through this bar-ren land; {
{ I am weak, but Thou art might-y; Hold me with Thy powerful hand: }

Consecration.

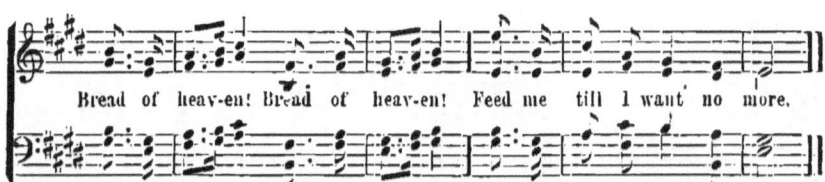

Bread of heav-en! Bread of heav-en! Feed me till I want no more.

2 Open now the crystal Fountain,
  Whence the healing streams do flow;
Let the fiery cloudy pillar
  Lead me all my journey through:
    Strong Deliverer!
Be Thou still my Strength and Shield.

3 When I tread the verge of Jordan,
  Bid my anxious fears subside;
Bear me through the swelling current;
  Land me safe on Canaan's side:
    Songs of praises,
I will ever give to Thee.
              William Williams, 1771.

456 Bethany. 6s & 4s.   Lowell Mason, 1858.

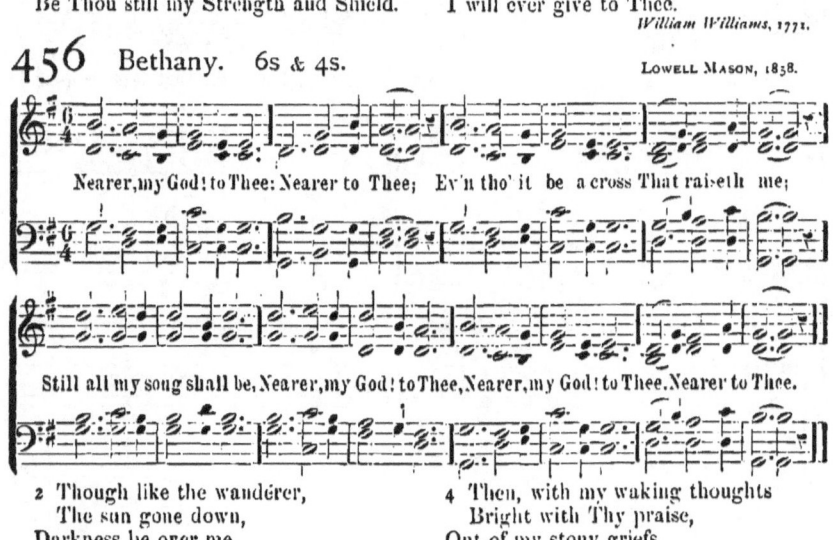

Nearer, my God! to Thee: Nearer to Thee; Ev'n tho' it be a cross That raiseth me;

Still all my song shall be, Nearer, my God! to Thee, Nearer, my God! to Thee, Nearer to Thee.

2 Though like the wanderer,
    The sun gone down,
  Darkness be over me,
    My rest a stone,
  Yet, in my dreams, I'd be
  Nearer, my God! to Thee,—
    Nearer to Thee.

3 There let the way appear,
    Steps unto heaven,
  All that Thou send'st to me,
    In mercy given;
  Angels to beckon me
  Nearer, my God! to Thee,—
    Nearer to Thee.

4 Then, with my waking thoughts
    Bright with Thy praise,
  Out of my stony griefs
    Bethel I'll raise;
  So by my woes to be
  Nearer, my God! to Thee,
    Nearer to Thee.

5 Or if, on joyful wing,
    Cleaving the sky,
  Sun, moon and stars forgot,
    Upward I fly,
  Still all my song shall be,
  Nearer, my God! to Thee,—
    Nearer to Thee.
              Sarah Flower Adams, 1840.

Consecration.

457   He Leadeth Me.   L. M.   Wm. B. Bradbury, 1864.

He lead-eth me: Oh bless-ed thought, Oh words with heavenly comfort fraught,
What-e'er I do, wher-e'er I be, Still 'tis God's hand that lead-eth me.

CHORUS.
He lead-eth me, He lead-eth me, By His own hand He lead-eth me;
His faithful follower I would be, For by His hand He lead-eth me.

2 Sometimes 'mid scenes of deepest gloom,
Sometimes where Eden's bowers bloom,
By waters still, o'er troubled sea,
Still 'tis His hand that leadeth me.

3 Lord, I would clasp Thy hand in mine,
Nor ever murmur nor repine;
Content, whatever lot I see,
Since 'tis my God that leadeth me.

4 And when my task on earth is done,
When, by Thy grace, the victory's won,
E'en death's cold wave I will not flee,
Since God thro' Jordan leadeth me.
                                         Jos. H. Gilmore, 1861.

Consecration.

458 St. Andrew. 6s & 5s. J. B. Dykes, 1868.

Christian, dost thou see them On the holy ground, How the powers of darkness Rage thy steps around? Christian, up and smite them, Counting gain but loss; In the strength that cometh By the Holy Cross. A-men.

2 Christian! dost thou feel them,
  How they work within,
Striving, tempting, luring,
  Goading into sin?
Christian! never tremble;
  Never be down-cast;
Gird thee for the battle,
  Watch and pray and fast.

3 Christian! dost thou hear them,
  How they speak thee fair?
"Always fast and vigil?
  Always watch and prayer?"
Christian! answer boldly:
  "While I breathe I pray!"
Peace shall follow battle,
  Night shall end in day.

Tr. *J. M. Neale*, 1862.

Consecration.

459 St. Gertrude. 6s & 5s.   A. S. SULLIVAN, 1872.

  2 Like a mighty army,
     Moves the Church of God:
  Brothers, we are treading
     Where the saints have trod.
  We are not divided,
     All one body we,
  One in hope, in doctrine,
     One in charity.

  3 Crowns and thrones may perish,
     Kingdoms rise and wane,
  But the Church of Jesus
     Constant will remain.

Gates of hell can never
    'Gainst that Church prevail:
We have Christ's own promise,
    And that cannot fail.

4 Onward, then, ye faithful,
    Join our happy throng,
Blend with ours your voices,
    In the triumph-song:
Glory, laud, and honor,
    Unto Christ the King:
This, through countless ages,
    Men and angels sing.
             S. Baring-Gould, 1865.

Consecration.

460 St. Albans. 6s & 5s.   F. J. Haydn.

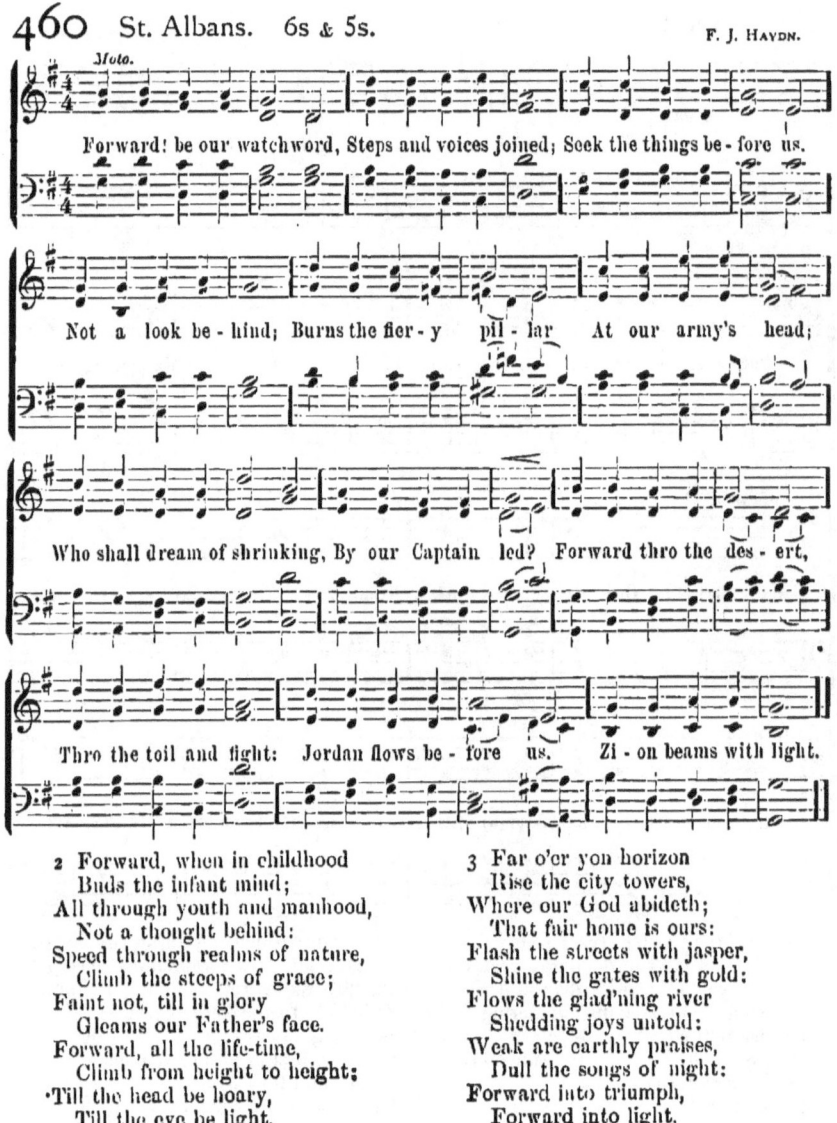

Forward! be our watchword, Steps and voices joined; Seek the things be-fore us. Not a look be-hind; Burns the fier-y pil-lar At our army's head; Who shall dream of shrinking, By our Captain led? Forward thro the des-ert, Thro the toil and fight: Jordan flows be-fore us. Zi-on beams with light.

2 Forward, when in childhood
  Buds the infant mind;
All through youth and manhood,
  Not a thought behind:
Speed through realms of nature,
  Climb the steeps of grace;
Faint not, till in glory
  Gleams our Father's face.
Forward, all the life-time,
  Climb from height to height;
Till the head be hoary,
  Till the eve be light.

3 Far o'er yon horizon
  Rise the city towers,
Where our God abideth;
  That fair home is ours:
Flash the streets with jasper,
  Shine the gates with gold:
Flows the glad'ning river
  Shedding joys untold:
Weak are earthly praises,
  Dull the songs of night:
Forward into triumph,
  Forward into light.

Henry Alford, 1865.

Consecration.

461 Victoria. L. M.   Henry Lahee.

When, marshaled on the night-ly plain, The glittering host be-stud the sky,

One star a-lone of all the train, Can fix the sin-ner's wandering eye:

Marcato.
Hark! hark! to God the chorus breaks, From ev-ery host, from ev-ery gem;

But one a-lone the Saviour speaks;— It is the Star of Beth-le-hem.

2 Once on the raging seas I rode;
   The storm was loud, the night was dark;
The ocean yawned, and rudely blowed
   The wind, that tossed my foundering bark:
Deep horror then my vitals froze;
   Death-struck, I ceased the tide to stem;
When suddenly a star arose;—
   It was the Star of Bethlehem.

3 It was my guide, my light, my all;
   It bade my dark forebodings cease;
And, thro the storm, and danger's thrall,
   It led me to the port of peace:
Now, safely moored, my peril's o'er,
   I'll sing, first in night's diadem,
For ever and for evermore,
   The Star—the Star of Bethlehem!
                      Henry Kirke White, 1804.

Consecration.

462

Arm these Thy soldiers, mighty Lord,
With shield of faith and Spirit's sword;
Forth to the battle may they go,
And boldly fight against the foe.
With banner of the cross unfurl'd,
And by it overcome the world;
And so at last receive from Thee
The palm and crown of victory.

2 Come, ever blessèd Spirit, come,
And make Thy servant's heart Thy home;
May each a living temple be,
Hallow'd for ever, Lord, to Thee;
Enrich that temple's holy shrine
With sevenfold gifts of grace divine;
With wisdom, light, and knowledge bless,
Strength, counsel, fear, and godliness.
Christopher Wordsworth, 1862.

463 Siloam. C. M.   I. B. WOODBURY, 1842.

Oh! for a heart to praise my God,—A heart from sin set free;
A heart that al-ways feels Thy blood So free-ly spilt for me!—

2 A heart resigned, submissive, meek,
My dear Redeemer's throne;
Where only Christ is heard to speak,
Where Jesus reigns alone!—

3 An humble, lowly, contrite heart,
Believing, true, and clean,
Which neither life nor death can part
From Him that dwells within!—

4 A heart in every thought renewed,
And filled with love divine;
Perfect, and right, and pure, and good,
A copy, Lord! of Thine.

5 Thy nature, gracious Lord! impart;
Come quickly from above;
Write Thy new name upon my heart,—
Thy new, best name of Love.
Charles Wesley, 1742.

464

Oh! may my heart, by grace renewed,
Be my Redeemer's throne;
And be my stubborn will subdued,
His government to own.

2 Let deep repentance, faith, and love,
Be joined with godly fear;
And all my conversation prove
My heart to be sincere.

3 Preserve me from the snares of sin,
Through my remaining days;
And in me let each virtue shine
To my Redeemer's praise.

4 Let lively hope my soul inspire;
Let warm affections rise;
And may I wait with strong desire,
To mount above the skies!
John Fawcett, 1782.

Submission.

465 Diman. L. M.   J. E. SWEETSER, 1870. (?)

Oh, deem not they are blest a-lone, Whose lives a peace-ful ten-or keep;
For God, who pit-ies man, hath shown A blessing for the eyes that weep.

2 The light of smiles shall fill again
   The lids that overflow with tears;
And weary hours of woe and pain
   Are promises of happy years.

3 There is a day of sunny rest
   For every dark and troubled night;
And grief may bide an evening guest,
   But joy shall come with early light.

4 Nor let the good man's trust depart,
   Though life its common gifts deny;
Though with a pierced and broken heart,
   And spurned of men, he goes to die.

5 For God has marked each sorrowing day
   And numbered every secret tear,
And heaven's long age of bliss shall pay,
   For all His children suffered here.
                 William Cullen Bryant, 1824.

466

IF life in sorrow must be spent,
So be it; I am well content;
And meekly wait my last remove,
Desiring only trustful love.

2 No bliss I'll seek, but to fulfil
In life, in death, Thy perfect will;
No succor in my woes I want,
But what my Lord is pleased to grant.

3 Our days are numbered; let us spare
Our anxious hearts a needless care;
'Tis Thine to number out our days;
'Tis ours to give them to Thy praise.

4 Faith is our only business here—
Faith, simple, constant, and sincere;
Oh, blessed days Thy servants see!
Thus spent, O Lord! in pleasing Thee.
                 Madame Guyon, 1710.

467

FRIEND of the friendless and the faint!
Where shall I lodge my deep complaint?
Where, but with Thee, whose open door
Invites the helpless and the poor?

2 Did ever mourner plead with Thee,
And Thou refuse that mourner's plea?
Does not the word still fixed remain,
That none shall seek Thy face in vain?

3 That were a grief I could not bear,
Didst Thou not hear and answer prayer;
But a prayer-hearing, answering God
Supports me under every load.

4 Poor though I am, despised, forgot,
Yet God, my God, forgets me not;
And he is safe, and must succeed,
For whom the Lord vouchsafes to plead.
                 William Cowper, 1772.

Submission.

468 · Baxter. 6s. U. C. Burnap, 1868.

Thy way, not mine, O Lord, How-ev-er dark it be:
Lead me by Thine own hand, Choose out the path for me.
Smooth let it be or rough, It will be still the best;
Wind-ing or straight, it leads Right on-ward to Thy rest. A-men.

2 I dare not choose my lot;
  I would not, if I might;
Choose Thou for me, my God;
  So shall I walk aright.
Take Thou my cup, and it
  With joy or sorrow fill,
As best to Thee may seem,
  Choose Thou my good and ill.

3 Choose Thou for me my friends,
  My sickness or my health;
Choose Thou my cares for me,
  My poverty or wealth.
Not mine, not mine the choice,
  In things or great or small;
Be Thou my guide, my strength,
  My wisdom, and my all.
            Tr. *Horatius Bonar*, 1856.

Submission.

469 Jewett. 6s. CARL MARIA VON WEBER, 1820.

My Jesus, as Thou wilt: Oh may Thy will be mine; Into Thy hand of love I would my all resign. Through sorrow or through joy, Conduct me as Thine own, And help me still to say, My Lord, Thy will be done.

2 My Jesus! as Thou wilt!
  Though seen through many a tear.
Let not my star of hope
  Grow dim or disappear:
Since Thou on earth hast wept,
  And sorrowed oft alone,
If I must weep with Thee,
  My Lord! Thy will be done!

3 My Jesus! as Thou wilt!
  All shall be well for me;
Each changing future scene
  I gladly trust with Thee:
Straight to my home above
  I travel calmly on,
And sing, in life or death,—
  My Lord! Thy will be done!
    Ger., *Benjamin Schmolke*, 1716.
    Tr., *Jane Borthwick*, 1854.

470 Manchester. C. M. R. WAINWRIGHT, 1774. (f)

O Thou whose bounty fills my cup With every blessing meet!

Submission.

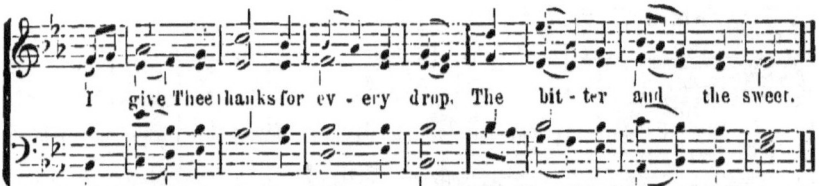

I give Thee thanks for ev-ery drop, The bit-ter and the sweet.

2 I praise Thee for the desert road,
And for the river-side,
For all Thy goodness hath bestowed,
And all Thy grace denied.

3 I thank Thee both for smile and frown,
And for the gain and loss;
I praise Thee for the future crown,
And for the present cross.

4 I bless Thee for the glad increase,
And for the waning joy;
And for this strange, this settled peace,
Which nothing can destroy.
Jane Fox Crewdson, 1860.

471 Troyte's Chant. A. H. D. TROYTE, 1857.

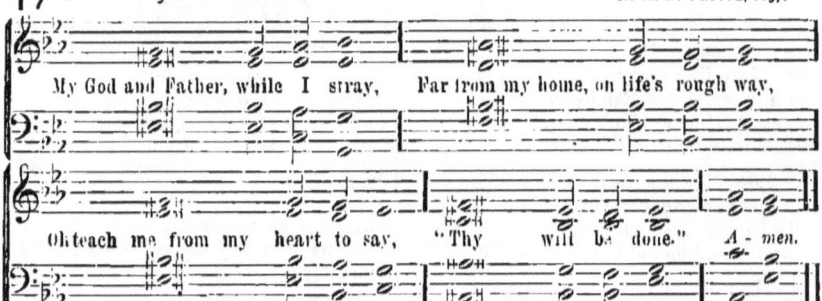

My God and Father, while I stray, Far from my home, on life's rough way,
Oh teach me from my heart to say, "Thy will be done." A-men.

472

2 Though dark my path, and | sad my | lot,
Let me be still and | murmur | not,
And breathe the prayer di-| vinely | taught,
   " Thy | will be | done."

3 If Thou shouldst call me | to re-| sign
What most I prize—it | ne'er was | mine;
I only yield Thee | what was | Thine—
   " Thy | will be | done."

4 Renew my will from | day to | day,
Blend it with Thine, and | take a-| way
All that now makes it | hard to | say,
   " Thy | will be | done."

5 Let but my fainting | heart be | blest
With Thy sweet Spirit | for its | Guest,
My God, to Thee I | leave the | rest;
   " Thy | will be | done." Amen.
Charlotte Elliott, 1834.

God of my life! Thy | boundless | grace;
Chose, pardoned, and a-| dopted | me;
My Rest, my Home, my | Dwelling | place,
Father! I | come to | Thee.

2 Jesus, my Hope, my | Rock, my | Shield!
Whose precious blood was | shed for | me,
Into Thy hands my | soul I | yield;
Saviour! I | come to | Thee.

3 Spirit of glory | and of | God!
Long hast Thou deigned my | guide to | be;
Now, be Thy comfort | sweet be-| stowed!
My God! I | come to | Thee.

4 I come to join that | countless | host,
Who praise Thy name un-| ceasing-| ly;
Bless'd Father, Son, and | Holy | Ghost!
My God! I | come to | Thee.
Charlotte Elliott, 1841.

Submission.

473. Mercy. 7s.
L. M. Gottschalk, 1854, ad. by H., 1865.

Day by day the man-na fell; Oh, to learn this les-son well! Still by con-stant mer-cy fed, Give us, Lord, our dai-ly bread.

2 "Day by day," the promise reads,
Daily strength for daily needs;
Cast foreboding fears away,
Take the manna of to-day.

3 Lord, our times are in Thy hand;
All our sanguine hopes have plann'd
To Thy wisdom we resign,
And would mould our wills to Thine.

4 Thou our daily task shalt give;
Day by day to Thee we live;
So shall added years fulfil
Not our own, our Father's will.
Josiah Conder, 1836.

474
Wait, my soul! upon the Lord,
To His gracious promise flee,
Laying hold upon His word,—
"As thy days, thy strength shall be."

2 If the sorrows of thy case
Seem peculiar still to thee,
God has promised needful grace;
"As thy days thy strength shall be."

3 Days of trial, days of grief,
In succession thou mayest see;
This is still thy sweet relief,—
"As thy days thy strength shall be."

4 Rock of ages! I'm secure,
With Thy promise, full and free,
Faithful, positive, and sure,—
"As thy days thy strength shall be."
William F. Lloyd, 1835.

475
Thine for ever—God of love!
Hear us from Thy throne above;
Thine for ever may we be,
Here and in eternity.

2 Thine for ever—Lord of life!
Shield us through the earthly strife;
Thou, the Life, the Truth, the Way,
Guide us to the realms of day.

3 Thine for ever—Oh! how bless'd
They who find in Thee their rest;
Saviour, Guardian, heavenly Friend!
Oh! defend us to the end.
Mary F. Maude, 1848.

476
Cast thy burden on the Lord,
Only lean upon His word;
Thou wilt soon have cause to bless
His eternal faithfulness.

2 He sustains thee by His hand,
He enables thee to stand;
Those, whom Jesus once hath loved,
From His grace are never moved.
John Cennick, 1745.

Submission

477 St. Bede. C. M.   John B. Dykes, 1856.

Father, I know that all my life Is portioned out for me;
The changes that will surely come I do not fear to see;
I ask Thee for a present mind, Intent on pleasing Thee.

2 I would not have the restless will
   That hurries to and fro,
Seeking for some great thing to do,
   Or secret thing to know:
I would be treated as a child,
   And guided where I go.

3 And if some things I do not ask
   Among my blessings be,
I'd have my spirit filled the more
   With grateful love to Thee;
More careful, not to serve Thee much,
   But please Thee perfectly.

4 Briars and thorns beset my path
   That call for patient care;
There is a cross in every lot,
   And earnest need for prayer;
But lowly hearts, that lean on Thee,
   Are happy anywhere.

5 In service which Thy will appoints
   There are no bonds for me;
My inmost heart is taught the truth
   That makes Thy children free;
A life of self-renouncing love
   Is one of liberty.

Anna Laetitia Waring, 1850, alt.

Submission.

478 Peace. S. M.   Alex. E. Ffsca.

"My times are in Thy hand:" My God! I wish them there;
My life, my soul, my all, I leave Entirely to Thy care.

2 "My times are in Thy hand,"
  Whatever they may be;
Pleasing or painful, dark or bright,
  As best may seem to Thee.

3 "My times are in Thy hand,"
  Why should I doubt or fear?
My Father's hand will never cause
  His child a needless tear.

4 "My times are in Thy hand;"
  I'll always trust in Thee,
Till I possess the promised land,
  And all Thy glory see.
                  William F. Lloyd, 1835.

479

Commit thou all thy griefs
  And ways into His hands,
To His sure truth and tender care,
  Who earth and heaven commands.

2 Give to the winds thy fears;
  Hope, and be undismayed;
God hears thy sighs and counts thy tears,
  God shall lift up thy head.

3 Through waves, and clouds, and storms,
  He gently clears thy way;
Wait thou His time; so shall this night
  Soon end in joyous day.

4 Leave to His sovereign sway
  To choose, and to command;
So shalt thou wondering, own His way
  How wise, how strong His hand!
           Ger., *Paul Gerhardt,* 1666.
              Tr., *John Wesley,* 1739.

480

Rest for the toiling hand,
  Rest for the anxious brow,
Rest for the weary, way-worn feet,
  Rest from all labor now;—

2 Rest for the fevered brain,
  Rest for the throbbing eye;
Thro these parched lips of thine no more
  Shall pass the moan or sigh.

3 Soon shall the trump of God
  Give out the welcome sound,
That shakes thy silent chamber-walls,
  And breaks the sealed ground.

4 Ye dwellers in the dust,
  Awake! come forth and sing;
Sharp has your frost of winter been,
  But bright shall be your spring.

5 'T was sown in weakness here:
  'Twill then be raised in power;
That which was sown an earthly seed,
  Shall rise a heavenly flower!
                 H. Bonar, 1857.

Submission.

481 Gorton. S. M. — L. van Beethoven.

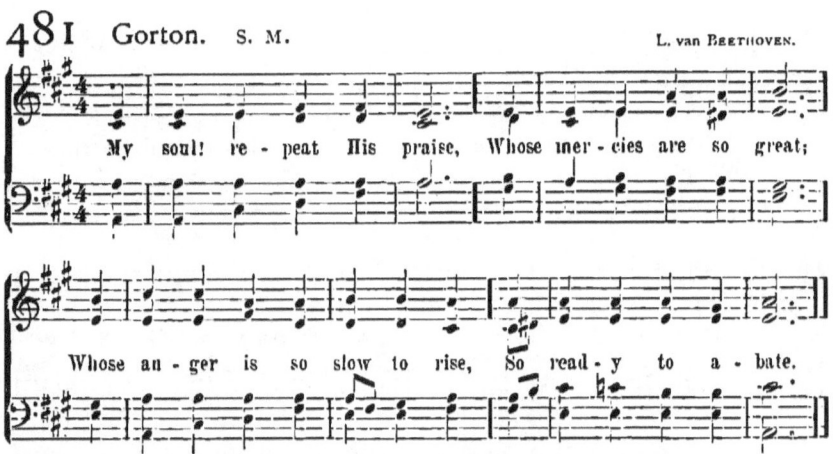

My soul! re-peat His praise, Whose mer-cies are so great;
Whose an-ger is so slow to rise, So read-y to a-bate.

2 God will not always chide;
  And, when His strokes are felt,
His strokes are fewer than our crimes,
  And lighter than our guilt.

3 High as the heavens are raised
  Above the ground we tread,
So far the riches of His grace
  Our highest thoughts exceed.

4 His power subdues our sins,
  And His forgiving love,
Far as the east is from the west,
  Doth all our guilt remove.
                    Isaac Watts, 1719.

4 I know Thy will is right,
  Though it may seem severe;
Thy path is still unsullied light,
  Though dark it may appear.

5 Jesus for me hath died;
  Thy Son Thou didst not spare;
His pierced hands, His bleeding side,
  Thy love for me declare.

6 Here my poor heart can rest;
  My God! it cleaves to Thee:
Thy will is Love; Thine end is bless'd;
  All work for good to me.
                    James George Deck, 1843.

482

It is Thy hand, my God!
  My sorrow comes from Thee;
I bow beneath Thy chastening rod,
  'Tis love that bruises me.

2 I would not murmur, Lord!
  Before Thee I am dumb;
Lest I should breathe one murm'ring word,
  To Thee for help I come.

3 My God! Thy name is Love;
  A Father's hand is Thine;
With tearful eyes I look above,
  And cry, "Thy will be mine!"

483

Jesus, who knows full well
  The heart of every saint,
Invites us, all our grief to tell,
  To pray and never faint.

2 Jesus, the Lord, will hear
  His chosen when they cry;
Yes, though He may awhile forbear,
  He'll help them from on high.

3 Then let us earnest cry,
  And never faint in prayer;
He sees, He hears, and, from on high,
  Will make our cause His care.
                    John Newton, 1779. a.

Submission.

484 Lucius. C. M.   GEORGE KINGSLEY, 1853.

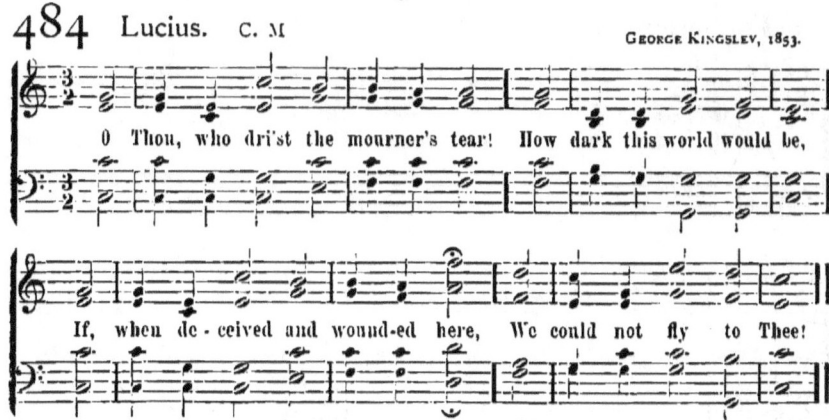

O Thou, who dri'st the mourner's tear! How dark this world would be,
If, when deceived and wounded here, We could not fly to Thee!

2 The friends, who in our sunshine live,
  When winter comes, are flown;
And he, who has but tears to give,
  Must weep those tears alone.

3 Oh! who would bear life's stormy doom,
  Did not Thy wing of love
Come, brightly wafting, thro the gloom,
  Our peace-branch from above?

4 Then sorrow, touched by Thee, grows bright,
  With more than rapture's ray;
As darkness shows us worlds of light
  We never saw by day.
  Thomas Moore, 1816.

485

IF Christ is mine, then all is mine,
  And more than angels know;
Both present things and things to come,
  And grace and glory too.

2 If He is mine, let friends forsake,
  And earthly comforts flee:
He, the Dispenser of all good,
  Is more than these to me.

3 Let Jesus tell me He is mine;
  I nothing want beside:
My soul shall at the Fountain live,
  When all the streams are dried.
  Benjamin Beddome, 1776.

486

I LOVE to kiss each print where Thou
  Hast set Thine unseen feet:
I cannot fear Thee, blessèd Will,
  Thine empire is so sweet.

2 I have no cares, O blessèd Will,
  For all my cares are Thine;
I live in triumph, Lord, for Thou
  Hast made Thy triumphs mine.

3 Ill that He blesses is our good,
  And unblest good is ill;
And all is right that seems most wrong,
  If it be His sweet will.
  F. W. Faber, 1849.

487

WHATE'ER my God ordains is right;
  His will is ever just;
Howe'er He orders now my cause,
  I will be still and trust.

2 Whate'er my God ordains is right;
  Though I the cup must drink
That bitter seems to my faint heart,
  I will not fear nor shrink;

3 Whate'er my God ordains is right;
  My Light, my Life is He,
Who cannot will me aught but good;
  I trust Him utterly.
  Fr. S. Rodigast, 1675.
  Tr. Catherine Winkworth, 1858, alt.

Submission.

488 Comfort. 11S & 10S. HUBERT P. MAIN, 1881.

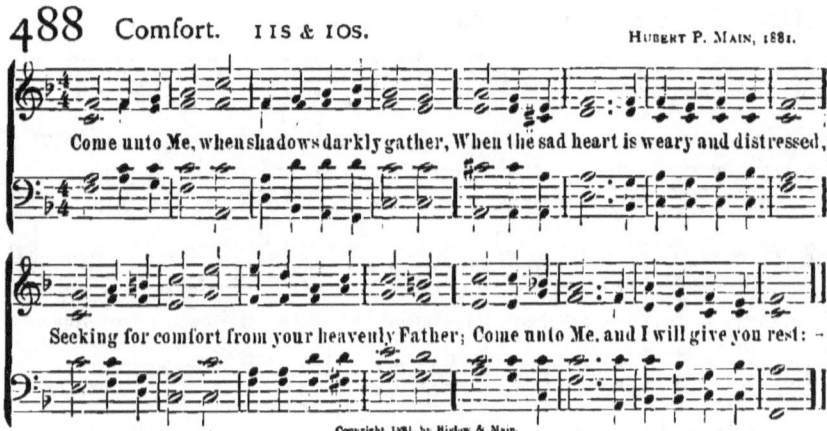

Come unto Me, when shadows darkly gather, When the sad heart is weary and distressed, Seeking for comfort from your heavenly Father; Come unto Me, and I will give you rest:—

Copyright, 1881, by Biglow & Main.

2 Ye, who have mourned, when the spring flowers were taken,
  When the ripe fruit fell richly to the ground,
When the loved slept, in brighter homes to waken,
  Where their pale brows with spirit-wreaths are crowned.

3 Large are the mansions in thy Father's dwelling,
  Glad are the homes that sorrows never dim;
Sweet are the harps in holy music swelling,
  Soft are the tones which raise the heavenly hymn.

4 There, like an Eden blossoming in gladness,
  Bloom the fair flowers the earth too rudely pressed;
Come unto Me, all ye who droop in sadness,
  Come unto Me, and I give you rest!
                            Catherine H. Waterman, 1848.

489 Thy Will be Done. LOWELL MASON, 1841.

"Thy will be | done!" || In devious way
The hurrying stream of | life may | run; ||
Yet still our grateful hearts shall say, |
    "Thy will be | done!"

2 "Thy will be | done!" || If o'er us shine,
A gladdening and a | pros-perous | sun, ||
This prayer will make it more divine—|
    "Thy will be | done!"

3 "Thy will be done!" || Tho' shrouded o'er
Our | path with | gloom, || one comfort—one
Is ours:—to breathe, while we adore, |
    "Thy will be | done!"
                            John Bowring, 1823.

Submission.

490 Paraclete. 11s & 10s. SAMUEL WEBBE, 1790.

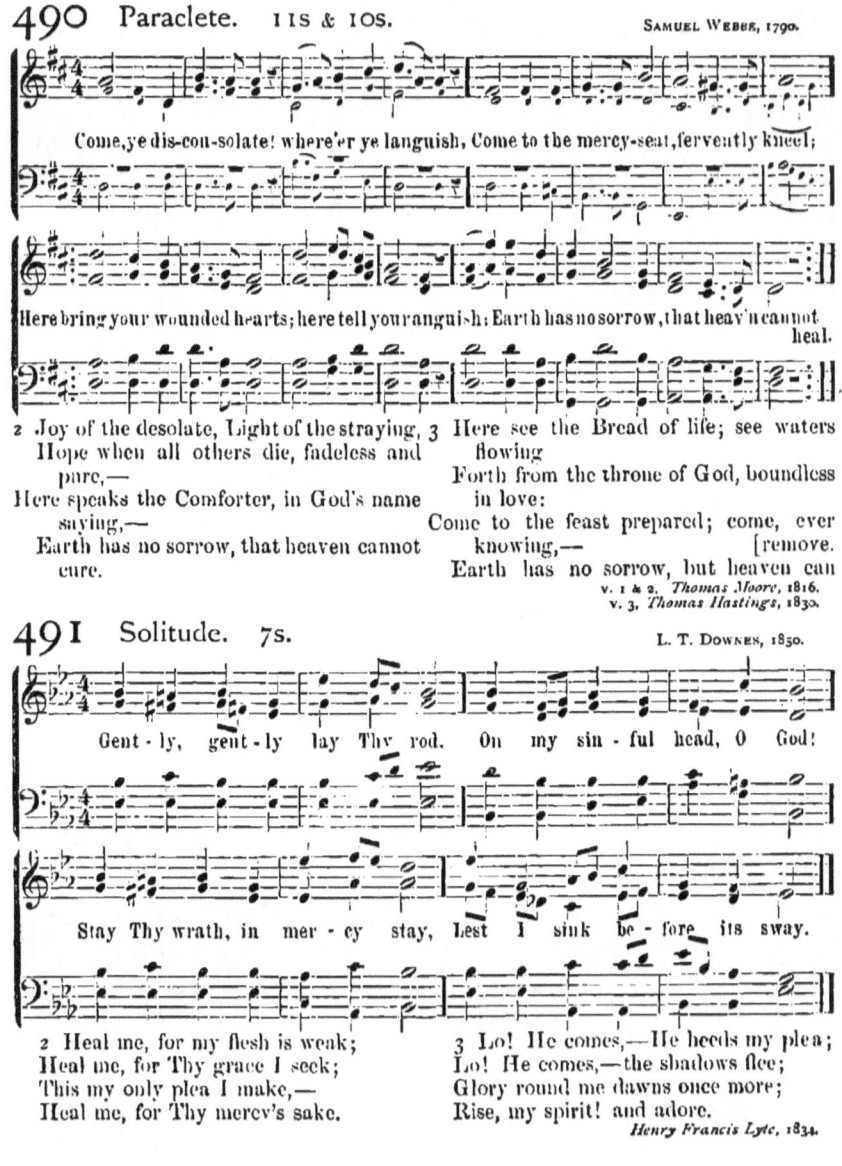

Come, ye dis-con-solate! where'er ye languish, Come to the mercy-seat, fervently kneel;

Here bring your wounded hearts; here tell your anguish; Earth has no sorrow, that heav'n cannot heal.

2 Joy of the desolate, Light of the straying,
Hope when all others die, fadeless and pure,—
Here speaks the Comforter, in God's name saying,—
Earth has no sorrow, that heaven cannot cure.

3 Here see the Bread of life; see waters flowing
Forth from the throne of God, boundless in love:
Come to the feast prepared; come, ever knowing,— [remove.
Earth has no sorrow, but heaven can
v. 1 & 2. *Thomas Moore*, 1816.
v. 3. *Thomas Hastings*, 1830.

491 Solitude. 7s. L. T. DOWNES, 1850.

Gent-ly, gent-ly lay Thy rod, On my sin-ful head, O God!

Stay Thy wrath, in mer-cy stay, Lest I sink be-fore its sway.

2 Heal me, for my flesh is weak;
Heal me, for Thy grace I seek;
This my only plea I make,—
Heal me, for Thy mercy's sake.

3 Lo! He comes,—He heeds my plea;
Lo! He comes,—the shadows flee;
Glory round me dawns once more;
Rise, my spirit! and adore.
Henry Francis Lyte, 1834.

The Ministry.

492 Medway. L. M.   G. B. PERGOLESI. 1730.

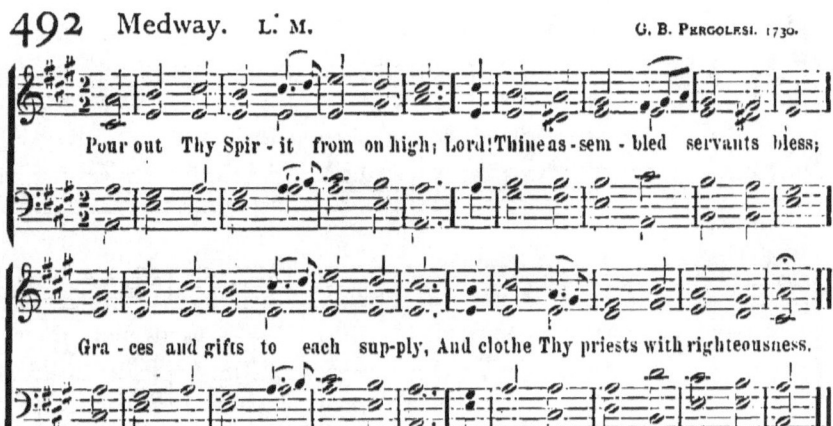

Pour out Thy Spirit from on high, Lord! Thine assembled servants bless; Graces and gifts to each supply, And clothe Thy priests with righteousness.

2 Within Thy temple, when we stand,
To teach the truth, as taught by Thee,
Saviour! like stars in Thy right hand,
The angels of the churches be!

3 Wisdom and zeal, and faith impart,
Firmness with meekness from above,
To bear Thy people on our heart,
And love the souls whom Thou dost love:

4 To watch and pray, and never faint;
By day and night, strict guard to keep;
To warn the sinner, cheer the saint,
Nourish Thy lambs, and feed Thy sheep.

5 Then, when our work is finished here,
In humble hope, our charge resign;
When the chief Shepherd shall appear,
O God! may they and we be Thine.
James Montgomery, 1825.

493
The solemn service now is done;
The vow is pledged, the toil begun;
Seal Thou, O God! the oath above,
And ratify the pledge of love.

2 The Shepherd of Thy people bless;
Gird him with Thine own holiness:
In duty may his pleasure be,
His glory in his zeal for Thee.

3 Here let the ardent prayer arise,
Faith fix its grasp beyond the skies,
The tear of penitence be shed,
And myriads to the Saviour led.

4 Come, Spirit! here consent to dwell;
The mists of earth and sin dispel:
Bless'd Saviour! Thine own rights maintain;
Supreme in every bosom reign.

5 Oh! let our humble worship be
A grateful tribute, Lord! to Thee;
And may these hallowed scenes of love
Fit us for purer joys above.
Samuel F. Smith, 1843.

494
We bid Thee welcome, in the name
Of Jesus, our exalted Head;
Come as a servant; so He came,
And we receive thee in His stead.

2 Come as a shepherd; guard and keep
This fold from hell, and earth, and sin;
Nourish the lambs, and feed the sheep,
The wounded heal, the lost bring in.

3 Come as a teacher, sent from God,
Charged His whole counsel to declare;
Lift o'er our ranks the prophet's rod,
While we uphold Thy hands with prayer.
James Montgomery, 1825.

The House of God.

495 Lenox. H. M. — Lewis Edson, 1781.

Christ is our Cor-ner-Stone; On Him alone we build; With His true saints alone The courts of heaven are filled: On His great love our hopes we place, On His great love our hopes we place, Of present grace and joys a-bove.

2 Oh! then, with hymns of praise,
These hallowed courts shall ring;
Our voices we will raise
The Three in One to sing,
And thus proclaim, in joyful song,
Both loud and long, that glorious name.

3 Here, gracious God! do Thou
For evermore draw nigh;
Accept each faithful vow,

And mark each suppliant sigh:
In copious shower, on all who pray,
Each holy day, Thy blessings pour.

4 Here may we gain from heaven
The grace which we implore,
And may that grace, once given,
Be with us evermore;
Until that day, when all the bless'd
To endless rest are called away.

Tr. *John Chandler*, 1837.

496 Ordinal. C. M. — Thomas Tallis, 1565.

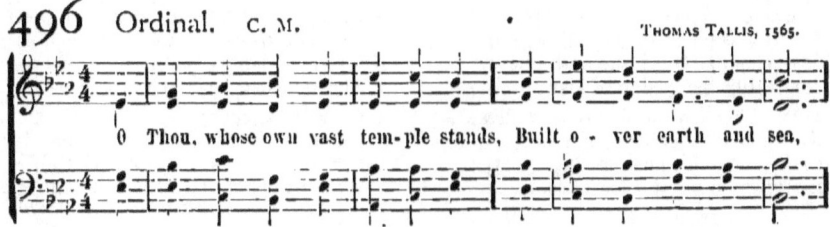

O Thou, whose own vast tem-ple stands, Built o-ver earth and sea,

The House of God.

Accept the walls that human hands Have raised to worship Thee.

2 Lord, from Thine inmost glory send,
Within these courts to bide,
The peace that dwelleth without end,
Serenely by Thy side!

3 May erring minds that worship here
Be taught the better way;
And they who mourn, and they who fear,
Be strengthened as they pray.

4 May faith grow firm, and love grow warm,
And pure devotion rise,
While round these hallow'd walls the storm
Of earth-born passion dies.

William Cullen Bryant, 1835.

497 Rockingham. L. M.   Lowell Mason, 1830.

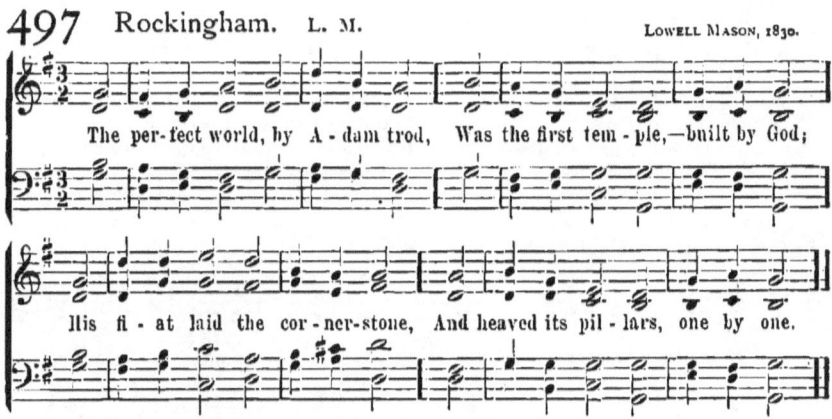

The perfect world, by Adam trod, Was the first temple,—built by God; His fiat laid the cornerstone, And heaved its pillars, one by one.

2 He hung its starry roof on high—
The broad, illimitable sky;
He spread its pavement green and bright,
And curtained it with morning light.

3 The mountains in their places stood,
The sea, the sky, and "all was good;"
And, when its first pure praises rang,
The "morning stars together sang."

4 Lord! 'tis not ours to make the sea
And earth and sky a house for Thee;
But, in Thy sight, our offering stands,—
An humbler temple, "made with hands."

Nathaniel P. Willis, 1826.

498

Within these walls let heavenly peace
And holy love and concord dwell;
Here give the burden'd conscience ease,
And here the wounded spirit heal.

2 When children's voices raise the song—
"Hosanna!"—to their heavenly King,
Let heaven with earth the strain prolong;
"Hosanna!" let the angels sing.

3 Here, when Thy messengers proclaim
The blessèd gospel of Thy Son,
Still, by the power of His great name,
Be mighty signs and wonders done

James Montgomery, 1825.

Baptism.

499 St. Agnes. C. M.   J. B. Dykes, 1858.

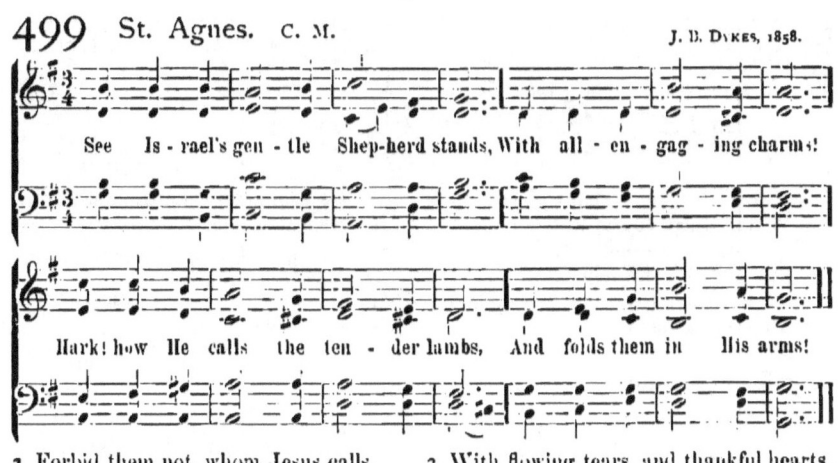

See Is-rael's gen-tle Shep-herd stands, With all - en - gag - ing charms!
Hark! how He calls the ten - der lambs, And folds them in His arms!

2 Forbid them not, whom Jesus calls,
  Nor dare the claim resist,
Since His own lips to us declare—
  Of such will heaven consist.

3 With flowing tears, and thankful hearts,
  We give them up to Thee;
Receive them, Lord! into Thine arms,—
  Thine may they ever be.

v. 1, *Philip Doddridge*, 1740.
v. 2 & 3, *John Peacock*, 1776.

500 Uxbridge. L. M.   Lowell Mason, 1824.

With thankful hearts our songs we raise, To cel - e - brate the Sav - iour's praise;
Yet who, but saints in heaven a - bove, Can tell the rich - es of His love?

2 He, the good Shepherd, kindly leads
The wanderer, and the hungry feeds;
Deigns in His arms the lambs to bear,
And makes them His peculiar care.

3 Jesus! to Thy protecting wing,
Our helpless little ones we bring;
Oh! grant them grace and strength, that they
May find and keep the heavenward way.

Edward Bickersteth, 1841.

Baptism.

501 Anvern. L. M.   Lowell Mason, 1839.

Oh, happy day, that fixed my choice On Thee, my Saviour, and my God! Well may this glowing heart rejoice, And tell its raptures all a-broad; And tell its raptures all a-broad.

2 Oh, happy bond, that seals my vows
   To Him who merits all my love!
Let cheerful anthems fill His house,
   While to that sacred shrine I move.

3 'Tis done, the great transaction's done:
   I am my Lord's, and He is mine;
He drew me, and I followed on,
   Charmed to confess the voice divine.
                       Philip Doddridge, 1740.

502 Germany. L. M.   L. van Beethoven.

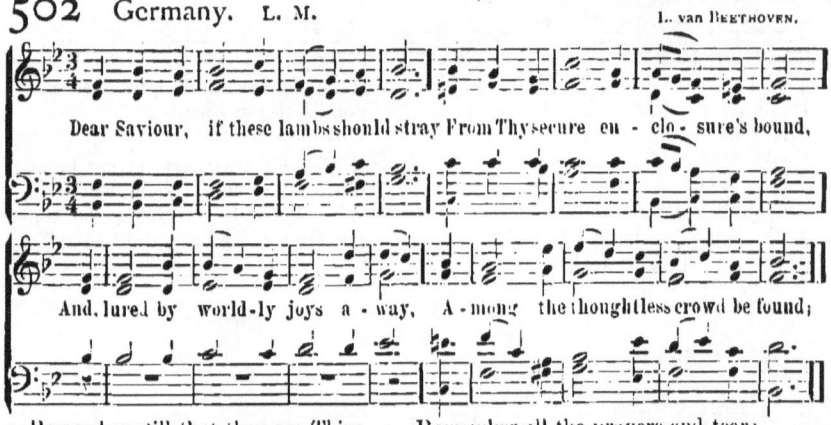

Dear Saviour, if these lambs should stray From Thy secure en-clo-sure's bound, And, lured by world-ly joys a-way, A-mong the thoughtless crowd be found;

2 Remember still that they are Thine,
   That Thy dear sacred name they bear;
Think that the seal of love divine,
   The sign of cov'nant grace, they wear.

3 In all their erring, sinful years,
   O let them ne'er forgotten be;

Remember all the prayers and tears
   Which consecrated them to Thee.

4 And when these lips no more can pray,
   These eyes can weep for them no more,
Turn Thou their feet from folly's way,
   The wand'rers to Thy fold restore.
                       Abby B. Hyde, 1824.

The Lord's Supper.

503 Rock of Ages. 7s. JOHN B. DYKES, 1871.

Rock of Ages, cleft for me, Let me hide myself in Thee!
Let the water and the blood, From Thy riven side which flowed,
Be of sin the double cure, Cleanse me from its guilt and power.

2 Not the labors of my hands
Can fulfil Thy law's demands;
Could my zeal no respite know,
Could my tears for ever flow,—
All for sin could not atone;
Thou must save, and Thou alone!

3 Nothing in my hand I bring;
Simply to Thy cross I cling;
Naked, come to Thee for dress,
Helpless, look to Thee for grace;
Foul, I to the Fountain fly,
Wash me, Saviour! or I die.

4 Whilst I draw this fleeting breath,
When my eyelids close in death,
When I soar thro realms unknown,
See Thee on Thy judgment throne,
Rock of ages, cleft for me,
Let me hide myself in Thee!

Augustus M. Toplady, 1776.
Three words in 4th stanza alt.

504 Toplady. 7s. T. HASTINGS, 1830.

Bless-ed Sav-iour, Thee I love, All my oth-er joys a-bove;
D.S. Ev-er shall my glo-ry be, On-ly, on-ly, on-ly Thee!

The Lord's Supper.

D. C.

All my hopes in Thee a-bide, Thou my Hope, and naught be-side:

Geo. Duffield, 1859.

505 Pax Dei. 10s.

E. J. Hopkins, 1866.

Sav-iour, a-gain to Thy dear name we raise With one ac-cord our part-ing hymn of praise; Once more we bless Thee ere our wor-ship cease, Then, low-ly stoop-ing, wait Thy word of peace.

2 Grant us Thy peace upon our homeward way;
With Thee began, with Thee shall end the day;
Guard Thou the lips from sin, the hearts from shame,
That in this house have called upon Thy name.

3 Grant us Thy peace throughout our earthly life,
Our balm in sorrow, and our stay in strife;
Then, when Thy voice shall bid our conflict cease,
Call us, O Lord, to Thine eternal peace.

John Ellerton, 1866.

The Lord's Supper.

506 Spanish Hymn. 7s. — Spanish Melody.

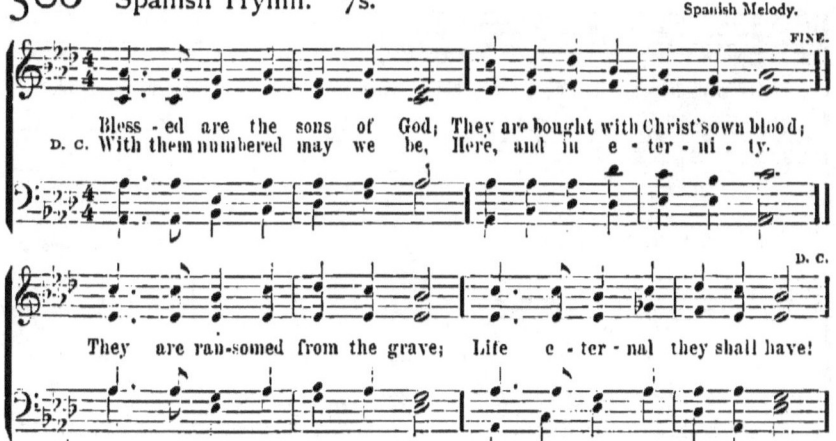

Bless-ed are the sons of God; They are bought with Christ's own blood;
With them numbered may we be, Here, and in e-ter-ni-ty.
They are ran-somed from the grave; Life e-ter-nal they shall have!

2 They are justified by grace;
They enjoy a solid peace;
All their sins are washed away;
They shall stand in God's great day:
With them numbered may we be,
Here, and in eternity.

3 They are lights upon the earth,—
Children of a heavenly birth,—
One with God, with Jesus one;
Glory is in them begun:
With them numbered may we be,
Here, and in eternity.
Joseph Humphreys, 1743. ab.

3 All who bear the Saviour's name,
Here their common faith proclaim;
Though diverse in tongue or rite,
Here, one body we unite;
Breaking thus one mystic bread,
Members of one common Head.

4 Come, the blessèd emblems share,
Which the Saviour's death declare;
Come, on truth immortal feed;
For His flesh is meat indeed;
Saviour! witness with the sign,
That our ransomed souls are Thine.
Josiah Conder, 1836. alt.

507

Many centuries have fled
Since our Saviour broke the bread,
And this sacred feast ordained,
Ever by His church retained:
Those His body who discern,
Thus shall meet till His return.

2 Through the churches' long eclipse,
When, from priest or pastor's lips,
Truth divine was never heard,—
'Mid the famine of the word,
Still these symbols witness gave
To His love who died to save.

508

"Till He come:" oh, let the words
Linger on the trembling chords;
Let the little while between
In their golden light be seen;
Let us think how heaven and home
Lie beyond that—"Till He come."

2 See, the feast of love is spread,
Drink the wine, and break the bread;
Sweet memorials,—till the Lord
Call us round His heavenly board;
Some from earth, from glory some,
Severed only—"Till He come."
Edward H. Bickersteth, 1861. ab.

The Lord's Supper.

509 St. Sebastian. 7s. — S. S. Wesley, 1872.

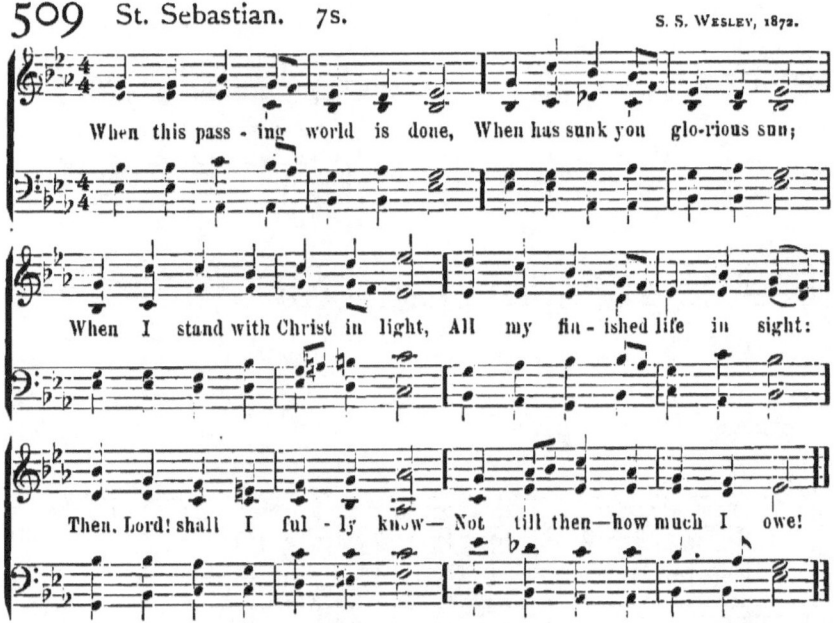

When this passing world is done, When has sunk yon glorious sun;
When I stand with Christ in light, All my finished life in sight:
Then, Lord! shall I fully know— Not till then—how much I owe!

2 When I stand before the throne
Clothed in beauty not my own,
When I see Thee as Thou art,
Love Thee with unsinning heart,
Then, Lord! shall I fully know—
Not till then—how much I owe!

3 When the praise of heaven I hear
Loud as thunders to the ear,
Loud as many waters' noise,
Sweet as harps' melodious voice,
Then, Lord! shall I fully know—
Not till then—how much I owe!

4 Chosen not for good in me,
Wakened up from wrath to flee,
Hidden in the Saviour's side,
By the Spirit sanctified,
Teach me, Lord! on earth to show
By my love how much I owe.
Robert M. McCheyne, 1837.

510

Christ, whose glory fill the skies!
 Christ, the true, the only Light!
Sun of righteousness! arise,
 Triumph o'er the shades of night:
Dayspring from on high! be near;
Daystar! in my heart appear.

2 Dark and cheerless is the morn,
 Unaccompanied by Thee;
Joyless is the day's return,
 Till Thy mercy's beams I see:
Till they inward light impart,
Glad my eyes, and warm my heart.

3 Visit then this soul of mine;
 Pierce the gloom of sin and grief;
Fill me, Radiancy divine!
 Scatter all my unbelief:
More and more Thyself display,
Shining to the perfect day.
Charles Wesley, 1740.

The Lord's Supper.

511 Penitence. 7s 6s & 8. W. H. Oakley, 1836.

Lamb of God! whose dying love
We now recall to mind.
Send the answer from above,
And let us mercy find:
Think on us who think on Thee,
And every struggling soul release;
Oh! remember Calvary,
And bid us go in peace!

2 By Thine agonizing pain,
  And bloody sweat, we pray,—
By Thy dying love to man,—
  Take all our sins away:
Burst our bonds, and set us free;
From all iniquity release;
Oh, remember Calvary,
  And bid us go in peace!

3 Let Thy blood, by faith applied,
  The sinner's pardon seal;
Speak us freely justified,
  And all our sickness heal:
By Thy passion on the tree,
Let all our griefs and troubles cease;
Oh, remember Calvary,
  And bid us go in peace!
                Charles Wesley, 1745.

512

Other knowledge I disdain;
  'Tis all but vanity:
Christ, the Lamb of God, was slain,—
  He tasted death for me.
Me to save from endless woe
The sin-atoning Victim died:
Only Jesus will I know,
  And Jesus crucified.

2 Him to know is life and peace,
  And pleasure without end;
This is all my happiness,
  On Jesus to depend;
Daily in His grace to grow,
And ever in His faith abide;
Only Jesus will I know,
  And Jesus Crucified.
              Charles Wesley, 1747, ab.

The Lord's Supper.

513 Shirland. S. M.   Samuel Stanley, 1805.

Grace,—'tis a charming sound, Harmonious to mine ear; Heaven with the echo shall resound, And all the earth shall hear.

2 Grace first contrived a way
  To save rebellious man;
And all the steps that grace display,
  Which drew the wondrous plan.

3 Grace led my wandering feet
  To tread the heavenly road;
And new supplies each hour I meet,
  While pressing on to God.

4 Grace all the work shall crown,
  Through everlasting days;
It lays in heaven the topmost stone,
  And well deserves the praise.
                    Philip Doddridge, 1740.

514

Sweet feast of love divine!
  'Tis grace that makes us free
To feed upon this bread and wine,
  In mem'ry, Lord! of Thee.

2 That blood, that flowed for sin,
  In symbol here we see,
And feel the blessèd pledge within,
  That we are loved of Thee.

3 Oh! if this glimpse of love
  Is so divinely sweet,
What will it be, O Lord! above,
  Thy gladdening smile to meet?—

4 To see Thee face to face,
  Thy perfect likeness wear,
And all Thy ways of wondrous grace
  Through endless years declare!
                    Edward Denny, 1839.

515

Jesus, we thus obey
  Thy last and kindest word,
And in thine own appointed way
  We come to meet Thee, Lord!

2 Thus we remember Thee,
  And take this bread and wine
As Thine own dying legacy,
  And our redemption's sign.

3 Thy presence makes the feast;
  Now let our spirits feel
The glory not to be expressed,—
  The joy unspeakable!

4 With high and heavenly bliss
  Thou dost our spirits cheer;
Thy house of banqueting is this,
  And Thou hast brought us here.

5 Now let our souls be fed
  With manna from above,
And over us Thy banner spread
  Of everlasting love.
                    Charles Wesley, 1745.

The Lord's Supper.

516 Nettleton. 8s & 7s. ANON, 1813.

{ Come, Thou Fount of ev-ery bless-ing! Tune my heart to sing Thy grace;
{ Streams of mer-cy, nev-er ceas-ing, Call for songs of loud-est praise:
D. C. Praise the mount; I'm fixed up-on it, Mount of God's un-changing love.

Teach me some me-lo-dious son-net, Sung by flam-ing tongues a-bove;

2 Oh! to grace how great a debtor,
   Daily I'm constrained to be!
Let that grace now, like a fetter,
   Bind my wandering heart to Thee;

Jesus sought me when a stranger,
   Wandering from the fold of God;
He, to rescue me from danger,
   Interposed His precious blood.
Robert Robinson, 1758.

517 Eucharist. 9s & 8s. J. S. B. HODGES, 1858.

Bread of the world, in mer-cy bro-ken, Wine of the soul, in mer-cy shed,

By whom the words of life were spok-en; And in whose death our sins are dead.

2 Look on the hearts by sorrow broken
  Look on the tears by sinners shed;
And be Thy feast to us the token
  That by Thy grace our souls are fed.
Reginald Heber, 1827.

The Lord's Supper.

518 Nuremberg. 7s.   Johann Rudolf Ahle, 1664.

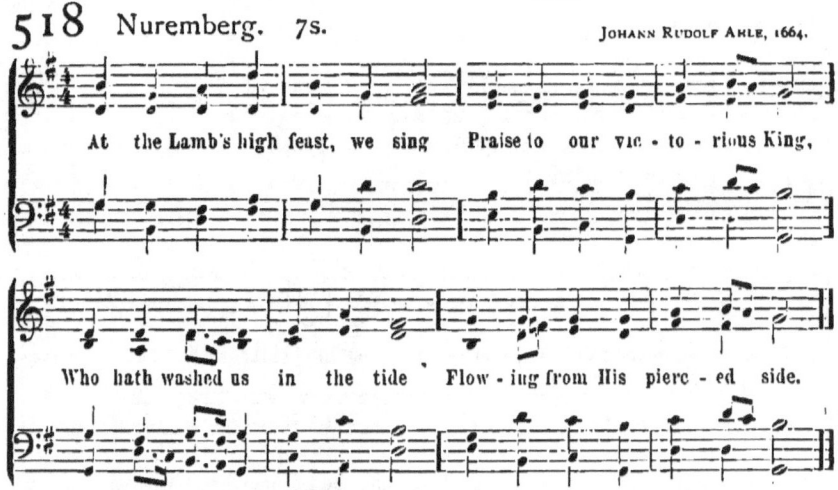

At the Lamb's high feast, we sing Praise to our vic-to-rious King, Who hath washed us in the tide Flow-ing from His pierc-ed side.

2 Praise we Him, whose love divine
Gives His sacred blood for wine,
Gives His body for the feast,—
Christ, the Victim,—Christ, the Priest.

3 Where the paschal blood is poured,
Death's dark angel sheathes his sword;
Israel's hosts triumphant go,
Through the wave that drowns the foe.

4 Praise we Christ whose blood was shed,
Paschal Victim, paschal Bread;
With sincerity and love,
Eat we manna from above.

5 Mighty Victim from the sky!
Hell's fierce powers beneath Thee lie;
Thou hast conquered in the fight,
Thou hast brought us life and light.

6 Hymns of glory and of praise,
Risen Lord! to Thee we raise;
Holy Father! praise to Thee,
With the Spirit, ever be!

          Lat., *Roman Breviary.*
       Tr., *Robert Campbell,* 1850, a.

519

Hark! my soul! it is the Lord;
'Tis thy Saviour—hear His word;
Jesus speaks, and speaks to thee,
"Say, poor sinner, lovest thou Me?

2 "I delivered thee when bound,
And when bleeding, healed thy wound;
Sought thee wandering, set thee right,
Turned thy darkness into light.

3 "Can a woman's tender care
Cease towards the child she bare?
Yes, she may forgetful be,
Yet will I remember thee.

4 "Mine is an unchanging love,
Higher than the heights above;
Deeper than the depths beneath—
Free and faithful—strong as death.

5 "Thou shalt see My glory soon,
When the work of grace is done;
Partner of My throne shalt be!
Say, poor sinner! lovest thou Me?"

6 Lord! it is my chief complaint,
That my love is weak and faint;
Yet I love Thee, and adore;—
Oh, for grace to love Thee more.

         Wm. Cowper, 1772.

The Lord's Supper.

520 Rolland. L. M.   WM. B. BRADBURY, 1844.

At Thy command, our dearest Lord! Here we attend Thy dying feast; Thy blood, like wine, adorns Thy board, And Thine own flesh feeds every guest, And Thine own flesh feeds every guest.

2 Our faith adores Thy bleeding love,
  And trusts for life in One that died;
We hope for heavenly crowns above,
  From a Redeemer crucified.

3 Let the vain world pronounce it shame,
  And fling their scandals on Thy cause;
We come to boast our Saviour's name,
  And make our triumphs in His cross.

4 With joy we tell the scoffing age,
  He that was dead has left His tomb;
He lives above their utmost rage,
  And we are waiting till He come.
Isaac Watts, 1707.

521

Poor, weak, and worthless, though I am,
I have a rich, almighty Friend;
Jesus, the Saviour, is His name,
He freely loves, and without end.

2 But ah! my inmost spirit mourns,
And well my eyes with tears may swim,
To think of my perverse returns,
I've been a faithless friend to Him.

3 Often my gracious Friend I grieve,
Neglect, distrust, and disobey;
And often Satan's lies believe
Sooner than all my Friend can say.

4 Sure, were I not most vile and base,
I could not thus my Friend requite!
And were not He the God of Grace,
He'd frown and spurn me from His sight.
John Newton, 1779.

522 Swanwick. C. M.   JAMES LUCAS, 1805.

Here at Thy ta-ble, Lord! we meet, To feed on food di-vine; Thy bo-dy

The Lord's Supper.

is the bread we eat, Thy precious blood the wine, Thy precious blood the wine.

2 Sure, there was never love so free,
Dear Saviour! so divine;
Well may'st Thou claim that heart of me,
Which owes so much to Thine.

3 Yes, Thou shalt surely have my heart,
My soul, my strength, my all;
With life itself I'll freely part,
My Jesus! at Thy call.
Samuel Stennett, 1787.

523
Sweet is the mem'ry of His name,
Who blessed us in His will,
And, to His testament of love,
Made His own life the seal.

2 Thy light, and strength, and pard'ning
And glory shall be mine;   [grace,
My life and soul, my heart and flesh,
And all my powers are Thine.
Isaac Watts, 1707.

524 Hanford. 8s & 4.   A. S. SULLIVAN, 1872.

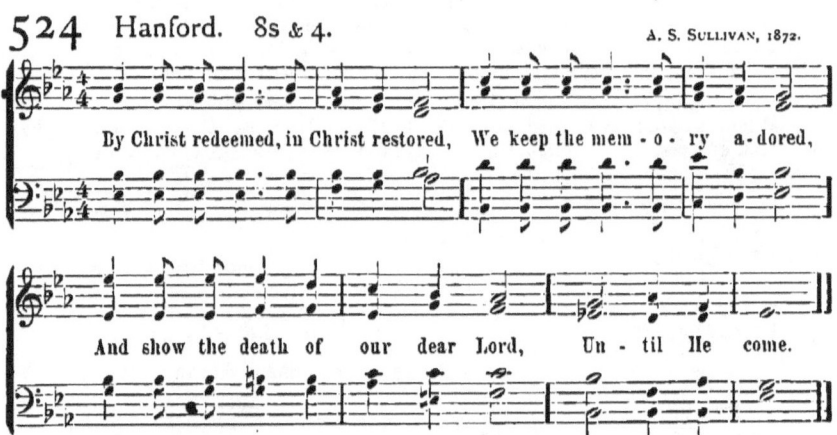

By Christ redeemed, in Christ restored, We keep the mem-o-ry a-dored, And show the death of our dear Lord, Un-til He come.

2 His body broken in our stead
Is here, in this memorial bread;
And so our needy love is fed,
   Until He come.

3 His fearful drops of agony,
His life-blood shed for us we see;
The cup shall tell the mystery,
   Until He come.

4 And thus that dark betrayal night,
With the last advent we unite—
The shame, the glory, by this rite,
   Until He come.

5 Oh, blesséd hope! with this elate,
Let not our hearts be desolate,
But, strong in faith, in patience wait,
   Until He come!
George Rawson, 1853. (?)

The Lord's Supper.

525 Canonbury. L. M.   Robert Schumann.

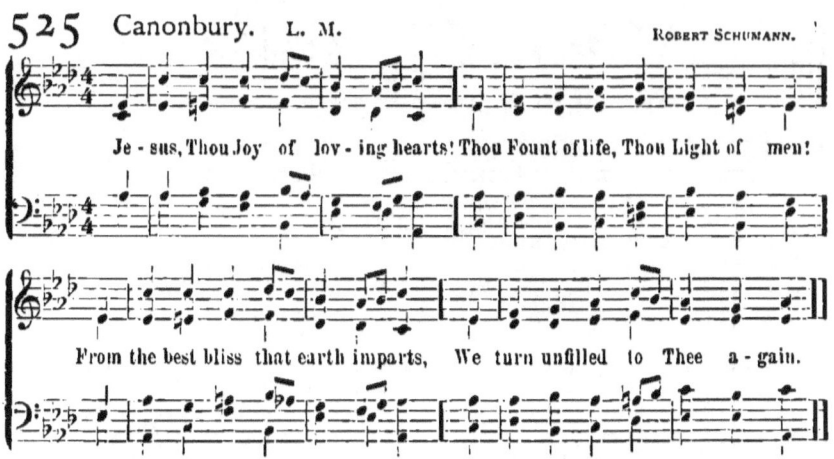

Jesus, Thou Joy of loving hearts! Thou Fount of life, Thou Light of men!
From the best bliss that earth imparts, We turn unfilled to Thee again.

2 Thy truth unchanged hath ever stood;
   Thou savest those that on Thee call;
To them that seek Thee, Thou art good,
   To them that find Thee,—All in all!

3 We taste Thee, O Thou living Bread!
   And long to feast upon Thee still;
We drink of Thee, the Fountain Head,
   And thirst, our souls from Thee to fill.

4 Our restless spirits yearn for Thee,
   Where'er our changeful lot is cast;
Glad, when Thy gracious smile we see,
   Bless'd, when our faith can hold Thee fast.

5 O Jesus! ever with us stay;
   Make all our moments calm and bright;
Chase the dark night of sin away;
   Shed o'er the world Thy holy light.

Lat., Bernard of Clairvaux, 1140.
Tr., Ray Palmer, 1858.

526 Dundee. C. M.   Andro Hart's "Psalter." 1615.

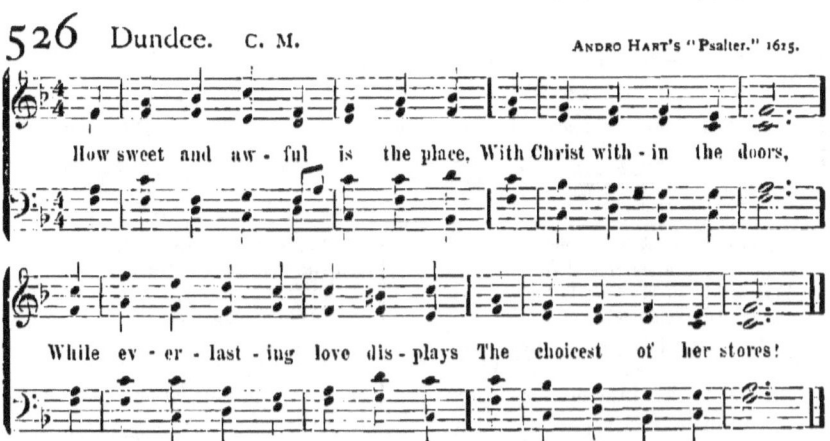

How sweet and awful is the place, With Christ within the doors,
While everlasting love displays The choicest of her stores!

The Lord's Supper.

2 While all our hearts, and all our songs,
  Join to admire the feast;
Each of us cry, with thankful tongues,—
  "Lord! why was I a guest?"

3 "Why was I made to hear Thy voice,
  And enter while there's room,
When thousands make a wretched choice,
  And rather starve than come?"

4 'Twas the same love that spread the feast,
  Compelled us sweetly in;
Else we had still refused to taste,
  And perished in our sin.

5 Pity the nations, O our God!
  Constrain the earth to come;
Send Thy victorious word abroad,
  And bring the strangers home.

6 We long to see Thy churches full,
  That all the chosen race
May, with one voice, and heart, and soul,
  Sing Thy redeeming grace.
  Isaac Watts, 1707.

527

Arise, my soul! my joyful powers!
  And triumph in my God;
Awake, my voice! and loud proclaim
  His glorious grace abroad.

2 He raised me from the deeps of sin,
  The gates of gaping hell;
And fixed my standing more secure,
  Than 't was before I fell.

3 The arms of everlasting love,
  Beneath my soul He placed;
And on the Rock of Ages set
  My slippery footsteps fast.

4 Jesus the Lord, invites us here,
  To His triumphal feast;
And brings immortal blessings down
  For each redeemed guest.

5 Arise, my soul! awake, my voice!
  And tunes of pleasure sing;
Loud hallelujahs shall address
  My Saviour and my King.
  Isaac Watts, 1707.

528 St. Salvador. L. M.
Emilio Pirraccini, 1848.

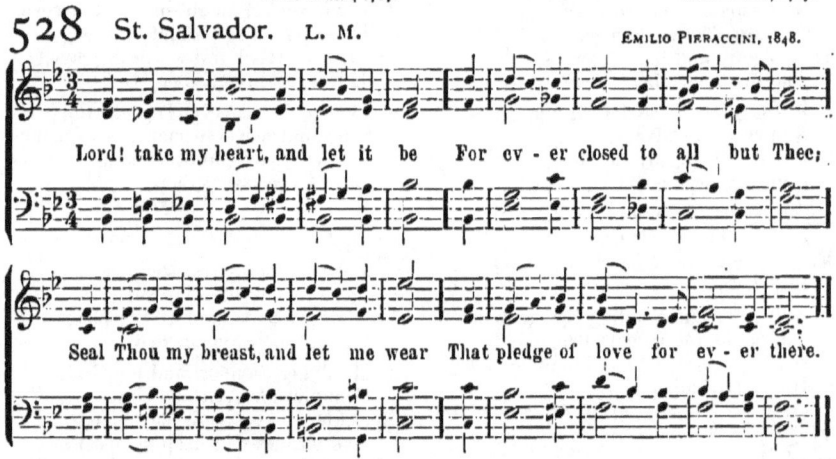

Lord! take my heart, and let it be For ev-er closed to all but Thee;
Seal Thou my breast, and let me wear That pledge of love for ev-er there.

2 How blest are they, who still abide
Close sheltered in Thy bleeding side!
Who thence their life and strength derive,
And by Thee move, and in Thee live.

3 What are our works but sin and death,
Till Thou Thy quick'ning Spirit breathe?
Thou giv'st the power Thy grace to move;
Oh! wondrous grace! Oh! boundless love!
  N. L. Zinzendorf. Tr. *John Wesley*, 1739.

The Lord's Supper.

529 St. John. C. M. JAMES TURLE, 1862.

According to Thy gracious word, In meek humili-
This will I do, my dying Lord, I will remember Thee.

2 Thy body, broken for my sake,
  My bread from heaven shall be;
Thy testamental cup I take,
  And thus remember Thee.

3 Gethsemane can I forget?
  Or there Thy conflict see,
Thine agony and bloody sweat,
  And not remember Thee?

4 When to the cross I turn mine eyes,
  And rest on Calvary,
O Lamb of God, my sacrifice!
  I must remember Thee:—

5 Remember Thee, and all Thy pains,
  And all Thy love to me!—
Yea, while a breath, a pulse remains,
  Will I remember Thee.

6 And when these failing lips grow dumb,
  And mind and mem'ry flee;
When Thou shalt in Thy kingdom come,
  Jesus! remember me.
          James Montgomery, 1825.

530
IF human kindness meets return,
  And owns the grateful tie;
If tender thoughts within us burn,
  To feel a friend is nigh;—

2 Oh! shall not warmer accents tell
  The gratitude we owe
To Him, who died, our fears to quell—
  Our more than orphan's woe?

3 While yet His anguished soul surveyed
  Those pangs He would not flee,
What love His latest words displayed,—
  "Meet, and remember Me!"

4 Remember Thee!—Thy death, Thy shame,
  Our sinful hearts to share!—
O mem'ry! leave no other name
  But His recorded there.
          Gerard T. Noel, 1813.

531
For ever here my rest shall be,
  Close to Thy bleeding side;
This all my hope, and all my plea,—
  For me the Saviour died.

2 My dying Saviour, and my God!
  Fountain for guilt and sin!
Sprinkle me ever with Thy blood!
  And cleanse and keep me clean.

3 Th' atonement of Thy blood apply,
  Till faith to sight improve,
Till hope shall in fruition die,
  And all my soul be love.
          Charles Wesley, 1740.

The Lord's Supper.

532 Phuvah. C. M.   MELCHOIR VULPIUS, 1609

See! Jesus stands, with open arms; He calls;—He bids you come;
Guilt holds you back, and fear alarms; But, see! there yet is room.

2 Room, in the Saviour's bleeding heart;
  There love and pity meet;
Nor will He bid the soul depart,
  That trembles at His feet.

3 Oh! come, and, with His children, taste
  The blessings of His love:
While hope attends the sweet repast
  Of nobler joys above.

4 There, with united heart and voice,
  Before th' eternal throne,
Ten thousand thousand souls rejoice,
  In ecstasies unknown.

5 And yet ten thousand thousand more
  Are welcome still to come;
Ye longing souls! the grace adore,
  Approach, there yet is room.
               Anne Steele, 1760.

533

There is a fountain filled with blood,
  Drawn from Immanuel's veins;
And sinners, plunged beneath that flood,
  Lose all their guilty stains.

2 The dying thief rejoiced to see
  That fountain in his day;
And there have I, as vile as he,
  Washed all my sins away.

3 Dear dying Lamb! Thy precious blood
  Shall never lose its power,
Till all the ransomed church of God
  Be saved to sin no more.

4 E'er since, by faith, I saw the stream
  Thy flowing wounds supply,
Redeeming love has been my theme,
  And shall be, till I die.

5 Then, in a nobler, sweeter song,
  I'll sing Thy power to save,
When this poor lisping, stamm'ring tongue
  Lies silent in the grave.
               William Cowper, 1772.

534

Thy head, the crown of thorns that wears,
  With brightest radiance glows;
That face, so marred with blood and tears,
  Transcendent beauty shows.

2 Those wounded hands, stretched out so wide,
  Proclaim the sinner's Friend,
And, from the cleft of Thy pierc'd side,
  Life-giving streams descend.

3 By men despised, rejected, scorned,—
  No beauty they can see,—
With grace and glory all adorned,
  The loveliest form to me.
               Thomas Haweis, 1792.

The Lord's Supper.

535 Hebron. L. M.   Lowell Mason, 1830.

No more, my God! I boast no more, Of all the du-ties I have done; I quit the hopes I held be-fore, To trust the mer-its of Thy Son.

2 Now, for the love I bear His name,
  What was my gain, I count but loss;
My former pride I call my shame,
  And nail my glory to His cross.

3 Yes, and I must, and will, esteem
  All things but loss for Jesus' sake;
Oh! may my soul be found in Him,
  And of His righteousness partake.

4 The best obedience of my hands
  Dares not appear before Thy throne;
But faith can answer Thy demands,
  By pleading what my Lord has done.
                Isaac Watts, 1709.

536
Lord! I am Thine, entirely Thine,
Purchased and saved by blood divine;
With full consent Thine I would be,
And own Thy sovereign right in me.

2 Grant one poor sinner more a place,
Among the children of Thy grace;
A wretched sinner, lost to God,
But ransomed by Immanuel's blood.

3 Thine would I live, Thine would I die,
Be Thine through all eternity;
The vow is past beyond repeal;
Now will I set the solemn seal.

4 Here, at that cross, where flows the blood
That bought my guilty soul for God,
Thee my new Master now I call,
And consecrate to Thee my all.
                Samuel Davies, 1760.

537
Now I resolve, with all my heart,
  With all my powers, to serve the Lord;
Nor from His precepts e'er depart,
  Whose service is a rich reward.

2 Oh! be His service all my joy!—
  Around let my example shine,
Till others love the blest employ,
  And join in labors so divine.

3 Be this the promise of my soul,
  My solemn, my determined choice,
To yield to His supreme control,
  And, in His kind commands, rejoice.

4 Oh! may I never faint nor tire,
  Nor wand'ring leave His sacred ways;
Great God! accept my soul's desire,
  And give me strength to live Thy praise.
                Anne Steele, 1760.

The Lord's Supper.

538 Cooling. C. M.   A. J. Abbey, 1863.

All that I was,—my sin, my guilt, My death was all my own;
All that I am, I owe to Thee, My gracious God! alone.

2 The evil of my former state
   Was mine, and only mine;
The good in which I now rejoice,
   Is Thine, and only Thine.

3 The darkness of my former state,
   The bondage, all was mine;
The light of life, in which I walk,
   The liberty is Thine.

4 Thy grace first made me feel my sin,
   It taught me to believe;
Then, in believing, peace I found,
   And now I live, I live.

5 All that I am, ev'n here on earth,
   All that I hope to be,
When Jesus comes, and glory dawns,
   I owe it, Lord! to Thee.
                Horatius Bonar, 1850.

539

My God! accept my heart this day,
   And make it always Thine,
That I from Thee no more may stray,
   No more from Thee decline.

2 Before the cross of Him who died,
   Behold I prostrate fall;
Let every sin be crucified;
   Let Christ be all in all.

3 May the dear blood once shed for me,
   My blessed atonement prove,
That I, from first to last, may be
   The purchase of Thy love.

4 Let every thought, and work, and word,
   To Thee be ever given;
Then life shall be Thy service, Lord!
   And death the gate of heaven.
                Matthew Bridges, 1848.

540

O Father, Son, and Holy Ghost,
   One God in persons Three!
We come in faith to count the cost,
   And give ourselves to Thee.

2 We seek to serve no other King,
   Follow no other Guide,
Nor earth, nor any earthly thing
   Shall tear us from Thy side.

3 We seek to know no other love,
   Save what we love in Thee;
And Thee we choose, all else above,
   Our chiefest love to be.

4 Thy blood our only treasure is,
   Thy cross our chosen part;
Thy sacrament our highest bliss,
   Our home, Thy sacred heart.
                Anon, 1862.

The Lord's Supper.

541 Olivet. 6s & 4s.   LOWELL MASON, 1832.

My faith looks up to Thee, Thou Lamb of Cal-va-ry, Sav-iour divine! Now hear me while I pray, Take all my guilt a-way, Oh! let me from this day, Be whol-ly Thine!

2 May Thy rich grace impart
Strength to my fainting heart;
  My zeal inspire;
As Thou hast died for me,
Oh! may my love to Thee
Pure, warm, and changeless be,
  A living fire!

3 While life's dark maze I tread,
And griefs around me spread,
  Be Thou my Guide;
Bid darkness turn to day,
Wipe sorrow's tears away,
Nor let me ever stray
  From Thee aside.

4 When ends life's transient dream,
When death's cold, sullen stream
  Shall o'er me roll,
Blest Saviour! then, in love,
Fear and distrust remove;
Oh! bear me safe above,
  A ransomed soul!
Ray Palmer, 1830.

542

PEACE, peace I leave with you,
My peace I give to you,
  Trust to My care!
Thus the Redeemer said,
And bowed His sacred head,
Lone in the garden shade,
  Wrestling in prayer.

2 Peace, peace I leave with you,
My peace I give to you,
  Perfect and pure;
Not as the world doth give,
Words that the soul deceive,
Ye who in Me believe
  Shall rest secure.

3 Peace, peace, I leave with you,
My peace I give to you,
  Though foes invade;
All power is given to Me,
I will your refuge be,
Now and eternally,
  Be not dismayed!
Thomas Hastings, 1856.

543

To GOD,—the Father, Son,
And Spirit,—Three in One,
  All praise be given!
Crown Him in every song:
To Him your hearts belong;
Let all His praise prolong—
  On earth, in heaven.
Edwin F. Hatfield, 1843.

The Lord's Supper

544 Louvan. L. M.   Virgil C. Taylor, 1847.

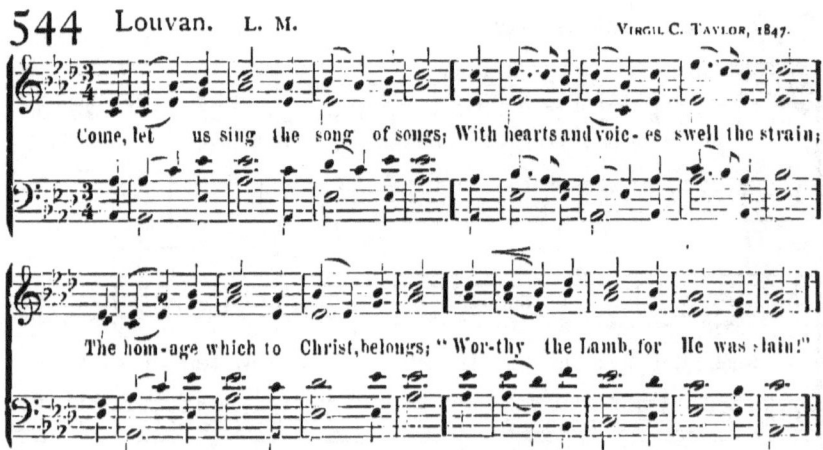

Come, let us sing the song of songs; With hearts and voic-es swell the strain; The hom-age which to Christ, belongs; "Wor-thy the Lamb, for He was slain!"

2 Slain to redeem us by His blood,
  To cleanse from every sinful stain,
And make us kings and priests to God;
  "Worthy the Lamb, for He was slain!"

3 To Him who suffered on the tree,
  Our souls, at His soul's price to gain,
All blessing, praise, and glory be!—
  "Worthy the Lamb, for He was slain!"

4 To Him, enthroned by filial right,
  All power in heaven and earth pertain,
All honor, majesty, and might;—
  "Worthy the Lamb, for He was slain!"

5 Come, Holy Spirit! from on high,
  Our faith, our hope, our love sustain,
Through life we sing, and dying, cry,—
  "Worthy the Lamb, for He was slain!"
              James Montgomery, 1853.

545

Now to the Lord, that makes us know
  The wonders of His dying love,
Be humble honors paid below.
  And strains of nobler praise above.

2 'T was He that cleansed our foulest sins,
  And washed us in His richest blood;
'T is He that makes us priests and kings,
  And brings us rebels near to God.

3 To Jesus, our atoning Priest,
  To Jesus, our superior King,
Be everlasting power confessed,
  And every tongue His glory sing.

4 Behold on flying clouds He comes,
  And every eye shall see Him move;
Tho with our sins we pierced Him once,
  Still He displays His pard'ning love.

5 The unbelieving world shall wail,
  While we rejoice to see the day;
Come, Lord! nor let Thy promise fail,
  Nor let Thy chariots long delay.
              Isaac Watts, 1707.

546

Jesus, Thou everlasting King!
Accept the tribute which we bring;
Accept the well-deserved renown,
And wear our praises as Thy crown.

2 Let every act of worship be,
Like our espousals, Lord! to Thee;—
Like the dear hour, when, from above,
We first received Thy pledge of love.

3 Each foll'wing minute as it flies,
Increase Thy praise, improve our joys;
Till we are raised to sing Thy name,
At the great supper of the Lamb.
              Isaac Watts, 1707.

The Lord's Supper.

547 Communion. 10s. FELIX MENDELSSOHN.

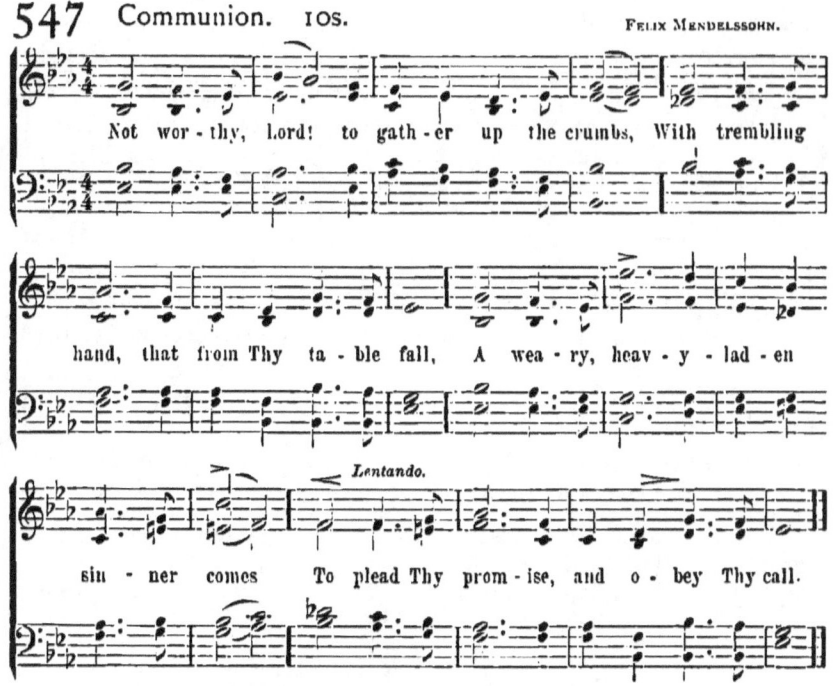

Not worthy, Lord! to gather up the crumbs, With trembling hand, that from Thy table fall, A weary, heavy-laden sinner comes To plead Thy promise, and obey Thy call.

2 I am not worthy to be thought Thy child,
  Nor sit the last and lowest at Thy board;
Too long a wanderer and too oft beguiled,
  I only ask one reconciling word.

3 And is not mercy Thy prerogative—
  Free mercy, boundless, fathomless, divine?
Me, Lord!—the chief of sinners,—me forgive,
  And Thine the greater glory,—only Thine.

4 I hear Thy voice; Thou bid'st me come and rest;
  I come, I kneel, I clasp Thy piercéd feet;
Thou bid'st me take my place, a welcome guest,
  Among Thy saints, and of Thy banquet eat.

5 My praise can only breathe itself in prayer,
  My prayer can only lose itself in Thee,
Dwell Thou forever in my heart, and there,
  Lord! let me sup with Thee: sup Thou with me.

E. H. Bickersteth.

The Lord's Supper.

548

Here, O my Lord, I see Thee face to face;
  Here would I touch and handle things unseen;
Here grasp with firmer hand the eternal grace,
  And all my weariness upon Thee lean.

2 Here would I feed upon the bread of God;
  Here drink with Thee the royal wine of heaven;
Here would I lay aside each earthly load,
  Here taste afresh the calm of sin forgiven.

3 This is the hour of banquet and of song,
  This is the heavenly Table spread for me;
Here let me feast, and, feasting, still prolong
  The brief bright hour of fellowship with Thee.

4 Too soon we rise; the symbols disappear;
  The Feast, though not the Love, is past and gone;
The Bread and Wine remove; but Thou art here,
  Nearer than ever; still my Shield and Sun.

5 I have no help but Thine; nor do I need
  Another arm save Thine to lean upon:
It is enough, my Lord: enough, indeed;
  My strength is in Thy might, Thy might alone.

6 I have no wisdom, save in Him Who is
  My Wisdom and my Teacher, both in one;
No wisdom can I lack while Thou art wise,
  No teaching do I crave, save Thine alone.

7 Mine is the sin, but Thine the Righteousness;
  Mine is the guilt, but Thine the cleansing Blood;
Here is my robe, my refuge, and my peace,
  Thy blood, Thy Righteousness, O Lord my God!

8 I know that deadly evils compass me,
  Dark perils threaten, yet I would not fear,
Nor poorly shrink, nor feebly turn to flee;
  Thou! O my Christ, art buckler, sword, and spear.

9 But see, the Pillar-Cloud is rising now,
  And moving onward through the desert night;
It beckons, and I follow; for I know
  It leads me to the heritage of Light.

10 Feast after feast thus comes, and passes by;
  Yet, passing, points to the glad Feast above,
Giving sweet foretastes of the festal joy,
  The Lamb's great bridal feast of bliss and love.

Horatius Bonar, 1856.

The Lord's Supper.

549 Oswestry. 12S & 11S. J. B. DYKES.

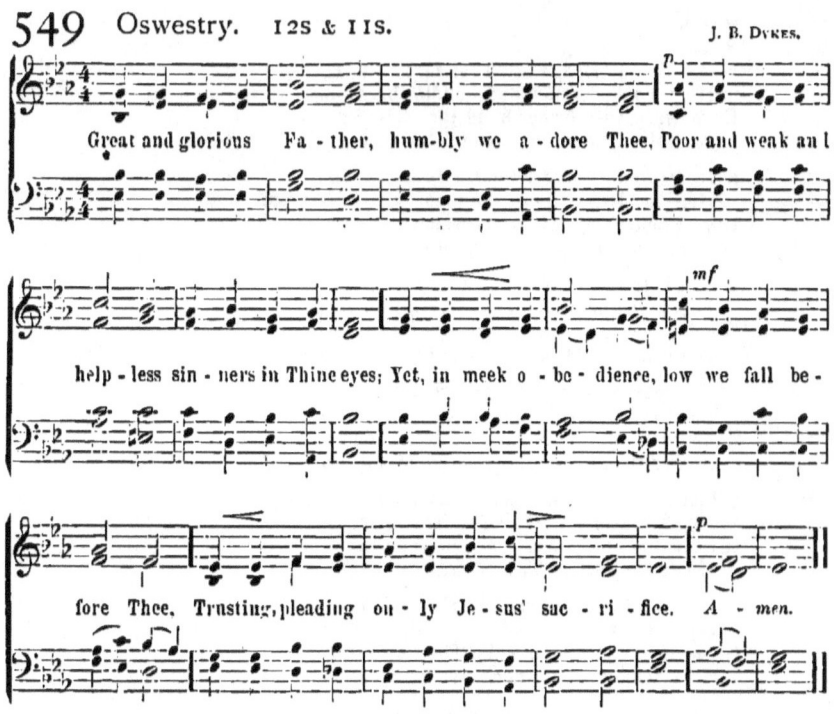

Great and glorious Father, humbly we adore Thee, Poor and weak and helpless sinners in Thine eyes; Yet, in meek obedience, low we fall before Thee, Trusting, pleading only Jesus' sacrifice. A-men.

2 Bowed beneath Thy footstool, yet with boldness pleading
This the only plea on which our hope relies,
Unto Thee, O Father, all Thy mercy needing,
Make we this memorial of Christ's sacrifice.

3 To our fellow sinners we repeat the story,
'Tis the gospel story pictured to our eyes,
Ever in this service, till He comes in glory,
Showing forth the Saviour's priceless sacrifice.

4 Then, O gracious Father, bent in reverence lowly,
We would taste the pledges we so dearly prize,
Food that none may dare to take with hands unholy,
Feasting on the once accepted sacrifice.

5 Lo! the Lamb once offered reigneth now victorious,
And the angel choirs adore His sacrifice!
We too would adore Thee, Saviour, ever raising
Praises to the Lamb who reigns above the skies. Amen.

Anon, 1874.

Childhood.

550 Shelter. P. M.   Samuel Smith, 1871.

There's a Friend for lit-tle children A-bove the bright blue sky, A Friend that never changes, Whose love will nev-er die: Un-like our friends by nature, Who change with changing years, This Friend is always wor-thy The precious name He bears.

2 There's a rest for little children
   Above the bright blue sky,
Who love the blessèd Saviour
   And to His Father cry,—
A rest from every trouble,
   From sin and danger free,
There every little pilgrim
   Shall rest eternally.

3 There's a home for little children
   Above the bright blue sky,
Where Jesus reigns in glory,
   A home of peace and joy;
No home on earth is like it,
   Nor can with it compare,
For every one is happy,
   Nor can be happier there.

4 There's a crown for little children
   Above the bright blue sky,
And all who look to Jesus,
   Shall wear it by-and-by.
A crown of brightest glory,
   Which He shall sure bestow
On all who love the Saviour,
   And walk with Him below.

5 There's a song for little children
   Above the bright blue sky,
And harps of sweetest music,
   And palms of victory:
And all above is pleasure,
   And found in Christ alone:
Oh come, dear little children,
   That all may be your own.
                   Albert Midlane, 1860.

Childhood.

551 Childhood. C. M.   St. Alban's Tune Book, 1855.

By cool Si-lo-am's shad-y rill How fair the lil-y grows! How sweet the breath, beneath the hill, Of Sharon's dew-y rose! A-men.

2 Lo! such the child, whose early feet
 The paths of peace have trod,
Whose sacred heart, with influence sweet,
 Is upward drawn to God.

3 By cool Siloam's shady rill
 The lily must decay;
The rose that blooms beneath the hill
 Must shortly fade away.

4 And soon, too soon, the wint'ry hour
 Of man's maturer age

Will shake the soul with sorrow's power,
 And stormy passion's rage.

5 O Thou, whose infant feet were found
 Within Thy Father's shrine,
Whose years, with changeless virtue crown'd,
 Were all alike divine:

6 Dependent on Thy bounteous breath,
 We seek Thy grace alone,
In childhood, manhood, age and death,
 To keep us still Thine own. Amen.
    Reginald Heber, 1812.

552 Starlight. L. M.   John B. Dykes, 1858.

O come, dear child, a-long with me, And look on yon-der clear blue sky, The moon is shin-ing bright, you see, And stars are twinkling up on high.

Childhood.

2 'Tis there, my child, far, far above,
  That heaven's eternal kingdom lies,
There holy angels dwell in love,
  And tears are wiped from all our eyes.

3 It is a happy, happy place,
  Without a sorrow, pain, or care,
There you may see the Saviour's face,
  Who loves to take good children there.

4 O pray each night that God may bless,
  And keep you while on earth you stay,
And give you endless happiness,
  When from the earth you pass away.
  Cecil F. Alexander, 1848.

553 St. Sylvester. 8s & 7s. JOHN B. DYKES, 1860.

Je-sus, ten-der Shepherd, hear me, Bless Thy lit-tle lamb to-night;

Through the darkness be Thou near me, Keep me safe till morn-ing light.

2 All this day Thy hand has led me,
  And I thank Thee for Thy care;
Thou hast clothed me, warmed and fed me,
  Listen to my evening prayer.

3 Let my sins be all forgiven,
  Bless the friends I love so well;
Take me when I die to heaven,
  Happy there with Thee to dwell.
  Mary Lundie Duncan, 1839.

554

Ever would I fain be reading,
  In the ancient holy Book,
Of my Saviour's gentle pleading,
  Truth in every word and look.

2 How, when children came, He bless'd them,
  Suffered no man to reprove,
Took them in His arms, and pressed them
  To His heart, with words of love.

3 How, to all the sick and tearful,
  Help was ever gladly shown;
How He sought the poor and fearful,
  Called them brothers and His own.

4 How no contrite soul e'er sought Him,
  And was bidden to depart;
How, with gentle words, He taught him,
  Took the death from out his heart.

5 Still I read the ancient story,—
  And my joy is ever new,—
How for us He left His glory,
  How He still is kind and true;

6 Let me kneel, my Lord! before Thee,
  Let my heart in tears o'erflow,
Melted by Thy love adore Thee,
  Bless'd in Thee, 'mid joy or woe.
  Ger. Luise Hensel, 1829.
Tr. Catherine Winkworth, 1858.

Childhood.

555 Christchild. 8s 7s 7 7.
H. J. Gauntlett, 1868.

Once in royal David's City, Stood a lowly cattle shed,
Where a mother laid her Baby, In a manger for His bed:
Mary was that mother mild, Jesus Christ that little child.

2 Oh, our eyes at last shall see Him,
  Through His own redeeming love,
 For that child so dear and gentle,
  Is our God in heaven above;
 And He leads His children on
  To the place where He is gone.

3 Not in that poor lowly stable,
  With the oxen standing by,
 We shall see Him; but in heaven,
  Set at God's right hand on high;
 When like stars His children crowned
  All in white shall wait around.

Cecil F. Alexander, 1848.

556 Pastor. 8s 7s & 4.
J. H. Wilcox.

Saviour, like a shepherd lead us, Much we need Thy tender care;
In Thy pleasant pastures feed us; For our use Thy folds prepare.

Childhood.

Bless-ed Je-sus, Bless-ed Je-sus, Thou hast bought us, Thine we are.

2 Thou hast promised to receive us,
  Poor and sinful though we be;
Thou hast mercy to relieve us;
  Grace to cleanse, and power to free!
    Blessèd Jesus!
Let us early turn to Thee.

3 Early let us seek Thy favor,
  Early let us do Thy will;
Holy Lord, our only Saviour!
  With Thy grace our bosom fill:
    Blessèd Jesus!
Thou hast loved us, love us still.
Dorothy Ann Thrupp, 1838.

557

Once was heard the song of children,
  By the Saviour, when on earth;
Joyful, in the sacred temple,
  Shouts of youthful praise had birth,
    And hosannas
Loud to David's Son broke forth.

2 God o'er all, in heaven reigning!
  We this day Thy glory sing;
Not with palms Thy pathway strewing,
  We would loftier tribute bring,—
    Glad hosannas
To our Prophet, Priest and King.
Anon, 1843.

558 Innocents. 7s.   F. A. G. Ouseley, 1867.

Je-sus, Sav-iour, Son of God, Who for me life's path-way trod,
Who for me be-came a child; Make me hum-ble, meek, and mild.

2 I Thy little lamb would be
Jesus, I would follow Thee;
Samuel was Thy child of old
Take me, too, within Thy fold.

3 Teach me how to pray to Thee,
Make me holy, heavenly;
Let me love what Thou dost love,
Let me live with Thee above.
Anon, 1833.

Childhood.

559 Hosanna. 7s & 6s. BERTHOLD TOURS, 1872.

When, His salvation bringing, To Sion Jesus came,
The children all stood singing, Hosannas to His name;
Nor did their zeal offend Him, But, as He rode along,
He let them still attend Him, And smil'd to hear their song.

2 And, since the Lord retaineth
   His love for children still,
Though now as King He reigneth
   On Sion's heavenly hill;
We'll flock around His banner
   Who sits upon His throne,
And cry aloud,—" Hosanna
   To David's royal Son!"

3 For, should we fail proclaiming
   Our great Redeemer's praise,
The stones, our silence shaming,
   Would their hosannas raise:
But shall we only render,
   The tribute of our words?
No! while our hearts are tender,
   They, too, shall be the Lord's.

John King. 1850.

Childhood.

560 Hermas. 6s & 5s. FRANCES RIDLEY HAVERGAL, 1871.

Brightly gleams our banner, Pointing to the sky, Waving on Christ's soldiers To their home on high! Marching thro the desert, Gladly thus we pray, Still with hearts united, Singing on our way.—Brightly gleams our banner, Pointing to the sky, Waving on Christ's soldiers, To their home on high.

2 Pattern of our childhood,
　Once Thyself a child,
Make our childhood holy,
　Pure, and meek, and mild.
All our days direct us
　In the way we go,
Lead us on victorious,
　Over every foe.
　　Brightly gleams, etc.

3 Then with Saints and Angels
　May we join above,
Offering prayers and praises
　At Thy throne of love;
When the toil is over
　Then comes rest and peace,
Jesus in His beauty,—
　Songs that never cease.
　　Brightly gleams, etc.

Thomas J. Potter, 1860 ab.

Wedlock.

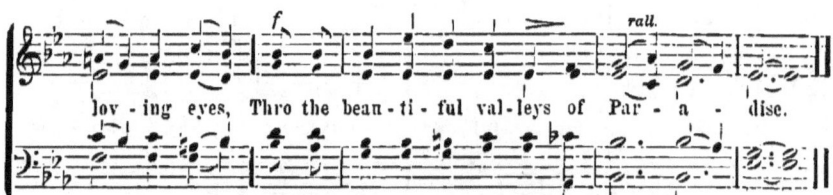

2 Hosanna we sing, for He bends His ear,
And rejoices the hymns of His own to hear;
We know that His heart will never wax cold
To the lambs that He feeds in His earthly fold.
Alleluia we sing in the church we love,
Alleluia resounds in the church above;
To Thy little ones, Lord, may such grace be given,
That we lose not our part in the song of heaven.

George Samuel Hodges, 1874.

562 Eden. 7s & 6s. St. Alban's Tune Book, 1865.

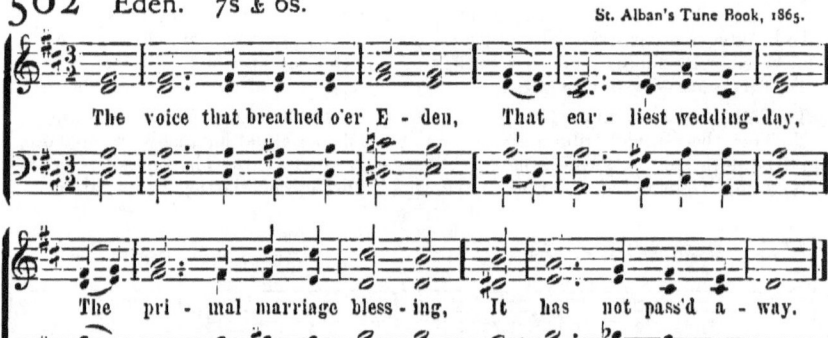

2 Still in the pure esponsal
  Of christian man and maid,
The holy Three are with us,
  The threefold grace is said.

3 Be present, heav'nly Father,
  To give away this bride,
As Eve Thou gav'st to Adam
  Out of his own pierc'd side:

4 Be present, Son of Mary,
  To join their loving hands,
As Thou didst bind two natures
  In Thine eternal bands!

5 Be present, holiest Spirit,
  To bless them as they kneel,
As Thou, for Christ the Bridegroom,
  The heavenly spouse dost seal!

6 O spread Thy pure wing o'er them,
  Let no ill power find place,
When onward to Thine altar
  Their hallowed path they trace.

7 To cast their crowns before Thee
  In perfect sacrifice,
Till to the home of gladness
  With Christ's own Bride they rise.

John Keble, 1857.

The Year.

563 Thanksgiving. L. M. 　　　FRANCIS R. STATHAM, 1872.

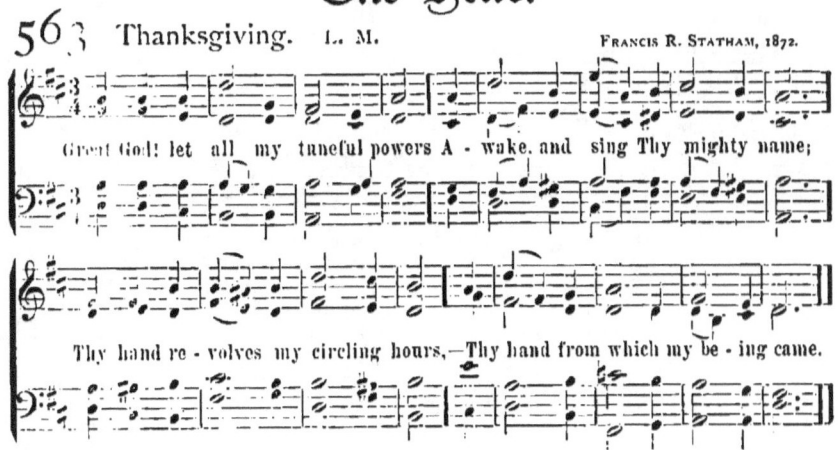

Great God! let all my tuneful powers Awake, and sing Thy mighty name;
Thy hand revolves my circling hours,—Thy hand from which my being came.

2 Seasons and moons still rolling round,
　In beauteous order speak Thy praise;
And years, with smiling mercy crowned,
　To Thee successive honors raise.

3 To Thee I raise the annual song,
　To Thee the grateful tribute give;
My God doth still my years prolong,
　And, midst unnumbered deaths, I live.

4 My life, my health, my friends, I owe
　All to Thy vast, unbounded love;
Ten thousand precious gifts below,
　And hope of nobler joys above.

5 Thus will I sing, till nature cease,
　Till sense and language are no more,
And, after death, Thy boundless grace,
　Through everlasting years, adore.
　　　　　　　Ottiwell Heginbothom, 1768.

564 Benevento. 7s. 　　　SAMUEL WEBBE, 1770. (?).

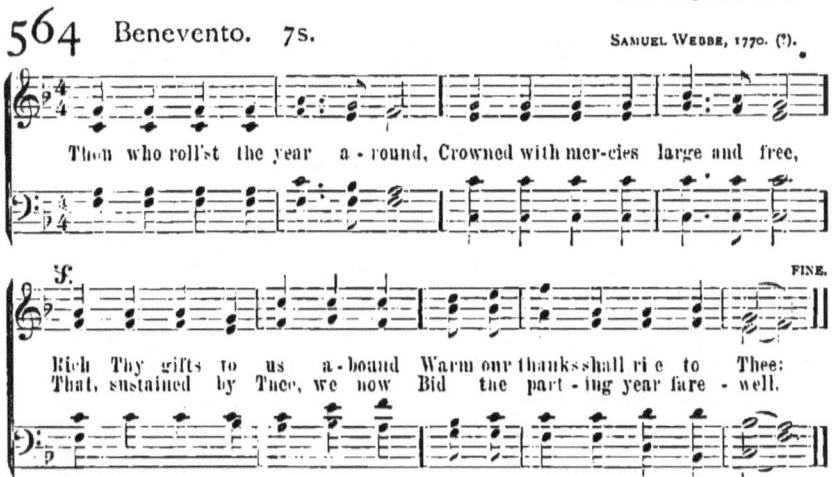

Thou who roll'st the year around, Crowned with mercies large and free,
Rich Thy gifts to us abound, Warm our thanks shall rise to Thee;
That, sustained by Thee, we now Bid the parting year farewell.

The Year.

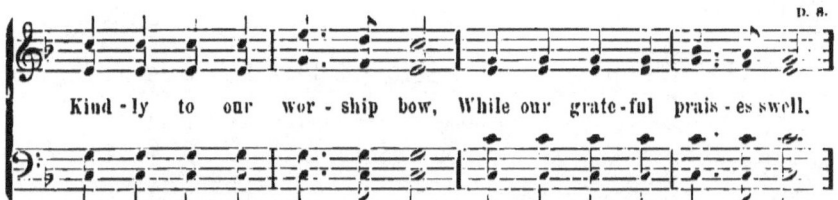

2 All its numbered days are sped,
  All its busy scenes are o'er,
All its joys for ever fled,
All its sorrows felt no more:
Mingled with th' eternal past,
  Its remembrance shall decay;
Yet to be revived at last
  At the solemn judgment-day.

3 All our follies, Lord! forgive;
  Cleanse each heart and make us Thine;
Let Thy grace within us live,
  As our future suns decline;
Then, when life's last eve shall come,
  Happy spirits, let us fly
To our everlasting home,
  To our Father's house on high.
      Ray Palmer, 1832.

565 Windsor. C. M.   GEORGE KIRBYE, 1592.

2 On all the wings of time it flies,
    Each moment brings it near;
  Then welcome each declining day,
    Welcome each closing year!

3 Ye wheels of nature! speed your course;
    Ye mortal powers! decay;
  Fast as ye bring the night of death,
    Ye bring eternal day.
        Philip Doddridge, 1740.

The Year.

566 Hummel. C. M.   H. C. ZEUNER, 1832.

To praise the ev-er-boun-te-ous Lord; My soul! wake all thy powers;
He calls—and at His voice come forth The smil-ing har-vest-hours.

2 His covenant with the earth He keeps;
   My tongue! His goodness sing;
Summer and winter know their time—
   His harvest crowns the spring.

3 Well-pleased the toiling workmen see
   The waving yellow crop;
With joy they bear the sheaves away,
   And sow again in hope.

4 Thus teach me, gracious God! to sow
   The seeds of righteousness;
Smile on my soul, and, with Thy beams,
   The ripening harvest bless.
                    John Needham, 1768.

4 His hoary frost, His fleecy snow,
   Descend and clothe the ground;
The liquid streams forbear to flow,
   In icy fetters bound.

5 He sends His word and melts the snow,
   The fields no longer mourn;
He calls the warmer gales to blow,
   And bids the spring return.

6 The changing wind, the flying cloud,
   Obey His mighty word:
With songs and honors sounding loud,
   Praise ye the sovereign Lord.
                    Isaac Watts, 1719.

567

WITH songs and honors sounding loud,
   Address the Lord on high;
Over the heavens He spreads His cloud,
   And waters veil the sky.

2 He sends His showers of blessing down,
   To cheer the plains below;
He makes the grass the mountains crown,
   And corn in valleys grow.

3 His steady counsels change the face
   Of the declining year;
He bids the sun cut short his race,
   And wintry days appear.

568

WHILE beauty clothes the fertile vale,
   And blossoms on the spray,
And fragrance breathes in every gale,
   How sweet the vernal day!

2 Oh! let my wondering heart confess
   With gratitude and love,
The bounteous hand, that deigns to bless
   The garden, field, and grove.

3 O God of nature, God of grace!
   Thy heavenly gifts impart,
And bid sweet meditation trace
   Spring blooming in my heart.
                    Anne Steele, 1760.

Harvest.

569 St. George's. 7s. G. J. Elvey, 1860.

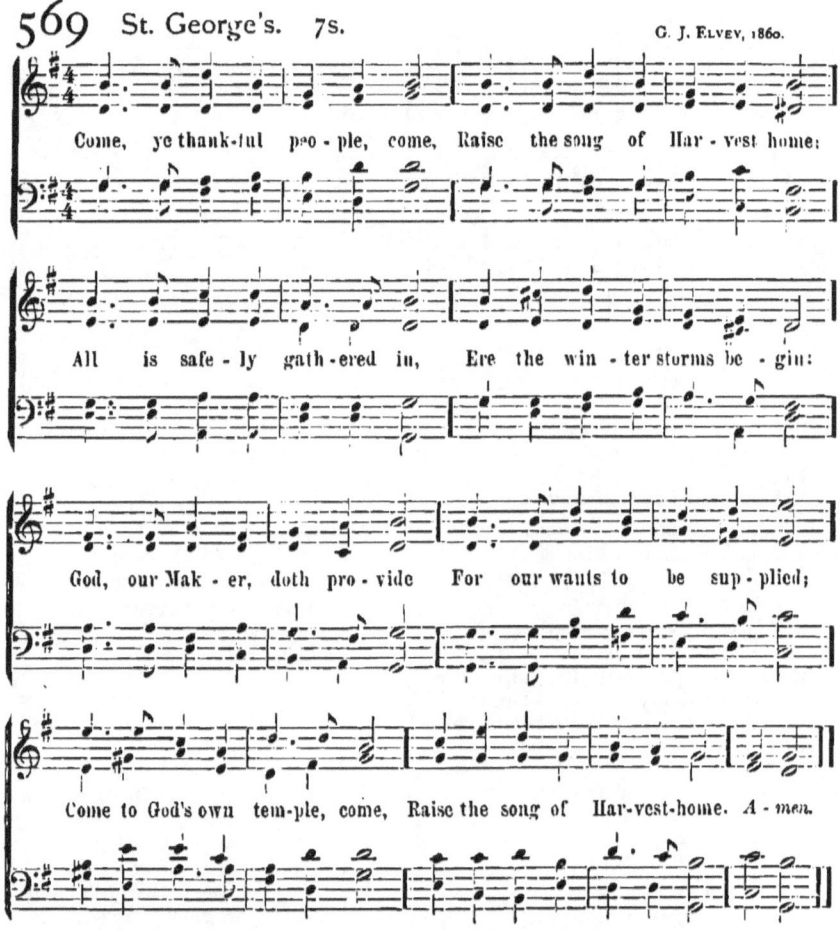

Come, ye thankful people, come, Raise the song of Harvest-home;
All is safely gathered in, Ere the winter storms begin:
God, our Maker, doth provide For our wants to be supplied;
Come to God's own temple, come, Raise the song of Harvest-home. Amen.

2 All the world is God's own field,
Fruit unto His praise to yield:
Wheat and tares together sown,
Unto joy or sorrow grown:
First the blade, and then the ear,
Then the full corn shall appear:
Lord of harvest, grant that we
Wholesome grain and pure may be.

3 Even so, Lord, quickly come
To Thy final Harvest-home;
Gather Thou Thy people in,
Free from sorrow, free from sin;
There for ever purified,
In Thy presence to abide:
Come with all Thine angels, come,
Raise the glorious Harvest-home. Amen.

Henry Alford 1844.

Harvest.

570 Luther. S. M.
Thomas Hastings, 1835.

Sow in the morn thy seed, At eve hold not thy hand; To doubt and fear give thou no heed; Broadcast it o'er the land, Broadcast it o'er the land.

2 And duly shall appear,
In verdure, beauty, strength,
The tender blade, the stalk, the ear,
And the full corn at length.

3 Thou canst not toil in vain;
Cold, heat, and moist, and dry,
Shall foster and mature the grain,
For garners in the sky.

4 Thence, when the glorious end,
The day of God, shall come,
The angel-reapers shall descend,
And heaven cry " Harvest-home!"
James Montgomery, 1832.

571
Lord of the harvest! hear
Thy needy servant's cry;
Answer our faith's effectual prayer,
And all our wants supply.

2 On Thee we humbly wait;
Our wants are in Thy view;

The harvest, truly, Lord! is great,
The laborers are few.

3 Convert and send forth more
Into Thy church abroad,
And let them speak Thy word of power,
As workers with their God.

4 Oh! let them spread Thy name,
Their mission fully prove;
Thy universal grace proclaim,—
Thine all redeeming love.
Charles Wesley, 1742.

572
The harvest dawn is near,
The year delays not long;
And he who sows with many a tear,
Shall reap with many a song.

2 Sad to his toil he goes,
His seed with weeping leaves;
But he shall come at twilight's close,
And bring his golden sheaves.
Geo. Burgess, 1839.

573 Stockwell. 8s & 7s.
Darius E. Jones, 1847.

He, that go-eth forth with weep-ing, Bearing pre-cious seed in love,

Harvest.

2 Soft descend the dews of heaven,
   Bright the rays celestial shine;
   Precious fruits will thus be given,
   Through an influence all divine.

3 Sow thy seed, be never weary,
   Let no fears thy soul annoy;
   Be the prospect ne'er so dreary,
   Thou shalt reap the fruits of joy:

4 Lo! the scene of verdure bright'ning,
   See the rising grain appear!
   Look again; the fields are whitening,
   For the harvest time is near.
   Thomas Hastings, 1835.

574 Stow. H. M.   LOWELL MASON, 1832.

2 In rich luxuriance dressed,
   Behold the spacious plain!
   Its bounty stands confessed,
   In fields of yellow grain:
   In lofty songs, your voices raise,
   The God of harvest claims your praise.

3 Fair plenty fills the land;
   His mercies never cease;—
   The husbandman doth smile,
   To see the large increase:
   In lofty songs, your voices raise,
   The God of harvest claims your praise.

4 The precious fruits He gives,
   Oh! may we ne'er abuse;
   But, through our future lives,
   To His own glory use,
   Then rise to heaven, and sing His praise
   In sweeter strains, and nobler lays.
   Anon, 1843.

Harvest.

575 Pæan. 7s.   W. A. Mozart, 1779. (?).

Let us with a gladsome mind Praise the Lord, for He is kind;
For His mercies shall en-dure, Ev-er faith-ful, ev-er sure.

REFRAIN. *Staccato.*
Al-le-lu-ia! A-men, Al-le-lu-ia! A-men.

2 Let us sound His name abroad,
God of gods He is the God,
Who by wisdom did create,
Heaven's expanse and all its state.
    Alleluia! Amen.

3 All His creatures God doth feed,
His full hand supplies their need;
Let us therefore warble forth
His high majesty and worth.
    Alleluia! Amen.
        John Milton, 1623.

576

Praise to God, immortal praise,
For the love that crowns our days;
Bounteous Source of every joy!
Let Thy praise our tongues employ.

2 All that spring, with bounteous hand,
Scatters o'er the smiling land,
All that liberal autumn pours
From her rich o'erflowing stores;—

3 Lord! for these our souls shall raise
Grateful vows, and solemn praise;
And, when every blessing's flown,
Love Thee for Thyself alone,
        Anna L. Barbauld, 1799.

577

Swell the anthem, raise the song;
Praises to our God belong:
Saints and angels! join to sing,
Praise to heaven's almighty King.

2 Blessings, from His liberal hand,
Pour around this happy land;
Let our hearts, beneath His sway,
Hail the bright, triumphant day.

3 Here, beneath a virtuous sway,
Lawful rulers we obey;
Here, we feel no tyrant's rod,
Here, we own and worship God.
        Nathan Strong, 1799.

National.

578 America.   6s & 4s.   HENRY CAREY, 1743. Ad. fr. JOHN BULL.

My country! 'tis of thee, Sweet land of lib-er-ty, Of thee I sing; Land, where my fathers died! Land of the pilgrims' pride! From every mountain side, Let freedom ring!

2 My native country! thee,—
Land of the noble, free,—
Thy name—I love;
I love thy rocks and rills,
Thy woods and templed hills:
My heart with rapture thrills
Like that above.

3 Our fathers' God! to Thee,
Author of liberty,
To Thee we sing:
Long may our land be bright,
With freedom's holy light;
Protect us by Thy might,
Great God, our King!
Samuel F. Smith, 1832.

579 Lowry.   C. M.   HUBERT P. MAIN, 1881.

Lord! while for all man-kind we pray, Of ev-ery clime and coast,—
Oh! hear us for our na-tive land,— The land we love the most.

Copyright, 1881, by Biglow & Main.

2 Unite us in the sacred love
Of knowledge, truth and Thee;
And let our hills and valleys shout
The songs of liberty.

3 Lord of the nations! thus to Thee
Our country we commend;
Be Thou her Refuge and her Trust,
Her everlasting Friend.
John R. Wreford, 1837.

National.

580 Nun Danket Alle Gott. P. M.   Johann N. Cruger, 1648.

Now thank we all our God, With hearts and hands and voic-es.
Who wondrous things hath done, In Whom His world re-joic-es;
Who from our moth-er's arms Hath bless'd us on our way
With count-less gifts of love, And still is ours to-day.

2 Lord God, we worship Thee:
Thou didst indeed chastise us;
Yet still Thy goodness spares,
And still Thy mercy tries us.
Once more our Father's hand
Has bid our sorrows flee,
And peace rejoice our land:
Lord God, we worship Thee.

3 Lord God, we worship Thee,
Whose goodness reigneth o'er us:
We praise Thy love and power
In loud and happy chorus,
To heaven our song shall soar;
For ever shall it be
Resounding o'er and o'er;
Lord God, we worship Thee.
M. Rinkart, 1644. Tr. Catherine Winkworth, 1858.

581 Ames. L. M.   Sigismund Neukomm, 1837.

O God, beneath Thy guid-ing hand, Our ex-iled fathers crossed the sea;

National.

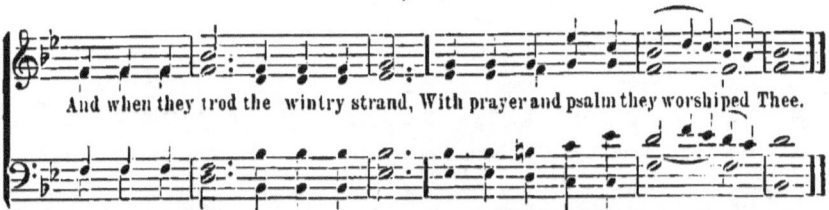

And when they trod the wintry strand, With prayer and psalm they worshiped Thee.

2 Thou heard'st, well-pleased, the song, the prayer;
Thy blessing came; and still its power
Shall onward through all ages bear
The memory of that holy hour!

3 Laws, freedom, truth, and faith in God
Came with those exiles o'er the waves;

And where their pilgrim feet have trod,
The God they trusted guards their graves.

4 And here Thy name, O God of love!
Their children's children shall adore,
Till these eternal hills remove,
And spring adorns the earth no more.

Leonard Bacon, 1838, 1845.

582   Russian Hymn.   11s, 10 & 9.   ALEXIS LWOFF, 1830.

O God, All ter-ri-ble! Thou who or-dain-est Thunder Thy clarion, and lightning Thy sword; Show forth Thy pit-y on high where Thou reignest; Give to us Peace in our time, O Lord!

2 O God, omnipotent, mighty Avenger!
Watching unseen, wielding judgment unheard,
Show us compassion,—oh! save us from danger,—
Give to us peace in our time, O Lord!

3 O God, all-merciful! Earth hath forsaken
Thy ways all-holy,—hath slighted Thy word,—
Let not Thy wrath, in its terror, awaken,—
Give to us pardon and peace, O Lord!

4 So shall we glorify, filled with devotion,
Thy grace that saved us from peril and sword;
Shouting in chorus, from Ocean to Ocean,
"Not unto us, but to Thee, O Lord!"

Henry F. Chorley, 1854, alt.

Fasting-Days.

583 Martyrs. C. M.   Scotch Psalter, 1615.

See, gracious God! before Thy throne, Thy mourning people bend! 'Tis on Thy sovereign grace alone, Our humble hopes depend.

2 Tremendous judgments, from Thy hand,
  Thy dreadful power display;
Yet mercy spares this guilty land,
  And still we live to pray.

3 Great God! why is our country spared,
  Ungrateful as we are?
Oh! be Thine awful warnings heard,
  While mercy cries,—"Forbear!"

4 How changed, alas! are truths divine,
  For error, guilt, and shame!
What impious numbers, bold in sin,
  Disgrace the Christian name!

5 Oh! turn us, turn us, mighty Lord!
  By Thy resistless grace;
Then shall our hearts obey Thy word,
  And humbly seek Thy face.
            Anne Steele, 1756.

584

Once more the solemn season calls,
  A holy fast to keep;
And now, within the temple walls,
  Let priest and people weep.

2 Yet all in vain the sound of woe,
  To reach the Father's ear,
If from the heart it does not flow,
  To prove our grief sincere.

3 Vain, vain, in ashes though we mourn,
  Our garments rend in twain,
Unless the smitten heart is torn
  With penitential pain.

4 Then let us cry to God betimes,
  Nor let His anger flow;
Lest, mindful of our numerous crimes,
  It deal the threatened blow.

5 O Father, righteous Judge, and God!
  Thy wrath be slow to burn;
Thou givest time to mark the rod—
  Give also hearts to turn.
        Lat., *Charles Coffin*, 1700.
        Tr., *William Mercer*, 1864.

585

Lord! Thou hast scourged our guilty land;
  Behold Thy people mourn!
Shall vengeance ever guide Thy hand?
  And mercy ne'er return?

2 Beneath the terrors of Thine eye,
  Earth's haughty towers decay;
Thy frowning mantle spreads the sky,
  And mortals melt away.

3 Our Zion trembles at Thy stroke,
  And dreads Thy lifted hand;
Oh! heal the people Thou hast broke,
  And save the sinking land.
            Isaac Watts, 1719. a.

The Church.

586 Aurelia. 7s & 6s.   S. S. Wesley, 1864.

The Church's one foun-da-tion Is Je-sus Christ her Lord;
She is His new cre-a-tion By wa-ter and the Word:
From heav'n He came and sought her, To be His ho-ly Bride;
With His own blood He bought her, And for her life He died.

2 Though with a scornful wonder,
  Men see her sore opprest,
By schisms rent asunder,
  By heresies distrest;
Yet saints their watch are keeping,
  Their cry goes up, "How long?"
And soon the night of weeping
  Shall be the morn of song.

3 'Mid toil and tribulation,
  And tumult of her war,
She waits the consummation
  Of peace for evermore;
Till with the vision glorious
  Her longing eyes are blest,
And the great Church victorious
  Shall be the Church at rest.

S. J. Stone, 1865.

The Church.

587 Maidstone. 7s. WALTER B. GILBERT, 1862.

Pleas-ant are Thy courts a-bove, In the land of light and love:
Pleas-ant are Thy courts be-low, In this land of sin and woe.
O, my spir-it longs and faints For the con-verse of Thy saints, For the bright-ness of Thy face, King of glo-ry, God of grace!

2 Happy souls! their praises flow,
Ever in this vale of woe;
Waters in the desert rise,
Manna feeds them from the skies;
On they go from strength to strength,
Till they reach Thy throne at length;
At Thy feet adoring fall,
Who hast led them safe through all.

3 Lord, be mine this prize to win;
Guide me through a world of sin,
Keep me by Thy saving grace,
Give me at Thy side a place;
Sun and shield alike Thou art,
Guide and guard my erring heart;
Grace and glory flow from Thee,
Shower, oh show'r them, Lord, on me.

Henry F. Lyte, 1834.

The Church.

588 Zerah. C. M.   LOWELL MASON, 1837.

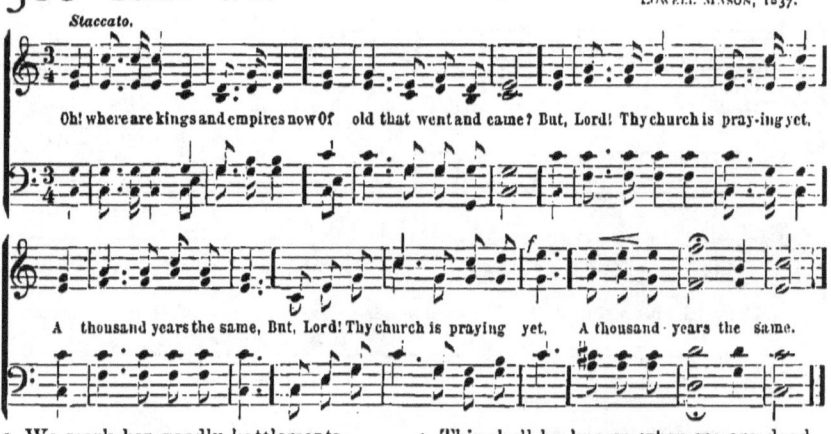

Oh! where are kings and empires now Of old that went and came? But, Lord! Thy church is pray-ing yet, A thousand years the same, But, Lord! Thy church is praying yet, A thousand years the same.

2 We mark her goodly battlements,
And her foundations strong;
We hear within the solemn voice
Of her unending song.

3 For, not like kingdoms of the world,
Thy holy church, O God!
Though earthquake shocks are threatening her,
And tempests are abroad;

4 Unshaken as eternal hills,
Immovable she stands,
A mountain that shall fill the earth,
A house not made by hands.
Arthur Cleveland Coxe, 1839, a.

589

Let Zion and her sons rejoice;
Behold the promised hour!
Her God hath heard her mourning voice,
And comes t' exalt His power.

2 Her dust and ruins that remain,
Are precious in our eyes;
Those ruins shall be built again,
And all that dust shall rise.

3 The Lord will raise Jerusalem,
And stand in glory there;
Nations shall bow before His name,
And kings attend with fear.

4 This shall be known when we are dead,
And left on long record,
That ages yet unborn may read,
And trust, and praise the Lord.
Isaac Watts, 1719.

590

Trust in the Lord, forever trust,
And banish all your fears;
Strength in the Lord Jehovah dwells,
Eternal as His years.

2 Lift up the everlasting gates,
The doors wide open fling;
Ye nations enter, that obey
The statutes of our King.

3 Behold the Morning Star arise,
Ye that in darkness sit;
He marks the path that leads to peace,
And guides our doubtful feet.

4 Be every vale exalted high,
Sink every mountain low;
The proud must stoop, and humble souls
Shall His salvation know.

5 The heathen realms with Israel's land
Shall join in sweet accord;
And all that's born of man shall see
The glory of the Lord!
Isaac Watts, 1707.

All Saints.

591 St. Thomas. S. M. — Aaron Williams, 1763.

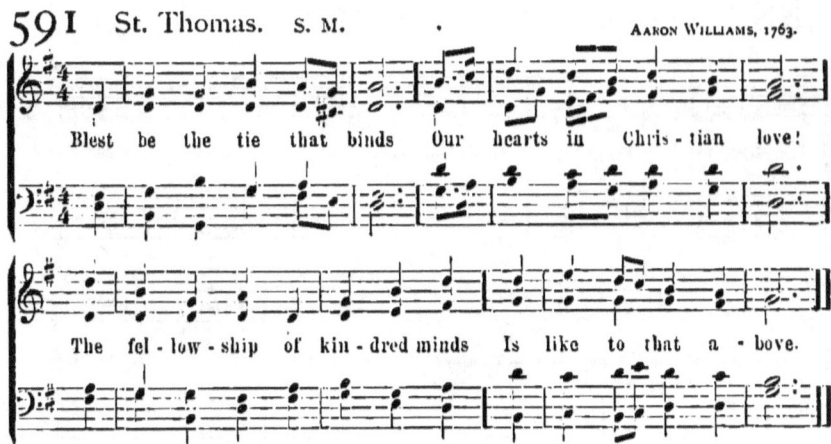

Blest be the tie that binds
Our hearts in Chris-tian love!
The fel-low-ship of kin-dred minds
Is like to that a-bove.

2 Before our Father's throne,
  We pour our ardent prayers;
Our fears, our hopes, our aims are one,
  Our comforts and our cares.

3 We share our common woes;
  Our common burdens bear;
And often for each other flows
  The sympathizing tear.

4 From sorrow, toil, and pain,
  And sin we shall be free;
And perfect love and friendship reign
  Through all eternity.
            John Fawcett, 1772.

592

1 Love Thy kingdom, Lord!
  The house of Thine abode,
The church, our blest Redeemer saved
  With His own precious blood.

2 I love Thy church, O God!
  Her walls before Thee stand,
Dear as the apple of Thine eye,
  And graven on Thy hand.

3 For her my tears shall fall,
  For her my prayers ascend;
To her my cares and toils be given,
  Till toils and cares shall end.

4 Beyond my highest joy
  I prize her heavenly ways,
Her sweet communion, solemn vows,
  Her hymns of love and praise.

5 Jesus, thou Friend divine,
  Our Saviour and our King!
Thy hand, from every snare and foe
  Shall great deliv'rance bring.

6 Sure as Thy truth shall last,
  To Zion shall be given
The brightest glories earth can yield,
  And brighter bliss of heaven.
            Timothy Dwight, 1800.

593

1 This is the glorious day,
  That our Redeemer made;
Let us rejoice, and sing, and pray,
  Let all the church be glad.

2 Hosanna to the King
  Of David's royal blood!
Bless Him, ye saints! He comes, to bring
  Salvation from your God.

3 We bless Thy holy word,
  Which all this grace displays;
And offer on Thine altar, Lord!
  Our sacrifice of praise.
            Isaac Watts, 1719.

All Saints.

594 Wavertree. L. M.   Wm. Shore.

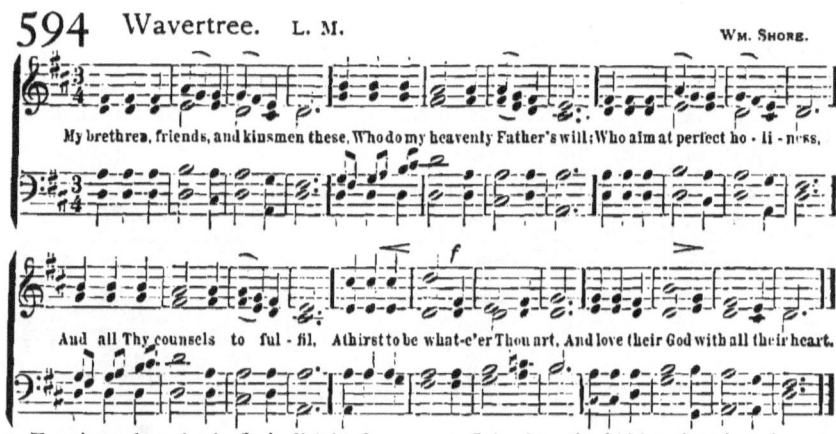

My brethren, friends, and kinsmen these, Who do my heavenly Father's will; Who aim at perfect ho-li-ness, And all Thy counsels to ful-fil, Athirst to be what-e'er Thou art, And love their God with all their heart.

2 For these, howe'er in flesh disjoined
   Where'er dispersed o'er earth abroad,
Unfeigned, unbounded love I find,
   And constant as the life of God;
Fountain of life! from thence it sprung,
As pure, as even, and as strong.

3 Joined to the hidden church unknown
   In this sure bond of perfectness,
Obscurely safe, I dwell alone,
   And glory in th' uniting grace,
To me—to each believer given,
To all Thy saints in earth and heaven.
Charles Wesley. 1755.

595 Hummel. C. M.   H. C. Zeuner, 1832.

Let saints be-low in con-cert sing With those to glo-ry gone; For all the serv-ants of our King In earth and heaven are one.

2 One family, we dwell in Him,—
   One church above, beneath,
Though now divided by the stream,—
   The narrow stream of death.

3 One army of the living God,
   To His command we bow;
Part of the host have crossed the flood,
   And part are crossing now.
Charles Wesley. 1759. ab.

All Saints.

596　Eltham.　7s.　　　　　　　　　Lowell Mason, 1840.

Hast-en, Lord! the glo-rious time, When, be-neath Mes-si-ah's sway,
Ev-ery na-tion, ev-ery clime, Shall the gos-pel's call o-bey.
D.C. Sa-tan and his host o'erthrown, Bound in chains, shall hurt no more.

Mightiest kings His pow'r shall own; Heathen tribes His name a-dore;

2 Then shall wars and tumults cease;
　Then be banished grief and pain;
Righteousness, and joy, and peace,
　Undisturbed shall ever reign.

Bless we, then, our gracious Lord:
　Ever praise His glorious name;
All His mighty acts record;
　All His wondrous love proclaim.
　　　　　Harriet Auber, 1829.

597　Unity.　8s & 4.　　　　　　　Henry John Gauntlett, 1874.

Fa-ther of all, from land and sea The na-tions sing, "Thine Lord are we;"

Count-less in num-ber, but in Thee May we be one.

2 O Son of God, whose love so free
　For men, did make Thee man to be,—
United to our God in Thee
　　May we be one.

3 O Trinity in Unity,
　One only God, in Persons Three,

Dwell ever in our hearts; like Thee
　May we be one.

4 So when the world shall pass away,
May we awake with joy and say,
"Now in the bliss of endless day,
　We all are one."
　　　　Christopher Wordsworth, 1865.

All Saints.

598 Aurora. 10S & 4S. MAX PIUTTI, 1879.

Copyright, 1880, by Biglow & Main

2 Thou wast their Rock, their Fortress and their Might;
Thou, Lord, their Captain in the well-fought fight;
Thou, in the darkness drear their one true Light. Alleluia!

3 Oh, blest communion, fellowship divine!
We feebly struggle; they in glory shine!
Yet all are one in Thee, for all are Thine. Alleluia!

4 The golden evening brightens in the west;
Soon, soon, to faithful warriors cometh rest;
Sweet is the calm of Paradise the blest. Alleluia!

5 But lo! there breaks a yet more glorious day;
The saints triumphant rise in bright array;
The King of Glory passes on His way! Alleluia!

6 From earth's wide bounds, from ocean's farthest coast,
Through gates of pearl streams in the countless host,
Singing to Father, Son, and Holy Ghost—Alleluia!

William W. How, 1854, ab.

All Saints.

599 St. Olave. C. M.   Joseph Barnby, 1861.

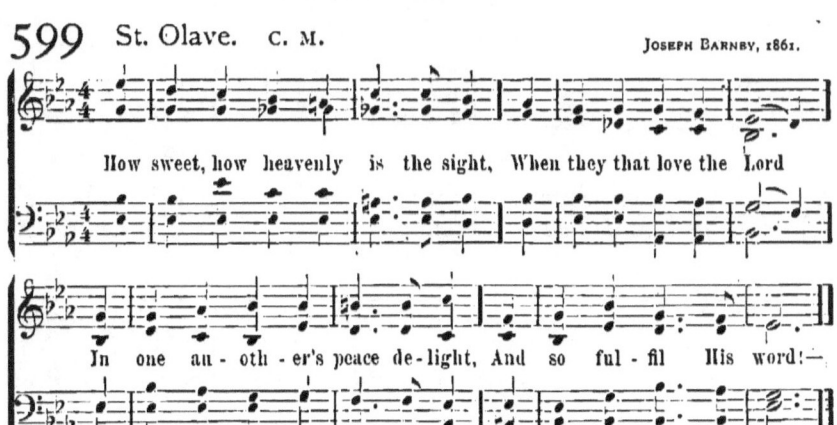

How sweet, how heavenly is the sight, When they that love the Lord
In one an-oth-er's peace de-light, And so ful-fil His word:—

2 When each can feel his brother's sigh,
   And with him bear a part;
When sorrow flows from eye to eye,
   And joy from heart to heart:—

3 When, free from envy, scorn, and pride,
   Our wishes all above,
Each can his brother's failings hide,
   And show a brother's love.
                  Joseph Swain, 1792 ab.

600

Happy the souls to Jesus joined,
   And saved by grace alone!
Walking in all Thy ways, we find
   Our heaven on earth begun.

2 The church, triumphant in Thy love,—
   Their mighty joys we know;
They sing the Lamb in hymns above,
   And we, in hymns below.

3 Thee, in Thy glorious realm they praise,
   And bow before Thy throne;
We, in the kingdom of Thy grace;
   The kingdoms are but one.

4 The holy to the holiest leads;
   From thence our spirits rise;
And he, that in Thy statutes treads,
   Shall meet Thee in the skies.
                  Charles Wesley, 1745.

601

Oh! let Thy grace perform its part,
   And let contention cease;
And shed abroad in every heart
   Thine everlasting peace.

2 Thus chastened, cleansed, entirely Thine,
   A flock by Jesus led,
The Sun of righteousness shall shine
   In glory on our head.

3 And Thou wilt turn our wandering feet,
   And Thou wilt bless our way;
Till worlds shall fade, and faith shall greet
   The dawn of lasting day!
                  Henry Kirke White, 1803, ab.

602

Among the saints that fill Thy house,
   My offerings shall be paid;
There shall my zeal perform the vows
   My soul in anguish made.

2 How much is mercy Thy delight,
   Thou ever-blessèd God!
How dear Thy servants in Thy sight,
   How precious is their blood!

3 Now I am Thine, for ever Thine,
   Nor shall my purpose move;
Thy hand hath loosed my bonds of pain,
   And bound me with Thy love.
                  Isaac Watts, 1719, ab.

All Saints.

603 Laurel. 7s & 6s p.   Joseph Barnby, 1868.

Let our choir new anthems raise; Wake the song of gladness;
God Himself to joy and praise Turns the martyrs' sadness:
Bright the day that won their crown, Opened Heaven's bright portal,
As they laid the mortal down To put on th' immortal.

2 Never flinched they from the flame,
  From the torture, never;
Vain the foeman's sharpest aim,
  Satan's best endeavor:
For by faith they saw the land
  Decked in all its glory,
Where triumphant now they stand
  With the victor's story.

3 Up and follow, Christian men!
  Press through toil and sorrow;
Spurn the night of fear, and then,
  Oh, the glorious morrow!
Who will venture on the strife?
  Who will first begin it;
Who will seize the land of life?
  Warriors, up and win it!
        Tr. *John M. Neale*, 1863.

Revival.

604 Baca. L. M.   Wm. B. Bradbury, 1857.

We all, O Lord, have gone astray, And wandered from Thy heavenly way: The wilds of sin our feet have trod, Far from the paths of Thee, our God, Far from the paths of Thee, our God.

2 Hear us, great Shepherd of Thy sheep!
Our wanderings heal, our footsteps keep:
We seek Thy sheltering fold again,
Nor shall we seek Thee, Lord, in vain.

3 Teach us to know and love Thy way;
And grant, to life's remotest day,
By Thine unerring guidance led,
Our willing feet Thy paths to tread.
Josiah Pratt's Coll., 1829.

605

Return, my roving heart! return,
And chase these shad'wy forms no more,
Seek out some solitude, to mourn,
And Thy forsaken God implore.

2 And Thou, my God! whose piercing eye,
Distinct surveys each deep recess,
In these devoted hours draw nigh,
And with Thy presence fill the place.

3 Through all the mazes of my heart,
My search let heavenly wisdom guide,
And still its radiant beams impart,
Till all be searched and purified.

4 Then, with the visits of Thy love,
Vouchsafe my inmost soul to cheer;
Till every grace shall join to prove,
That God has fixed His dwelling there.
Philip Doddridge, 1740.

606

Great Shepherd of Thine Israel!
Who didst between the cherubs dwell,
And led the tribes, Thy chosen sheep,
Safe through the desert and the deep;

2 Thy church is in the desert now;
Shine from on high and guide us through;
Turn us to Thee, Thy love restore;
We shall be saved, and sigh no more.
Isaac Watts, 1719.

607

O Lord! how joyful 'tis to see
The brethren join in love to Thee!
On Thee alone their heart relies;
Their only strength Thy grace supplies.

2 Oh! may we love the house of God,
Of peace and joy the blest abode!
Oh! may no angry strife destroy
That sacred peace, that holy joy!

3 The world without may rage, but we
Will only cling more close to Thee,
With hearts to Thee more wholly given,
More weaned from earth, more fixed on heaven.

4 Lord! show'r upon us, from above,
The sacred gift of mutual love;
Each other's wants may we supply,
And reign together in the sky.
Tr., John Chandler, 1837.

Revival.

608 Gloucester. C. M. RICHARD FARRANT, 1580.

Lord! let Thy sav-ing mer-cy heal The wounds it made be-fore;

Now on our hearts im-press Thy seal, That we may doubt no more.

2 The fear, which Thy convictions wrought,
Oh! let Thy grace remove;
And may the souls, which Thou hast taught
To weep, now learn to love.

3 Complete the work Thou hast begun,
And make our darkness light,—
That we a glorious race may run,
Till faith be lost in sight.
Wm. Hiley Bathurst, 1830. ab.

609 Wycliffe. 8 8 7 7. WÜRTTEMBERG GESANGBUCH.

Mighty God, Thy church re-cov-er, Bid the sleep of death be o-ver,

Purge our hearts, Thou Ho-ly Ghost! Light the flames of Pen-te-cost.

2 By the Saviour's intercession,
Blot, in mercy, our transgression;
Thou, O God, wilt not despise
Broken-hearted sacrifice!

3 Turn Thy people's desolation
To the joy of Thy salvation;
So our tongues aloud shall sing
Of Thy righteousness, our King!
M. W. Stryker, 1881.

Missions.

610 Webb. 7s & 6s. GEORGE JAMES WEBB, 1830.

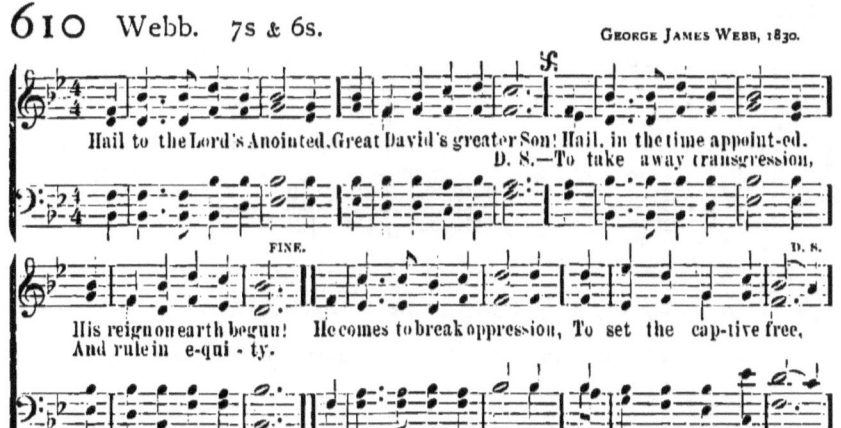

Hail to the Lord's Anointed, Great David's greater Son! Hail, in the time appoint-ed.
D. S.—To take away transgression,
His reign on earth begun! He comes to break oppression, To set the cap-tive free,
And rule in e-qui-ty.

2 He comes, with succor speedy,
  To those who suffer wrong:
To help the poor and needy,
  And bid the weak be strong;
To give them songs for sighing,
  Their darkness turn to light,
Whose souls, condemned and dying,
  Were precious in His sight.

3 He shall come down, like showers
  Upon the fruitful earth,
And joy, and hope, like flowers,
  Spring in His path to birth:
Before Him on the mountains,
  Shall peace, the herald, go;
And righteousness, in fountains,
  From hill to valley flow.

4 For Him shall prayer unceasing
  And daily vows ascend;
His kingdom still increasing,—
  A kingdom without end:
The tide of time shall never
  His covenant remove;
His name shall stand for ever;
  That name to us is—Love.
  James Montgomery. 1821.

611

STAND up, stand up for Jesus,
  Ye soldiers of the cross!
Lift high His royal banner,
  It must not suffer loss:
From vict'ry unto vict'ry
  His army shall He lead,
Till every foe is vanquished
  And Christ is Lord indeed.

2 Stand up, stand up for Jesus,
  The trumpet call obey;
Forth to the mighty conflict,
  In this His glorious day:
Ye that are men! now serve Him,
  Against unnumbered foes;
Your courage rise with danger,
  And strength to strength oppose.

3 Stand up, stand up for Jesus;
  Stand in His strength alone;
The arm of flesh will fail you;
  Ye dare not trust your own:
Put on the gospel armor,
  And, watching unto prayer,
Where duty calls, or danger,
  Be never wanting there.

Missions.

612

4 Stand up, stand up for Jesus;
   The strife will not be long;
This day, the noise of battle,—
   The next, the victor's song:
To him that overcometh,
   A crown of life shall be;
He, with the King of glory,
   Shall reign eternally!
George Duffield, 1858.

The whole wide world for Jesus;
   Once more before we part,
Ring out the joyful watchword
   From every grateful heart:
The whole wide world for Jesus;
   We'll wing the song with prayer,
And link the prayer with labor,
   Till Christ His crown shall wear.
Katharine H. Johnson, 1872.

613 Faben.. 8s & 7s. JOHN H. WILCOX, 1849.

Glorious things of thee are spoken, Zi-on, cit-y of our God! He, whose word cannot be broken, Formed thee for His own a-bode: On the Rock of A-ges founded, What can shake thy sure repose? With salvation's walls surrounded, Thou may'st smile at all thy foes.

2 See! the streams of living waters,
   Springing from eternal love,
Well supply Thy sons and daughters,
   And all fear of want remove:
Who can faint, while such a river
   Ever flows their thirst t'assuage?—
Grace, which, like the Lord, the Giver,
   Never fails from age to age.
John Newton, 1779.

Missions.

614   Aithlone.   C. P. M.   HEINRICH ISAAC, 1490.

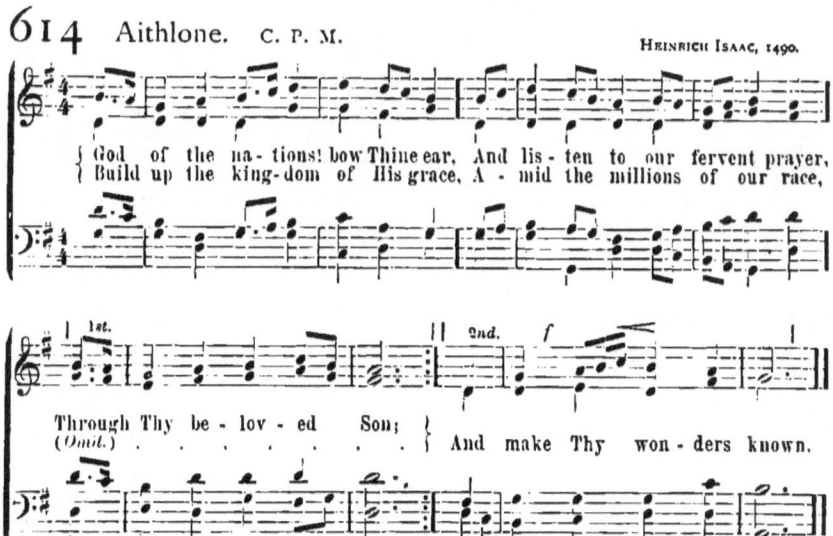

{ God of the na-tions! bow Thine ear, And lis-ten to our fervent prayer,
{ Build up the king-dom of His grace, A-mid the millions of our race,
Through Thy be-lov-ed Son;
(Omit.) . . . . . . And make Thy won-ders known.

2 Send forth the heralds in His name;
Bid them a Saviour's love proclaim,
　With every fleeting breath;
Till distant lands shall hear the sound,
And send the joyful echoes round,
　Amid the shades of death.

3 Hast Thou not given the heavenly word,
That all the earth shall know the Lord,
　And to His sceptre bow?
And is not this the favored hour,
When many a realm shall feel His power,
　And pay the solemn vow?

4 Oh! let the nations rise, and bring
Their offerings to th' almighty King,
　And trust in Him alone;
Renounce their idols, and adore
The God of gods for evermore,
　Upon His lofty throne.

5 The dying millions thus shall prove
The matchless power of bleeding love,
　And feel their sins forgiven;
Shall join the converts' joyful throng,
And raise on high redemption's song,
　Along the path to heaven.
　　　　　　　　Thomas Hastings, 1834.

615   Rockingham.   L. M.   LOWELL MASON, 1830.

O Spir-it of the liv-ing God! In all Thy plen-i-tude of grace,

Missions.

Where'er the foot of man hath trod, De-scend on our a-pos-tate race.

2 Give tongues of fire, and hearts of love,
  To preach the reconciling word;
  Give power and unction from above,
  Whene'er the joyful sound is heard.

3 Be darkness, at Thy coming, light;
  Confusion—order, in Thy path;
  Souls without strength inspire with might;
  Bid mercy triumph over wrath.

4 Baptize the nations; far and nigh,
  The triumphs of the cross record;
  The name of Jesus glorify,
  Till every kindred call Him Lord.

5 God, from eternity, hath willed,—
  All flesh shall His salvation see;
  So be the Father's love fulfilled,
  The Saviour's suff'rings crown'd, thro thee.
  James Montgomery, 1823.

616 Dawn. 7s & 5.   C. STEGGALL, 1872.

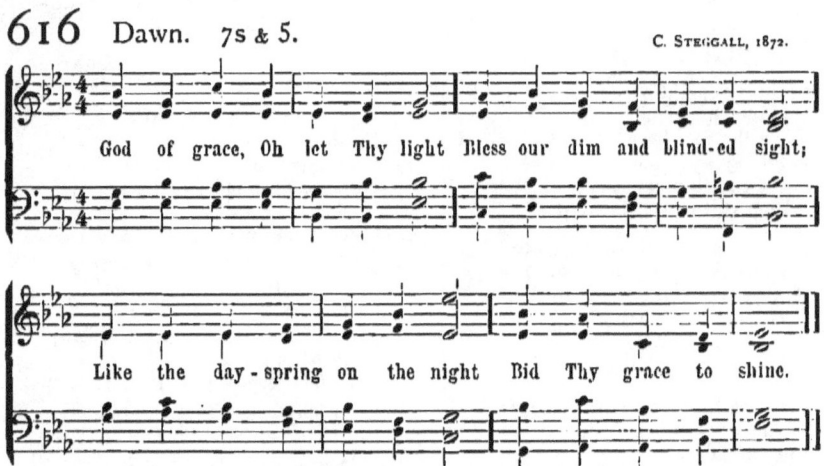

God of grace, Oh let Thy light Bless our dim and blind-ed sight;

Like the day-spring on the night Bid Thy grace to shine.

2 To the nations led astray
  Thine eternal love display;
  Let Thy truth direct their way
  Till the world be Thine.

3 Praise to Thee, the faithful Lord;
  Let all tongues in glad accord
  Learn the good thanksgiving word,
  Ever praising Thee.

4 Let them, moved to gladness, sing,
  Owning Thee their Judge and King;
  Righteous truth shall bloom and spring
  Where Thy rule shall be.
  Edward Churton, 1854.

Missions.

617 Zion. 8s 7s & 4. THOMAS HASTINGS, 1830.

On the mountain's top appearing,
Lo! the sacred herald stands,
Welcome news to Zion bearing—
Zion, long in hostile lands;
  Mourning captive!
God Himself shall loose thy bands.

2 Has thy night been long and mournful?
Have thy friends unfaithful proved?
Have thy foes been proud and scornful,
By thy sighs and tears unmoved?
  Cease thy mourning;
Zion still is well beloved.

3 Every human tie may perish;
Friend to friend unfaithful prove;
Mothers cease their own to cherish;
Heaven and earth at last remove:
  But no changes
Can attend Jehovah's love.

4 In the furnace God may prove thee,
Thence to bring thee forth more bright;
But can never cease to love thee;
Thou art precious in His sight;
  God is with thee—
God, thine everlasting light.

5 Peace and joy shall now attend thee;
All thy warfare now is past;
God thy Saviour will defend thee;
Victory is thine at last:
  All thy conflicts
End in everlasting rest.
  Thomas Kelly, 1806.

618

CHRIST is coming! let creation
Bid her groans and travail cease:
Let the glorious proclamation
Hope restore and faith increase;
  Christ is coming!
Come, Thou blessèd Prince of peace!

2 Earth can now but tell the story
Of Thy bitter cross and pain;
She shall yet behold Thy glory
When Thou comest back to reign;
  Christ is coming!
Let each heart repeat the strain.

3 Long Thy exiles have been pining,
Far from rest, and home, and Thee:
But, in heavenly vesture shining,
Soon they shall Thy glory see;
  Christ is coming!
Haste the joyous jubilee.

4 With that "blessèd hope" before us,
Let no harp remain unstrung;
Let the mighty advent chorus
Onward roll from tongue to tongue;
  Christ is coming!
Come, Lord Jesus, quickly come.
  J. R. Macduff, 1851.

Missions.

619

O'er the gloomy hills of darkness,
Cheered by no celestial ray,
Sun of righteousness! arising,
  Bring the bright, the glorious day;
    Send the gospel,
  To the earth's remotest bound.

2 Kingdoms wide that sit in darkness,—
Grant them, Lord! the glorious light;
And, from eastern coast to western,
  May the morning chase the night;
    And redemption,
  Freely purchased, win the day.

3 Fly abroad, thou mighty gospel!
Win and conquer, never cease;
May thy lasting, wide dominions,
  Multiply and still increase;
    Sway Thy sceptre,
  Saviour! all the world around.
William Williams, 1772, a.

620

Yes, we trust, the day is breaking;
Joyful times are near at hand;
God, the mighty God, is speaking
  By His word in every land;
    Mark His progress!
  Darkness flies, at His command.

2 While the foe becomes more daring,
While he enters like a flood,
God, the Saviour, is preparing
  Means to spread His truth abroad:
    Every language
  Soon shall tell the love of God.

3 God of Jacob, high and glorious!
Let Thy people see Thy hand;
Let the gospel be victorious,
  Through the world, in every land;
    Let the idols
  Perish, Lord! at Thy command.
Thomas Kelly, 1809.

621 New Haven. 6s & 4s.
THOS. HASTINGS, 1833.

Christ for the world we sing; The world to Christ we bring, With loving zeal; The poor, and them that mourn, The faint and overborne, Sin-sick and sorrow-worn, Whom Christ doth heal.

2 Christ for the world we sing;
The world to Christ we bring,
  With one accord;
With us the work to share,
With us reproach to dare,
With us the cross to bear,
  For Christ our Lord.

3 Christ for the world we sing,
The world to Christ we bring,
  With joyful song;
The new-born souls, whose days,
Reclaimed from error's ways,
Inspired with hope and praise,
  To Christ belong.
Samuel Wolcott, 1869.

Missions.

622 Missionary Hymn. 7s & 6s. LOWELL MASON, 1823.

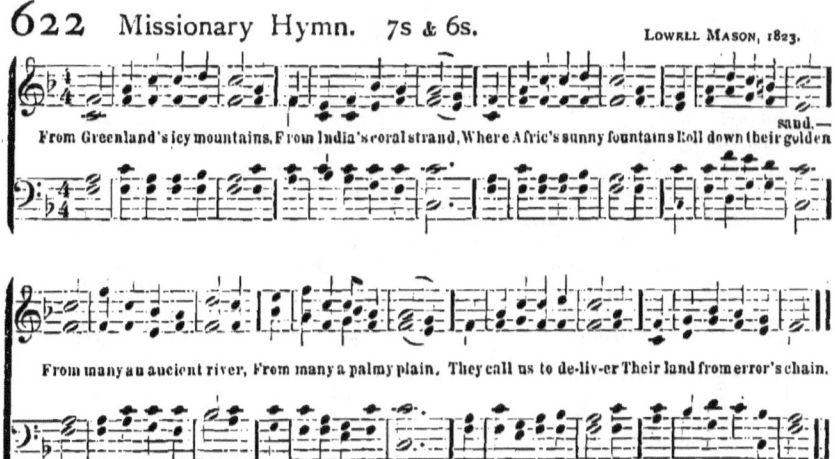

From Greenland's icy mountains, From India's coral strand, Where Afric's sunny fountains Roll down their golden sand.
From many an ancient river, From many a palmy plain, They call us to de-liv-er Their land from error's chain.

2 What, though the spicy breezes
  Blow soft o'er Ceylon's isle;
Though every prospect pleases,
  And only man is vile?
In vain with lavish kindness
  The gifts of God are strewn;
The heathen, in his blindness,
  Bows down to wood and stone!

3 Can we, whose souls are lighted
  With wisdom from on high,—
Can we, to men benighted,
  The lamp of life deny?
Salvation, Oh! salvation!—
  The joyful sound proclaim,
Till each remotest nation
  Has learned Messiah's name.

4 Waft, waft, ye winds! His story,
  And you, ye waters! roll,
Till, like a sea of glory,
  It spreads from pole to pole;
Till, o'er our ransomed nature,
  The Lamb, for sinners slain,
Redeemer, King, Creator,
  In bliss returns to reign!
                Reginald Heber, 1819.

623

The morning light is breaking;
  The darkness disappears;
The sons of earth are waking
  To penitential tears;
Each breeze, that sweeps the ocean,
  Brings tidings, from afar,
Of nations in commotion,
  Prepared for Zion's war.

2 See heathen nations bending
  Before the God we love,
And thousand hearts ascending
  In gratitude above;
While sinners, now confessing,
  The gospel call obey,
And seek the Saviour's blessing,—
  A nation in a day.

3 Blest river of salvation!
  Pursue thine onward way;
Flow thou to every nation,
  Nor in thy richness stay:—
Stay not, till all the lowly
  Triumphant reach their home;
Stay not, till all the holy
  Proclaim, "The Lord is come."
                Samuel F. Smith, 1831.

Missions.

624 Arlington. C. M.   Thomas A. Arne, 1762.

Light of the lonely pilgrim's heart! Star of the coming day!
Arise, and with Thy morning beams Chase all our griefs away.

2 Come, blessèd Lord! let every shore
And answering island sing
The praises of Thy royal name,
And own Thee as their King.

3 Jesus! Thy fair creation groans,—
The air, the earth, the sea,—
In unison with all our hearts,
And calls aloud for Thee.
      Edward Denny.

625.
Lord! send Thy word, and let it fly,
Armed with Thy Spirit's power;
Ten thousands shall confess its sway,
And bless the saving hour.

2 Beneath the influence of its grace,
The barren wastes shall rise,
With sudden greens and fruits arrayed,—
A blooming paradise.

3 Peace, with her olives crowned, shall
Her wings from shore to shore; [stretch
No trump shall rouse the rage of war,
Nor murderous cannon roar.

4 Lord! for these days we wait;—these
Are in Thy word foretold;   [days
Fly swifter, sun and stars! and bring
This promised age of gold.

5 "Amen!"—with joy divine, let earth's
Unnumbered myriads cry;
"Amen!"—with joy divine, let heaven's
Unnumbered choirs reply.
      Thomas Gibbons, 1769.

626
Daughter of Zion! from the dust
Exalt thy fallen head;
Again in thy Redeemer trust,—
He calls thee from the dead.

2 Awake, awake, put on thy strength,—
Thy beautiful array;
Thy day of freedom dawns at length,—
The Lord's appointed day.

3 Rebuild thy walls, thy bounds enlarge,
And send thy heralds forth;
Say to the south,—"Give up thy charge,"
And,—"Keep not back, O north!"

4 They come! they come! thine exil'd bands,
Where'er they rest or roam,
Have heard thy voice in distant lands,
And hasten to their home.

5 Thus, when our God the world shall burn,
And all its works destroy,
With songs, the ransomed shall return,
And everlasting joy.
      James Montgomery, 1825, a.

Missions.

627 Park Street. L. M.   F. M. A. VENUA, *cir.* 1810.

E-ter-nal Fa-ther! Thou hast said, That Christ all glo-ry shall ob-tain; That He who once a sufferer bled, Shall o'er the world a conq'ror, reign, Shall o'er the world a conq'ror, reign.

2 We wait Thy triumph, Saviour King!
   Long ages have prepared Thy way;
Now all abroad Thy banner fling,
   Set Time's great battle in array.

3 On mountain-tops the watch-fires glow,
   Where scatter'd wide the watchmen stand;
Voice echoes voice, and onward flow
   The joyous shouts, from land to land.

4 Oh, fill Thy church with faith and power!
   Bid her long night of weeping cease;
To groaning nations haste the hour,
   Of life and freedom, light and peace.

5 Come, Spirit, make Thy wonders known!
   Fulfil the Father's high decree;
Then earth, the might of hell o'erthrown,
   Shall keep her last great jubilee!
                      Ray Palmer, 1860.

628

JESUS shall reign where'er the sun
   Doth his successive journeys run;
His kingdom spread from shore to shore,
   Till moons shall wax and wane no more!

2 For Him shall endless prayer be made,
   And praises throng to crown His head;
His name, like sweet perfume, shall rise
   With every morning sacrifice.

3 People and realms of every tongue
   Dwell on His love, with sweetest song;
And infant voices shall proclaim
   Their early blessings on His name.

4 Where He displays His healing power,
   Death and the curse are known no more;
In Him the tribes of Adam boast
   More blessings than their father lost.

5 Let every creature rise and bring
   Peculiar honors to our King;
Angels descend with songs again,
   And earth repeat the loud Amen!
                      Isaac Watts, 1719.

629

JESUS! Thy church, with longing eyes,
   For Thine expected coming waits;
When will the promised light arrive,
   And glory beam from Zion's gates?

2 E'en now, when tempests round us fall,
   And wint'ry clouds o'ercast the sky,
Thy words with pleasure we recall,
   And deem that our redemption's nigh.

3 Teach us, in watchfulness and prayer,
   To wait for the appointed hour;
And fit us, by Thy grace, to share
   The triumps of Thy conquering power.
                   William H. Bathurst, 1829.

Missions.

630

Triumphant Zion! lift thy head
From dust, and darkness, and the dead;
Though humbled long, awake at length,
And gird thee with thy Saviour's strength.

2 Put all thy beauteous garments on,
And let thy various charms be known;
The world thy glories shall confess,
Decked in the robes of righteousness.

3 No more shall foes unclean invade,
And fill thy hallowed walls with dread;
No more shall hell's insulting host
Their vict'ry and thy sorrows boast.

4 God, from on high, thy groans will hear;
His hand thy ruins shall repair;
Nor will thy watchful Monarch cease
To guard thee in eternal peace.
Philip Doddridge, 1740.

631 Bray. C. M.   Nicolaus Hermann, 1561.

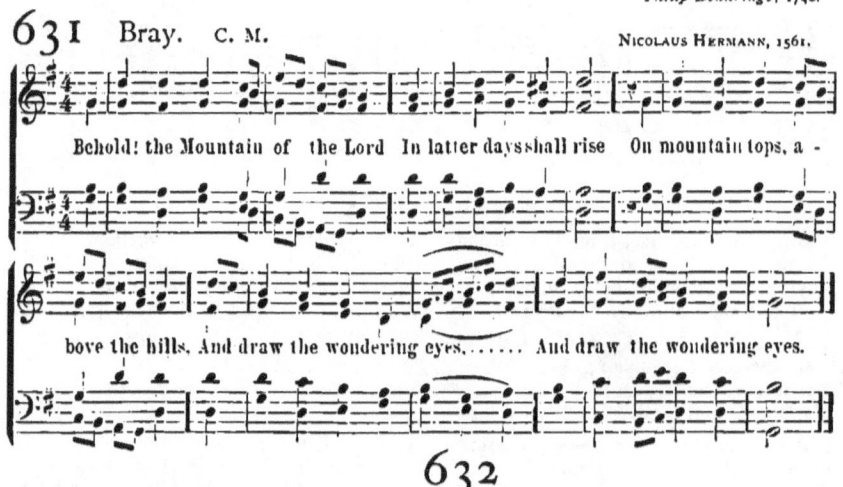

Behold! the Mountain of the Lord In latter days shall rise On mountain tops, above the hills, And draw the wondering eyes...... And draw the wondering eyes.

2 The beam that shines from Zion's hill
Shall lighten every land;
The King who reigns in Salem's towers
Shall all the world command.

3 No strife shall vex Messiah's reign,
Or mar the peaceful years;
To ploughshares men shall beat their swords,
To pruning-hooks their spears.

4 No longer hosts encountering hosts
Their millions slain deplore;
They hang the trumpet in the hall,
And study war no more.

5 Come, then! Oh come, from every land,
To worship at His shrine;
And, walking in the light of God,
With holy beauties shine.
Michael Bruce, 1768.

632

Behold the sure foundation stone,
Which God in Zion lays,
To build our heavenly hopes upon,
And His eternal praise.

2 Chosen of God, to sinners dear;
And saints adore His name:—
They trust their whole salvation here,
Nor shall they suffer shame.

3 The foolish builders, scribe and priest,
Reject it with disdain;
Yet on this rock the church shall rest,
And envy rage in vain.

4 What, though the gates of hell withstood?
Yet must this building rise;
'Tis Thine own work, almighty God!
And wondrous in our eyes.
Isaac Watts, 1719.

Missions.

633 Missionary Chant. L. M.   H. C. Zeuner, 1832.

Arm of the Lord! awake, awake; Put on thy strength, the nations shake; And let the world, adoring, see Triumphs of mercy, wrought by Thee.

2 Say to the heathen, from Thy throne,
"I am Jehovah—God alone!"
Thy voice their idols shall confound,
And cast their altars to the ground.

3 No more let human blood be spilt,
Vain sacrifice for human guilt;
But to each conscience be applied
The blood, that flowed from Jesus' side.

4 Almighty God! Thy grace proclaim,
In every clime, of every name,
Till adverse powers before Thee fall,
And crown the Saviour—Lord of all.
William Shrubsole Jr., 1790.

634

Soon may the last glad song arise
Through all the millions of the skies,—
That song of triumph, which records,
That all the earth is now the Lord's.

2 Let thrones, and powers, and kingdoms be
Obedient, mighty God! to Thee;
And, over land, and stream, and main,
Wave Thou the sceptre of Thy reign.

3 Oh! that the anthem now might swell,
And host to host the triumph tell,—
That not one rebel heart remains,
But over all the Saviour reigns.
Mrs. Voke, 1816.

635

Ye Christian heralds, go, proclaim
Salvation in Immanuel's name;
To distant climes the tidings bear,
And plant the Rose of Sharon there.

2 He'll shield you with a wall of fire—
With holy zeal your hearts inspire;
Bid raging winds their fury cease,
And calm the savage breast to peace.

3 And when our labors all are o'er,
Then shall we meet to part no more;
Meet—with the blood-bought throng to fall,
And crown our Jesus—Lord of all.
Mrs. Voke, (?) 1803.

636

O Thou to whom, in ancient time,
  The psalmist's sacred harp was strung,
Whom kings adored in song sublime,
  And prophets praised with glowing tongue!

2 From every place below the skies,
  The grateful song, the fervent prayer,
The incense of the heart may rise
  To heaven, and find acceptance there.

3 O Thou to whom, in ancient time,
  The holy prophets' harp was strung!
To Thee at last, in every clime,
  Shall temples rise, and praise be sung.
John Pierpont, 1824. alt.

Labor.

637 Watchman. S. M.   JAMES LEACH, 1788.

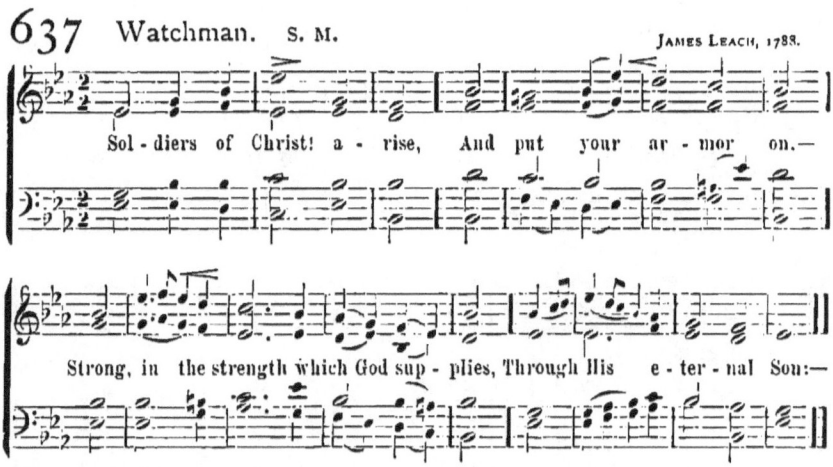

Sol-diers of Christ! a-rise, And put your ar-mor on.—
Strong, in the strength which God sup-plies, Through His e-ter-nal Son:—

2 Strong, in the Lord of hosts,
  And in His mighty power;
Who in the strength of Jesus trusts,
  Is more than conqueror.

3 Stand, then, in His great might,
  With all His strength endued;
And take, to arm you for the fight,
  The panoply of God:—

4 That, having all things done,
  And all your conflicts past,
You may o'ercome through Christ alone,
  And stand entire at last.

5 From strength to strength go on;
  Wrestle, and fight, and pray;
Tread all the powers of darkness down,
  And win the well-fought day.

6 Still let the Spirit cry,
  In all His soldiers, "Come,"
Till Christ, the Lord, descends from high,
  And takes the conquerors home.
                Charles Wesley, 1749.

638

TEACH me, my God and King,
  In all things Thee to see,
And what I do in anything,
  To do it as for Thee;

2 All may of Thee partake;
  Nothing so small can be
But draws, when acted for Thy sake,
  Greatness and worth from Thee.

3 If done to obey Thy laws,
  E'en servile labors shine;
Hallowed is toil, if this the cause,
  The meanest work, divine.
                George Herbert, 1635.

639

MY soul, weigh not thy life
  Against thy heavenly crown;
Nor suffer Satan's deadliest strife
  To beat thy courage down.

2 With prayer and crying strong,
  Hold on the fearful fight,
And let the breaking day prolong
  The wrestling of the night.

3 The battle soon will yield,
  If thou thy part fulfill:
For strong as is the hostile shield,
  Thy sword is stronger still.

4 Thine armor is divine,
  Thy feet with victory shod;
And on thy head shall quickly shine
  The diadem of God.
                Leonard Swain, 1858.

Labor.

640 Southport. C. M. — George Kingsley, 1853.

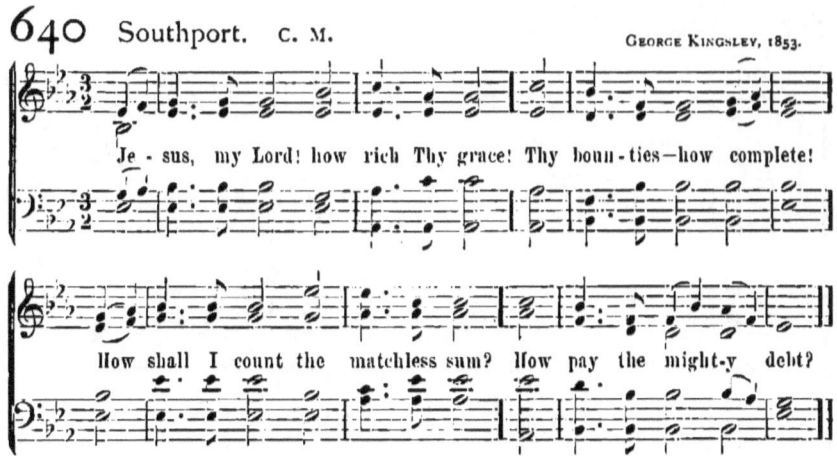

Jesus, my Lord! how rich Thy grace! Thy bounties—how complete!
How shall I count the matchless sum? How pay the mighty debt?

2 High on a throne of radiant light,
 Dost Thou exalted shine;
What can my poverty bestow,
 When all the worlds are Thine?

3 But Thou hast brethren here below,
 The partners of Thy grace,
And wilt confess their humble names
 Before Thy Father's face.

4 In them may'st Thou be cloth'd, and fed,
 And visited, and cheered;
And, in their accents of distress,
 My Saviour's voice be heard.
  Philip Doddridge, 1740.

641

Lord! lead the way the Saviour went,
 By lane and cell obscure,
And let love's treasure still be spent,
 Like His, upon the poor.

2 Like Him, thro' scenes of deep distress,
 Who bore the world's sad weight,
We, in their crowded loneliness,
 Would seek the desolate.

3 For Thou hast placed us side by side,
 In this wide world of ill;
And, that Thy followers may be tried,
 The poor are with us still.

4 Mean are all offerings we can make;
 Yet Thou hast taught us, Lord!
If given for the Saviour's sake,
 They lose not their reward.
  William Croswell, 1831.

642

Workman of God, oh lose not heart,
 But learn what God is like;
And in the darkest battle-field
 Thou shalt know where to strike.

2 Thrice blest is he to whom is given
 The instinct that can tell
That God is on the field, when He
 Is most invisible.

3 Blest too is he who can divine,
 Where real right doth lie,
And dares to take the side that seems
 Wrong to man's blindfold eye.

4 Then learn to scorn the praise of men,
 And learn to lose with God;
For Jesus won the world through shame,
 And beckons thee His road.

5 For right is right, since God is God
 And right the day must win;
To doubt would be disloyalty,
 To falter would be sin.
  Frederick W. Faber, 1849, ab.

Aspiration.

643 Seasons. L. M.   IGNACE PLEYEL.

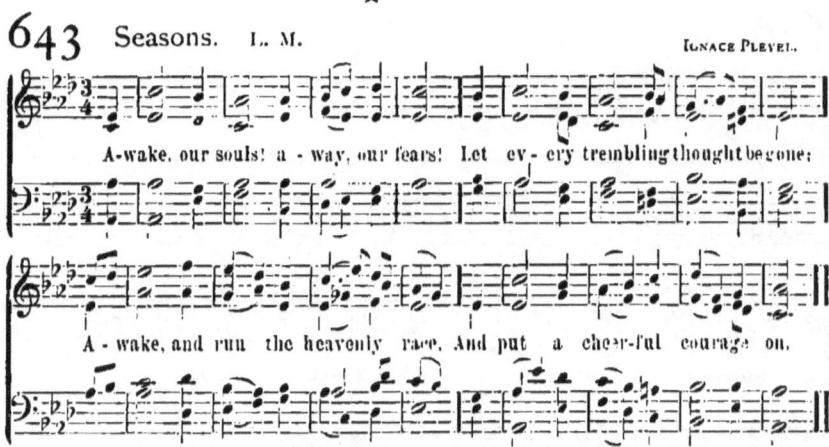

A-wake, our souls! a-way, our fears! Let ev-ery trembling thought be gone;
A-wake, and run the heavenly race, And put a cheer-ful courage on.

2 True,—'tis a strait and thorny road,
   And mortal spirits tire and faint;
But they forget the mighty God,
   Who feeds the strength of every saint:

3 Thee, mighty God! whose matchless
   Is ever new, and ever young, [power
And firm endures while endless years
   Their everlasting circles run.

4 From Thee, the overflowing spring,
   Our souls shall drink a fresh supply;
While such as trust their native strength,
   Shall melt away, and droop, and die.

5 Swift as an eagle cuts the air,
   We'll mount aloft to Thine abode;
On wings of love, our souls shall fly,
   Nor tire amidst the heavenly road.
                    Isaac Watts, 1707.

644

Rest for my soul I long to find;
   Saviour of all! if mine Thou art,
Give me Thy meek and lowly mind,
   And stamp Thine image on my heart.

2 Break off the yoke of inbred sin,
   And fully set my spirit free;
I cannot rest, till pure within,
   Till I am wholly lost in Thee.

3 Fain would I learn of Thee, my God!
   Thy light and easy burden prove,—
The cross, all stained with hallowed blood,
   The labor of Thy dying love.

4 I would, but Thou must give the power;
   My heart from every sin release;
Bring near, bring near the joyful hour,
   And fill me with Thy perfect peace!
                    Charles Wesley, 1742, ab.

645

O Thou, to whose all-searching sight
The darkness shineth as the light!
Search, prove my heart; it pants for Thee;
Oh! burst these bonds, and set it free.

2 Wash out its stains, refine its dross;
Nail my affections to the cross;
Hallow each thought; let all within
Be clean, as Thou, my Lord! art clean.

3 When rising floods my soul o'erflow,
When sinks my heart in waves of woe,
Jesus! Thy timely aid impart,
And raise my head and cheer my heart.

4 Saviour! where'er Thy steps I see,
Dauntless, untired, I follow Thee;
Oh! let Thy hand support me still,
And lead me to Thy holy hill.
        Ger., *Gerhard Tersteegen, 1731.*
        Tr., *John Wesley, 1738.*

Death.

646 Raven. S. M.   U. C. Burnap, 1868.

A few more years shall roll, A few more seasons come, And we shall be with those that rest Asleep within the tomb.

A few more storms shall beat / On this wild, rocky shore; / And we shall be where tempests cease, / And surges swell no more.

2 A few more struggles here,
  A few more partings o'er,
A few more toils, a few more tears,
  And we shall weep no more.
A few more Sabbaths here
  Shall cheer us on our way,
And we shall reach the endless rest,
  Th' eternal Sabbath day:

3 'Tis but a little while,
  And He shall come again,
Who died that we might live, who lives
  That we with Him may reign.
Then, O my Lord! prepare
  My soul for that glad day;
Oh! wash me in Thy precious blood,
  And take my sins away.
Horatius Bonar, 1844.

647

Thou art gone up on high
  To mansions in the skies,
And round Thy throne unceasingly
  The songs of praise arise.
But we are lingering here
  With sin and care oppressed:
Lord! send Thy promised Comforter,
  And lead us to Thy rest!

2 Thou art gone up on high:
  But Thou didst first come down,
Through earth's most bitter misery
  To pass unto Thy crown.
And girt with griefs and fears
  Our onward course must be;
But only let that path of tears
  Lead us at last to Thee!
Emma Toke, 1851

648

"For ever with the Lord!"—
  Amen! so let it be;
Life from the dead is in that word;
  'Tis immortality.
Here, in the body pent,
  Absent from Him I roam,
Yet nightly pitch my moving tent
  A day's march nearer home.

2 So when my latest breath
  Shall rend the veil in twain,
By death I shall escape from death,
  And life eternal gain.
Knowing as I am known,
  How shall I love that word,
And oft repeat before the throne,
  "For ever with the Lord!"
James Montgomery, 1835. ab

Death.

649 Frederick. 11s. GEORGE KINGSLEY, 1834.

I would not live al-way; I ask not to stay Where storm after storm ris-es dark o'er the way; The few lu-rid mornings, that dawn on us here, Are e-nough for life's woes, full e-nough for its cheer.

2 I would not live alway, thus fettered by sin,
Temptation without and corruption within;
E'en the rapture of pardon is mingled with fears,
And the cup of thanksgiving with penitent tears.

3 I would not live alway; no, welcome the tomb;
Since Jesus hath lain there, I dread not its gloom;
There sweet be my rest, till He bid me arise,
To hail Him in triumph descending the skies.

4 Who, who would live alway, away from his God;
Away from yon heaven, that blissful abode,
Where the rivers of pleasure flow o'er the bright plains,
And the noontide of glory eternally reigns?

5 Where the saints of all ages in harmony meet,
Their Saviour and brethren transported to greet;
While the anthems of rapture unceasingly roll,
And the smile of the Lord is the feast of the soul.

William A. Muhlenburg, 1823.

Death.

650 St. Sylvester. 8s 7s 8s & 9.   John B. Dykes, 1860.

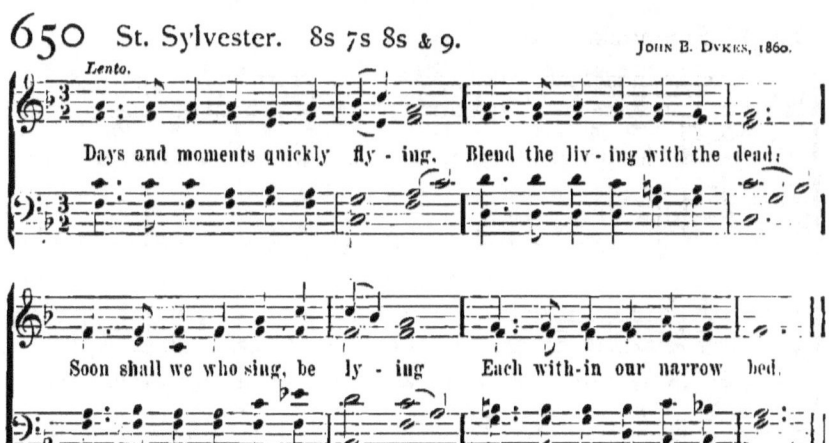

Days and moments quickly fly-ing, Blend the liv-ing with the dead;
Soon shall we who sing, be ly-ing Each with-in our narrow bed.

2 Soon our souls to God who gave them
  Will have sped their rapid flight;
Able now by grace to save them,
  Oh, that while we can we might!

3 Jesus, infinite Redeemer,
  Maker of this mighty frame,
Teach, oh, teach us to remember
  What we are, and whence we came;

    4 Whence we came, and whither wending
      Soon we must through darkness go,
    To inherit bliss unending,
      Or eternity of woe.

Life passeth soon: death draweth near: Keep us, good Lord, 'till Thou appear; With Thee to live, with Thee to die. With Thee to reign thro e-ter - ni-ty! A-men.

Edward Caswall, 1858.

Death.

651 Valentine. 8s & 7s. HUBERT P. MAIN, 1874.

{ Tar-ry with me, O my Saviour! For the day is passing by;
{ See! the shades of evening gather, And the night is drawing nigh.
Deeper, deeper grow the shadows, Paler now the glowing west,
Swift the night of death advances, Shall it be the night of rest?

2 Lonely seems the vale of shadow;
  Sinks my heart with troubled fear;
Give me faith for clearer vision,
  Speak Thou, Lord! in words of cheer;
Let me hear Thy voice behind me,
  Calming all these wild alarms;
Let me, underneath my weakness,
  Feel the everlasting arms.

3 Feeble, trembling, fainting, dying,
  Lord! I cast myself on Thee;
Tarry with me through the darkness;
  While I sleep, still watch by me.
Tarry with me, O my Saviour!
  Lay my head upon Thy breast
Till the morning; then awake me;
  Morning of eternal rest!
        Caroline Sprague Smith, 1853.

652

TIME, thou speedest on but slowly,
  Hours, how tardy is your pace!
Ere with Him, the high and holy,
  I hold converse face to face.
Here is naught but care and mourning;
  Comes a joy, it will not stay;
Fairly shines the sun at dawning,
  Night will soon o'ercloud the day.

2 Onward then! not long I wander
  Ere my Saviour comes for me,
And with Him abiding yonder,
  All His glory I shall see.
Oh, the music and the singing
  Of the host redeemed by love!
Oh, the hallelujahs ringing
  Through the halls of light above!
        Johann Georg Albinus, 1652.
        Tr. *Cath. Winkworth*, 1858.

Death.

653 Requiem. L. M. — S. Burt Saxton, 1857.

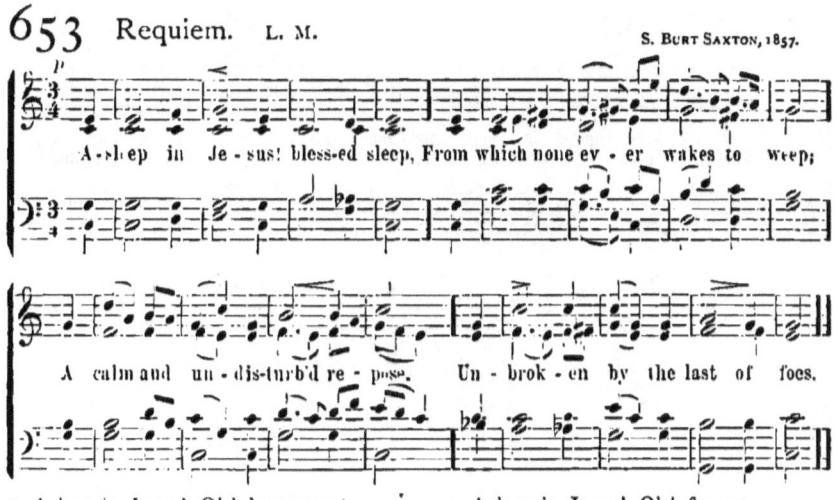

Asleep in Jesus! blessed sleep, From which none ever wakes to weep;
A calm and undisturb'd repose, Unbroken by the last of foes.

2 Asleep in Jesus! Oh! how sweet
To be for such a slumber meet,
With holy confidence to sing—
That death has lost his venomed sting!

3 Asleep in Jesus! peaceful rest,
Whose waking is supremely blest;
No fear, no woe, shall dim that hour
That manifests the Saviour's power.

4 Asleep in Jesus! Oh! for me
May such a blissful refuge be!
Securely shall my ashes lie,
Waiting the summons from on high.

5 Asleep in Jesus! far from Thee
Thy kindred and their graves may be;
But thine is still a blessèd sleep,
From which none ever wakes to weep.

Margaret Mackay, 1832. ab.

654 Rest. L. M. — William B. Bradbury, 1843, arr.

"Death cannot make my soul afraid, If God my Lord be with me there;
I can walk thro its darkest shade, And never understand a fear."

Death.

2 For He, alone yet not alone,
    Who trod that path, leads still the way;
  And guides His pilgrims, one by one,
    Within the gates of cloudless day.
3 My sins are lost in Love's embrace,
    He stays my heart, Who did redeem:
  My soul is kept in perfect peace,
    Because my trust is fixed on Him.
4 Assured forever of my Friend,
    Upon His word my faith can stand,
  Who, having loved, loves to the end;
    And naught shall pluck me from His hand.
5 What tho these daybeams disappear,—
    My candle now the Lord will light:
  Sun of my soul! Thou Saviour dear,
    If Thou art near, it is not night.
6 Thine everlasting arms beneath,
    Twixt love and life,—how should I weep?
  I cannot die,—there is no death!
    In Jesus' clasp, I'm laid to sleep.
      M. Woolsey Stryker, 1881.

655 Surrey Chapel. L. M. Hubert P. Main. 1881.

Gent-ly my Sav-iour! let me down, To slumber in the arms of death;
I rest my soul on Thee a-lone, Ev'n till my last, ex-pir-ing breath.

Copyright, 1881, by Biglow & Main.

656

2 Bid me possess sweet peace within;
    Let childlike patience keep my heart,
  Then shall I feel my heaven begin,
    Before my spirit hence depart.
3 Soon will the storm of life be o'er,
    And I shall enter endless rest;
  There I shall live to sin no more,
    And bless Thy name, forever blessed.
4 There shall my raptured spirit raise
    Still louder notes than angels sing,—
  High glories to Immanuel's grace,
    My God, my Saviour, and my King!
      Rowland Hill, 1796. ab.

Let me be with Thee, where Thou art,
    My Saviour, my eternal Rest;
  Then only will this longing heart
    Be fully and for ever blest.
2 Let me be with Thee, where Thou art,
    Where spotless saints Thy name adore;
  Then only will this sinful heart
    Be evil and defiled no more.
3 Let me be with Thee, where Thou art,
    Where none can die, where none remove;
  Where life nor death my soul can part
    From Thy bless'd presence and Thy love
      Charlotte Elliott, 1841. ab.

Death.

657 Meinhold. 7s & 8s. J. S. BACH.

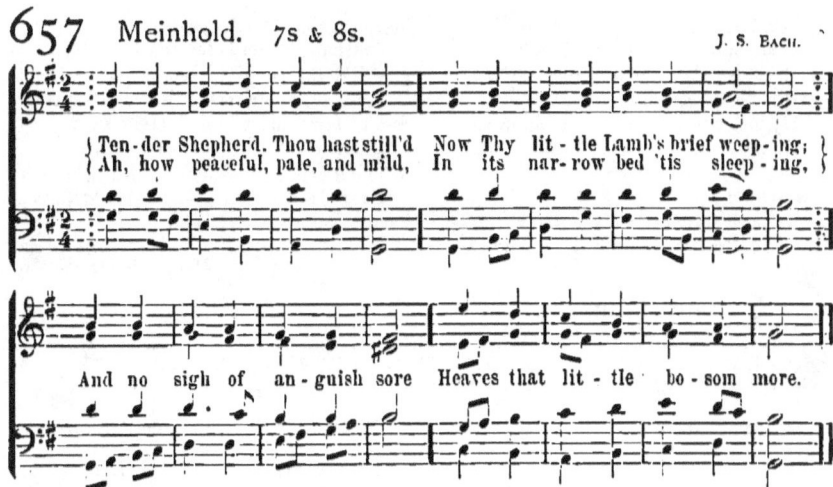

Tender Shepherd, Thou hast still'd Now Thy little Lamb's brief weeping;
Ah, how peaceful, pale, and mild, In its narrow bed 'tis sleeping,
And no sigh of anguish sore Heaves that little bosom more.

2 In this world of care and pain,
  Lord, Thou wouldst no longer leave it;
  To the sunny heavenly plain
  Thou dost now with joy receive it;
  Clothed in robes of spotless white,
  Now it dwells with Thee in light.

3 Ah, Lord Jesus, grant that we
  Where it lives may soon be living,
  And the lovely pastures see
  That its heavenly food are giving;
  Then the gain of death we prove,
  Though Thou take what most we love.
      Tr. *Catherine Winkworth*, 1858.

658 St. Millicent. 7s & 4. ARTHUR S. SULLIVAN, 1873.

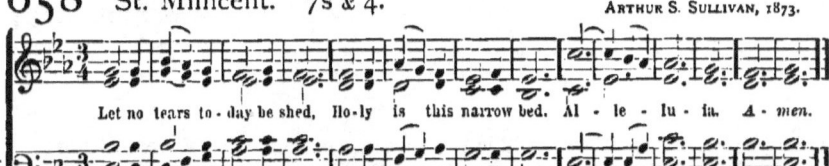

Let no tears to-day be shed, Holy is this narrow bed. Alleluia. Amen.

2 Not salvation hardly won,
  Not the meed of race well run!
      Alleluia!

3 But the pity of the Lord
  Gives His child a full reward;
      Alleluia!

4 Grants the prize without the course,
  Crowns, without the battle's force.
      Alleluia!

5 God, who loveth innocence,
  Hastes to take His darling hence.
      Alleluia!

6 Christ, when this sad life is done,
  Join us to Thy little one.
      Alleluia!

7 And in Thine own tender love,
  Bring us to the ranks above.
      Alleluia! Amen.
      Tr. *Richard F. Littledale*, 1864.

Death.

659 Woolsey. L. M. — Hubert P. Main, 1881.

My will, O Lord, to Thine I bow; No thought of fear disturbs me now, While I can see Thy love divine, With constant light, around me shine.

dolce. rit. What though my hour of death draws nigh, With Thee so close 'tis sweet to die,— To feel Thine arms about me thrown, And know that I am all Thine own.

Copyright, 1881, by Biglow & Main.

2 Not Jordan's stream my heart can chill;
Lo! at Thy voice its waves are still;
Thy gentle hand will guide my barque,
And steer it safe o'er waters dark.
Earth's transient scenes are waning fast,
Its toils and tears will soon be past,
And, strife all done, my soul shall rise
To reach its home beyond the skies.

3 Oh bliss untold! from sleep to wake
Where raptured songs of glory break;
Oh who would dwell forever here,
When joy, and heaven, and God are there!
On Thee, O Lord, my all I rest,
I lean my head upon Thy breast;
My latest breath Thy praise shall be,
I close my eyes, at peace with Thee.
Frances J. Van Alstyne, 1881.

Death.

660 Greenwood. S. M.
Joseph E. Sweetser, 1848.

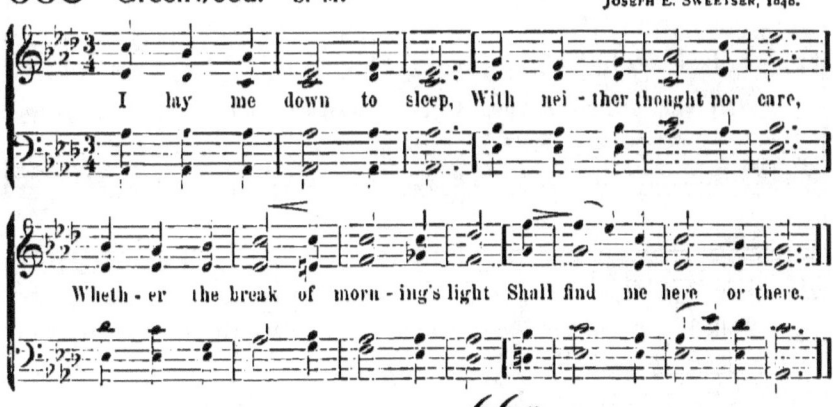

I lay me down to sleep, With nei-ther thought nor care, Wheth-er the break of morn-ing's light Shall find me here or there.

2 A bowing burdened head,
  That only asks to rest,
Unquestioned and unquestioning,
  Upon a loving breast.

3 My half day's work is done,
  And this is all my part,
I can but give a patient God
  An uncomplaining heart.
      Anon, 1862, a.

661

The pains of death are past;
  Labor and sorrow cease;
And, life's long warfare closed at last,
  His soul is found in peace.

2 Soldier of Christ! well done!
  Praise be thy new employ;
And, while eternal ages run,
  Rest in thy Saviour's joy!
      James Montgomery, 1835, ab.

662 Immanuel. 7s.
R. Redhead, 1852.

When our heads are bowed with woe, When our bit-ter tears o'er-flow, When we mourn the lost, the dear, Je-sus, Son of Ma-ry, hear!

Death.

2 Thou our throbbing flesh hast worn;
Thou our mortal griefs hast borne;
Thou hast shed the human tear;
Jesus, Son of Mary, hear!

3 When the solemn death-bell tolls
For our own departing souls,
When our final doom is near,
Jesus, Son of Mary! hear.

4 When the heart is sad within,
With the thought of all its sin;
When the spirit sinks with fear,
Jesus, Son of Mary, hear!

5 Thou the shame, the grief, hast known,
Though the sins were not Thine own,
Thou hast bowed their load to bear;
Jesus, Son of Mary, hear!

Henry H. Milman, 1821

663 Requiescat. 4s & 6s. J. BARNBY, 1868.

Sleep thy last sleep, Free from care and sorrow; Rest, where none weep, Till th' e-ter-nal mor-row; Though dark waves roll O'er the si-lent riv-er, Thy faint-ing soul Je-sus can de-liv-er. A-men.

2 Life's dream is past,
　All its sin, its sadness,
Brightly at last
　Dawns a day of gladness;
Under thy sod,
　Earth, receive our treasure,
To rest in God,
　Waiting all His pleasure.

3 Though we may mourn
　Those in life the dearest,
They shall return,
　Christ, when Thou appearest!
Soon shall Thy voice
　Comfort those now weeping,
Bidding rejoice,
　All in Jesus sleeping. Amen.

Edward A. Dayman, 1868.

Death.

664 Pilgrim. 10s 9 & 11. HENRY SMART, 1868.

2 Go to the grave; at noon from labor cease;
   Rest on thy sheaves, thy harvest-task is done;
   Come from the heat of battle, and in peace,
   Soldier, go home; with thee the fight is won.

3 Go to the grave, for there thy Saviour lay
   In death's embraces, ere He rose on high;
   And all the ransomed, by that narrow way
   Pass to eternal life beyond the sky.

James Montgomery, 1825, ab.

Resurrection.

665 Wareham. L. M.   William Knapp, 1738.

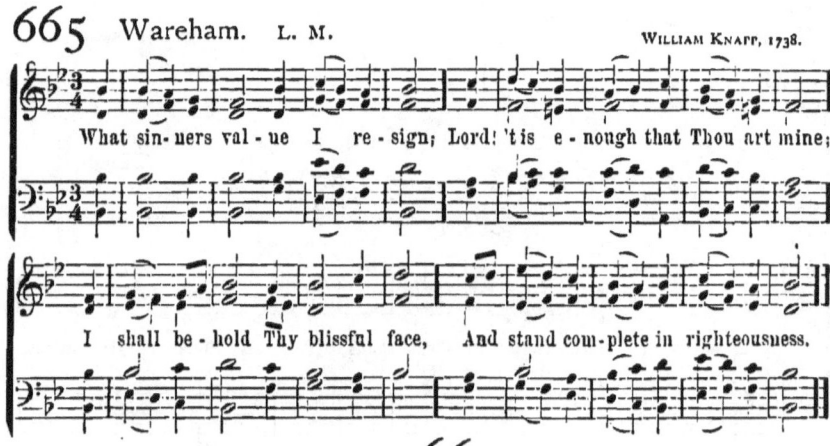

What sin-ners val-ue I re-sign; Lord! 'tis e-nough that Thou art mine; I shall be-hold Thy blissful face, And stand com-plete in righteousness.

2 This life's a dream—an empty show;
But the bright world, to which I go,
Hath joys substantial and sincere;
When shall I wake, and find me there?

3 Oh! glorious hour!—Oh! bless'd abode!
I shall be near and like my God;
And flesh and sin no more control
The sacred pleasures of the soul.

4 My flesh shall slumber in the ground,
Till the last trumpet's joyful sound:
Then burst the chains, with sweet surprise,
And in my Saviour's image rise.
Isaac Watts, 1719.

666

We sing His love, who once was slain,
Who soon o'er death revived again,
That all His saints, thro Him, might have
Eternal conquests o'er the grave.

2 The saints, who now in Jesus sleep,
His own almighty power shall keep,
Till dawns the bright illustrious day,
When death itself shall die away.

3 Hasten, dear Lord! the glorious day,
And this delightful scene display:
When all Thy saints from death shall rise,
Raptured in bliss beyond the skies.
Rowland Hill, 1796.

667

Faith sees the bright eternal doors
Unfold, to make His children way;
They shall be clothed with endless life,
And shine in everlasting day.

2 The trump shall sound; the dust awake,
From the cold tomb the slumberers spring;
Thro heaven, with joy, their myriads rise,
And hail their Saviour and their King.
Timothy Dwight, 1800.

668

Go, labor on; spend, and be spent,—
Thy joy to do the Father's will;
It is the way the Master went;
Should not the servant tread it still?

2 Go, labor on; 'tis not for naught;
Thine earthly loss is heavenly gain;
Men heed thee, love thee, praise thee not;
The Master praises;—what are men?

3 Go, labor on; enough, while here,
If He shall praise thee, if He deign
Thy willing heart to mark and cheer;
No toil for Him shall be in vain.

4 Toil on, and in thy toil rejoice;
For toil, comes rest, for exile, home;
Soon shalt thou hear the Bridegroom's voice,
The midnight peal:—"Behold! I come!"
Horatius Bonar, 1857.

Resurrection.

669 China. C. M.
Timothy Swan, 1800.

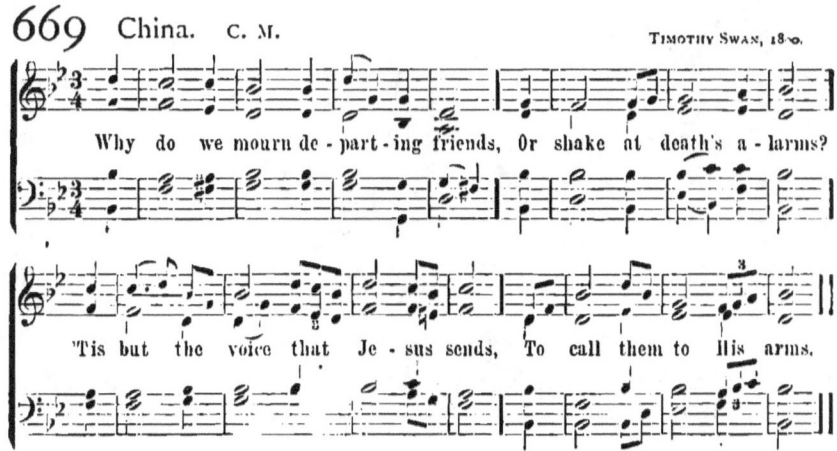

Why do we mourn departing friends, Or shake at death's alarms?
'Tis but the voice that Jesus sends, To call them to His arms.

2 Are we not tending upward too,
  As fast as time can move?
Nor would we wish the hours more slow,
  To keep us from our love.

3 Why should we tremble to convey
  Their bodies to the tomb?
There the dear flesh of Jesus lay,
  And left a long perfume.

4 The graves of all His saints He bless'd,
  And softened every bed;
Where should the dying members rest,
  But with their dying Head?

5 Thence He arose, ascending high,
  And showed our feet the way;
Up to the Lord our flesh shall fly
  At the great rising day.
  Isaac Watts, 1707.

670

Why should our tears in sorrow flow,
  When God recalls His own,
And bids them leave a world of woe,
  For an immortal crown?

2 Is not e'en death a gain to those,
  Whose life to God was given?
Gladly to earth their eyes they close,
  To open them in heaven.

3 Their toils are past—their work is done,
  And they are fully bless'd;
They fought the fight, the vict'ry won,
  And entered into rest.

4 Then let our sorrows cease to flow,—
  God has recalled His own;
But let our hearts, in every woe,
  Still say,—"Thy will be done!"
  William H. Bathurst, 1829.

671

The time draws nigh, when, from the clouds,
  Christ shall with shouts descend;
And the last trumpet's awful voice
  The heavens and earth shall rend.

2 Then they who live shall changed be,
  And they who sleep shall wake;
The graves shall yield their ancient charge,
  And earth's foundations shake.

3 The saints of God, from death set free,
  With joy shall mount on high;
The heavenly host, with praises loud,
  Shall meet them in the sky.

4 Together to their Father's house,
  With joyful hearts, they go;
And dwell for ever with the Lord,
  Beyond the reach of woe.
  Michael Bruce, 1766.

The Second Advent.

672 Lancashire. 7s & 6s.   HENRY SMART, 1836. (?)

Rejoice, rejoice believers! And let your lights appear;
The evening is advancing, And darker night is near.
The Bridegroom is a-rising, And soon He draweth nigh;
Up, pray, and watch, and wrestle,— At midnight comes the cry!

2 See that your lamps are burning,
  Replenish them with oil;
And wait for your salvation,
  The end of earthly toil.
The watchers on the mountain
  Proclaim the Bridegroom near;
Go meet Him as He cometh,
  With hallelujahs clear.

3 O wise and holy virgins,
  Now raise your voices higher,
Till, in your jubilations,
  Ye meet the heavenly choir.
The marriage feast is waiting,
  The gates wide open stand;
Up, up, ye heirs of glory!
  The Bridegroom is at hand.

Laurentius Laurenti, 1690.
... ane Borthwick, 1853.

The Second Advent.

673 Midnight Cry. 14s.   G. A. MACFARREN, 1872.

Be-hold the Bridegroom com-eth in the mid-dle of the night,
And blest is he whose loins are girt, whose lamp is burn-ing bright;
But woe to that dull serv-ant, whom his Mas-ter shall sur-prise
With lamp untrimmed, un-burn-ing, and with slum-ber in his eyes.

2 That day, the day of fear, shall come; my soul slack not thy toil,
But light thy lamp, and feed it well, and make it bright with oil;
Who knowest not how soon may sound the cry at eventide,
"Behold the Bridegroom comes. Arise! go forth to meet the Bride."

3 Beware, my soul, take thou good heed, lest thou in slumber lie,
And, like the five, remain without, and knock, and vainly cry;
But watch, and bear thy lamp undimmed, and Christ shall gird thee on
His own bright wedding-robe of light, the glory of the Son.

Gerard Moultrie, 1867.

The Second Advent.

674 Archangel. 8s 7s & 4. MAX PIUTTI, 1880.

Maestoso.

Lo! He comes, with clouds descending,
Once for favored sinners slain;
Thousand thousand saints attending
Swell the triumph of His train;
Hallelujah!
Jesus comes, and comes to reign!

2 Every island, sea and mountain,
  Heaven and earth shall flee away;
All who hate Him must, confounded,
  Hear the trump proclaim the day:—
    "Come to judgment!
  Come to judgment! come away."

3 Now redemption, long expected,
  See, in solemn pomp appear!
All His saints, by man rejected,
  Now shall meet Him in the air:
    Hallelujah!
  See the day of God appear!

v. 1. *Charles Wesley*, 1758, a.
v. 2 & 3, *John Cennick*, 1749, a.

675

O'ER the distant mountains breaking,
  Comes the reddening dawn of day;
Rise, my soul, from sleep awaking,
  Rise, and sing, and watch, and pray;
    'Tis thy Saviour!
  On his bright returning way.

2 O Thou long-expected, weary
    Waits my anxious soul for Thee;
  Life is dark, and earth is dreary
    Where Thy light I do not see:
      O my Saviour,
    When wilt Thou return to me?

3 Long, too long, in sin and sadness,
    Far away from Thee I pine;
  When, oh when, shall I the gladness
    Of Thy Spirit feel in mine?
      O my Saviour,
    When shall I be wholly Thine?

4 Nearer is my soul's salvation,
    Spent the night, the day at hand;
  Keep me in my lowly station,
    Watching for Thee, till I stand,—
      O my Saviour,
    In Thy bright and promised land.

John S. B. Monsell, 1863.

The Second Advent.

676 Elisabeth. 10s & 7. HENRY SMART, 1872.

"Thy king-dom come!" O bless-ed Son of God, Ful-fil-ing all the prom-ise of Thy word: Cov-er with Thy ma-jes-ty The earth, as might-y wa-ter-floods the sea! A-men.

2 Let lust, and anarchy, and falsehood yield
To signs and wonders of the Holy Child:
　All earth's kingdoms now be one,—
The kingdom of our God, and Christ His Son.

3 The winds Thy sandals, and the tides Thy path,
Break all oppression with Thy rod of wrath;
　Everlasting righteousness
Bring in, and reign, Thou Holy Prince of Peace!

4 Bring tears of joy to long expectant eyes,
Above the noonday let Thy light arise:
　Far and wide Thy truth advance,
And take Thine uttermost inheritance.

5 Thine unseen kingdom rises in our midst,
Amid the candles walks the living Christ;
　O reveal Thy wondrous way
Brighter and brighter to Thy perfect day!

6 Thy blesséd Gospel conq'ring all earth's gloom,
Lord, even so, Thy kingdom quickly come!
　Thine the might was, Thine the power,
And Thine shall be the glory evermore. Amen.

M. Woolsey Stryker, 1883.

The Second Advent.

677

Burst forth, O Bridegroom, from Thy chamber bright!
That, all earth's darkness swallowed up of light,
Forth may stand Thy holy Bride,—
The travail of Thy soul be satisfied.

2 Fair as the moon, and clear as Thou her Sun,
Thine undivided garment putting on,
Thou wilt take her then, and own
The love no waters quenched, nor floods could drown.

3 Long has she waited, watched, and mourned apart,
But now is set a seal upon Thy heart,
Joyful reads the way she trod
Submissive to the righteousness of God.

4 Rejoice with trembling, serve the Lord with fear,
Though we know not the day He shall appear,
Even time shall still be light,
And joyful morning follow heavy night.

5 Oh glorious day, when Christ, our Sun, shall rise;
And heaven's high morning fill the unfolding skies:
None shall say, "Lo here!"—"Lo there!"
For lo! the shining light is everywhere!
M. Woolsey Stryker, 1880.

678 Louise. 8s & 7s. Hubert P. Main, 1869.

Zi-on, drear-y and in an-guish, In the des-ert hast Thou stray'd?
Oh, thou wea-ry, cease to lan-guish, Jesus shall lift up thy head.

2 Still lamenting and bemoaning,
  'Mid thy follies and thy woes;
Soon repenting and returning,
  All thy solitude shall close.

3 Though benighted and forsaken,
  Though afflicted and distressed,—
His almighty arm shall waken:
  Zion's King shall give thee rest.

4 Cease thy sadness, unbelieving,
  Soon His glory thou shalt see,
Joy, and gladness, and thanksgiving,
  And the voice of melody.
Thomas Hastings, 1836.

The Second Advent.

2 Watchman! tell us of the night;
  Higher yet that star ascends;—
Trav'ler! blessedness and light,
  Peace and truth, its course portends;—
Watchman! will its beams alone
  Gild the spot that gave them birth?—
Trav'ler! ages are its own;
  See, it bursts o'er all the earth!—

3 Watchman! tell us of the night,
  For the morning seems to dawn;—
Trav'ler! darkness takes its flight,
  Doubt and terror are withdrawn;—
Watchman! let thy wanderings cease;
  Hie thee to thy quiet home!—
Trav'ler! lo! the Prince of peace,
  Lo! the Son of God, is come!

John Bowring, 1825.

680 Winchcombe. 4s & 6s.   JOHN B. CALKIN, 1866.

The Bridegroom comes; Bride of the Lamb, a-wake! The midnight cry is heard; Thy sleep for-sake. The marriage-day Has come; lift up thy head. Put on thy bri-dal robe, The feast is spread. A-men.

2 Shake off earth's dust,
    And wash thy weary feet;
  Arise, make haste, go forth,
    The Bridegroom greet.
  Sing the new song!
    Thy triumph has begun;
  Thy tears are wiped away,
    Thy night is done! Amen.

Horatius Bonar, 1861.

The Second Advent.

681 Nuremberg. 7s. JOHANN R. AHLE, 1664.

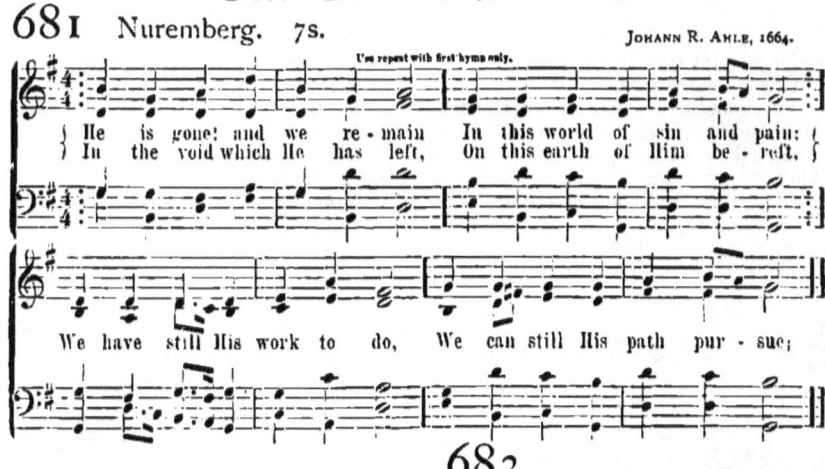

He is gone! and we remain
In this world of sin and pain:
In the void which He has left,
On this earth of Him bereft,
We have still His work to do,
We can still His path pursue;

2 He is gone! we heard Him say,
"Good that I should go away;"
Gone is that dear form and face,
But not gone His present grace;
Though Himself no more we see,
Comfortless we cannot be;

3 He is gone! unto their goal
World and church must onward roll;
Far behind we leave the past;
Forward all our glances cast;
Still His words before us range
Through the ages, as they change;

4 He is gone! but we once more
Shall behold Him as before,
In the heaven of heavens the same
As on earth He went and came:
In that world, unseen, unknown,
He and we shall yet be one.
Arthur P. Stanley, 1859.

682

HASTEN, Lord! the promised hour;
Come in glory, come in power;
Still Thy foes are unsubdued;
Nature sighs to be renewed.

2 Time has nearly reached its sum;
All things, with Thy bride, say, "Come!"
Jesus! whom all worlds adore,
Come,—and reign for evermore.
Josiah Conder, 1830.

683

IN the sun, and moon, and stars,
Signs and wonders there shall be;
Earth shall quake with inward wars,
Nations with perplexity.

2 Soon shall ocean's hoary deep,
Tossed with stronger tempests, rise;
Wilder storms the mountains sweep,
Louder thunder rock the skies.

3 Dread alarms shall shake the proud,
Pale amazement, restless fear;
And amid the thunder cloud
Shall the Judge of man appear.

4 But, though from His awful face,
Heaven shall fade, and earth shall sigh,
Fear not ye, His chosen race,
Your redemption draweth nigh.
Reginald Heber, 1827.

684

EARTH is passed away and gone,
All her glories, every one,
All her pomp is broken down;
God is reigning, God alone!

2 No more sorrow, no more night;
Perfect joy and purest light!
With His spotless saints and bright,
God is reigning in the height!
Henry Alford, 1844.

The Second Advent.

685 Orion. L. M.   John Zundel, 1852.

Come, quickly come, dread Judge of all, For, awful though Thine advent be,
All shadows from the truth will fall, And falsehood die, in sight of Thee:
Come, quickly come: for doubt and fear Like clouds dissolve when Thou art near.
Come, quickly come: for Thou alone Canst make Thy scattered people one.

2 Come, quickly come, true Life of all;
The curse of death is on the ground;
On every home his shadows fall,
On every heart his mark is found:
Come, quickly come, great King of all;
Let sin no more our souls enthral,
Reign all around us, and within,
Let pain and sorrow die with sin.

3 Come, quickly come, sure Light of all,
For gloomy night broods o'er our way;
And fainting souls begin to fall
With weary watching for the day:
Come, quickly come: for grief and pain
Can never cloud Thy glorious reign:
Come, quickly come: for round Thy throne
No eye is blind, no night is known.

Lawrence Tuttiett, 1868. arr.

The Second Advent.

686 Laban. S. M.   Lowell Mason, 1830.

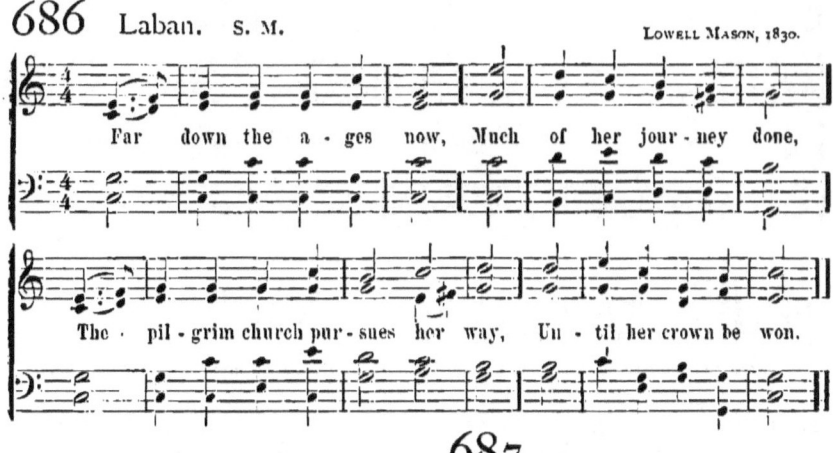

Far down the ages now, Much of her journey done,
The pilgrim church pursues her way, Until her crown be won.

2 'Tis the same story still
Of sin and weariness,
Of grace and love yet flowing down
To pardon and to bless.

3 No slacker grows the fight,
No feebler is the foe,
Nor less the need of armor tried,
Of shield and spear and bow.

4 Thus onward still we press
Through evil and through good,
Through pain and poverty and want,
Through peril and through blood.

5 Still faithful to our God,
And to our Captain true,
We follow where He leads the way,
The kingdom in our view.
Horatius Bonar, 1857, ab.

687

Ye servants of the Lord!
Each in his office wait,
Observant of His heavenly word,
And watchful at His gate.

2 Let all your lamps be bright,
And trim the golden flame;
Gird up your loins as in His sight,
For awful is His name.

3 Watch! 'tis your Lord's command;
And, while we speak, He's near:
Mark the first signal of His hand,
And ready all appear.

4 Oh! happy servant he,
In such a posture found!
He shall his Lord with rapture see,
And be with honor crowned.
Philip Doddridge, 1740.

688 St Ann's. C. M.   William Croft, 1708.

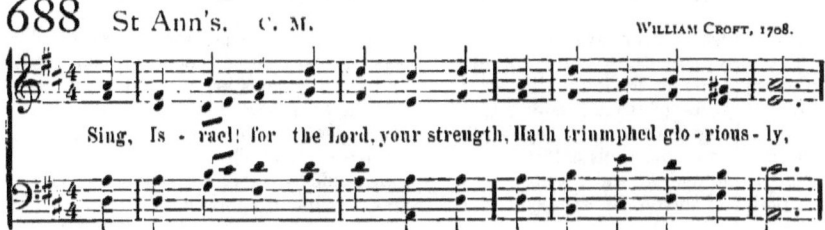

Sing, Israel! for the Lord, your strength, Hath triumphed gloriously,

The Second Advent.

Rid-er and horse your fa-ther's God Hath thrown in-to the sea.

2 The floods were parted at Thy word,
　The waters upright stood,
And through the depths, as by dry land,
　Thy ransomed millions trod.

3 Foes with hot haste, and clamoring wrath,
　Outstretched their angry hands;
But from His fists the watching God
　Flung forth the gathered winds.

4 The mighty waters came again,
　And down they sank as stone!
Thou—holy, fearful, wondrous Lord—
　Art God!—and Thou alone.

5 Nations that hear shall fear and dread
　The greatness of Thine arm,
And shall be still, till Israel pass
　Secure from threatened harm.

6 Till all Thy purchased people pass
　Up to Thy citadel,
The sure inheritance, O Lord!
　Where saints in light shall dwell.

7 There as with voice of many seas,
　Shall Israel sing again,
The Lord who triumphs gloriously,—
　Who evermore shall reign.
　　　　　　　M. Woolsey Stryker, 1878.

689　Austrian Hymn.. 8s & 7s.　　　F. J. Haydn, 1797.

{ He is coming, He is coming, Not as once He came be-fore, }
{ Wailing infant, born in weakness On a low-ly sta-ble floor; } But up-on His cloud of glo-ry
In the crimson-tint-ed sky, Where we see the golden sun-rise In the ros-y distance lie.

2 He is coming, He is coming,
　Not in pain, and shame and woe,
With the thorn-crown on His forehead,
　And the blood-drops trickling slow;
But with diadem upon Him,
　And the sceptre in His hand,
And the dead all ranged before Him,
　Raised from death, hell, sea, and land.

3 He is coming, He is coming;
　Let His lowly first estate,
And His tender love, so teach us
　That in faith and hope we wait,
Till in glory eastward burning,
　Our redemption draweth near;
And we see the sign in heaven
　Of our Judge and Saviour dear.
　　　　　　Cecil Frances Alexander, 1858.

The Second Advent.

690 Gottland. 7s & 6s. *Swedish Choral.*

Awake, awake, O Zion! Put on thy strength divine;
Thy garments bright in beauty, The bridal dress be thine:
Jerusalem the holy, To purity restored,
Meek Bride, all fair and lowly, Go forth to meet thy Lord.

2 The Lamb who bore our sorrows,
  Comes down to earth again;
No Sufferer now, but Victor,
  For evermore to reign;
To reign in every nation,
  To rule in every zone:
Oh, wide-world coronation,
  In every heart a throne.

3 Awake, awake, O Zion!
  The bridal day draws nigh,
The day of signs and wonders,
  And marvels from on high:
Thy sun uprises slowly,
  But keep thou watch and ward;
Fair Bride, all pure and lowly,
  Go forth to meet thy Lord.

4 Lift up thy voice, O watchman!
  And shout, from Zion's towers,
Thy hallelujah chorus,—
  "The victory is ours!"
The Lord shall build up Zion
  In glory and renown,
And Jesus, Judah's lion,
  Shall wear His rightful crown.

5 Break forth in hymns of gladness;
  O waste Jerusalem!
Let songs, instead of sadness,
  Thy jubilee proclaim;
The Lord, in strength victorious,
  Upon thy foes hath trod;
Behold, O earth! the glorious
  Salvation of our God!
  Benjamin Gough, 1865.

691

My soul, there is a country
  Afar beyond the stars,
Where stands a winged sentry,
  All skilful in the wars.
There, above noise and danger,
  Sweet Peace sits, crowned with smiles,
And One, born in a manger,
  Commands the beauteous files.

2 If thou canst get but thither!
  There grows the flower of peace,
The rose that cannot wither,
  Thy fortress and thine ease.
Leave then thy foolish ranges,
  For none can thee secure,
But One, who never changes,
  Thy God, thy Life, thy Cure.
  Henry Vaughan, 1650.

The Second Advent.

692 Parousia. 7s.   Max Piutti, 1881.

Copyright, 1881, by Bigelow & Main.

2 Hallelujah!—hark!—the sound,
　From the depths unto the skies,
Wakes, above, beneath, around,
　All creation's harmonies:
See Jehovah's banners furled!
　Sheathed His sword! He speaks—'tis done,
And the kingdoms of this world
　Are the kingdoms of His Son.

3 He shall reign from pole to pole
　With illimitable sway;
He shall reign, when, like a scroll,
　Yonder heavens have passed away;
Then the end;—beneath His rod,
　Man's last enemy shall fall;
Hallelujah!—Christ in God,
　God in Christ, is all in all.

James Montgomery, 1819.

Judgment.

693 Pearsall. 7s & 6s. Arr. St. Gall. Katholische Gesangbuch, 1868.

The world is ve-ry e-vil, The times are wax-ing late,
Be so-ber and keep vi-gil, The Judge is at the gate;
The Judge Who comes in mer-cy, The Judge Who comes with might,
Who comes to end the e-vil, Who comes to crown the right.

2 Arise, arise, good Christian,
　Let right to wrong succeed;
Let penitential sorrow
　To heavenly gladness lead,
To light that has no evening,
　That knows nor moon nor sun,
The light so new and golden,
　The light that is but one.

3 For now we fight the battle,
　But then shall wear the crown
Of full and everlasting
　And passionless renown.

And He whom now we trust in
　Shall then be seen and known;
And they that know and see Him
　Shall have Him for their own.

4 Behold the morn shall waken,
　And shadows shall decay,
And each true-hearted servant
　Shall shine as doth the day,
And God, our King and Portion,
　In fullness of His grace,
Shall we behold for ever,
　And worship face to face.

Tr. J. M. Neale, 1851.

Judgment.

694 Luther's Hymn. 8s & 7s. P. — Martin Luther, 1535.

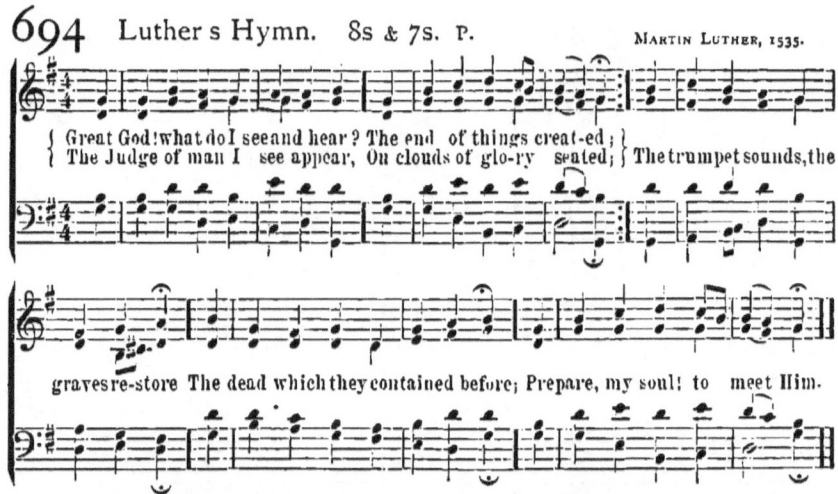

Great God! what do I see and hear? The end of things creat-ed;
The Judge of man I see appear, On clouds of glo-ry seated; The trumpet sounds, the graves re-store The dead which they contained before; Prepare, my soul! to meet Him.

2 The dead in Christ shall first arise,
   At the last trumpet's sounding,
Caught up to meet Him in the skies,
   With joy their Lord surrounding;
No gloomy fears their souls dismay,
His presence sheds eternal day
   On those prepared to meet Him.

3 And see!—they take the mansions bright,
   Where God prepared their dwelling;
Like angels now;—and, to their sight,
   Their joys are onward swelling;
They knew in part,—now, all is clear;
Nor doubt, nor sorrow enters here,
   To break their bliss unceasing.

4 O God, to Thee our prayers we pour,
   In deep abasement bending;
O shield us through the last dread hour,
   Thy wondrous love extending:
May we, in this our trial day,
With faithful hearts Christ's word obey,
   And thus prepare to meet Him.

v. 1 & 2. Tr. *Wm. B. Collyer* 1812.
v. 3. Tr. *Henry Mills*, 1845.

695

When my last hour is close at hand,
   My last sad journey taken,
Do Thou, Lord Jesus! by me stand;
   Let me not be forsaken:
O Lord! my spirit I resign
Into Thy loving hands divine;
   'Tis safe within Thy keeping.

2 Countless as sands upon the shore,
   My sins may then appall me;
Yet, though my conscience vex me sore,
   Despair shall not enthrall me;
For as I draw my latest breath,
I'll think, Lord Christ! upon Thy death,
   And there find consolation.

3 I shall not in the grave remain,
   Since thou death's bonds hast severed,
But hope with Thee to rise again,
   From fear of death delivered;
I'll come to Thee, where'er Thou art,
With Thee I'll live, and never part;
   Therefore I die in rapture.

4 And so to Jesus Christ I'll go,
   My longing arms extending;
So fall asleep, in slumber deep,
   The sleep that knows no waking,—
Till Jesus Christ, God's only Son,
Opens the gates of bliss, leads on
   To heaven, to life eternal.

Tr. from the German.

Judgment.

696 Dies Iræ. 7s.
JOHN STAINER, 1871.

Day of wrath,—oh dreadful day! When this world shall pass away;
And the heavens together roll, Shrivelling like a parched scroll,
When the Archangel's trumpet-tone Summons all before the throne. Amen.

2 Then the writing shall be read,
Which shall judge the quick and dead;
Then the Lord of all our race
Shall appoint to each his place;
Every wrong shall be set right,
Every secret brought to light.

3 King of kings, enthroned on high,
In Thine awful Majesty,
Thou Who of Thy mercy free
Savest those who saved shall be:
In Thy boundless charity,
Fount of pity, save Thou me.

4 Thou Who bad'st the sinner cease
From her tears, and go in peace;
Thou Who to the dying thief
Spakest pardon and relief;
Thou, O Lord, to me hast given,
E'en to me, the hope of heaven!

5 Naught of Thee my prayers can claim,
Save in Thy free mercy's name.
Worthless is each tear and cry:
Yet, Good Lord, in grace comply;
Make me with Thy sheep to stand,
Severed from the guilty band;

6 Full of tears, and full of dread,
Is the day that wakes the dead,
Calling all, with solemn blast,
From the ashes of the past;
Lord of Mercy, Jesus Blest,
Grant us Thine eternal rest. Amen.

Tr. *Arthur P. Stanley*, ab.

Judgment.

697 St. Cross. L. M.
JOHN B. DYKES, 1860.

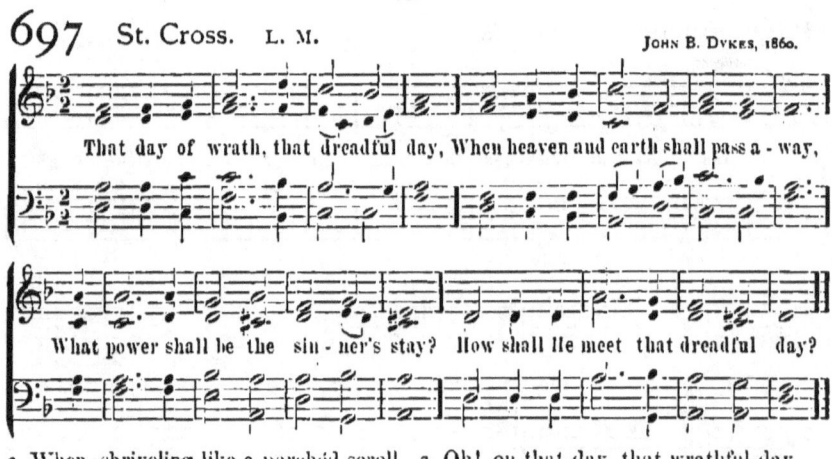

That day of wrath, that dreadful day, When heaven and earth shall pass a-way,
What power shall be the sin-ner's stay? How shall He meet that dreadful day?

2 When, shriveling like a parched scroll,
The flaming heavens together roll;
When louder yet, and yet more dread,
Swells the high trump that wakes the dead;

3 Oh! on that day, that wrathful day,
When man to judgment wakes from clay,
Be Thou, O Christ! the sinner's stay,
Tho' heaven and earth shall pass away.
Lat., *Thomas of Celano*, 1230.
Tr. *Walter Scott*, 1805.

698 St. Jerome. L. M.
C. H. GRAUN, 1720.

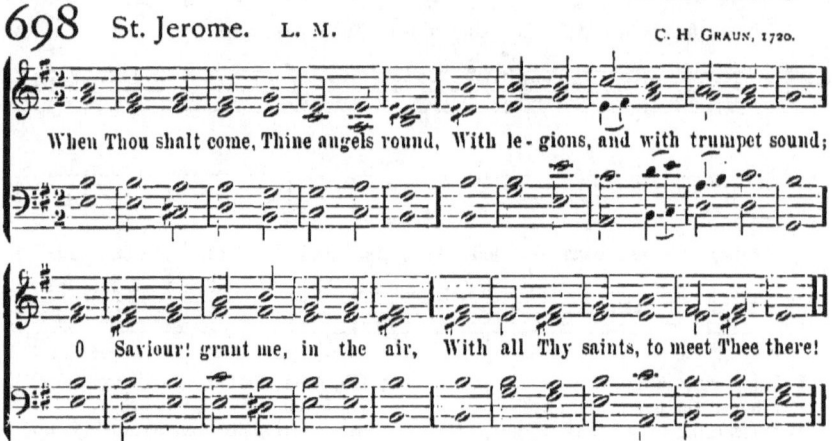

When Thou shalt come, Thine angels round, With le-gions, and with trumpet sound;
O Saviour! grant me, in the air, With all Thy saints, to meet Thee there!

2 Weep, O my soul! ere that great day,
When God shall shine in great array;
Oh! weep thy sin, that thou may'st be
In that severest judgment free!

3 O Christ! forgive, remit, protect,
And set Thy servant with th' elect;
That I may hear the voice, that calls
The righteous to Thy heavenly halls!
Lat. *Theodore*, cir., 820.
Tr. *John M. Neale*, 1862.

Heaven.

699 Alford. 7s 6s & 8s.   JOHN B. DYKES, 1875.

Ten thousand times ten thousand, In sparkling raiment bright,
The armies of the ransomed saints Throng up the steeps of light;
'Tis finished, all is finished, Their fight with death and sin;
Fling open wide the golden gates, And let the victors in.

2 What rush of hallelujahs
  Fills all the earth and sky!
What ringing of a thousand harps
  Bespeaks the triumph nigh!
Oh, day, for which creation
  And all its tribes were made!
Oh, joy, for all its former woes
  A thousand fold repaid!

3 Oh, then what raptured greetings
  On Canaan's happy shore,
What knitting severed friendships up,
  Where partings are no more!
Then eyes with joys shall sparkle,
  That brimmed with tears of late,—
Orphans no longer fatherless,
  Nor widows desolate.

Henry Alford, 1. 66.

Heaven.

700 Shining Shore. 8s & 7s. Geo. F. Root, 1859.

My days are glid-ing swift-ly by, And I, a pil-grim stran-ger,
Would not de-tain them, as they fly. Those hours of toil and dan-ger;
D. S.—just be-fore, the shin-ing shore We may al-most dis-cov-er.

CHORUS.

For, Oh! we stand on Jordan's strand; Our friends are pass-ing o-ver; And,

2 Should coming days be cold and dark,
    We need not cease our singing;
That perfect rest naught can molest,
    Where golden harps are ringing;
        For, Oh! we stand, etc.

3 Let sorrow's rudest tempest blow,
    Each cord on earth to sever;
Our King says—"Come!"—and there's our [home,
    For ever, Oh! for ever!
        For, Oh! we stand, etc.
                                        David Nelson, 1835.

701

The tribes of faith, from all the earth,
    Press up to thee, O Zion!
For God hath broke our captive yoke,
    And burst the gates of iron:
Within thy land our feet shall stand,
    In spite of Satan's malice,
Our conquering King His Church shall
    Triumphant to His palace.   [bring,

2 Our thirsty hearts cry out to God—
    The living Rock is riven;
Our hungry souls believe the Word,
    And eat the Bread of heaven:
Sun shall not smite, nor moon by night,—
    The Lord doth stand beside us;
'Tis He that keeps Who never sleeps,
    And home His hand shall guide us

3 We shout for joy as on we march,
    With Christ our Captain glorious;
In Him the promise is Amen
    That we shall be victorious:
'Mid flame and flood, 'neath calm and cloud,
    Through wilderness and river,
We tread the road that leads to God,
    To dwell with Him forever.
                            M. Woolsey Stryker, 1881.

Heaven.

702 Vox Angelica. P. M. JOHN B. DYKES, 1868.

Hark! hark! my soul! an-gel-ic songs are swell-ing O'er earth's green fields, and ocean's wave-beat shore: How sweet the truth those blessed strains are tell - ing Of that new life when sin shall be no more! An-gels of Je - sus, An-gels of light, Sing-ing to welcome the pil - grims of the night, Sing-ing to wel-come the pilgrims,—the pilgrims of the night.

2 Onward we go, for still we hear them singing,
"Come, weary souls, for Jesus bids you come;"
And, through the dark, its echoes sweetly ringing,
The music of the Gospel leads us home.
    Angels of Jesus, etc.

Heaven.

3 Far, far away, like bells at evening pealing,
   The voice of Jesus sounds o'er land and sea,
And laden souls, by thousands meekly stealing,
   Kind Shepherd! turn their weary steps to Thee.
     Angels of Jesus, etc.

4 Rest comes at length, though life be long and dreary,
   The day must dawn, and darksome night be past;
All journeys end in welcomes to the weary,
   And heaven, the heart's true home, will come at last.
     Angels of Jesus, etc.

5 Cheer up, my soul! faith's moonbeam's softly glisten
   Upon the breast of life's most troubled sea;
And it will cheer thy drooping heart to listen
   To those brave songs which angels mean for thee.
     Angels of Jesus, etc.

6 Angels, sing on! your faithful watches keeping;
   Sing us sweet fragments of the songs above;
Till morning's joy shall end the night of weeping,
   And life's long shadows break in cloudless love.
     Angels of Jesus, etc.

Frederick W. Faber, 1849. ab. and sl. changed.

[SECOND TUNE.]

Carmen Cœli.   P. M.   JOSEPH BARNBY, 1868

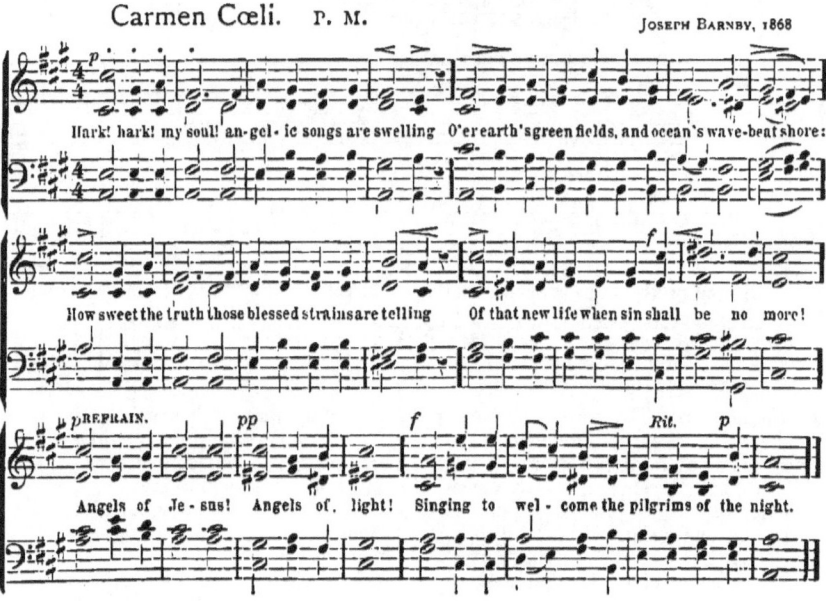

Heaven.

703 Sanctuary. 8s & 7s. JOHN B. DYKES, 1867.

Hark! the sound of ho-ly voic-es Chant-ing at the crys-tal sea,
Al-le-lu-ia, Al-le-lu-ia, Al-le-lu-ia, Lord, to Thee;
Mul-ti-tude, which none can number, Like the stars in glo-ry stands,
Clothed in white ap-par-el, holding Palms of vic-t'ry in their hands. A-men.

2 Marching with Thy cross their banner,
   They have triumphed, following
Thee, the Captain of salvation,
   Thee, their Saviour and their King:
Mocked, imprisoned, stoned, tormented,
   Sawn asunder slain with sword,
They have conquered death and Satan
   By the might of Christ the Lord.

3 Now they reign in heavenly glory,
   Now they walk in golden light,
Now they drink, as from a river,
   Holy bliss and infinite:
Love and peace they taste for ever,
   And all truth and knowledge see
In the beatific vision
   Of the Blessèd Trinity. Amen.

Christopher Wordsworth, 1862.

Heaven.

704

Hear what God, the Lord, hath spoken;
  O my people, faint and few,
Comfortless, afflicted, broken!
  Fair abodes I build for you;
Themes of heartfelt tribulation
  Shall no more perplex your ways;
You shall name your walls "Salvation,"
  And your gates shall all be "Praise."

2 Still in undisturbed possession,
  Peace and righteousness shall reign;
Never shall you feel oppression,
  Hear the voice of war again:
God shall rise, and shining o'er you,
  Change to day the gloom of night;
He, the Lord, shall be your Glory,
  God, your everlasting Light. Amen.
  William Cowper, 1772.

705 Rest for the Weary. 8s 7s & 5.   Wm. McDonald, 1857.

In the Christian's home in glory, There remains a land of rest;
There my Saviour's gone before me, [Omit.]
To fulfil my soul's request. There is rest for the weary, There is rest for the weary, There is rest for the weary. There is rest for you.

2 He is fitting up my mansion,
  Which eternally shall stand.
For my stay shall not be transient,
  In that holy, happy land.
    There is rest, etc.

3 Death itself shall then be vanquished,
  And his sting shall be withdrawn·

Shout for gladness, O ye ransomed!
  Hail with joy the rising morn.
    There is rest, etc.

4 Sing, Oh! sing, ye heirs of glory!
  Shout your triumph as you go;
Zion's gate will open for you,
  You shall find an entrance through.
    There is rest, etc.
  Samuel Young Harmer, 1856.

Heaven.

706 Paradise P. M.   John B. Dykes, 1868.

O Par-a-dise, O Par-a-dise, Who doth not crave for rest? Who would not seek the hap-py land Where they that loved are blest? Where loy-al hearts and true / hearts and true Stand ev-er in the light; All rap-ture thro and thro, In God's most ho-ly sight. A-men

2 O Paradise, O Paradise,
   The world is growing old;
Who would not be at rest and free
   Where love is never cold?
     Where loyal hearts, etc.

3 O Paradise, O Paradise,
   'Tis weary waiting here;
I long to be where Jesus is,
   To feel, to see Him near;
     Where loyal hearts, etc.

4 O Paradise, O Paradise,
   I want to sin no more,
I want to be as pure on earth
   As on Thy spotless shore;
     Where loyal hearts, etc.

5 Lord Jesus, King of Paradise,
   O keep me in Thy love,
And guide me to that happy land
   Of perfect rest above;
     Where loyal hearts, etc. Amen.
                      F. W. Faber, 1849.

Heaven.

707 Rutherford. 7s & 6s.
CHAS. D'URHAN, arr. 1845.

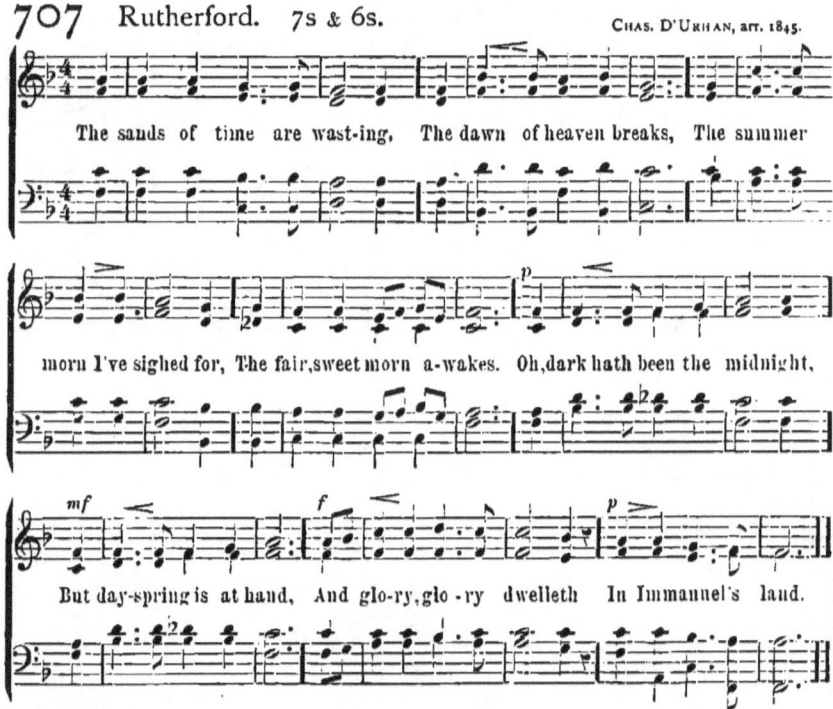

The sands of time are wast-ing, The dawn of heaven breaks, The summer morn I've sighed for, The fair, sweet morn a-wakes. Oh, dark hath been the midnight, But day-spring is at hand, And glo-ry, glo-ry dwelleth In Immanuel's land.

2 Oh! Christ He is the fountain;
  The deep, sweet well of love;
The streams of earth I've tasted,
  More deep I'll drink above.
There to an ocean fullness
  His mercy doth expand,
And glory, glory dwelleth
  In Immanuel's land.

3 With mercy and with judgment,
  My web of time He wove,
And aye the dews of sorrow
  Were lustered with His love.
I'll bless the hand that guidéd,
  I'll bless the heart that planned,
When throned where glory dwelleth,
  In Immanuel's land.

4 Oh! I am my Beloved's,
  And my Beloved's mine,
He brings a poor, vile sinner,
  Into His house divine.
Upon the Rock of Ages
  My soul redeemed shall stand,
Where glory, glory dwelleth
  In Immanuel's land.

5 The bride eyes not her garment,
  But her dear bridegroom's face;
I will not gaze at glory,
  But on my King of Grace—
Not at the crown He giftéth,
  But on His piercéd hand;—
The Lamb is all the glory
  Of Immanuel's land.
          Annie Ross Cousin, 1857.

Heaven.

708　Brightland.　7s 5s & 7s P.　　　John B. Dykes, 1868.

Ev-ery morn the glow-ing sun Ris-es warm and bright;
But the eve-ning com-eth on, And the dark, cold night;
There's a bright land far a-way, Where is nev-er end-ing day.

2 Ev'ry spring the sweet young flowers
　Open fresh and gay;
Till the chilly autumn hours
　Wither them away:
There's a land we have not seen,
Where the trees are always green!

3 Christ our Lord is ever near
　Those who follow Him!
But we cannot see Him here,
　For our eyes are dim:
There's a blissful happy place
Where men always see His face.
　　　　　　　Cecil F. Alexander, 1848.

709　Saints' Rest.　6s & 4s.　　　Arthur S. Sullivan, 1872.

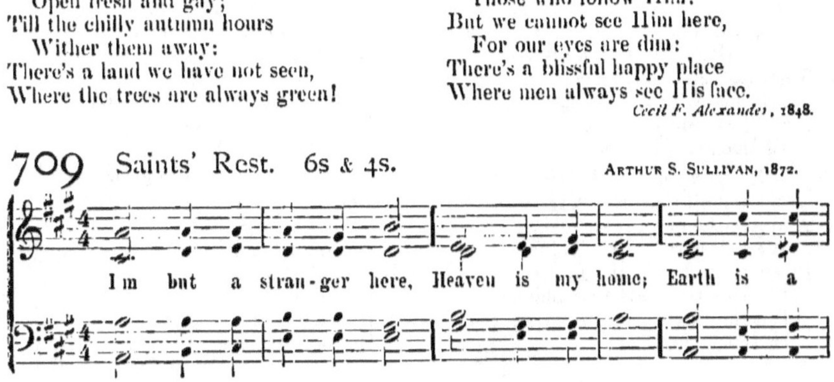

I'm but a stran-ger here, Heaven is my home; Earth is a

Heaven.

des - ert drear, Heaven is my home; Dan - ger and sorrow stand Round me on ev - ery hand; Heaven is my fa - ther - land, Heaven is my home.

2 What, though the tempest rage,
　Heaven is my home;
Short is my pilgrimage,
　Heaven is my home:
And time's wild wintry blast
Soon shall be overpast;
I shall reach home at last,
　Heaven is my home.

3 There, at my Saviour's side,—
　Heaven is my home;
I shall be glorified;—
　Heaven is my home:
There are the good and blest,
Those I love most and best;
And there I too shall rest,
　Heaven is my home.
　　　　　Thomas Rawson Taylor, 1834.

710

Now I have found a Friend;
　Jesus is mine;—
His love shall never end;
　Jesus is mine:
Though earthly joys decrease,
Though earthly friendships cease,
Now I have lasting peace;
　Jesus is mine.

2 Though I grow poor and old,
　Jesus is mine;
Though I grow faint and cold,
　Jesus is mine:
He shall my wants supply;
His precious blood is nigh,
Naught can my hope destroy;
　Jesus is mine.

3 When earth shall pass away,—
　Jesus is mine,—
In the great judgment day,—
　Jesus is mine,—
Oh! what a glorious thing,
Then to behold my King,
On tuneful harp to sing,
　Jesus is mine.

4 Farewell, mortality!
　Jesus is mine:
Welcome, eternity!
　Jesus is mine:
Welcome, ye scenes of rest!
Welcome, ye mansions blest!
Welcome, a Saviour's breast;
　Jesus is mine!
　　v. 1, 2 & 3, Henry J. McC. Hope, 1852.
　　　　v. 4, Catherine Jane Bonar, 1843.

Heaven.

711 Anchorage. H. M.
ARTHUR S. SULLIVAN, 1872.

Safe home, safe home in port! Rent cordage, shattered deck, Torn sails, provisions short,
And on-ly not a wreck: But, oh! the joy, upon the shore! To tell our voyage per-ils o'er.

2 The prize, the prize secure!
   The wrestler nearly fell;
Bare all he could endure,
   And bare not always well:
But he may smile at troubles gone
Who sets the victor-garland on!

3 No more the foe can harm!
   No more of leaguered camp,
And cry of night alarm,
   And need of ready lamp:—
And yet how nearly had he failed—
How nearly had that foe prevailed!

4 The exile is at home!
   Oh, nights and days of tears!
Oh, longings not to roam!
   Oh, sins and doubts and fears!
What matters now grief's darkest day,
When God has wiped all tears away!
— *Tr. J. M. Neale, 1863.*

712 Civitas Dei. 8s 7 8s 7.
J. B. CALKIN, 1866. arr.

Up-ward where the stars are burn-ing, Si - lent, si - lent in their turning,
Round the nev - er - chang-ing pole; Up-ward where the sky is bright-est,

Copyright, 1880, by Biglow & Main.

Heaven.

Up-ward where the blue is light-est.—Lift I now my long-ing soul.

2 Far beyond that arch of gladness,
Far beyond these clouds of sadness,
  Are the many mansions fair.
Far from pain and sin and folly,
In that palace of the holy—
  I would find my mansion there.

3 Where the Lamb on high is seated,
By ten thousand voices greeted,
  Lord of lords, and King of kings;
Son of Man, they crown, they crown Him,
Son of God, they own, they own Him.
  With His name the palace rings.
    Horatius Bonar, 1866.

713 Bernard. C. M.
BERTHOLD TOURS, 1866, alt.

O moth-er dear, Je-ru-sa-lem! When shall I come to thee?
When shall my sor-rows have an end? Thy joys when shall I see?

2 O happy harbor of God's saints!
  O sweet and pleasant soil!
In thee no sorrow may be found,
  No grief, no care, no toil.

3 Thy walls are made of precious stones,
  Thy bulwarks diamond-square;
Thy gates are all of orient pearl;—
  O God! if I were there!

4 Oh! passing happy were my state,
  Might I be worthy found
To wait upon my God and King,
  His praises there to sound.
    David Dickson, 1612.

714

These are crowns, that we shall wear,
  When all Thy saints are crowned;
These are the palms, that we shall bear
  On yonder holy ground.

2 That is the city of the saints,
  Where we so soon shall stand,
When we shall strike these desert tents,
  And quit this desert sand.

3 Then welcome toil, and care, and pain!
  And welcome sorrow, too!
All toil is rest, all grief is gain,
  With such a prize in view.
    Horatius Bonar, 1857.

Heaven.

715 Varina. C. M.   G. F. Root, 1848, Fr. J. C. H. Rinck.

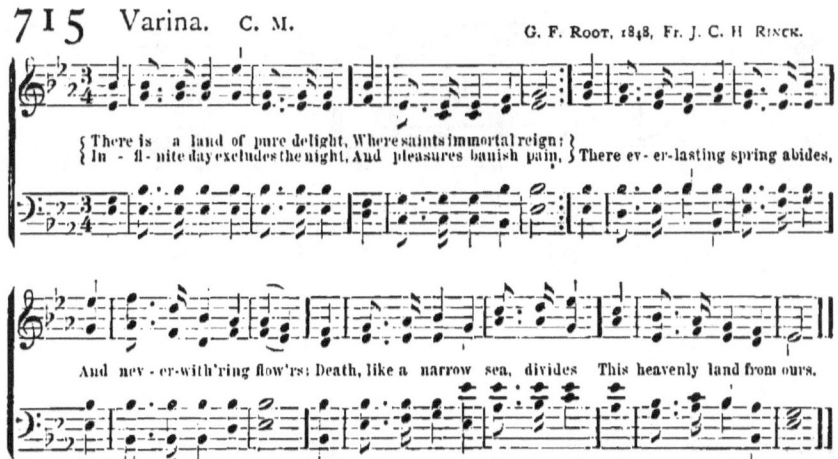

There is a land of pure delight, Where saints immortal reign;
In-fi-nite day excludes the night, And pleasures banish pain,
There ev-er-lasting spring abides, And nev-er-with'ring flow'rs:
Death, like a narrow sea, divides This heavenly land from ours.

2 Sweet fields beyond the swelling flood
   Stand dressed in living green;
So to the Jews old Canaan stood,
   While Jordan rolled between.
But timorous mortals start and shrink
   To cross this narrow sea;
And linger, shivering on the brink,
   And fear to launch away.

3 Oh, could we make our doubts remove,
   These gloomy doubts that rise,
And see the Canaan that we love
   With unbeclouded eyes:—
Could we but climb where Moses stood,
   And view the landscape o'er,
Not Jordan's stream, nor death's cold flood,
   Should fright us from the shore.
                      Isaac Watts, 1707.

716

Lo! what a glorious sight appears
   To our believing eyes;
The earth and seas are passed away,
   And the old, rolling skies.
From the third heav'n, where God resides,
   That holy, happy place,
The new Jerusalem comes down,
   Adorned with shining grace.

2 "His own soft hand shall wipe the tears
   From every weeping eye;
And pains and groans and griefs and fears
   And death itself shall die."
How long, dear Saviour, oh how long
   Shall this bright hour delay?
Fly swifter round, ye wheels of time,
   And bring the welcome day.
                      Isaac Watts, 1709.

717

Nor eye has seen, nor ear has heard,
   Nor sense, nor reason known,
What joys the Father has prepared,
   For those that love the Son.
But the good Spirit of the Lord
   Reveals a heaven to come:
The beams of glory, in His word,
   Allure and guide us home.

2 Pure are the joys above the sky,
   And all the region peace;
No wanton lips, nor envious eye,
   Can see or taste the bliss.
Those holy gates for ever bar
   Pollution, sin, and shame;
None can obtain admittance there
   But foll'wers of the Lamb.
                      Isaac Watts, 1709.

Heaven.

718 Tranquillity. L. M.   John Marson.

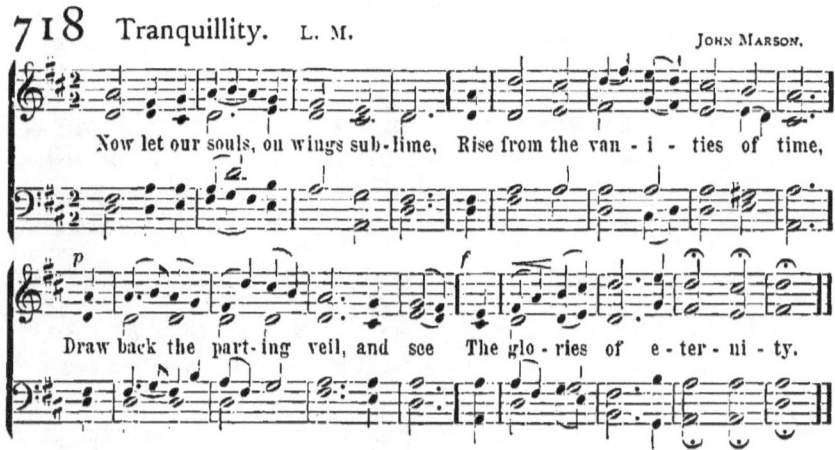

Now let our souls, on wings sub-lime, Rise from the van-i-ties of time, Draw back the part-ing veil, and see The glo-ries of e-ter-ni-ty.

2 Shall aught beguile us on the road,
  While we are traveling back to God?
For strangers into life we come,
  And dying is but going home.

3 As, when the weary traveler gains
  The height of some o'erlooking hill,
His heart revives, if 'cross the plains
  He eyes his home, though distant still;

4 So, when the Christian pilgrim views,
  By faith, his mansion in the skies,
The sight his fainting strength renews,
  And wings his speed to reach the prize.
v. 1 & 2, Thomas Gibbons, 1762.
v. 3 & 4, John Newton, 1779.

719

Hark! how the choral song of heaven
  Swells, full of peace and joy, above;
Hark! how they strike their golden harps,
  And raise the tuneful notes of love!

2 No anxious care, nor thrilling grief,
  No deep despair, nor gloomy woe
They feel, while high their lofty strains
  In noblest, sweetest concord flow.

3 When shall we join the heavenly host,
  Who sing Immanuel's praise on high,
And leave behind our fears and doubts,
  To swell the chorus of the sky?
Robert S. McAll, 1812.

720

Lord! Thou wilt bring the joyful day;
  Beyond earth's weariness and pains,
Thou hast a mansion far away,
  Where, for Thine own, a rest remains.

2 No sun there climbs the morning sky,
  There never falls the shade of night,
God and the Lamb, for ever nigh,
  O'er all shed everlasting light.

3 The bow of mercy spans the throne,—
  Emblem of love and goodness there;
While notes, to mortals all unknown,
  Float on the calm celestial air.

4 Around the throne bright legions stand,
  Redeemed by blood from sin and hell;
And shining forms, an angel band,
  The mighty chorus join to swell.

5 There, Lord! Thy way-worn saints shall find
  The bliss for which they longed before;
And holiest sympathies shall bind
  Thine own to Thee for evermore.

6 O Jesus! bring us to that rest,
  Where all the ransomed shall be found,
In Thine eternal fullness blessed,
  While ages roll their cycles round.
Ray Palmer, 1853.

Heaven.

721 Hope. 7s & 6s. St. Alban's Tune Book, 1865.

D.C. For thee, O dear, dear Coun-try, Mine eyes their vig-ils keep;
For ver-y love be-hold-ing, Thy hap-py name they weep.
The men-tion of Thy glo-ry Is unc-tion to the breast,
And med-i-cine in sick-ness, And love, and life and rest.

2 There grief is turned to pleasure;
　Such pleasure as below
No human voice can utter,
　No human heart can know:
And, after fleshly scandal,
　And, after this world's night,
And, after storm and whirlwind,
　Is calm, and joy, and light.
　　　For thee, &c

3 O sweet and blessèd country!
　Shall I e'er see thy face?
O sweet and blessèd country!
　Shall I e'er win thy grace?—
Exult, O dust and ashes!
　The Lord shall be thy part;
His only, His for ever,
　Thou shalt be, and thou art!
　　　For thee, &c.

Lat. *Bernard de Morlaix*, 1150.
Tr. *J. M. Neale*, 1851.

Heaven.

722 Amaranth. 6s & 4s P.   G. ROSSINI, 1823, ad.

E-ternal day hath dawned; The Prince of Life is throned! Thro gates of amethyst, Up to the heavenly feast, The Church of God, Purchased with blood, Pour in,—a ransomed throng, Up-lift-ing endless song; On ev-ery brow the name Brighter than diadem.

Copyright, 1881, by Biglow & Main.

2 These that confessed that Name,
These that despised the shame,
They have passed through the flood,
They stand before their God:
  Kept they the faith;
  Loved unto death.
White-robed in righteousness,
Transformed beneath His face,
Long as eternity,
The Blessed One they see.

3 God hath wiped every tear,
Ended all doubt and fear;
Crying and pain are o'er,
And death shall be no more;
  All things are new:
  Faithful and true,
The King of kings hath come,
Fetched all His banished home;
Jesus hath kept His word,—
The Bride is with her Lord!

4 Perfected peace at last!
Sin, curse, and woe, are past;
There is no longer night,
The Lamb doth give them light:
  Immanuel
  God all in all!
Lord! make our spirits thirst
Ever to be with Christ!
Hasten Thy Holy reign;
Come quickly, Lord! Amen.

M. Woolsey Stryker, 1881.

Heaven.

723 Ewing. 7s & 6s. — ALEXANDER EWING, 1853.

Je-ru-sa-lem, the gold-en, With milk and honey blest! Beneath thy contem-pla-tion Sink heart and voice oppressed: I know not, oh, I know not What social joys are there, What radiancy of glo-ry, What light beyond compare.

2 They stand, those halls of Zion,
  All jubilant with song,
And bright with many an angel,
  And all the martyr throng;
The Prince is ever in them,
  The daylight is serene;
The pastures of the blessèd
  Are decked in glorious sheen.

3 There is the throne of David;
  And there, from care released,
The song of them that triumph,
  The shout of them that feast:
And they, who with their Leader,
  Have conquered in the fight,
For ever and for ever
  Are clad in robes of white.

Lat. *Bernard de Morlaix*, ab. 1150.
Tr. *John Mason Neale*, 1851.

724

O LAMB of God! still keep me
  Near to Thy wounded side;
'Tis only there in safety
  And peace can I abide!
What foes and snares surround me!
  What doubts and fears within!
The grace that sought and found me,
  Alone can keep me clean.

2 Soon shall my eyes behold Thee,
  With rapture face to face;
One half hath not been told me
  Of all Thy power and grace;
Thy beauty, Lord! and glory,
  The wonders of Thy love,
Shall be the endless story
  Of all Thy saints above.

James George Deck, 1857.

Heaven.

725

There is a land immortal,
  The beautiful of lands;
Beside its ancient portal
  A silent sentry stands;
He only can undo it,
  And open wide the door;
And mortals who pass through it,
  Are mortal nevermore.

2 Though dark and drear the passage
  That leadeth to the gate,
Yet grace comes with the message,
  To souls that watch and wait;
And at the time appointed,
  A messenger comes down,
And leads the Lord's anointed
  From cross to glory's crown.

3 Their sighs are lost in singing,
  They're blessèd in their tears;
Their journey heavenward winging,
  They leave on earth their fears:
Death like an angel seemeth:
  "We welcome thee," they cry;
Their face with glory beameth—
  'Tis life for them to die!

Thomas Mackellar, 1846.

726 All Saints. 8s 7s 7 7. *German Choral,* 1693.

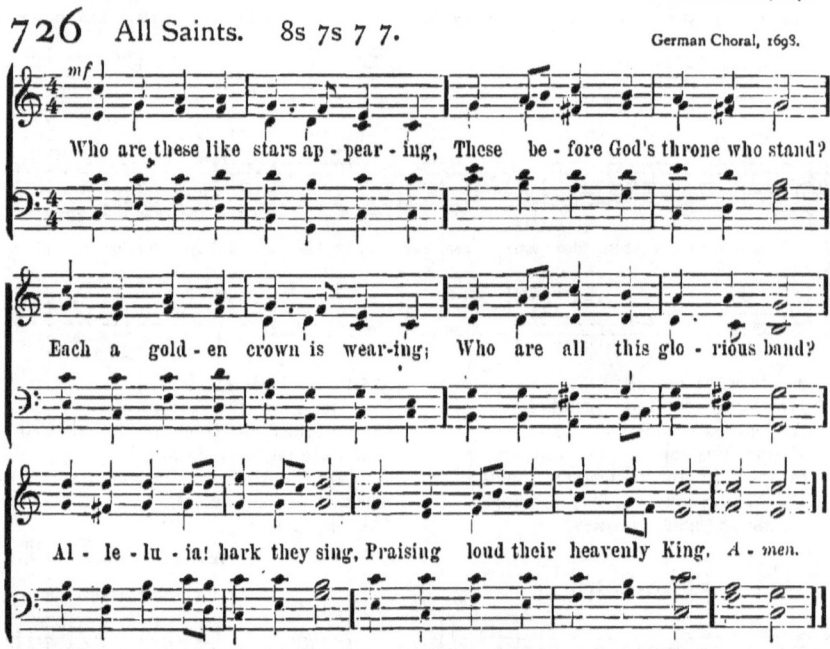

Who are these like stars appearing, These before God's throne who stand?
Each a golden crown is wearing; Who are all this glorious band?
Alleluia! hark they sing, Praising loud their heavenly King. A-men.

2 These are they who have contended
  For their Saviour's honor long,
Wrestling on till life was ended,
  Following not the sinful throng:
These, who well the fight sustained,
Triumph by the Lamb have gained.

3 These are they whose hearts were riven,
  Sore with woe and anguish tried,
Who in prayer full oft have striven
  With the God they glorified:
Now, their painful conflict o'er,
God has bid them weep no more.

H. F. Schenck, Tr. Frances E. Cox, 1841, ab.

Eternity.

727 Eternity. P.
JOSEPH E. SWEETSER, 1871. (?)

Eternity! eternity! How long art thou, eternity!
And yet to thee time hastes away, Like as the war-horse to the fray, Or swift as couriers homeward go,
Or ships to port, or shaft from bow; Ponder, O man, eternity, eternity!

2 Eternity! eternity!
How long art thou, eternity!
As long as God is God, so long
Endure the pains of hell and wrong,
So long the joys of heaven remain;
Oh, lasting joy! oh, lasting pain!
Ponder, O man, eternity!

3 Eternity! eternity!
How long art thou, eternity!
O man, full oft thy thoughts should dwell
Upon the pains of sin and hell,
And on the glories of the pure,
That do beyond all time endure;
Ponder, O man, eternity!
D. Wulffer, 1648.
Tr. Cath. Winkworth, 1855.

728 Gloria Patri.
RICHARD FARRANT, 1570.

Glory be to the Father, and.......... to the | Son, || And.......... to the | Ho-ly | Ghost;
As it was in the beginning is now, and | ev - er | shall be, || World.......... with-out | end. A- | men.

INDEX OF COMPOSERS.

A

Abbey, Alonzo Judson (1825-   ), 538.
Abt, Franz (1819-   ), 679.
Ahle, Johann Rudolph (1625-1673), 518, 681.
Allen, George Nelson (1812-1877), 446.
Andro Hart's *Psalter* (1615), 526.
Armes, Philip, D. M. (1836-   ), 445.
Arne, Thomas Augustine, D. M. (1710-1778), 350, 624.
Arrangements by H., 84, 110, 115, 123, 152, 159, 168, 182, 227, 276, 279, 280, 309, 315, 320, 336, 347, 371, 401, 421, 426, 429, 441, 469, 473, 490, 582, 588, 604, 627, 654, 679, 685, 705, 722.

B

Bach, Johann Christoph (1643-1703), 213.
Bach, Johann Sebastian (1685-1750), 657.
Baker, Sir Henry Williams, Bart. (1821-1877), 401.
Barnby, Joseph (1838-   ), 12, 128, 145, 369, 402, 432, 599, 603, 663, 702.
Barrett, William Alexander (1836-   ), 164.
Beethoven, Ludwig van (1770-1827), 84, 171, 280, 421, 481, 502.
Blancks, Edward (*Este's Psalter*, 1592), 253.
Blumenthal, Jacques (1829-   ), 276.
Bortniansky, Dimitri (1751-1825), 47, 351.
Bost, Rev. Paul-Ami-Isaac-David, (1790-1874), 182.
Bourgeois, Louis (-   ?), 89, 98.
Bowman, Rev. Thomas (1728-1792), 108.
Boyd, William (?-   ), 319.
Bradbury, William Batchelder (1816-1868), 13, 131, 169, 183, 256, 315, 323, 331, 335, 353, 457, 520, 604, 654.
Bryan, C (?-   ), 22.
Bull, John, D. M. (1563?-1628), 578.
Burder, Rev. George (1752-1832), 6.
Burnap, Uzziah Christopher (1834-   ), 184, 229, 310, 468, 646.
Burney, Charles, D. M., F. R. S. (1726-1814), 72.
Burrowes, John Freckleton (1787-1852), 147, 250.

C

Calkin, John Baptiste (1827-   ), 680, 712.
Carey, Henry (1680?-1743), 578.
Carter, Rev. Edmund S. (?-   ), 93.
Cherubini, Maria Luigi Carlo Zenobi Salvatore (1760-1842), 300.
Chetham, Rev. John (1700?-1760?), 38.
Cole, John (1774?-1855), 120.
Conkey, Ithamar (1815-1867), 224.
Cornell, John Henry (1828-   ), 325.
Croft, William, D. M. (1677-1727), 49, 688.
Cruger, Rev. Johann (1598-1662), 580.
Cuzens, Benjamin (-   ?), 341.

D

Darwall, Rev. John, B. A. (1731-1789), 212.
Decius, Nicholas (1519?-1541), 309.
Dixon, William (-   ?), 64.
Downes, Lewis T. (1824-   ), 491.
D'Urhan, Charles (-   ?), 707.
Dykes, Rev. John Bacchus, M. A., D. M. (1823-1876), 5, 17, 61, 153, 185, 238, 245, 329, 366, 372, 427, 458, 477, 499, 503, 549, 552, 553, 561, 650, 697, 699, 702, 703, 706, 708.

E

Edson, Lewis (1748-1820), 495.
Elvey, Sir George Job, D. M. (1816-   ), 569.

Emerson, Luther Orlando, D.M. (1826-   ), 282.
Ewing, Alexander (1830-   ), 723.

F

Farrant, Richard (1530?-1580), 608(?), 728.
Fesca, Alexander Ernst (1820-1849), 478.
Fischer, William Gustavus (1835-   ), 397.
Flemming, Friederich Ferdinand, M. D. (1778-1813), 85.
Flint, James (1822-   ), 328.
Freylinghausen, Rev. Johann Anastasius (1670-1739), 303.

G

Gauntlett, Henry John, D. M. (1806-1876), 201, 555, 597.
German Chorals, 23, 71, 102, 150, 215, 398, 609, 693, 726.
Giardini, Felice (1716-1796), 78.
Gibbons, Orlando, D. M. (1583-1625), 142, 399.
Gilbert, Walter Bond, Mus. Bac. (1829-   ), 587.
Goss, Sir John, D. M. (1800-1880), 20, 82, 165.
Gottschalk, Louis Moreau (1829-1869), 473.
Gould, John Edgar (1822-1875), 272, 327, 408.
Gould, Nathaniel Duren (1781-1864), 269.
Gounod, Charles François (1818-   ), 157.
Graun, Karl Heinrich (1701-1759), 698.
Greatorex, Henry Wellington (1811-1858), 52, 86, 115, 373.

H

Hamilton, Edward (1812-1870), 368.
Handel, George Frideric (1685-1759), 154, 166, 384, 447.
Harrison, Rev. Ralph (1748-1810), 28.
Harwood, Edward (-1787), 105.
"Hasler," John Leonard (1564-1612), 191.
Hastings, Thomas, D. M. (1784-1872), 195, 198, 260, 376, 395, 429, 434, 504, 570, 617, 621.
Hatton, John (-1793), 2.
Hatton, John Liphot (1809-   ), 308.
Havergal, Frances Ridley (1836-1879), 560.
Haweis, Rev. Thomas (1734-1820), 380.
Haydn, Franz Joseph, D. M. (1732-1809), 103, 109, 135, 320, 347, 460, 689.
Hayes, William, D. M. (1707-1777), 415.
Hermann, Nicholaus, (-1561), 631.
Herold, Louis Joseph Ferdinand (1791-1833), 206.
Hewlett, Thomas, Mus. Bac. (1845-1874), 307.
Hews, George, (1806-1873), 31.
Heywood, John (-   ?), 440.
Hiles, Henry, D. M. (1826-   ), 16.
Hodges, John Seb. Bach, S. T. D. (1830-   ), 517.
Holbrook, Joseph Perry, D.M. (1822-   ), 274, 333, 342.
Holden, Oliver (1765-1844), 220.
Hopkins, Edward John (1818-   ), 1, 10, 505.
Hopkins, John Henry, S. T. D (1820-   ), 111, 190.
Horsley, William, Mus. Bac (1774-1858), 178.
Husband, Rev. E. (-   ?), 317, 422.

I

Isaac, Heinrich (1440?-1528?), 614.

J

Johnson, James Anthony, (1820-   ), 122.
Jones, Rev. Darius Eliot (1815-1881), 573.
Jones, Rev. William (1726-1800), 360.

K.

Kingsley, George (1811- ---), 221, 381, 484, 640, 649.
Kirbye, George (--- ?- ---?), 565.
Knapp, William (1698-1768), 665.
Kocher, Conrad, Ph. D. (1786- ---), 76, 176.

L.

Lahee, Henry (1826- ---), 211, 461.
Langran, James (1835- ---), 306.
Leach, James (1762-1797), 637.
Lockhart, Charles (1745-1815), 455.
Löhr, G. A. (--- ?- ---), 114, 174.
Lowry, Robert, D.D. (1826- ---), 173.
Lucas, James (1762- ---?), 522.
Luther, Martin, D.D. (1483-1546), 123, 170, 694.
Lwoff, Alexis (1799-1870), 582.
Lyra Davidica, (1708), 196.

M.

Macdonald, A. (--- ?- ---), 448.
Macfarren, George Alexander, D. M. (1813- ---), 673.
Main, Hubert Platt (1839- ---), 140, 337, 391, 396, 403, 407, 423, 437, 443, 488, 579, 651, 655, 659, 678.
Malan, Rev. Cæsar Henri Abraham (1787-1864), 58.
Marsh, Simeon Butler (1798-1875), 334.
Marson, John (--- ?- ---?), 718.
Mason, Lowell, D. M. (1792-1872), 7, 46, 68, 70, 159, 187, 214, 241, 261, 290, 293, 339, 355, 363, 393, 410, 433, 452, 456, 489, 497, 500, 501, 535, 541, 574, 586, 596, 615, 622, 686.
Mazzinghi, Joseph (1765-1844), 279.
McDonald, Rev. William (1820- ---), 705.
Mehul, Etienne Henri (1763-1817), 251.
Mendelssohn-Bartholdy, Felix Jacob Ludwig, Ph. D. (1809-1847), 21, 90, 163, 547.
Monk, William Henry (1823- ---), 19, 263.
Mornington, Garrett Colley Wellesley, Earl of, D. M. (1735-1781), 370.
Mozart, Johannes Chrysostomus Wolfgang Theophilus Gottlieb (1756-1791), 45, 202, 441, 575.

N.

Nageli, Johann Georg (1768-1836), 453.
Nares, James, D. M. (1715-1783), 80, 313.
Neander, Rev. Joachim (1640-1688), 209.
Neukomm, Sigismund, Chevalier, (1778-1858), 581.

O.

Oakley, William Henry (1809-1881), 511.
Oliver, Gen. Henry Kemble (1800- ---), 230, 281, 382, 388.
Ouseley, Rev. Sir Frederick Arthur Gore, Bart., D. M. (1825- ---), 558.

P.

Palestrina, Giovanni Pierluigi da, (1524?-1594), 207.
Pelton, Jeremiah Morehouse (1821- ---), 326.
Pergolesi, Giovanni Battista (1710-1736), 492.
Pieraccini, Emilio (1828- ---), 528.
Piutti, Max (1852- ---), 210, 598, 674, 692.
Pleyel, Ignaz Joseph (1757-1831), 246, 352, 426, 444, 643.
Pond, Sylvanus Billings (1792-1871), 96.
Portugal, Marcos (--- -1834), 168, 336?
Purcell, Henry (1658-1695), 318.

R.

Randall, John, D. M. (1715-1799), 264.
Read, Daniel (1757-1836), 254.
Redhead, Richard (1820- ---), 192, 662.
Reinagle, Alexander Robert (1799-1877), 116.
Rinck, Johann Christian Heinrich (1770-1846), 715.
Ritter, Peter (1760?-1846), 29, 33.
Root, George Frederick, D.M. (1820- ---), 126, 700, 715.

Rosenmüller, Johann (1610?-1686), 271.
Rossini, Gioacchino (1792-1868), 722.
Rousseau, Jean-Jacques (1712-1778), 55.

S.

Saxton, S. Burt (1827- ---), 653.
Schein, Johann Hermann (1586-1630), 129, 449.
Schneider, Friedrich (1786-1853), 25.
Schnyder, Xavier, von Wartensee, (1786-1868), 152.
Schubert, Franz (1797-1828), 110.
Schumann, Robert, Ph. D. (1810-1856), 525.
Scotch Psalter (1615), 112, 128, 358, 583.
Sherwin, William Fisk (1826- ---), 125.
Shore, William (--- - ---), 36, 594.
Shrubsole, William (1758-1806), 220.
Smart, Henry (1812-1879), 338, 664, 672, 676.
Smith, Isaac (--- -1800), 26.
Smith, Samuel (1804-1873), 107, 550.
Spohr, Louis, D. M. (1784-1859), 43, 248, 450.
St. Alban's Tune Book (1865), 551, 562, 721.
Stainer, John, M A., D. M. (1840- ---), 696.
Stanley, Samuel (1767-1822), 69, 513.
Statham, Francis Reginald (1844- ---), 563.
Steggall, Charles, D. M. (1826- ---), 616.
Sullivan, Arthur Seymour, D. M. (1842- ---), 200, 459, 524, 658, 709, 711.
Swan, Timothy (1758-1842), 669.
Sweetser, Joseph Emerson (1825-1873), 73, 285, 465, 660, 727.

T.

Tallis, Thomas (1529-1585), 8, 496.
Tansur, William (1700-1783), 137, 208.
Taylor, Virgil Corydon (1817- ---), 188, 544.
Thalberg, Sigismund (1812-1871), 24.
Thorne, Edward Henry (1834- ---), 409.
Tours, Berthold (1838- ---), 559, 713.
Tucker, Isaac (1761-1825), 121.
Tuckerman, Samuel Parkman, D. M. (1819- ---), 97, 288.
Turle, James (1802- ---), 132, 529.
Troyte, Arthur Henry Dyke (Ackland) (1811-1857), 471.

U.

Uglow, J. (--- - ---?), 11.
Unknown. 18, 23, 63, 71, 102, 112, 150, 189, 196, 215, 262, 296, 324, 358, 367, 398, 506, 516, 526, 551, 562, 583, 609, 690, 693, 721, 726.

V.

Venua, Frederick Marc Antoine (1788- ---?), 627.
Vulpius, Melchior (1560?-1616), 532.

W.

Wainwright, John (--- -1768), 162.
Wainwright, Robert, D. M. (1748-1782), 412, 470.
Wallace, William Vincent (1815-1865), 354.
Walter, William Henry, D.M. (1825- ---), 106.
Warren, Nathan Boutou, D. M. (--- ?- ---), 268.
Webb, George James (1803- ---), 316, 610.
Webbe, Samuel (1740-1816), 151, 346, 490, 564.
Weber, Carl Maria von (1786-1826), 431, 469.
Wesley, Samuel Sebastian, D. M. (1810-1876), 509, 586.
Wheall, William, Mus. Bac. (--- -1745), 234.
Wilcox, John Henry, D. M. (1827-1875), 556, 613.
Wilkes, John P., A. R. A. (--- ?- ---), 60, 419.
Williams, Aaron (1731-1776), 65, 591.
Willing, Charles Edward (--- ?- ---), 11.
Willis, Richard Storrs (1819- ---), 158, 394.
Wilson, Hugh (--- ?- ---?), 243.
Woodbury, Isaac Baker (1819-1858), 167, 371, 463.

Z.

Zeuner, Heinrich Christopher (1795-1857), 203, 566, 595, 633.
Zundel, John (1815- ---), 217, 219, 227, 685.

INDEX OF HYMN WRITERS.

A.

Adams, Mrs. Sarah (Flower) (1805-1848), 456.
Addison, Joseph, (1672-1719), 109, 115, 120.
Adolphus, Gustavus (1594-1632), 415.
Albinus, Rev. Johann Georg (1624-1679), 652.
Alexander, Mrs. Cecil Frances (1823-   ), 184, 208, 321, 361, 552, 555, 689, 708.
Alexander, James Waddell, D.D. (1804-1859), 191.
Alexander, Joseph Addison, D.D. (1809-1860), 288.
Alexander, William Lindsay, D. D., F. R. S. E. (1808-   ), 231.
Alford, Henry, D.D. (1810-1871), 430, 460, 569, 684, 699.
Allen, Rev. James (1734-1804), 442.
Allen, Oswald (1816-   ), 316.
Ambrose (340-397), 9, 73.
Anatolius (-458), 328.
Anstice, Prof. Joseph (1808-1836), 416.
Auber, Miss Harriet (1773-1862), 39, 203, 206, 245, 596.
Austin, John (1613-1699), 258.

B.

Bacon, Leonard, D.D. (1802-   ), 15, 581.
Baker, Rev. Sir Henry Williams, Bart. (1821-1877), 198, 338, 411.
Barbauld, Mrs. Anna Lætitia (1743-1825), 42, 576.
Barlow, Joel (1755-1812), 119.
Baring-Gould, Rev. Sabine, M.A. (1834-   ), 12, 459.
Bathurst, Rev. William Hiley, M.A. (1796-1877), 360, 608, 623, 670.
Baxter, Rev. Richard (1615-1691), 354.
Beddome, Rev. Benjamin, M.A. (1717-1795), 232, 242, 252, 485.
Bernard de Clairvaux (1091-1153), 380, 412, 525.
Bernard de Morlaix (1120?-   ?), 721, 723.
Bethune, George Washington, D.D. (1805-1862), 150.
Bickersteth, Rev. Edward (1786-1850), 500.
Bickersteth, Rev. Edward Henry, M.A. (1825-   ), 297, 508, 547.
Boden, Rev. James (1757-1841), 141.
Bonar, Mrs. Catherine Jane (1811?-   ), 710.
Bonar, Horatius, D.D. (1808-   ), 310, 329, 395, 468, 480, 538, 548, 646, 668, 680, 686, 712, 714.
Borthwick, Miss Jane (1825-   ), 304, 422, 432, 469, 672.
Bowring, Sir John, LL.D., F.R.S. (1792-1872), 91, 224, 327, 489, 679.
Bridges, Matthew (1800-   ), 219, 221, 539.
Brown, Mrs. Phœbe Hinsdale (1782-1862), 13.
Browne, Rev. Simon (1680-1732), 233.
Bruce, Michael (1746-1767), 160, 436, 631, 671.
Bryant, William Cullen (1794-1878), 465, 496.
Bulfinch, Stephen Greenleaf (1809-1870), 22.
Burgess, George, D.D. (1809-1866), 572.
Burnham, Rev. Richard (1749-1810), 296.
Burns, Rev. James Drummond, M.A. (1823-1864), 52.
Byrom, John, M.A., F. R. S. (1691-1763), 162.

C.

Campbell, Robert (1799?-1868), 205, 518.
Campbell, Thomas (1777-1844), 169.
Caswall, Rev. Edward (1814-1878), 380, 388, 390, 412, 650.
Cawood, Rev. John, M.A. (1775-1852), 171.
Cennick, Rev. John (1718-1755), 305, 444, 476, 674.
Chambers, John David, M.A. (1804?-   ), 144.
Chandler, Rev. John, M.A. (1806-1876), 9, 289, 389, 495, 607.
Charles, Mrs Elizabeth (1818-   ), 85, 454.
Chorley, Henry Fothergill (1808-1872), 582.

Churton, Edward, D.D. (1800-   ), 616.
Cleveland, Rev. Benjamin (--?--?), 437.
Codner, Mrs. Elizabeth (1835?-   ), 315.
Coffin, Charles (1676-1749), 584.
Collins, Rev. Henry, M.A. (1834?-   ), 145.
Collyer, William Bengo, D.D. (1782-1854), 48, 283, 694.
Conder, Josiah (1789-1855), 75, 278, 391, 473, 507, 682.
Cotterill, Rev. Thomas, M.A. (1779-1823), 239.
Cousin, Mrs. Annie Ross (--?--   ), 707.
Cowper, William (1731-1800), 247, 351, 418, 424, 451, 467, 519, 533, 704.
Cox, Miss Frances Elizabeth (--?--   ), 152, 201, 726.
Coxe, Arthur Cleveland, D.D. (1818-   ), 588.
Crewdson, Mrs. Jane (Fox) (1809-1863), 343, 470.
Crosby, Fanny (see Van Alstyne).
Crosswell, William, D.D. (1804-1854), 641.
Cruger, Johann (1598-1662), 271.

D.

Davies, Rev. Samuel, M.A. (1724-1761), 536.
Dayman, Rev. Edward Arthur, B.D. (1807-   ), 663.
Decius, Rev. Nicholas (Von Hofe) (--?-1529), 309.
Deck, James George (1802-   ), 140, 369, 482, 724.
Denny, Sir Edward, Bart. (1796-   ), 178, 179, 417, 514, 624.
Dickson, Rev. David (1583-1663), 713.
Dix, William Chatterton (1837-   ), 176.
Doane, George Washington, D.D. (1799-1859), 31, 181.
Doddridge, Philip, D.D. (1702-1751), 43, 62, 86, 155, 311, 375, 386, 447, 499, 501, 513, 565, 605, 630, 640, 687.
Duffield, George, D.D. (1818-   ), 504, 611.
Duncan, Mrs. Mary (Lundie) (1814-1840), 553.
Dryden, John, M.A. (1631-1700), 229.
Dwight, Timothy, D.D. (1752-1817), 592, 667.

E.

Eastburn, James Wallis (1798-1819), 74.
Edmeston, James (1791-1867), 44, 47, 50, 92.
Ellerton, Rev. John (1826-   ), 54, 505.
Elliott, Miss Charlotte (1789-1871), 323, 331, 427, 428, 445, 471, 472, 656.
Elven, Rev. Cornelius (1797-   ), 301.
Evans, Rev. James Harrington (1785-1849), 419.

F.

Faber, Frederic William, D.D. (1814-1863), 132, 149, 330, 486, 642, 702, 706.
Fawcett, John, D.D. (1739-1817), 57, 94, 266, 359, 367, 464, 591.
Finch, Francis Miles (1827-   ), 449.
Fortunatus, Venantius Honorius Clementianus (530-609), 389.
Francis, Rev. Benjamin (1734-1799), 382.
Fulbert, of Chartres, (--?-1029?), 205.

G.

Gellert, Christian Fürchtegott (1715-1769), 201.
Gerhard, Rev. Paul (1606-1676), 191, 422, 479.
Gibbons, Thomas, D.D. (1720-1785), 625, 718.
Gill, Thomas Hornblower (1819-   ), 53, 235, 257, 438, 439.
Gilmore, Rev. Prof. Joseph Henry (1834-   ), 457.
Goode, Rev. William, M.A. (1762-1816), 56.
Gough, Benjamin (1805-   ), 690.
Grant, Sir Robert (1785-1838), 135, 308, 349.
Gregory I. (550-604), 143.

INDEX OF HYMN WRITERS.

Grigg, Rev. Joseph (1723?-1768), 286, 382.
Gurney, Rev. Archer Thompson (1820- ——), 200.
Guyon, Jeannie Bouvier de la Motte (1648-1717), 89, 106, 351, 418, 466.

H.

Hammond, Rev. William, B.A. (1719-1783), 58, 199, 222.
Hankey, Miss Catherine (— ?- ——), 397.
Harmer, Rev. Samuel Young (1809- ——), 705.
Hart, Rev. Joseph (1712-1768), 241, 275.
Hastings, Thomas, D. M. (1784-1872), 29, 195, 260, 280, 490, 542, 573, 614, 678.
Hatfield, Edwin Francis, D.D. (1807- ——). 40, 73, 543.
Havergal, Rev. William Henry, M.A. (1793-1870), 148.
Haweis, Rev. Thomas, LL.B., M.D. (1732-1820), 237, 244, 534.
Hayward (*Dobell's Collection*, 1806), 25.
Heath, Rev. George (— ?- ——?), 452.
Heber, Reginald, D.D. (1783-1826), 5, 10, 164, 448, 517, 551, 622, 683.
Heginbotham, Rev. Ottiwell (1744-1768), 116, 563.
Hensel, Miss Luise (1798- ——). 554.
Herbert, Rev. George, M.A. (1593-1632), 638.
Hill, Rev. Rowland, M.A. (1744-1833), 655, 666.
Hillhouse, Augustus Lucas (1792-1859), 396.
Hodges, George Samuel (— ?- ——), 561.
Holmes, Oliver Wendell, LL.D. (1809- ——), 103, 371.
Hone, William (1780-1842), 270.
Hope, Henry Joy McCracken (1809-1872), 710.
Hopkins, John Henry, S.T.D. (1820- ——), 111.
Hoskins, Rev. Joseph (1745-1788), 236.
How, Rev. William Walsham, M.A. (1823- ——), 107, 317, 345, 598.
Humphreys, Rev. Joseph (1720- ——?), 506.
Hunter, William, D.D. (1811-1877), 409.
Huntington, Rev. Frederic Dan, S.T.D. (1819- ——), 264.
Hupton, Rev. Job (1762-1849), 151, 209.
Hyde, Mrs. Abby (Bradley) (1799-1872), 273, 502.

J.

Johnson, Mrs. Katharine (Hardenbergh) (1835- ——), 612.
Johnson, Rev. Nathaniel Emmons (1804-1847), 186.
Julius, Mrs. A. (— ?- ——), 435.
Judkin, Rev. Thomas James (1788-1871), 223.

K.

Keble, Rev. John, M.A. (1792-1866), 3, 33, 562.
Keith, George (— ?- ——?), 336.
Kelly, Rev. Thomas (1769-1855), 41, 55, 198, 213, 214, 215, 216, 225, 267, 399, 420, 617, 620.
Ken, Rev. Thomas (1637-1711), 2, 8, 101.
Kethe, Rev. William (1510-1580), 100.
Key, Francis Scott (1779-1843), 122.
King, Rev. John (1788-1858), 559.
Kirby, W. H. (— ?- ——), 440.
Knyaston, Herbert, D.D. (1809- ——), 307.

L.

Langford, Rev. John (— ?- 1790), 276.
Laurenti, Laurentius (1660-1722), 672.
Littledale, Rev. Richard Frederick, LL.D. (1833- ——), 658.
Lloyd, William Freeman (1791-1853), 474, 478.
Luther, Martin, D.D. (1483-1546), 123, 170.
Lyte, Rev. Henry Francis, M.A. (1793-1847), 19, 77, 129, 295, 325, 407, 441, 443, 491, 587.

M.

Macduff, John Ross, D.D. (1818- ——), 618.
Mackay, Mrs. Margaret (1801- ——), 653.
Mackellar, Thomas (1812- ——), 725.
Madan, Rev. Martin (1726-1790), 222.

Mant, Richard, D.D. (1776-1848), 90, 110, 161, 246.
Marriott, Rev. John (1780-1825), 79.
Mason, Rev. John, M.A. (— ?- 1694), 45, 234, 374.
Maude, Mrs. Mary Fawler (— ?- ——), 475.
McAll, Rev. Robert Stephens (1792-1838), 719.
McCheyne, Rev. Robert Murray (1813-1843), 509.
Medley, Rev. Samuel (1738-1799), 156, 207, 364, 379, 393.
Mercer, Rev. William, M.A. (1811-1873), 10, 168, 584.
Metrical Psalm, 174.
Midlane, Rev. Albert (1825- ——), 550.
Mills, Rev. Henry, D.D. (1786-1867), 694.
Milman, Henry Hart, D.D. (1791-1868), 185, 190, 662.
Milton, John (1608-1674), 575.
Monsell, Rev. John Samuel Bewley, LL.D. (1811-1875), 84, 128, 344, 675.
Montgomery, James (1771-1854), 27, 32, 34, 59, 173, 192, 227, 243, 256, 326, 406, 429, 492, 494, 498, 529, 544, 570, 610, 615, 626, 648, 661, 664, 692.
Moore, Thomas (1779-1852), 484, 490.
Morrison, John, D.D. (1749-1798), 159.
Moultrie, Rev. Gerard, M.A. (1839- ——), 193, 673.
Muhlenberg, William Augustus, D.D. (1796-1877), 84, 408, 649.

N.

Neale, John Mason, D.D. (1818-1866), 112, 157, 175, 328, 401, 458, 603, 693, 698, 711, 721, 723.
Neander, Rev. Joachim (1640-1680), 398.
Needham, Rev. John (— ?- ——?), 133, 566.
Nelson, Rev. David, M.D. (1793-1844), 700.
Nelson, Earl, Horatio (1823- ——), 153.
Newman, John Henry, D.D. (1801- ——), 17.
Newton, Rev. John (1725-1807), 46, 60, 320, 334, 377, 381, 431, 483, 521, 613, 718.
Noel, Hon. and Rev. Gerard Thomas, M.A. (1782-1851), 530.

O.

Ogilvie, John, D.D. (1733-1814), 105.

P.

Palmer, Ray, D.D. (1808- ——), 95, 143, 269, 341, 346, 373, 405, 525, 541, 564, 627, 720.
Peacock, John (— ?- ——?), 499.
Perronet, Rev. Edward (— ?-1792), 220.
Pierpont, Rev. John (1785-1866), 636.
Plumptre, Rev. Edward Hayes (1821- ——), 180.
Pollock, Thomas Benson (1836- ——), 189.
Pott, Rev. Francis, M.A. (1832- ——), 207.
Potter, Rev. Thomas J— (1827-1873), 560.
Prentiss, Mrs. Elizabeth (Payson) (1818-1878), 372.
Procter, Miss Adelaide Anne (1825-1864), 16.
Psalm cxxx., 324.

R.

Rawson, George (1807- ——), 524.
Reed, Andrew, D.D. (1787-1862), 165, 240.
Rinkart, Rev. Martin (1586-1649), 580.
Robinson, Rev. Robert (1735-1790), 516.
Rodigast, Rev. Samuel (1640-?- ——?), 487.
Russell, Rev. Arthur Tozer, B.C.L. (1806-1874), 170.

S.

Saffery, Mrs. Maria Grace (1773-1858), 51.
Santolius Maglorianus (1628-1684), 338.
Scheffler, Rev. Johann, M.D. (1624-1677), 152, 348.
Schenck, Henry Theodore (— -1727), 726.
Schmolke, Rev. Benjamin (1672-1737), 469.
Scotch Version (1641), 350.
Scott, Sir Walter (1771-1832), 697.
Seagrave, Rev. Robert, M.A. (1693-1759?), 81.
Sears, Edmund Hamilton, D.D. (1810-1876), 158, 166.
Seymour, Aaron Crossley Hobart (1789- ——), 204.
Sherwin, William Fisk (1826- ——), 125.
Shirley, Mrs. Selina, Countess of Huntingdon (1707-1791), 291.

INDEX OF HYMN WRITERS. 371

Shirley, Hon. and Rev. Walter (1725-1786), 279, 442.
Shrubsole, Jr., William (1759-1829), 37, 633.
Sigourney, Mrs. Lydia Howard (Huntley) (1791-1865), 19.
Singleton, Rev. Robert Corbett, M.A. (—?-—), 123.
Smith, Mrs. Caroline Sprague (—?-—), 651.
Smith, Samuel Francis, D.D. (1808-—), 261, 493, 578, 623.
Spitta, Charles John Philip, D.D. (1801-1859), 342.
Stanley, Arthur Penrhyn, D.D. (1815-1881), 681, 696.
Steele, Miss Anne (1716-1778), 11, 36, 114, 248, 298, 312, 357, 384, 413, 433, 532, 537, 568, 583.
Stennett, Samuel, D.D. (1727-1795), 188, 322, 376, 522.
Sterling, Rev. John (1806-1844), 130.
Sternhold, Thomas (—?-1549). 96.
Stone, Rev. Samuel John, M.A. (1839-—), 306, 586.
Stowe, Mrs Harriet (Beecher) (1814-—), 21, 402.
Stowell, Rev. Hugh (1799-1865), 434.
Strong, Nathan, D.D. (1748-1816), 577.
Stryker, Rev. Melancthon Woolsey (1851-—), 1, 177, 398, 609, 654, 676, 677, 688, 701, 722.
Swain, Rev. Joseph (1761-(1796), 67, 274, 599.
Swain, Rev. Leonard (1821-1869), 639.

T.

Tappan, Rev. William Bingham (1794-1849), 183.
Tate and Brady's Collection (1696), 211, 372.
Tate, Nahum (1652-1715), 72, 167, 407.
Taylor, Rev. Thomas Rawson (1807-1835), 709.
Tersteegen, Rev. Gerhard (1697-1769), 304, 645.
Theodore of the Studium (759-826), 698.
Thomas of Celano (—?-—?), 697.
Thring, Rev. Godfrey (1823-—), 366.
Thrupp, Miss Dorothy Ann (1779-1847), 556.
Toke, Miss Emma (1812-1878), 647.
Toplady, Rev. Augustus Montague (1740-1778), 194, 292, 314, 368, 410, 503.
Tuttiett, Rev. Lawrence (1825-—), 685.

U.

Unknown, 14, 18, 30, 93, 174, 197, 211, 262, 268, 281, 350, 392, 394, 400, 423, 518, 540, 549, 557, 558, 574, 604, 650, 695.

V.

Van Alstyne, Mrs. Frances Jane (Crosby) (1823-—), 131, 659.

Vaughan, Henry, M.D. (1621-1695), 691.
Voke, Mrs. (—?-—?), 634, 635.

W.

Waring, Miss Anna Lætitia (1820-—), 337, 477.
Waterman, Miss Catherine H. (—?-—), 488.
Watts, Isaac, D.D. (1674-1748), 4, 6, 7, 26, 28, 35, 38, 61, 63, 64, 65, 66, 68, 69, 70, 71, 82, 83, 87, 97, 98, 99, 102, 104, 108, 113, 117, 118, 121, 127, 134, 137, 138, 139, 142, 147, 154, 182, 187, 230, 238, 249, 250, 251, 253, 254, 255, 263, 265, 272, 282, 285, 293, 294, 299, 302, 318, 335, 339, 340, 353, 355, 356, 358, 362, 363, 365, 370, 387, 403, 404, 414, 425, 446, 450, 481, 520, 523, 526, 527, 535, 545, 546, 567, 585, 589, 590, 593, 602, 606, 628, 632, 643, 665, 669, 715, 716, 717.
Weiss, Rev. Michael (—?-1540), 196.
Weissell, Rev. George (1590-1635), 303.
Wesley, Rev. Charles, M.A. (1708-1788), 78, 80, 136, 163, 172, 202, 210, 212, 217, 227, 228, 259, 271, 277, 290, 300, 313, 319, 333, 347, 378, 385, 421, 453, 463, 510, 511, 512, 515, 531, 571, 594, 595, 600. 637, 644, 674.
Wesley, Rev. John, M.A. (1703-1791), 98, 348, 352, 383, 479, 528, 645.
Whately, Richard, D.D. (1787-1863), 10.
White, Henry Kirke (1785-1806), 126, 284, 461, 601.
Whitfield, Rev. Frederick, M.A. (1829-—), 342, 375.
Whittingham, William Rollinson, D.D., LL.D. (1805-1879), 124.
Williams, Miss Helen Maria (1762-1827), 426.
Williams, Rev. William (1717-1791), 455, 619.
Willis, Nathaniel Parker (1807-1867), 497.
Winkworth, Miss Catherine (1829-1878), 23, 146, 196, 303, 415, 487, 554, 580, 652, 657, 727.
Wolcott, Samuel, D.D. (1813-—), 621.
Wolfe, Rev. Aaron Robarts (1821-—), 332.
Woodford, James Russell, D.D. (1820-—), 226.
Wordsworth, Christopher, D.D. (1807-—), 20, 24, 76, 218, 462, 597, 703.
Wreford, John Reynell, D.D., F.S.A. (1799?-—), 579.
Wulffer, Rev. Daniel (1617-1685), 727.

X.

Xavier, St. Francis (1506-1552), 388.

Z.

Zinzendorf, Nicholaus Ludwig von (1700-1760), 383, 528.

INDEX OF FIRST LINES.

ABIDE in me, O Lord, and I in Thee.	402
Abide with me! fast falls the	19
A broken heart, my God, my King..	293
According to Thy gracious word	529
A charge to keep I have	453
A few more years shall roll	646
Again the Lord of life and light	42
A glory gilds the sacred page	247
All hail the power of Jesus' name	220
All people, that on earth do dwell	100
All that I was,—my sin, my guilt	538
Alone with Thee, with Thee alone	439
Amazing grace! how sweet the	377
Am I a soldier of the cross	450
Among the saints that fill Thy house	602
And now another week begins	41
Angels from the realms of glory	173
A pilgrim and a stranger	422
A pilgrim through this lonely world.	179
A poor blind child I wander here	352
Approach, my soul! the mercy seat.	320
Arise, my soul! my joyful powers	527
Arise, O King of grace! arise	63
Arise, ye people! and adore	203
Arm of the Lord! awake, awake	633
Arm these, Thy soldiers, mighty	462
Art thou weary, art thou languid	401
Asleep in Jesus! blessed sleep	653
As pants the hart for cooling streams	407
As with gladness men of old	176
At the Lamb's high feast, we sing	518
At Thy command, our dearest Lord.	520
Awake, and sing the song	222
Awake, awake, O Zion	690
Awake, my soul! and with the sun.	2
Awake, my soul! in joyful lays	364
Awake, my soul! stretch every	447
Awake, my soul! to sound His	119
Awake, our souls! away, our fears	643
Awake, ye saints! and raise your	565
Away from every mortal care	35
BEFORE Jehovah's awful throne	98
Begin, my soul! th' exalted lay	105
Begin, my tongue! some heavenly	250
Behold! a Stranger's at the door	286
Behold! the Bridegroom cometh	673
Behold! the mountain of the Lord.	631
Behold the sure foundation stone	632
Blessed are the sons of God	506
Bless'd be Thy love, dear Lord	258
Blessed fountain, full of grace	399
Blessed Saviour, Thee I love	504
Blest be the tie that binds	591
Blest day of God! most calm, most.	45
Bound upon the accursed tree	190
Bread of the world, in mercy broken	517
Brightest and best of the sons of	164
Bright King of glory, wondrous God	137
Brightly gleams our banner	560
Buried in shadows of the night	294
Burst forth! O Bridegroom, from	677
By Christ redeemed, in Christ	524
By cool Siloam's shady rill	551
CALM on the listening ear of night.	166
Cast thy burden on the Lord	476
Child of sin and sorrow	260
Children of light! arise and shine	417
Children of the heavenly King	444
Christ, above all glory seated	226
Christ for the world we sing	621
Christ had His sorrows, when He	186
Christian, dost thou see them	458
Christians, awake, salute the happy.	162
Christian, seek not yet repose	445
Christ is coming! let creation	618
Christ is our Corner-Stone	495
Christ is risen! Christ is risen	200
Christ the Lord is risen again	196
"Christ, the Lord, is risen to-day!".	202
Christ, whose glory fills the skies,..	510
Come, all ye saints of God	141

Come and rejoice with me	454	Earth has a joy unknown to heaven.	396
Come, blessed Spirit, Source of light	232	Earth has nothing sweet or fair	152
Come, dearest Lord! descend and..	71	Earth is passed away and gone	684
"Come hither, all ye weary souls"..	285	Enthroned is Jesus now	223
Come, Holy Spirit! come	241	Enthroned on high, almighty Lord.	237
Come, Holy Spirit, heavenly Dove..	233	Ere the blue heavens were stretch'd.	138
Come, Holy Spirit, heavenly Dove..	238	Eternal day hath dawned	722
Come, let our voices join to raise...	272	Eternal Father! Thou hast said	627
Come, let us join our cheerful songs	147	Eternal Spirit! God of truth	239
Come, let us sing of Jesus	150	Eternal Spirit! we confess	230
Come, let us sing the song of songs.	544	Eternal Sun of Righteousness	385
Come, Lord! when grace has made.	354	Eternity! eternity! how long art...	727
Come, my soul! thy suit prepare ...	431	Ever would I fain be reading	554
Come, O Thou traveler unknown...	347	Every morn the glowing sun	708
Come, quickly come, dread Judge of	685		
Come, see the place where Jesus lay	198	FADING, still fading, the last beam is	18
Come, sinner! to the gospel feast...	264	Faint not, Christian! though the...	419
Come, sound His praise abroad	26	Fairest Lord Jesus	394
Come, Thou almighty King	78	Fair shines the morning star	227
Come, Thou Fount of every blessing	516	Faith sees the bright eternal doors..	667
Come, Thou long-expected Jesus...	172	Far down the ages now	686
Come unto Me, when shadows..,...	488	Father, I know that all my life	477
Come, we that love the Lord	68	Father of all, from land and sea	597
Come, ye disconsolate! where'er ye.	490	Father of mercies! in Thy word	248
Come, ye faithful, raise the anthem.	209	Father! whate'er of earthly bliss	433
Come, ye saints! and raise an	151	Fear not, O little flock, the foe	415
Come, ye sinners! poor and	275	Fierce raged the tempest o'er the...	366
Come, ye souls, by sin afflicted	274	Fierce was the billow wild..,......	328
Come, ye thankful people, come....	569	For all the saints, who from their...	598
Commit thou all thy griefs	479	Forever here my rest shall be	531
Complete in Thee! no work of mine	332	"Forever with the Lord!"	648
Creator, Spirit! by whose aid	229	For thee, O dear, dear country	721
Crown Him with many crowns	221	Forth to the fight, ye ransomed	440
		Forward! be our watchword	460
DAUGHTER of Zion! from the dust.	626	Friend of the friendless, and the....	467
Day by day the manna fell	473	From all that dwell below the skies.	99
Day by day we magnify Thee	93	From deep distress, and troubled...	255
Day of wrath, Oh, dreadful day	696	From every stormy wind that blows.	434
Days and moments quickly flying...	650	From Greenland's icy mountains ...	622
Dear Lord and Master mine	257	From the faint dayspring's eastern..	161
Dear Saviour, if these lambs should	502	From the recesses of a lowly spirit.	327
Dear Saviour! when my thoughts..	312		
"Death cannot make my soul .....'.	654	GENTLY, gently lay Thy rod	491
Deep in our hearts, let us record ...	282	Gently, my Saviour! let me down...	655
Depth of mercy, can there be	277	Give me the wings of faith, to rise...	362
Draw nigh, draw nigh, Immanuel...	157	Glorious things of Thee are spoken.	613
Drooping souls, no longer mourn...	280	Glory be to God on high	262
		Glory be to the Father	728
EARLY, my God, without delay	64	Glory to Thee, my God! this night.	8

INDEX OF FIRST LINES.

God calling yet!—shall not I hear .. 304
God hath made the moon, whose... 111
God, in the gospel of His Son...... 252
God is gone up on high............ 228
God is love; His mercy brightens.. 91
God is the Refuge of His saints.... 355
God moves in a mysterious way.... 424
God, my king, Thy might confessing 90
God of grace, oh, let Thy light..... 616
God of mercy, God of grace........ 77
God of my life! through all my days 86
God of my life! Thy boundless..... 472
God of the morning! at whose voice 6
God of the nations! bow Thine ear. 614
God of the sunlight hours! how sad 51
God that madest earth and heaven.. 10
Go, labor on; spend, and be spent.. 668
Good news from heaven the angels. 170
Go to dark Gethsemane............ 192
Go to the grave in all thy glorious.. 664
Grace,—'tis a charming sound...... 513
Grander than ocean's story........ 125
Great and glorious Father, humbly . 549
Great God! let all my tuneful...... 563
Great God! this sacred day of Thine 36
Great God, to Thee my evening.... 11
Great God! what do I see and hear. 694
Great Jehovah! we adore Thee..... 56
Great Shepherd of Thine Israel.... 606
Great Spirit! by whose mighty..... 244
Guide me, O Thou great Jehovah.. 455

Hail to the Lord's Anointed........ 610
Hail to the Sabbath day............ 22
Happy the souls to Jesus joined.... 600
Hark! hark! my soul! angelic..... 702
Hark! hark!—the notes of joy..... 165
Hark! how the choral song of..... 719
Hark! my soul! it is the Lord..... 519
Hark! ten thousand harps and..... 214
Hark! the song of Jubilee......... 692
Hark the glad sound! the Saviour.. 155
Hark! the herald angels sing...... 163
Hark the notes of angels, singing.. 225
Hark! the sound of holy voices.... 703
Hark! what mean those holy voices 171
Hasten, Lord! the glorious time.... 596
Hasten, Lord! the promised hour... 682
Haste, traveler, haste! the night.... 283

Hast thou within a care so deep.... 435
Head of the Church triumphant.... 421
Hear what God, the Lord, hath..... 704
Hearts of stone! relent, relent..... 271
He is coming; He is coming....... 689
He is gone! and we remain........ 681
He leadeth me, O blessed thought.. 457
He lives, the great Redeemer lives.. 357
Here at Thy table, Lord! we meet.. 522
Here, O my Lord, I see Thee face... 548
He, that goeth forth with weeping . 573
High in the heavens, eternal God... 104
Holy and reverend is the name..... 133
Holy, delightful day 53
Holy Father! Holy Son............ 197
Holy Ghost! my soul inspire....... 246
Holy, holy, holy is the Lord........ 131
Holy, holy, holy Lord.............. 76
Holy, holy, holy, Lord God Almighty 5
Hosanna! raise the pealing hymn.. 148
Hosanna we sing, like the children. 561
How are Thy servants bless'd, O ... 115
How calm and beautiful the morn... 195
How can I, Lord, abide with Thee... 438
How firm a foundation, ye saints of. 336
How oft, alas! this wretched heart.. 298
How pleasant, how divinely fair.... 70
How pleased and blessed was I..... 65
How sad our state by nature is..... 253
How sweet and awful is the place... 526
How sweet, how heavenly is the.... 599
How sweetly breaks the Sabbath... 40
How sweet the name of Jesus sounds 381
How sweet, thro' long-remembered. 15

If Christ is mine, then all is mine... 485
If human kindness meets return.... 530
If life in sorrow must be spent..... 466
If, thro' unruffled seas............. 368
I heard the voice of Jesus say...... 329
I lay me down to sleep 660
I love my God, but with no love of. 106
I love Thy kingdom, Lord.......... 592
I love to kiss each print where Thou 486
I love to steal awhile away......... 13
I love to tell the story 397
I'm but a stranger here............ 709
I'm not ashamed to own my Lord.. 446
In all my vast concerns with Thee.. 358

INDEX OF FIRST LINES.

I need Thee, precious Jesus........ 342
Infinite God! Thou great unrivaled .89
In heavenly love abiding.......... 337
In the Christian's home in glory.... 705
In the cross of Christ I glory...... 224
In the morning hear my voice...... 32
In the sun, and moon, and stars ... 683
In this calm impressive hour....... 29
In Thy great name, O Lord, we come 236
In Thy name, O Lord! assembling.. 55
I see the crowd in Pilate's hall..... 310
I sing th' almighty power of God... 134
It came upon the midnight clear.... 158
It is Thy hand, my God............ 482
I've found a joy in sorrow......... 343
I've found the Pearl of greatest.... 374
I was a wandering sheep........... 395
I would not live alway; I ask...... 649

Jerusalem the golden............. 723
Jesus! and shall it ever be........ 382
Jesus comes, His conflict over..... 213
Jesus, engrave it on my heart...... 287
Jesus, immortal King! arise........ 204
Jesus, I my cross have taken....... 441
Jesus, in Thy dying woes.......... 189
Jesus is God! the glorious bands... 149
Jesus lives! thy terrors now....... 201
Jesus, lover of my soul 333
Jesus, my All, to heaven is gone.... 305
Jesus, my Lord! how rich Thy..... 640
Jesus, my Lord, my God, my all ... 145
Jesus, my Saviour, look on me..... 428
Jesus, Saviour, Son of God........ 558
Jesus shall reign where'er the sun.. 628
Jesus, tender Shepherd, hear me.... 553
Jesus! these eyes have never seen . 373
Jesus, the sinner's Friend, to Thee.. 300
Jesus! the very thought of Thee.... 412
Jesus, Thou art the sinner's Friend. 296
Jesus, Thou everlasting King...... 546
Jesus, Thou Joy of loving hearts... 525
Jesus, Thy blood and righteousness. 383
Jesus, Thy church, with longing.... 629
Jesus, Thy name I love............ 140
Jesus, we thus obey............... 515
Jesus, who died a world to save 199
Jesus, who knows full well........ 483
Join all the glorious names........ 335

Joyful be the hours to-day......... 420
Joyfully, joyfully onward I move... 409
Joy to the world, the Lord is come. 154
Just as I am, without one plea...... 331

Keep silence, all created things 97
Know, my soul! thy full salvation.. 443

Laden with guilt and full of fears.. 249
Lamb of God, whose dying love.... 511
Lead, kindly Light, amid th' encir .. 17
Let all the people join.. 574
Let every heart exulting beat...... 144
Let every mortal ear attend........ 265
Let Israel, to the Prince of Peace., 160
Let me be with Thee, where Thou.. 656
Let me but hear my Saviour say.... 365
Let no tears to-day be shed........ 658
Let our choir new anthems raise.... 603
Let saints below in concert sing.... 595
Let us with a gladsome mind....... 575
Let Zion and her sons rejoice....... 589
Lift up your heads, eternal gates.... 211
Lift up your heads, ye mighty gates. 303
Light of light! enlighten me....... 23
Light of the lonely pilgrim's heart.. 624
Like sheep we went astray......... 340
Lo! He comes with clouds......... 674
Lo! hills and mountains shall bring. 174
Look! ye saints! the sight is....... 216
Lo! on a narrow neck of land...... 290
Lord, and is Thine anger gone..... 313
Lord! dismiss us with Thy blessing. 57
Lord God of my salvation.......... 325
Lord! I am Thine, entirely Thine... 536
Lord, I feel a carnal mind.......... 314
Lord! I hear of showers of blessing 315
Lord Jesus, are we one with Thee .. 369
Lord! lead the way the Saviour.... 641
Lord! let Thy saving mercy heal... 608
Lord, my weak thought in vain..... 346
Lord of all being! throned afar..... 103
Lord of the harvest! hear.......... 571
Lord of the worlds above.......... 61
Lord! send Thy word, and let it fly. 625
Lord! take my heart, and let it be.. 528
Lord! Thou hast scourged our..... 585
Lord, Thou hast searched and seen. 356
Lord! Thou wilt bring the joyful... 720

INDEX OF FIRST LINES.

Lord, Thy glory fills the heaven....	110
Lord! 'tis not that I did choose Thee	391
Lord! we come before Thee now ...	58
Lord! when my raptured thought..	114
Lord! while for all mankind we pray	579
Lord, with glowing heart I'd praise.	122
Love divine, all love excelling......	217
Lo! what a glorious sight appears..	716
MAJESTIC sweetness sits enthroned.	376
Maker of earth, to Thee alone......	112
Many centuries have fled..........	507
Mary to the Saviour's tomb........	334
Meet and right it is to sing........	80
Mighty God, Thy church recover...	609
Millions within Thy courts have met	34
More love to Thee, O Christ........	372
Mortals! awake, with angels join...	156
Music! bring thy sweetest treasures	92
My brethren, friends, and kinsmen..	594
My country, 'tis of thee............	578
My days are gliding swiftly by......	700
My dear Redeemer, and my Lord...	182
My faith looks up to Thee..........	541
My God! accept my heart this day..	539
My God and Father, while I stray...	471
My God! how endless is Thy love ..	4
My God, how wonderful Thou art...	132
My God, I love Thee, not because ..	388
My God! is any hour so sweet......	427
My God, my everlasting hope	113
My God, my King, Thy various.....	87
My God, my Life, my Love........	370
My God! the covenant of Thy love.	386
My God! the spring of all my joys .	387
My Jesus, as Thou wilt............	469
My Lord! how full of sweet content	351
My Saviour! my almighty Friend...	117
My sins, my sins, my Saviour.......	344
My soul, be on thy guard..........	452
My soul doth magnify the Lord.....	234
My soul! how lovely is the place...	69
My soul! repeat His praise........	481
My soul, there is a country........	691
My soul, weigh not thy life....	639
"My times are in Thy hand".......	478
My will, O Lord, to Thine I bow....	659
NATURE with open volume stands..	302
Nearer, my God! to Thee..........	456
Near the tomb where Christ hath...	193
New every morning is the love.....	3
No more, my God! I boast no more.	535
Nor eye has seen, nor ear has heard.	717
Not all the blood of beasts.........	339
Not worthy, Lord, to gather up the.	547
Now begin the heavenly theme.....	276
Now I have found a Friend	710
Now I resolve with all my heart....	537
Now let our souls on wings sublime.	718
Now may He, who, from the dead ..	60
Now, my soul! thy voice upraising.	338
Now thank we all our God.........	580
Now the day is over	12
Now to the Lord a noble song......	142
Now to the Lord, that makes us....	545
Now, with angels round the throne.	278
O CHRIST! our King, Creator, Lord.	143
O come, all ye faithful.............	168
O come, dear child, along with me..	552
O day of rest and gladness.........	24
O'er the distant mountains breaking	675
O'er the gloomy hills of darkness ..	619
O Father, Son, and Holy Ghost.....	540
O God, all-terrible! Thou who......	582
O God beneath Thy guiding hand ..	581
O God of mercy! hear my call	299
O God! Thou art my God alone....	406
O holy, holy, holy Lord............	74
O Jesus Christ! if aught there be..	390
O Jesus! King most wonderful.....	380
O Jesus, Lord of heavenly grace ...	9
O Jesus, Saviour of the lost........	297
O Jesus! sweet the tears I shed	341
O Jesus, Thou art standing........	317
O Lamb of God! still keep me.....	724
O Lord! how happy should we be..	416
O Lord! how joyful 'tis to see.....	607
O Lord! in sorrow I resign.........	418
O Love Divine! that stooped to....	371
O Love, who ere life's earliest dawn.	146
O mother dear, Jerusalem..........	713
O my soul! what means this sadness	367
Once in royal David's City.........	555
Once more, my soul, the rising day.	28
Once more the solemn season calls.	584
Once was heard the song of children	557

INDEX OF FIRST LINES.

On the mountain's top appearing...	617
Onward, Christian soldiers.........	459
O paradise, O paradise.............	706
O sacred Head, now wounded......	191
O sinner, bring not tears alone.....	289
O Source divine, and Life of all....	130
O Spirit of the living God...........	615
Other knowledge I disdain..........	512
O Thou, that hearest the prayer of..	292
O Thou to whom, in ancient time...	636
O Thou, to whose all-searching.....	645
O Thou, who by a star didst guide..	175
O Thou, who dri'st the mourner's...	484
O Thou, who hast Thy servants....	430
O Thou whose bounty fills my cup.	470
O Thou, whose own vast temple....	496
Our blest Redeemer, ere He........	245
Our God, our God! Thou shinest...	235
Our God, our help in ages past.....	425
Our God stands firm, a Rock and...	123
Our Lord is risen from the dead....	210
Out of the depths have I cried.....	324
Out of the depths of woe	326
O wisdom! spreading mightily	153
O word of God incarnate...........	345
O Zion! tune thy voice............	62
Oh, cease, my wandering soul	408
Oh! could I find from day to day...	437
Oh! could I speak the matchless...	393
Oh, deem not they are blest alone..	465
Oh, for a closer walk with God.....	451
Oh! for a faith that will not shrink.	360
Oh! for a heart to praise my God...	463
Oh! for a thousand tongues to sing.	378
Oh! gift of gifts! Oh! grace of	330
Oh, happy day, that fixed my choice	501
Oh! injured Majesty of heaven.....	311
Oh! let Thy grace perform its part.	601
Oh! may my heart, by grace	464
Oh! what amazing words of grace..	379
Oh! what if we are Christ's........	411
Oh! where are kings and empires..	588
Oh! where shall rest be found......	256
Oh! worship the King, all glorious.	135
PEACE, peace, I leave with you.....	542
Peace, troubled soul, whose plaintive	279
Pleasant are Thy courts above......	587
Poor, weak, and worthless, tho' I...	521
Pour out Thy Spirit from on high ..	492
Praise God, from whom all blessings	101
Praise, Lord, for Thee in Zion waits.	129
Praise the name of God most high..	30
Praises we're bringing to Jesus.....	398
Praise to God, immortal praise.....	576
Praise to Thee, Thou great Creator.	94
Praise ye the Father! for His loving	85
Praise ye the Lord, ye immortal....	127
Prayer is the soul's sincere desire ..	429
REJOICE, rejoice, believers	672
Rejoice! the Lord is King...........	212
Rest for my soul I long to find.....	644
Rest for the toiling hand............	480
Return, my roving heart! return...	605
Ride on! ride on in majesty........	185
Ring again, ye starry chime	177
Rise, glorious Conqueror! rise.....	219
Rise, my soul, and stretch thy wings	81
Rock of Ages, cleft for me.........	503
SAFE home, safe home in port......	711
Safely thro' another week..........	46
Salvation! O the joyful sound......	263
Saviour, again to Thy dear name we.	505
Saviour! breathe an evening.......	47
Saviour, like a Shepherd lead us....	556
Saviour! teach me, day by day.....	400
Saviour, when in dust to Thee.....	308
Says Christ our champion, follow...	449
Say, sinner! hath a voice within....	273
See, gracious God! before Thy.....	583
See Israel's gentle Shepherd stands.	499
See! Jesus stands with open arms..	532
See the clouds upon the mountains.	48
See, the Conqueror mounts in......	218
Show pity, Lord! O Lord, forgive ..	254
Since o'er Thy footstool here.......	84
Sing, Israel! for the Lord, your.....	688
Sing to the Lord a joyful song......	88
Sing to the Lord Jehovah's name...	118
Sinner! the voice of God regard...	266
Slain for my soul, for all my sins ...	307
Sleep thy last sleep.................	663
Softly now the light of day.........	31
Soldiers of Christ! arise	637
Soon may the last glad song arise...	634
Sow in the morn thy seed..........	570

INDEX OF FIRST LINES.

First line	No.
Spirit Divine! attend our prayers...	240
Spirit of power and might! behold.	243
Spirit of power, and truth, and love.	231
Stand up, and bless the Lord.......	27
Stand up, my soul! shake off thy...	403
Stand up, stand up for Jesus.......	611
Still, still with Thee, my God.......	52
Still, still with Thee, when purple..	21
Summer suns are glowing..........	107
Sun of my soul, Thou Saviour dear.	33
Surely Christ thy griefs hath borne.	194
Sweet feast of love divine..........	514
Sweet is the light of Sabbath eve...	44
Sweet is the memory of His name..	523
Sweet is the mem'ry of Thy grace..	121
Sweet is Thy mercy, Lord..........	128
Sweet the moments, rich in blessing.	442
Swell the anthem, raise the song....	577
TAKE me, O my Father! take me...	95
Tarry with me, O my Saviour.......	651
Teach me, my God and King.......	638
Tender Shepherd, Thou hast stilled.	657
Ten thousand times ten thousand...	699
That day of wrath, that dreadful day	697
The Bridegroom comes	680
The Church's one Foundation......	586
The day is gently sinking to a close.	20
The day of praise is done	54
Th' eternal gates lift up their heads.	208
Thee, Thee we praise, O God! and..	73
Thee will I love, my Strength, my..	348
The harvest dawn is near..........	572
The Head that once was crowned...	267
The heavens declare Thy glory...	251
The Lord descended from above.....	96
The Lord is King; lift up thy voice.	75
The Lord's my Shepherd, I'll not...	350
The Lord Jehovah reigns	66
The Lord, our God, is clothed with .	126
The morning light is breaking......	623
The oath and promise of the Lord..	404
The pains of death are past........	661
The perfect world, by Adam trod...	497
The proudest heart that ever beat..	270
Therefore with angels and archangels	268
There is a Fountain filled with blood	533
There's a Friend for little children..	550
There is a green hill far away.......	184
There is a land immortal...........	725
There is a land of pure delight.....	715
There is a name I love to hear	375
There is a time, we know not when.	288
The roseate hues of early dawn.....	361
The royal banner is unfurled	389
The sands of time are wasting......	707
These are the crowns, that we shall.	714
The solemn service now is done....	493
The Son of God goes forth to war..	448
The shadows of the evening hours..	16
The spacious firmament on high....	109
The strife is o'er, the battle done ...	207
The time draws nigh, when, from...	671
The tribes of faith, from all the.....	701
The twilight falls, the night is near .	14
The voice that breathed o'er Eden..	562
The whole wide world for Jesus	612
The world is very evil..............	693
Thine arm, O Lord, in days of old..	180
Thine earthly Sabbaths, Lord, we...	43
Thine forever, God of love.........	475
This is the day the Lord hath made.	38
This is the glorious day...........	593
Thou art gone up on high..........	647
Thou art the Way; to Thee alone...	181
Thou knowest, Lord, the weariness.	432
Thou lovely Source of true delight.	413
Thou, Saviour! art the Living bread	405
Thou who roll'st the year around...	564
Thou, whose almighty Word	79
Thus far the Lord has led me on ...	7
Thy head, the crown of thorns that.	534
"Thy Kingdom come!" O blessed..	676
Thy way, not mine, O Lord....,....	468
Thy way, O God! is in the sea......	359
"Thy will be done!" (Chant).......	489
"'Till He come:' Oh let the words.	508
Time, thou speedest on but slowly..	652
'Tis by the faith of joys to come....	363
"'Tis finished!" so the Saviour.....	188
'Tis God the Spirit leads	242
'Tis heaven begun below...........	67
'Tis midnight! and on Olive's brow.	183
To-day the Saviour calls	261
To-day Thy mercy calls me........	316
To Father, Son, and Holy Ghost....	124

INDEX OF FIRST LINES.

To Father, Son, and Holy Ghost ...	392
To God on high be thanks and.....	309
To God,—the Father, Son..........	543
To Him that chose us first.........	82
To our Redeemer's glorious name ..	384
To praise the ever-bounteous Lord.	566
To Thy temple I repair............	59
To us a child of hope is born.......	159
Triumphant Zion, lift thy head	630
Trust in the Lord, forever trust.....	590
Upward I lift mine eyes...........	353
Upward where the stars are burning	712
Wait, my soul! upon the Lord.....	474
Watchman! tell us of the night	679
We all, O Lord, have gone astray...	604
Weary of earth, and laden with my.	306
Weary of wandering from my God..	319
We bid Thee welcome, in the name.	494
We bless Thee for Thy peace, O....	423
We give immortal praise...........	83
Welcome, delightful morn..........	25
We sing His love, who once was....	666
We thank Thee, Father, for the day.	49
Whate'er my God ordains is right...	487
What equal honors shall we bring..	139
What grace, O Lord! and beauty...	178
What sinners value I resign........	665
When all Thy mercies, O my God ..	120
When at Thy footstool, Lord! I....	295
When gathering clouds around I...	349
When God's right arm is bared for..	284
When, His Salvation bringing......	559
When I can read my title clear.....	414
When I survey the wondrous cross.	187
When Jordan hushed his waters....	169
When, marshaled on the nightly....	461
When my last hour is close at hand.	695
When shall Thy love constrain.....	259
When, streaming from the eastern..	37
When our heads are bowed with....	662
When the Everlasting Lord........	1
When the worn spirit wants repose.	50
When this passing world is done ...	509
When Thou, my righteous Judge...	291
When Thou shalt come, Thine......	698
When wounded sore, the stricken ..	321
Where high the heavenly temple...	436
While beauty clothes the fertile...	568
While Shepherds watched their.....	167
While Thee I seek, protecting......	426
Who are these like stars appearing.	726
"Who is this that comes from Edom"	215
Why do we mourn departing friends	669
Why should our tears in sorrow....	670
Why should the children of a King.	318
"Wide, ye heavenly gates! unfold".	206
With all my powers of heart and...	102
With broken heart and contrite.....	301
Within these walls let heavenly.....	498
With joy we hail the sacred day....	39
With one consent, let all the earth..	72
With songs and honors sounding...	567
With tearful eyes I look around....	323
With tears of anguish I lament.....	322
With thankful hearts our songs we.	500
Workman of God, oh, lose not	642
Would'st thou eternal life obtain ...	269
Would you see Jesus? Come with.	281
Ye choirs of new Jerusalem........	205
Ye Christian heralds, go, proclaim..	635
Ye holy souls! in God rejoice	108
Ye servants of God! your Master..	136
Ye servants of the Lord............	687
Yes, I will bless Thee, O my God...	116
Yes, we trust, the day is breaking ..	620
Your harps, ye trembling saints	410
Zion dreary and in anguish.........	678

ALPHABETICAL INDEX.

A.

Achor 325
Adeste Fideles 168
Adrian 408
Affiance 402
Aithlone 614
Alford 699
Alleluia 1
All Saints 215, 726
Amantius 22
Amaranth 722
America 578
Ames 581
Amsterdam 80, 313
Anastasius 303
Anchorage 711
Angels 142
Antioch 154
Antiphon 110
Anvern 501
Archangel 674
Ariel 393
Arlington 350, 624
Arthur's Seat 82, 165
Ascension 210
Ashwell 187
Aurelia 586
Aurora 508
Austrian Hymn 689

B.

Baca 604
Baxter 468
Bedford 234
Beecher 217
Bemerton 115
Benediction 151
Benevento 564
Bera 272
Bernard 713
Bethany 456
Bethlehem 167
Bethune 229
Blumenthal 276
Boston 184
Bowen 103
Boylston 339
Braden 256
Bradford 384
Brattle Street 426
Bray 631
Bremen 198
Brightland 708
Brooklyn 227
Brown 13

Brownell 347
Burlington 147, 250
Byefield 429

C.

Calvary 271
Cambridge 264
Canonbury 525
Canterbury 253
Carey 391
Carmen Cœli 702
Carol 158
Cherith 248
Chesterfield 380
Childhood 551
China 669
Christchild 555
Christmas 166, 447
Christus Rex 150
Civitas Dei 712
Clare 337
Clarendon 121
Clark 423
Comfort 488
Communion 21, 547
Conqueror 219
Cooling 538
Coronation 220
Covenant 145
Coventry 341
Creation 109
Crusaders' Hymn 394

D.

Dalston 65
Darwall 212
Dawn 616
Day Star 679
Dennis 453
Devotion 93
Dewitt 310
Dies Iræ 696
Diman 465
Disciple 441
Dix 76, 176
Duke Street 2
Dundee 112, 526

E.

Easter Hymn 196
Eden 562
Ein Feste Burg 123
Eisenach 449
Elisabeth 676
Eloise 407

Eltham 596
Emmaus 20
Entreaty 260
Eucharist 517
Evening Hymn 8
Even Me 315
Eventide 19
Ewing 723

F.

Faben 613
Faith 328
Federal Street 230, 382
Ferguson 221
Festival 440
Forelight 409
Frankfort 213
Frederick 649

G.

Geer 373
Geneva 120
Germany 502
Gethsemane 192
Gilead 251
Gloria Paschali 309
Gloucester 608
God's Love 125
Gorton 481
Gottland 690
Gratitude 182
Greenville 55
Greenwood 660
Grostete 86
Guyon 106

H.

Halle 29
Hamburg 293
Hanford 524
Harmony Grove 281
Harwell 214
Hastings 195
Heber 381
Hebron 7, 535
He Leadeth Me 457
Hendon 58
Henry 96
Herald Angels 163
Hermas 560
Hodnet 24
Holley 31
Hope 721
Horbury 372
Horsley 178

Horton 152
Hosanna 559
Huguenot 89
Hummel 203, 566, 595
Hursley 33
Hymn to Joy 171

I.

Immanuel 662
Incarnation 170
Innocents 558
Integer 85
Italy 78

J.

Jerusalem 450
Jewett 469

K.

Kirke 351
König der Ehren 398

L.

Laban 68, 452, 686
Lancashire 672
Lanesboro' 64
Langran 306
Last Beam 18
Laurel 603
Laus Deo 122
Leighton 52
Lenox 495
Lintz 353
Lischer 25
Litany 308
Littledale 189
Liverpool 412
Logos 140
Louise 678
Louvan 544
Love Divine 371
Lowry 579
Lucius 484
Luther 570
Luther's Hymn 694
Luton 6
Lux Benigna 17
Lux Mundi 173
Lyman 84
Lyons 135

M.

Magdalene College 415
Maidstone 587

ALPHABETICAL INDEX.

381

Maitland	446	Paradise	706	Silver Street	26	**U.**	
Manchester	470	Park Street	627	Solitude	491	Unity	597
Manoah	320	Parousia	692	Southminster	399	Uxbridge	70, 500
Marlow	38	Passion Choral	191	Southport	640		
Martyn	334	Pastor	556	Spanish Hymn	506	**V.**	
Martyrdom	243	Pax Dei	505	Spohr	43		
Martyrs	583	Peace	478	Starlight	552	Valentine	651
Mear	63	Pearsall	693	Stephanos	401	Varina	715
Meditation	97, 288	Pelton	326	Stockwell	573	Veni Immanuel	157
Medway	492	Penitence	511	Stow	574	Victoria	461
Meinhold	23, 657	Pentecost	319	St. Ælred	366	Victory	207
Melcombe	346	Peterborough	28	St. Agnes	238, 499	Vigils	45
Melita	153	Phuvah	532	St. Alban's	460	Vox Angelica	702
Mendon	71	Pilgrim	664	St. Albinus	201	Vox Dilecti	329
Mercy	473	Pleiades	111	St. Andrew	458		
Mercy Seat	432	Pleyel	246, 444	St. Ann's	49, 688	**W.**	
Meribah	290	Portuguese Hymn	336	St. Anselm	190		
Merton	388	Prayer	427	St. Barnabas	263	Walsal	318
Messiah	206			St. Bartholomew	448	Ward	355
Midnight	188	**R.**		St. Bede	477	Wareham	665
Midnight Cry	673			St. Cross	697	Warwick	69
Migdol	363	Rapture	105	St. Cuthbert	245	Wartburg	129
Miles' Lane	220	Rathbun	224	St. Drostane	185	Watchman	637
Miller	396	Raven	646	St. Frances	114, 174	Wavertree	36, 594
Miriam	342	Redemption	300	St. George's	569	Webb	316, 610
Mishael	280	Refuge	333	St. Gertrude	459	Wellord	403
Missionary Chant	633	Regent Square	338	St. Godric	61	Westminster	132
Missionary Hymn	622	Remember Me	307	St. Hilda	317, 422	Winchcombe	680
Monkland	60, 419	Requiem	653	St. Jerome	698	Winchester	102
Monsell	128	Requiescat	663	St. John	529	Windham	254
Mornington	370	Resurrexit	200	St. Laura	164	Windsor	565
Mozart	202	Rest	654	St. Leonard	16	Woodland	269
		Rest for the Weary	705	St. Martin's	208	Woodworth	331
N.		Retreat	434	St. Millicent	658	Woolsey	659
		Rockingham	497, 615	St. Olave	369, 599	Wycliffe	609
Naomi	433	Rock of Ages	503	St. Peter	116		
Nativity	211	Rolland	520	St. Salvador	528	**Y.**	
Neander	209	Rose Hill	285	St. Sebastian	509		
Nebo	395	Roseville	443	St. Stephens	360	York	358
Nettleton	516	Rothwell	137	St. Sylvester	553, 650	Yorkshire	162
Newcourt	103	Russia	47	St. Thomas	591		
New Haven	621	Russian Hymn	582	St. Vincen	11	**Z.**	
Nicæa	5	Rutherford	707	Sunlight	107		
Nun Danket alle Gott	580			Surrey Chapel	655	Zephyr	169
Nuremberg	518, 681	**S.**		Sutherland	335	Zerah	159, 588
				Swanwick	522	Zion	617
O.		Sabaoth	131			Zion's King	561
		Sabbath	46	**T.**			
Old Hundredth	98	Saint's Rest	709				
Olive's Brow	183	Sanctuary	703	Tamworth	455		
Olivet	541	Seasons	352, 643	Te Deum	73	**INDEX TO CHANTS.**	
Olmutz	241, 410	Segur	274	Temple	10		
Ordinal	496	Sentinel	445	Tenderness	368		
Orion	685	Septuor	421	Teneriffe	126	Come to Me	323
Ortonville	376	Serenity	354	Thanksgiving	563	De Profundis	324
Oswestry	549	Sessions	282	The Old Story	397	Eternity	727
		Seymour	431	To-Day	261	Gloria in Excelsis	262
P.		Shelter	550	Toplady	504	Gloria Patri	728
		Shining Shore	700	Tranquillity	718	Gould's Chant	327
Packer	437	Shirland	513	Truro	72	Thy Will be Done	489
Pæan	575	Sicily	367	Trust	90	Trisagion	268
Palestrina	279	Siloam	463	Twilight	12	Troyte's Chant	471
Paraclete	490			Tyndal	296		

METRICAL INDEX.

C. M.
(8.6.8.6.)

Antioch	154
Arlington	350, 624
Bedford	234
Bemerton	115
Bernard	713
Boston	184
Bradford	384
Bray	631
Brown	13
Burlington	147, 250
Byefield	429
Cambridge	264
Canterbury	253
Cherith	248
Chesterfield	380
Childhood	551
China	669
Christmas	166, 447
Clarendon	121
Clark	423
Cooling	538
Coronation	220
Coventry	341
Dewitt	310
Dundee	112, 526
Eloise	407
Geer	373
Geneva	120
Gloucester	608
Heber	381
Henry	96
Horsley	178
Hummel	203, 566, 595
Lanesboro'	64
Liverpool	412
Lowry	579
Lucius	484
Maitland	446
Manchester	470
Manoah	320
Marlow	38
Martyrdom	243
Martyrs	583
Mear	63
Meditation	97, 288
Merton	388
Miles' Lane	220
Naomi	433
Nativity	211
Ordinal	496
Ortonville	376
Packer	437
Peterborough	28
Phuvah	532
Serenity	354
Siloam	463
Southport	640
St. Agnes	238, 499
St. Ann's	49, 688
St. Barnabas (with cho)	263
St. Frances	114, 174
St. John	529
St. Martin's	208
St. Olave	369, 599
St. Peter	116
St Stephens	360
Swanwick	522
Teneriffe	126
Tyndal	296
Vigils	45
Walsal	318
Warwick	69
Westminster	132
Windsor	565
York	358
Zerah	159, 568

C. M. 5 lines.
(8.6.8.8.6.)

Woodland	269

C. M. 6 lines.
(8.6.8.6.8.6.)

St. Bede	477

C. M. 8 lines.
(8.6.8.6.8.6.8.6.)

Bethlehem	167
Brattle Street	426
Carol	158
Jerusalem	450
St. Bartholomew	448
St. Leonard	16
Varina	715
Vox Dilecti	329

L. M.
(8.8.8.8.)

Ames	581
Anastasius	303
Angels	142
Anvern	501
Ashwell	187
Baca	604
Bera	272
Bowen	103
Canonbury	525
Come to Me	323
Diman	465
Duke Street	2
Evening Hymn	8
Federal Street	230, 382
Germany	502
Gilead	251
Gratitude	182
Grostete	86
Hamburg	293
Harmony Grove	281
Hebron	7, 535
Hursley	33
Incarnation	170
Kirke	351
Louvan	544
Love Divine	371
Luton	6
Medway	492
Melcombe	346
Mendon	71
Midnight	188
Migdol	363
Miller	396
Missionary Chant	633
Old Hundredth	98
Olive's Brow	183
Park Street	627
Pentecost	319
Redemption	300
Requiem	653
Rest	654
Retreat	434
Rockingham	497, 615
Rolland	520
Rose Hill	285
Rothwell	137
Seasons	352, 643
Sessions	282
Spohr	43
Starlight	552
St. Cross	697
St. Drostane	185
St. Jerome	698
St. Salvador	528
St. Vincent	11
Surrey Chapel	655
Te Deum	73
Thanksgiving	563
Tranquillity	718
Truro	72
Uxbridge	70, 500
Ward	355
Wareham	665
Wartburg	129
Wellerd	403
Winchester	102
Windham	254
Woodworth	331
Zephyr	169

L. M. 6 lines.

Bethune	229
Brownell	347
Covenant	145
Melita	153
Palestrina	279
Veni Immanuel	157
Wavertree	36, 594

L. M. 8 lines.

Ascension	210
Creation	109
He Leadeth Me	457
Orion	685
Victoria	461
Woolsey	659

S. M.
(6.6.8.6.)

Adrian	408
Amantus	22
Boylston	339
Braden	256
Dennis	453
Ferguson	221
Gorton	481
Greenwood	660
Laban	68, 452, 686
Leighton	52
Luther	570
Monsell	128
Mornington	370
Nebo	395
Olmutz	241, 410
Peace	478
Pelton	326
Shirland	513
Silver Street	26
St. Thomas	591
Tenderness	368
Watchman	637

METRICAL INDEX.

S. M. 8 lines.
Raven................ 646

4.6.4.6.4.6.4.6.
Requiescat........... 663

4.6.6.4.4.6.6.4.
Winchcombe......... 680

5.6.8.5.5.8.
Crusaders' Hymn.... 394

6s. 8 lines.
Baxter............... 468
Jewett............... 469

6.4.6.4.
To-Day............... 261

6.4.6.4.4.6.4.
Entreaty.............. 260

6.4.6.4.6.6.4.
Horbury.............. 372

6.4.6.4.6.6 6.4.
Bethany............. 456
Saint's Rest......... 709

6.5.6.5.
Twilight............. 12

6s & 5s. 8 lines.
Hermas............... 560
Sunlight.............. 107
St. Andrew.......... 458
St. Gertrude........ 459

6s & 5s. 12 lines.
St. Alban's.......... 460

6.6.4.6.6.6.4.
America............. 578
Conqueror........... 219
Italy.................. 78
Logos................ 140
New Haven.......... 621
Olivet................ 541

6.6.6.6.4.4.6.6.6.6.
Amaranth............ 722

11. M.
(6.6.6.6.8.8.)
Anchorage........... 711
Arthur's Seat......82, 165
Brooklyn............. 227
Darwall.............. 212
Lenox................. 495
Lintz.................. 353
Lischer................ 25
Lyman................. 84
Stow................... 574
St. Godric............ 61
Sutherland........... 335

S. P. M.
(6.6.8.6.6.8.)
Dalston................ 65

6.6.10.5.6,7.7.10.
Adeste Fideles....... 168

6.7.6.7.6.6.6.6.
Nun Danket alle Gott. 580

7s. 4 lines.
Hendon................ 58
Holley................. 31
Horton................. 152
Immanuel............. 662
Innocents............. 558
Mercy................. 473
Monkland.........60, 419
Mozart................. 202
Nuremberg........... 518
Pleyel............246, 444
Seymour............... 431
Solitude................ 491
Southminster......... 399

7s. 6 lines.
Calvary................ 271
Dies Iræ............... 696
Dix..................76, 176
Gethsemane.......... 192
Halle................... 29
Nuremberg.......... 681
Pœan................... 575
Rock of Ages........ 503
Spanish Hymn....... 506
St. Sebastian......... 509
Toplady............... 504

7s. 8 lines.
Alleluia................ 1
Benevento............ 564
Blumenthal........... 276
Day Star.............. 679
Eltham................ 596
Herald Angels....... 163
Litany................. 308
Maidstone............ 587
Martyn................ 334
Messiah................ 206
Parousia............... 692
Refuge................ 333
Sabbath................ 46
St. George's.......... 569

7s. 10 lines.
St. Anselm........... 190

7.4.7.4.7.4.7.4.
Easter Hymn......... 196

7.5.7.5.7.7.
Brightland............ 708

7.6.7.6.
Christus Rex......... 150
Eden................... 562

7.6.7.6. 8 lines.
Achor.................. 325
Aurelia................ 586
Clare................... 337
Ewing................. 723
Gottland.............. 690
Hodnet................. 24
Hosanna............... 559
Lancashire........... 672
Miriam................ 342
Missionary Hymn... 622
Passion Choral...... 191
Pearsall............... 693
Rutherford........... 707
St. Hilda.........317, 422
The Old Story....... 397
Webb.............316, 610

7s & 6s. 8 lines.
PECULIAR.
Amsterdam........80, 313
Festival............... 440
God's Love........... 125
Laurel................. 603
Mishael............... 280

7s & 6s. 12 lines.
Hope................... 721

7.6.7.6.7.8.7.6.
Penitence............. 511

7.6.8 6.7.6.8.6.
Alford................. 699

7.7.7.3.
Sentinel............... 445

7 7.4.
St. Millicent......... 658

7.7.7.5.
Dawn.................. 616

7.7.7.5. 8 lines.
Pleiades............... 111

7.7.7.6.
Littledale............. 189

7.7.8.7.7.7.8.7.
Septuor................ 421

7.8.7.8.4.
St. Albinus........... 201

7.8.7.8.7.7.
Meinhold..........23, 657

8.4.8.4.8.8.8,4.
Temple................ 10

8.5.8.3.
Stephanos............. 401

8.5.8.5. 8 lines.
Carey.................. 391

8.6.7.6.7.6.7.6.
Shelter................ 550

8.6.8.4.
St. Cuthbert......... 245

8.6.8.6.6.6.6.6.
Paradise............... 706

C. L. M.
(8.6.8 6.8.8.)
Hastings.............. 195

8.6.8.6.8.8.8.7.
St. Barnabas......... 263

8.7.8.7.6.7.
Even Me.............. 315

8.7.8.7.6.6 6.6.7.
Ein Feste Burg...... 123

8.7.8.7 7.5.7.5.8.7.8.7.
Resurrexit............ 200

8.7.8.7.7.7.
All Saints........215, 726
Christchild........... 555

8.7.8.7.7.7.7.5.
Rest for the Weary... 705

8 7.8.7.8.7.7.
Gloria Paschali...... 309

8.7.8.7.
Devotion.............. 93
Louise................. 678
Rathbun.............. 224
Stockwell............. 573
St. Sylvester......... 553
Trust.................. 90

8.7.8.7.8.7.
All Saints............. 215
Benediction........... 151
Frankfort............. 213
Neander.............. 209
Regent Square...... 338

METRICAL INDEX.

8.7.8.7.8.7.8.7.

Antiphon............ 110
Austrian Hymn...... 689
Beecher............. 217
Disciple............. 441
Faben............... 613
Harwell............. 274
Hymn to Joy........ 171
Laus Deo............ 122
Nettleton............ 516
Roseville............ 443
Russia............... 47
Sanctuary............ 703
Shining Shore....... 700
Valentine............ 651

8.7.8.7.4.7.

Archangel........... 674
Greenville........... 55
Lux Mundi........... 173
Pastor............... 556
Segur................ 274
Sicily................ 367
Tamworth............ 455
Zion................. 617

8.7.8.7.8.8.

Eisenach............. 449

8.7.8.7.8.8.7.

Luther's Hymn....... 694

8.7.8.7.8.8.8.9.

St. Sylvester........ 650

C. P. M.
(8.8.6.8.8.6.)

Aithlone............. 614
Ariel................. 393
Bremen.............. 198
Magdalene College... 415
Meribah............. 290
Rapture............. 105

8.8.7.7.

Wycliffe............. 609

8.8.7.8.8.7.

Civitas Dei.......... 712

8.8.8.3.

St. Ælred............ 366

8.8.8.4.

Hanford............. 524
Prayer............... 427
Unity................ 597
Victory.............. 207

L. P. M.
(8.8.8.8.8.8.)

Newcourt............ 108

9.8.9.8.

Eucharist............ 517

9.10.9.9.10.9.9.9.

Sabaoth............. 131

10.4.10.4.10.10.

Lux Benigna........ 17

10.6.10.6.10.10.

Guyon............... 106

10.10,10.4.4.

Aurora............... 598

10.10.7.10.

Elisabeth............ 679

10.10.10.10.

Affiance............. 402
Communion........21, 547
Emmaus............. 20
Eventide............. 19
Faith................. 328
Forelight............ 409
Huguenot........... 89
Langran............. 306
Pax Dei.............. 505
Remember Me....... 307

10.10.10.10.10.10.

Yorkshire............ 162

10.10.10.10.9.11.

Pilgrim.............. 664

10.10.11.11.

Lyons................ 135

10.11.10.11.11.11.11.

Zion's King......... 561

11.10.11.9.

Russian Hymn....... 582

11.10.11.10.

Comfort............. 488
St. Laura............ 164

11.10.11.10.
PECULIAR.

Paraclete............ 490

11.10.11.10.11.10.

Mercy Seat.......... 432

11.10.11.10.9.11.

Carmen Cœli........ 702

11.10.11.10.9.11.14.

Vox Angelica........ 702

11.11.10.10.12.9.10.11.

Last Beam........... 18

11.11.11.5.

Integer............... 85

11.11.11.11.

Frederick............ 649
Portuguese Hymn... 336

12.11.12.11.

Oswestry............ 549

12.12.12.10.

Nicæa............... 5

14.14.4.7.8.

König der Ehren..... 398

14.14.14.14.

Midnight Cry........ 673

www.ingramcontent.com/pod-product-compliance
Lightning Source LLC
Chambersburg PA
CBHW030350230426
43664CB00007BB/595